EVENINGS AT THE OPERA

EVENINGS AT THE OPERA

AN EXPLORATION OF THE BASIC REPERTOIRE

Jeffrey Langford

AMADEUS PRESS

AMADEUS PRESS
AN IMPRINT OF HAL LEONARD CORPORATION

Published in 2011 by Amadeus Press
An Imprint of Hal Leonard Corporation
7777 West Bluemound Road
Milwaukee, WI 53213

Trade Book Division Editorial Offices
33 Plymouth St., Montclair, NJ 07042

Grateful acknowledgment is made to the following for permission to reprint music examples from previously published operas:

European American Music Distributors LLC: Berg WOZZECK © 1931 by Universal Edition A.G., Wien. © Renewed. All rights reserved. Used by permission of European American Music Distributors LLC, U.S. and Canadian agent for Universal Edition A.G., Wien.

Boosey & Hawkes: *Peter Grimes* by Benjamin Britten, words by Montagu Slater. © Copyright 1945 by Boosey & Hawkes Music Publishers Ltd. Boosey & Hawkes, Inc., Sole Licensee. Reprinted by permission.

Printed in the United States of America

Book design by Michael Kellner

Library of Congress Cataloging-in-Publication Data

Langford, Jeffrey Alan.
  Evenings at the opera : an exploration of the basic repertoire / Jeffrey Langford.
    p. cm.
  Includes bibliographical references and index.
  ISBN 978-1-57467-187-2
  1. Operas–Analysis, appreciation. I. Title.
  MT95.L354 2011
  782.109–dc22
                          2011007704

www.amadeuspress.com

To Joanne and Julian
For their unflagging love and support

CONTENTS

ACKNOWLEDGMENTS

The writing of a book is a team effort, and this one would not have been possible without the assistance of innumerable colleagues and associates. Because the idea for a book on the basic opera repertoire grew out of preconcert lectures I have given over the years for the Opera Guild of the New York Metropolitan Opera, I am especially indebted to Ms. Dottie Allen, Director of Education at the Guild, for giving me the opportunity to try out some of my ideas before live audiences of opera aficionados. For the hours spent reading over the first drafts of this book, and for their helpful suggestions for revisions, I have to thank my Manhattan School of Music colleagues, Drs. Kariné Poghosyan and Kate Maroney. And for rescuing me from the quagmires of the Finale music-writing program, I will be eternally grateful to Evan Antonellis, a doctoral composition major and Finale guru par excellence at Manhattan School of Music.

John Pennino, Director of the Met Opera Archive was most helpful in directing me through the intricacies of the Met's large photo collection and for putting me in touch with the photographers Ken Howard and Marty Sohl, whose photos enliven the pages of this book.

Musical examples from Berg's *Wozzeck* are reprinted by permission of European American Music Distributors LLC, agent for Universal Edition A. G., Vienna. And the examples from Britten's *Peter Grimes* are reprinted by permission of Boosey & Hawkes Music Publishers Ltd.

My wife, pianist Joanne Polk, deserves special thanks for encouraging me to take on this project, and for pushing me to continually think of ways to make the whole book more user-friendly and generally more interesting. She too read the entire manuscript with the kind of critical eye that every author needs.

Lastly, to the staff at Hal Leonard Publishing Corp. I owe an especially big "thank you": to John Cerullo, whose positive reaction to my initial proposal for such a book got things going; to Iris Bass, who painstakingly pored over every word of the manuscript in her role as copy editor; and—most importantly—to my editor and main contact person, Jessica Burr, whose expertise in matters of editorial style, as well as her uncanny ability to spot errors in multiple languages, helped bring the disparate threads of these individual chapters together in a unified whole. Her standard of excellence in the production of the book—from beginning to end—has made an immense difference in the final product, and I am grateful for having had the opportunity to work with her.

INTRODUCTION

In 1852, Hector Berlioz, composer of the famous *Symphonie fantastique,* published his *Les soirées de l'orchestre* (*Evenings with the Orchestra*), a collection of fictional short stories and anecdotes told by the players of an anonymous opera orchestra during performances of bad operas. (Yes, they literally put down their instruments and start telling stories to pass the time.) Like that remarkably witty and insightful book, *Evenings at the Opera* is also a collection—not of satirical short stories, but of essays about specific operas, not bad, but all rather good. The operas these essays cover could be said to represent, in some very selective way, the basic repertoire one might encounter in any major opera house around the world. This book is therefore a survey or reexamination of a small part of this basic repertoire, written with the specific goal of determining what makes these particular operas successful (or sometimes not so successful) examples of drama in music. It was this term, *dramma per musica*, with which the seventeenth-century Italian inventors of opera chose to label their new genre. But through the ages, the term came to mean different things to different composers, working in different countries, at different times. This book is the story of those composers and their answers to the question of how music and drama can be made to work together.

Because the works I have chosen to examine represent a narrow 150-year slice of the broader four-hundred-year history of opera, this book cannot be said to portray a history of the genre, despite what appears to be a somewhat chronological arrangement of its topics. The essays have been organized, rather, around twelve different themes and categories, which, when taken together, suggest one possible way of organizing and understanding the vast diversity of musical styles and techniques that make up the history of opera. The various sections of the book have been designed to allow the reader to pick and choose from among them what he or she finds interesting, in any particular order. I have made no attempt along the way to review each opera in its entirety, or to synopsize the plots, or to catalogue all the characters involved, for the simple reason that such information is both readily available elsewhere and usually not relevant to the specific musical issues explored in each essay.

Throughout the book I have tried to address a general audience, limiting, wherever possible, my use of the technical vocabulary of music; but where I do delve into technical analysis, I have also tried to elucidate my basic points in a non-technical vocabulary that all readers will understand. When discussions of the music require reference to specific musical pitches, I have tried to use commonly understood expressions such as "the G above middle C," but on occasion have resorted (out of necessity) to the more professional nomenclature that represents middle C as "c^1," the octave below that as "c," and the octave above as "c^2." Each essay is also illustrated with musical examples that I hope will be useful whether one reads music or not. Certain aspects of music can be grasped as visual patterns on the page, even when the actual musical notation is not completely understood.

The idea for this book and the thoughts expressed in it grew out of regular preconcert lectures I have presented for several years at the Opera Guild of the Metropolitan Opera in New York City, and out of lectures given in an opera survey course I teach at Manhattan School of Music. My interaction with audiences at the Met and with my own students has inspired and sharpened my thinking about opera over the years. I am extremely grateful to have had the opportunity to share my ideas about opera with these many unnamed contributors to the genesis of this book.

In closing, I would like to relate a story that exemplifies one such intellectual interchange. Shortly after I came to New York to begin teaching at Manhattan School of Music, a student in my opera history class, interrupted my discussion of the often competing demands of drama and music in opera with the following observation: "Professor Langford," she boomed in a rather large and resonant voice, "this is all very nice, but what you don't seem to understand is that opera is really just about singing, pure and simple—what we singers refer to as 'park and bark.'" That young woman went on to have a very successful career as an operatic soprano, despite my insistence that opera was more than just nice singing. To all such believers in opera as "park and bark," I owe the impetus for this book. May we all come to know better!

Evenings at the Opera

PART I
THE EVOLUTION OF COMIC OPERA

CHAPTER 1

*D*on Giovanni is not only one of Mozart's best-known operas, it is also one of those works of art which, like the *Ring* cycle of Wagner, has given rise to volumes of polemical writing and has become over the years an opera about which musicologists and historians continue to find more to say while agreeing to disagree on some of its most basic points of interpretation. To be sure, *Don Giovanni* is one of Mozart's richest operas, replete with multiple and usually quite contradictory layers of dramatic meaning. Finding the real meaning of this opera has been complicated by the fact that it is a masterpiece that has meant different things to different audiences at different times. This investigation of *Don Giovanni* will attempt, through an examination of its historical context, to address some of these issues, and to come to grips with the perennial question of whether Mozart intended this opera to be interpreted as a comedy, or whether he was simply using a comic genre to mask a serious subject of moral dissolution.

As nearly every devotee of classical music knows, Wolfgang Amadeus Mozart lived a tragically short thirty-five years in the last half of the eighteenth century, from 1756 to 1791. His life and work thus fall squarely in the center of the high classical style in the history of music. Like many of his eighteenth-century contemporaries, Mozart was a prolific composer. The Köchel catalog of his complete works lists well over six hundred extant compositions. But what is remarkable about this list is that it contains masterpieces in nearly every musical genre then known. Mozart was truly a composer with the Midas touch, able time and again to transform routine compositional assignments into pure musical gold. As a composer of opera, he was especially prolific, with nineteen works that stretch across his life from the age of twelve all the way to the year of his death. These might be divided into two large groups, those written before 1781, during his itinerant years, and those written after 1781, when he settled in Vienna as an independent freelance composer. The earliest operas were nearly all the product of commissions obtained during trips Mozart made to foreign capitals in the company of his entrepreneurial father, Leopold. In the 1760s and '70s, when Mozart was actively traveling abroad, several different kinds of opera were popular across Europe. In Italy, where he began his career, opera seria and opera buffa were both common, while in Germany the only native opera was the comic Singspiel. This latter genre was a fairly unsophisticated comic form that used spoken dialogue in the place of sung recitative. Mozart wrote examples of all these kinds of opera, depending on where he was visiting at any given time. The only kind of opera he never wrote was French opera—either serious or comic.

Today, many of Mozart's nineteen operas are little more than titles in music history books, despite recent attempts by some well-respected conductors to resurrect a few of the more interesting early works. What matters to opera-goers, of course, are the Viennese works, the masterpieces written after Mozart broke away from indentured servitude in Salzburg to establish himself in what was then the most important center of German-speaking musical culture. Despite the fact that Vienna was the seat of the Austrian Empire, it was Italian opera that reigned supreme in the city's theaters, thanks mostly to the fact that all the major musical court positions were held by immigrant Italians—the Germans somehow having been bamboozled into believing that Italy was the only true center of vocal music in the world. Thus, five of Mozart's eight Viennese operas—some serious, some comic—were written in Italian. Of these Italian operas, the greatest, perhaps, are the three *buffa* operas written in collaboration with the librettist Lorenzo Da Ponte, who was himself one of those immigrant Italians—the official royal court poet—with whom Mozart was able to establish a personal connection that was essential to the successful procurement of opera commissions in Vienna and to his success as a freelance composer. The Da Ponte operas include three of Mozart's greatest comic operas: *Le nozze de Figaro*, *Don Giovanni*, and *Così fan tutte*, all written in the mid to late 1780s. To set the historical record straight about these Viennese operas, it should be noted that *Don Giovanni* was not actually written in Vienna, but was the result of a commission in 1787 from the opera house in Prague, after audiences in that city had gone wild over the production there of *Le nozze di Figaro*. *Don Giovanni* was then produced in Vienna the following year (1788).

Unlike the first Mozart/Da Ponte collaboration (*Le nozze di Figaro*), the libretto for *Don Giovanni* was not adapted from any single piece of great literature. The story of Don Juan was instead one that could be found in any number of versions, both oral and written, throughout Europe for centuries before Da Ponte took up the subject. One of the earliest written versions of the story was that of the Spanish monk, Tirso de Molina, who in 1630 published a three-act play on the subject titled *El burlador de Sevilla*. After that, the great French dramatist Molière produced a Don Juan play in 1665. Both of these were then pilfered for characters and ideas that could be put on as semi-improvised plays at carnival fairgrounds by itinerant theater troupes such as the Italian commedia dell'arte. In music, the Don Juan theme turned up several times before Mozart's opera. Most influential on Da Ponte's libretto was a one-act opera produced in Venice early in 1787 with music by Giuseppe Gazzaniga and a libretto by Giovanni Bertati. A comparison of the Bertati libretto with the one Da Ponte prepared for Mozart shows that the latter poet plagiarized nearly all of the earlier work in making Mozart's libretto.

The result of all the various musical and dramatic sources from which Da Ponte could, and did, draw inspiration for his own libretto is that there is a certain looseness of plot about Mozart's opera. That is to say, there is no single definitive version of the rake's story on which a librettist might base his drama, and thus, Da Ponte's libretto, like so many other of the Don Giovanni dramas, has little real dramatic continuity to it. Instead it is simply an elaborately patched-up collection of comic episodes all based on the simple idea that the good guys have to discover, catch, and punish the villain. By the beginning of act 2, this all seems rather difficult to keep going in an interesting fashion; and were it not for the quality of Mozart's music, there is little doubt that this opera would have vanished from the repertoire as quickly as Gazzaniga's now long-forgotten version.

Much has been made in the literature surrounding *Don Giovanni* of the fact that Mozart and Da Ponte described their work as a *dramma giocoso*. One even hears well read opera aficionados telling their friends (usually at intermission in the opera house) that because of this designation, the opera is not really an opera buffa at all. To clarify this little generic squabble, we need only understand that this term was used in the history of Italian comic opera to distinguish a special kind of comic libretto in which there appeared characters drawn from three different social classes: the so-called *parti serie* (usually the aristocrats), the *parti buffe* (the servants), and the middle-class characters referred to as the *parti di mezzo caraterre*. Comic operas of this type were not new with *Don Giovanni*. The form was created around 1750 by an earlier Italian librettist named Carlo Goldoni. And, in addition to *Don Giovanni*, a few of Mozart's other early operas also fall into this category. So *Don Giovanni* is not unique in carrying the designation *dramma giocoso*. What is also important to understand about this special kind of comic opera is that its three different levels of characters are manifested in highly differentiated musical styles: a folklike simplicity for the peasants, a more sophisticated but still unadorned lyricism for the middle-ground characters, and an elaborate, highly ornamented vocal style for the most serious, aristocratic characters. In *Don Giovanni*, Mozart clearly thought of Donna

Anna and Don Ottavio as *serie* characters, whose music is drawn directly from the world of opera seria. Mozart had considerable experience with this kind of opera throughout his career, and must have believed that mixing the serious style with the more folklike simplicity of the usual *buffa* style enabled a composer to achieve greater musical and dramatic sophistication through the juxtaposition of contrasting musical styles. What is truly special about Mozart's handling of the *dramma giocoso*, however, is that he allowed his characters to sing in styles that were not their own. Thus *serie* characters sometimes sing in a *buffa* style, whereas *buffa* characters sometimes cross over into the *seria* style. This is partly why the work is so open to multiple readings and interpretations.

One of the greatest difficulties in appreciating this opera revolves around the question of how to understand its protagonist. What are we to think of one who is such a bundle of contradictions: a villain, an aristocrat who disgraces the aristocracy, a rake who fails in all attempts to seduce his targeted victims, and an operatic leading man who has no big reflective arias to sing. Clearly, the Don is an enigma, or at the very least a tangle of perplexing paradoxes. As the opera opens, he is inside the home of Donna Anna, trying to seduce her, while his servant Leporello stands guard outside. The opening ensemble begins with a little solo for Leporello, in which he complains about his life and expresses a longing to be the master rather than the servant. Here we have an unusually complex and interesting comic character—himself a fascinating paradox. As we learn a little later in the opera, he knows full well that his master is an egotistic, self-serving rake, but here at the beginning, he wants nothing more than to be the same. The music Mozart writes for his opening solo perfectly captures the combination of moods at the outset of this scene—or at least it does if and when it is performed with insight into the character and all his emotional conflicts. At the outset, Leporello sings a repetitive pattern of equal quarter notes (Ex. 1-1).

Example 1-1. Leporello's opening solo.

As was always the case with composers of the eighteenth century, Mozart provided few suggestions as to how this music should actually sound in performance. One could, of course, take a literal approach to the notated rhythm of equal quarter notes, giving each its full value. The result would be a very broad and lyrical interpretation suggesting grandiosity. But the dramatic situation in which Leporello finds himself here suggests something different, something rather sneaky: the servant standing guard outside while the master is inside up to no good with Donna Anna. The text Leporello sings implies a bit of pent-up anger as well: "Night and day I slave away for one who doesn't appreciate me; enduring wind and rain, eating and sleeping badly." But none of this would be communicated in a literal reading of the music. Instead, what is needed is a performance that will suggest the emotion that lies behind the words—something that communicates a latent hostility about the injustice of the situation. A sensitive singer might thus alter the rhythm a little to shorten the quarter notes by putting some space between them. This more pointed delivery of the music would then allow the singer to project a feeling of controlled anger that would capture what Leporello most likely feels at this particular moment in the drama. Following this opening phrase, the music breaks into a broadly lyrical and suitably regal-sounding phrase at the point where the servant longs to be the master. Here the music borrows from the style of opera seria, as Leporello casts himself momentarily in his boss's role. Here the noble sound of French horns signals a new aristocratic mood, as Leporello boldly sings, "I would rather be the gentleman" (Ex. 1-2).

Example 1-2. Leporello's "noble" style.

Vo - glio far il gen - til - uo - mo   e   non vo - glio più ser - vir

The broad lyrical style of performance that was so inappropriate at the beginning is now completely in keeping with the implied dignity of the text, and a good performance must change accordingly, adopting a much more regal sound at this point. In this way Mozart's music can be made to support the changing moods through which Leporello moves, and to present this *buffa* character as one who operates beyond the boundaries of his social station as defined by the traditional categories of *dramma giocoso* stereotypes.

After Leporello's opening solo, Don Giovanni suddenly comes running out of the house with Donna Anna in hot pursuit. Again this is a paradoxical scene, with the victim now taking the role of attacker. What kind of hero is this who is being chased by his victim? Far too few opera lovers see the humor in this situation, and as a result, completely miss its importance in defining the comic aspect of the Don's character. This scene raises the question of whether Giovanni actually succeeded in his rape of Donna Anna—a question that has occupied opera historians and commentators for years. If we believe Donna Anna's later telling of the episode, her attacker failed to achieve his goal; but of course, what else could a noble lady say in such a circumstance? Given the fact that the victim is now chasing her attacker, it seems more than probable that Donna Anna did fend off the attack, and that Don Giovanni is actually more of an Inspector Clouseau–like character, rather than an invincible James Bond–like hero. This, of course, is part of the important paradox built into this opera. Mozart's music here—a trio—skillfully combines a sense of seriousness in the parts of Donna Anna and Don Giovanni, with a wonderfully comic undertone in the frightened mutterings of Leporello as he comments on the unfolding action. Thus the mixed comic/serious tone of the whole opera is established here at the outset.

Next Donna Anna's father (the Commandant) comes running out of the house to save his daughter. His confrontation with Don Giovanni leads to a sword fight and a trio for the three men in which the Commandant is killed. This very serious ensemble is then followed immediately by some comic dialogue in secco recitative (the driest, most speechlike variety of recitative) between Don Giovanni and Leporello, in which the servant asks his master, "Who's dead, you or the old man?" Quickly Mozart undercuts the seriousness of the murder trio and sets the opera back on a comic path, again sending mixed signals about this opera—is it serious or comic? The dramatic technique employed here is that of *irony*—a process by which the author undercuts or contradicts the very nature and style of the genre in which he seems to be working. By virtue of this self-contradictory technique, *Don Giovanni* becomes one of the first great examples of musical irony. The widespread use of this technique in both literature and music in the nineteenth century may account, in part, for the tremendous popularity of this opera throughout the century following its composition.

After Don Giovanni and Leporello exit the stage, Donna Anna and Don Ottavio (her fiancé) enter in the hope of helping the Commandant— but too late. This scene, in which they discover the dead body, is set by Mozart as an *accompanied recitative*. This is a special kind of recitative in which the voices are accompanied by the orchestra rather than just the harpsichord. It was used, especially in opera seria, for those moments in the dialogue that express an intense emotion. Mozart's use of this accompanied recitative here is one of the many ways in which he suggests the gravity of the moment, as well as the upper-class opera seria social station of Donna Anna and Don Ottavio.

Donna Anna and Don Ottavio discover the murdered Commandant.

DONNA ANNA:	DONNA ANNA:
Ma qual mai s'offre, oh Dei,	But what a dreadful sight, O God
Spettacolo funesto agli occhi miei!	Confronts my eyes!
Il padre ... padre mio ...	Father ... my father ...
Caro mio padre!	Dearest father!
DON OTTAVIO:	DON OTTAVIO:
Signore ...	Sir ...
DONNA ANNA:	DONNA ANNA:
Ah! l'assassino	Ah! The assassin
Mel trucidò. Quel sangue ...	Has struck him down. What blood.
Quella piaga ... quel volto ...	This wound ... his face
Tinto e coperto dei color di morte ...	Discolored with the pallor of death.
Ei non respira più ...	He has stopped breathing ...
Fredde ha le membra ...	His limbs are cold ...
Padre mio! Caro padre! Padre amato!	My father! Dear father! Beloved!
Io manco ... io moro ...	I'm fainting ... I'm dying.

This recitative leads then to a duet in which Anna asks Ottavio to avenge her father's murder (Ex. 1-3). This duet is fully in the opera seria style. It uses the sound and mood of the minor mode (instead of the major mode that was more usually associated with the *buffa* characters). It employs chromatic harmony in place of the simple diatonic harmony of most comic opera, and it involves expressive melodic gestures of the kind one finds most often in serious Italian opera of the time. The duet is especially expressive in the moment when Don Ottavio reassures Donna Anna that in him she shall find both husband and father. Here the use of chromatic harmony (unusual in the world of comic opera where simple diatonic harmony is the norm) combines with an unusual descending melodic leap of a minor seventh as Ottavio pours out his heart in music of a nearly romantic expressivity.

Example 1-3. Act 1, Donna Anna–Don Ottavio duet.

Example 1-3 *(continued)*

Here, too, the style of the performance can make a significant difference in the emotional impact of the music. Those conductors who favor the faster tempos now thought to be characteristic of performance in the eighteenth century sacrifice some of the expressivity of this music by whipping through it at such a rapid pace. On the other hand, some of the great conductors of the early twentieth century—Bruno Walter, for example—steeped in a more romantic tradition of Mozart performance, move through this duet with a loving elasticity of tempo that literally squeezes every ounce of musical expression out of this poignant music.

Of the five characters encountered thus far in the opera, four have been aristocrats and one a servant. Now a new character, Donna Elvira, enters the drama. She is a woman of noble birth whom Don Giovanni has already seduced and abandoned. She would thus appear to be a member of the *parti serie*. But again, Mozart and Da Ponte give us a character far more complex than that. Her social station may be aristocratic, but her behavior is most unaristocratic and undignified. Rarely has the world of opera seen a better example of the old adage "Hell hath no fury like that of a woman spurned." Elvira's propelling goal in life seems to be to unmask the fraudulent respectability of Giovanni, and she will do so whenever and wherever she can, absolutely without consideration of any embarrassment to her own person. Yet at the same time she wants nothing more than to take him back. She comes onstage actively engaged in a hunt for the traitor. Don Giovanni and Leporello notice this angry woman without recognizing who she is. She sings an aria here ("Ah! chi mi dice mai"), which, in its musical style, is reminiscent of the old "rage" arias so common in Italian opera seria of this time. The inclusion of such an aria, drawn from the world of serious opera, would make sense coming from a character of Elvira's social station. But in this aria we recognize something unusual: an exaggeration of the usual style of such rage arias that suggests that Mozart might have been making fun of both the musical tradition behind such operatic conventions and the character of Elvira herself. Most rage arias were built upon a melodic vocal line that featured a wide vocal range from high to low in a soprano's compass, along with dramatic leaps from one extreme of her range to another, all of which were far less common in every other kind of aria known to opera seria in the late eighteenth century. But Mozart's music for Elvira carries this vocal tradition over the edge, as it were, into the realm of parody. Of course, the communication of this parodistic effect lies in the hands of the singer. If she believes that Mozart wanted to make fun of Elvira, the classic spurned and angry woman, then an exaggerated performance of the aria could bring to this dramatic moment an element of the comic and ridiculous. A more subdued performance, on the other hand, would cause the aria to simply sound like any other rage aria, appropriately placed in the mouth of the angry heroine. While the dramatic situation here is (or can be) serious, the musical treatment is thus (or can be) comic, preventing the opera from taking on a truly tragic significance, and adding another instance of musical/dramatic irony to the whole. For those wishing to explore the sound of an exaggerated performance of this aria, I can recommend the old EMI recording (1959) with Elisabeth Schwarzkopf playing the part of Elvira.

The *buffa* characters in this opera are represented by Zerlina and Masetto. These are true country folk whose music is cast in the standard eighteenth-century pastoral style, which usually means a folklike simplicity and 6/8 meter. For example, when Zerlina first enters with Masetto, the two of them sing about the joys of young love. They do so in a fine example of this pastoral style, as seen in Ex. 1-4.

Example 1-4. Entrance of Masetto and Zerlina.

Throughout the opera, Mozart continues to allow his characters to cross over into styles that are not technically theirs by the "rules" of *dramma giocoso*. We saw at the very beginning of the opera how Leporello's opening solo partakes of both *buffa* and *seria* styles, suggesting a low-class character with noble pretensions. This crossing over into foreign vocal territory, for the purpose of illustrating something unusual about a character is carried into the *parti serie* as well. Thus, when Don Giovanni (an aristocratic *seria* character) tries to seduce Zerlina (a *buffa* character), he does so by temporarily adopting her pastoral, *buffa* style. In a musical sense he takes on a new identity by speaking to her in her own language.[1] The duet in which this happens is the famous "Là ci darem la mano." Here again, if singers recognize that Giovanni is moving into the musical realm of the *parte buffe*, then the duet will have its intended effect—which is to say we will recognize that Giovanni is faking his concern for Zerlina just to seduce her. To accomplish this temporary transition into the *buffa* style, the baritone must sing his part as lightly and simply as possible. This is not the moment for a full-voiced, big-vibrato sound. The duet must have a folklike simplicity that clarifies Don Giovanni's insincerity for the audience, allowing them to conclude, "That's not really him . . . he's faking." One of the best (i.e., least pretentious) performances of this famous duet is that by Håkan Hagegård and Barbara Bonney in a wonderful Decca recording from 1989 that was motivated throughout by the goal of achieving a lighter style of performance more accurately reflective of eighteenth-century performance practice.

In the next few scenes Don Giovanni busies himself with trying to seduce Zerlina, while Leporello is told to occupy the rest of her friends and her fiancé with food and drink at his master's palazzo. The finale of the first act represents this huge party, put on to lure Zerlina into a compromising position. But the party is interrupted by Donna Anna, Don Ottavio, and Elvira, who now know that Giovanni was the Commandant's murderer. Like all Mozart ensemble finales, this one is wonderfully complex. The usual structure of these extended musical numbers is something like a multimovement symphony—several different sections of music in contrasting tempos, keys, and meters, all strung together without recitative. We therefore have in these ensembles, a long uninterrupted stretch of music in which the action unfolds continuously. The basic formula was for the librettist to begin with two characters and gradually add more in

---

1. This technique of changing identity through music is extended to act 2 in a scene in which Giovanni actually trades clothing with Leporello for the same purpose.

each successive section, until he finally had all the principal singers and sometimes also a chorus onstage at the end of the act.

The finale of act 1 is most famous for its incorporation of multiple dance orchestras onstage playing simultaneously in three different rooms—a prime example of musical complexity far beyond what any other eighteenth-century composer of opera buffa would ever have dared try. These stage orchestras play different dances in different meters and tempos, each representing the kind of music that fits the three social levels of the characters in the opera: an aristocratic minuet (for Donna Anna and Don Ottavio), a contredanse (for Don Giovanni and Zerlina), and a peasant *Teitsch* (for Leporello and Masetto). The complexity of this scene actually led Mozart to plan it out through compositional sketches, something he rarely did for most of his works.

The second act of *Don Giovanni* is dramatically much less successful than the first, with the exception of its most important scene, the finale, in which the stone statue of the Commandant comes to dine with Don Giovanni and then drags him off to hell. Before getting to that famous scene, however, the opera has to pass through a considerable number of very ordinary *buffa*-style situations. In fact, much of the first half of this act was invented by Da Ponte solely to stretch the single act of Bertati's libretto, which he was copying, into two. In other words, the basic plot of discovering the Commandant's murderer and hunting him down was being padded by Da Ponte at this point to lengthen the opera. But the new scenes add little if any interest to the plot or to our understanding of the characters. Instead, they simply mark time by relying on well-worn opera buffa devices, such as the exchange of clothes between characters for the purpose of trading identities.

Interestingly enough, it is this part of the opera that exists in two distinctly different versions: the first created for the premiere in Prague, the second revised for a production the following year in Vienna. Clearly, Mozart must not have been entirely happy with this part of the libretto, and took the opportunity a year after its premiere to try fixing it. From a purely dramatic point of view, neither version is really satisfactory, but since the music of each is quite different, the choice of which version to do becomes an important one. There are two extra arias in the Vienna version that no one wants to lose by doing the Prague version; but the revised version also contains a meaningless duet added for Leporello and Zerlina (nearly always cut in performances today). For its part, the original Prague version contains an aria for Leporello and one for Don Ottavio, which were eliminated in rewriting the opera for Vienna. Without delving too deeply into the effect of all these changes on the overall impact of the opera, we can understand the basic problem with one isolated sample—the part of Don Ottavio. It is near the beginning of act 2 that Ottavio finally realizes that Don Giovanni is indeed the man who murdered the Commandant. In an intricately difficult aria, "Il mio tesoro" (Ex. 1-5), he announces that he will avenge the wrongs suffered by Donna Anna.

Example 1-5. "Il mio tesoro"—difficult passagework.

This wonderful aria was dropped in the Viennese version of the opera because the new singer was unable to negotiate the difficult vocal passagework. To keep the Viennese tenor happy, Mozart inserted a new aria in act 1 at the point where Donna Anna first tells Ottavio that she recognizes the voice of Giovanni as that of her attacker. His response is to doubt that this is possible, but to resolve to discover the truth and ease Anna's mind. This aria, "Dalla sua pace," is lyrical and far easier to sing than the one found in the Prague version. But besides making alterations to suit the strength or weaknesses of new singers in Vienna, Mozart and Da Ponte must surely have recognized that the second act was dramatically weak and incoherent in its original form, and needed fixing. Ironically, one might actually say that the fix (the Viennese version of the libretto) made matters worse, which is why parts of it are always suppressed in productions today. Another reason for the rewrite of act 2 may have been that Mozart and Da Ponte recognized that act 1 had slipped dangerously deep into the style of opera seria, from which it could only be rescued by the addition of new comic scenes. Perhaps they understood that the continual balanced juxtaposition of comic and serious elements was essential to the meaning of this opera. Thus, after the buffoonery of the opening of act 2, things turn serious once more as the opera moves to its deadly conclusion.

It is the penultimate scene of act 2—the supper scene—that is justifiably the opera's most famous, and most serious. This is where the stone statue of the Commandant pays Don Giovanni a dinner visit to offer him one last chance to repent his immoral behavior. This scene, more than any other, appealed to nineteenth-century audiences, and kept the opera in the repertoire throughout the whole of the romantic era. Partly, this appeal was based on the appearance of supernatural spirits from hell, which brought the work into alignment with romantic interest in the devil and reminded many of that quintessential romantic subject, Faust. In addition, Don Giovanni's defiant attitude, when confronted with his well deserved retribution, also called to mind another favorite romantic character type: the outlaw hero who boldly refuses to be forced to conform to societal mores that impinge on his own freedom. Mozart's music for this scene—in the ominously brooding key of D minor—bespeaks a seriousness of mood that even the comic grumblings of Leporello cannot undo.

Following this very romantic end to Don Giovanni, comes a comic ensemble in which all the surviving characters assemble to tell the audience what they intend to do with the rest of their lives. This kind of finale was traditional in comic opera, especially in France where it was known as the "vaudeville" finale. In *Don Giovanni*, this final scene is an essential part of the balance between the comic and serious elements with which Mozart imbued his opera. But this scene was frequently omitted in productions after Mozart's death, exactly because later audiences wanted to interpret in deadly earnestness that which Mozart designed as a parody. In the eyes of nineteenth-century musicians, the slapstick finale was incompatible with the real meaning of the opera. Today we recognize how this view falsifies Mozart's intention, which was not to instruct and moralize, but to entertain with a collection of ironic paradoxes that poke fun at both comic and serious opera of the eighteenth century. Ultimately, Don Giovanni is not, as E. T. A. Hoffmann claimed, a Faustian man in search of Goethe's "eternal feminine"; rather, like Mozart himself, a victim of his own audacious self-destructive behavior. He is a tragic hero undermined by his own buffoonery and fantasies of self-importance.

Like so much of Mozart's dramatic music, *Don Giovanni* contains an element of autobiographical self-projection, in which aspects of the composer's personality are projected onto the opera's protagonist. Like the Don, Mozart was a man who demanded more respect than he got. His behavior was often arrogantly entitled and inflexible, and in the end, self-damaging. Just as Don Giovanni was a man defined by a collection of paradoxes that shaped his life, so, too, was Mozart a serious musician whose career unraveled under the weight of irreconcilable paradoxes of his own. At best, he frequently undermined his own respectability with childish buffoonery. At worst he, like the Don, allowed his own arrogance and sense of self-importance to lead to his ultimate demise. These correlations between the composer and his musical alter-ego are an important key to understanding this opera. Just as Mozart often resorted to comedy to cover the tragedies of his life, so too did he use comedy to deal with serious issues in many of his greatest operas, including this one.

Most important, I would propose that this opera is best understood as an ironic work—that is, one that undercuts and contradicts it own suppositions. Don Giovanni is not what he appears to be. Unlike the great seducer and lover of legend, Mozart's hero is an inept antihero who is thwarted at every turn. His adamant defiance of the Commandant's demand that he repent is therefore not to be taken as a kind of romantic insistence on the primacy of individual will (which is how the nineteenth century wanted to understand the Don), but rather as one final instance of the comic self-delusion under which Giovanni labors throughout the opera. His defeat at the hands of the supernatural is just another of the many reversals that he suffers because of his delusional omnipotence. He is the ultimate ironic hero, who like Cervantes's Don Quixote, is not what he thinks he is. Both the hero and the opera are a tangle of contradictions that continually intrigue audiences by bringing the serious and the comic face to face.

CHAPTER 2

The shadow of Gioachino Rossini looms large across the landscape of early nineteenth-century Italian opera. He stands, along with Beethoven, at the threshold of a new era in the history of opera. Beethoven created German romantic opera, which culminated eventually in the tremendous achievements of Wagner later in the century, but Rossini was no less important. His works bridge the gap between the classical style of Mozart and the romantic melodramas of Donizetti, Bellini, and early Verdi, setting the style and form and general aesthetic of Italian opera for decades to come. Rossini was thus as important to nineteenth-century Italian opera as Beethoven was to German opera: both were progenitors of distinctly different national traditions that dominated the world of opera for the next hundred years. But unlike Beethoven, who wrote only one opera, Rossini was a prolific composer who wrote over seventy. He was born in 1792 (just one year after Mozart died) and lived a long life of seventy-six years. Ironically, only a part of that life was continuously productive, as Rossini's operatic career, which began early at age eighteen, abruptly came to a halt in 1829, before he had even turned thirty years of age. Early on, he wrote both serious and comic opera in Italy, until moving to Paris in 1824, a city that was then the operatic capital of Europe. There he produced several new operas, one in Italian, the rest in French, ending his career in 1829 with *Guillaume Tell* (William Tell), a serious French grand opera. After that Rossini ceded the operatic stage to a younger rising star by the name of Giacomo Meyerbeer, who, like Rossini himself, was also moving on to Paris from a successful career in Italy.

As a composer working at the crossroads of Italian opera history, Rossini found himself facing some serious artistic challenges. The first of these does not directly concern the subject of this chapter, because it has to do with serious opera. Nevertheless, Rossini's contribution to Italian serious opera in the early years of the nineteenth century is worth mentioning in passing just because it *is* so important. In fact, from a strictly historical point of view, Rossini was much more important for his work in serious opera than he was for his comic operas, despite the fact that it is really only the latter that remain popular with audiences today. In the final analysis, Rossini rescued serious opera from near total extinction at the end of the eighteenth century by transforming the genre in ways that made it relevant to the new middle-class audiences of post-Revolutionary Europe. He literally forged the path for the next generation of Italian composers to follow.

Rossini's historical importance as a composer of serious opera, only makes more difficult the evaluation of his contribution to comic opera. Unlike serious opera, which was centuries old, comic opera was new in the eighteenth century. Its birth and the nature of the subjects it treated were a response to the same sociological changes that doomed the old opera seria. Comic opera was all about the common man and his struggle to assume political power and social equality during the period of the Enlightenment. The style of this new kind of opera was the style of the people: simple and unsophisticated. Its harmonies were less complex, its melodies more folklike, and its orchestral accompaniments far less intricate. Its music bounced and flitted along, almost exclusively in the major mode, at fairly brisk tempos, and with lots of rhythmic animation. And its musical form was far more varied, thanks to the addition of ensembles to the monotonous sequence of arias on which opera seria had exclusively relied. Furthermore, these new comic operas were not based on stories drawn from ancient history and mythology, as had been the case with opera seria, but were instead based on stories drawn from real life, featuring characters to whom middle-class audiences could relate. So unlike opera seria, eighteenth-century opera buffa was not in danger of dying under the weight of its own sociological irrelevance, and was not in need of revitalization. Instead, the real dilemma for Rossini as a composer of comic opera in the nineteenth century was to find a way to go beyond the masterpieces of Mozart in this genre—to transcend the transcendent. His solution was based on the old principle of giving audiences what they wanted (or at least what Rossini thought they wanted). In this case that meant mixing one important element of the old opera seria with several other new elements drawn from opera buffa and even from French opera. Rossini recognized that while the form and subject matter of the old Italian opera seria was unpopular with new nineteenth-century blue-collar audiences, the elaborate virtuosic style of singing found in those operas was still appealing. This was the kind of singing practiced by the great castrati of the classical era. In many ways, serious opera had been a showcase and a vehicle for the artistry of this eerily artificial breed of singer—the male soprano. Castrati had been acceptable in opera as long as they played the parts of kings and other aristocratic figures of antiquity, but composers balked at the thought of asking them to take on the roles of the more common heroes found in the realistic contemporary dramas on which comic operas were based. Yet

Rossini gambled that their style of singing, with its beauty of tone, smooth legato phrasing, technical virtuosity, and ornate vocal improvisations, would continue to thrill audiences and would never really go out of favor in Italy. So while the castrati themselves—those creatures of the surgeon's barbarous knife—were far too artificial to survive the changes brought about by the invention of comic opera, there seemed to be no reason not to transplant their vocal style (usually known as *bel canto*) into opera buffa, which had for many years been a fairly simple, unsophisticated genre. In making this change, Rossini produced a kind of comic opera that was, in terms of its vocal style at least, indistinguishable from serious opera. What he set in motion was a rapprochement of comic and serious opera that would become the model for Italian composers of the next generation and beyond.

With this perspective on the historical significance of Rossini, we can now take a closer look at his *La Cenerentola* as an example of the new nineteenth-century comic opera style. Rossini was a very busy composer, much in demand in the second decade of the nineteenth century. After the production in February 1816 of his *Il barbiere di Siviglia* in Rome, Rossini was asked to return to the city later that same year to write a new opera for the opening of what was referred to as the "carnival season," which began right after Christmas. As it turned out, however, Rossini's arrival in Rome was delayed until mid-December, so work on the new opera got off to a late start. Additional complications arose when the libretto Rossini had agreed to set was objected to by the papal censors, whose job it was to make sure that all theatrical productions met specific standards with regard to moral, religious, and political issues. When negotiations with the censors broke down, Rossini and his impresario found themselves hunting for a new subject for the opera.

At this point, the impresario then approached a local librettist Jacopo Ferretti for help. According to Ferretti's published memoirs, it was he who suggested, in a late night brainstorming session, the subject of Cinderella. This idea was as much an act of desperation as it was one of inspiration, undoubtedly surfacing because both Ferretti and Rossini were familiar with an opera by Stefano Pavesi titled *Agatina, o la virtù premiata* (Agatina, or Virtue Rewarded), given in Milan just a couple of years earlier, in 1814. This opera was itself based on (which is to say plagiarized from) a French libretto for an opera by Nicolas Isouard called *Cendrillon*, produced at the Paris Opéra-Comique in 1810. All three of these operas (Rossini's and its two predecessors) are loosely based on the famous version of the Cinderella legend as told by Charles Perrault in his 1697 collection of Mother Goose tales.

But Rossini's opera features some important alterations of the usual fairy tale, caused mostly by the needs and traditions of comic opera. For instance, most opera buffa is populated with characters based on comic prototypes found in the improvised, spoken dramas of the Italian commedia dell'arte. One such character, which audiences had come to know and love, was that of an elderly gentleman who is the protector or guardian of a young lady, with whom he is in love, but whom he also mistreats—for example, the character of Dr. Bartolo in Rossini's other comic masterpiece, *Il barbiere di Siviglia*. But such a character could fit into Rossini's Cinderella story only by changing the wicked stepmother of the original into a vain, self-serving stepfather. In this opera he has the funny (and surely ironic) name Don Magnifico. Another tradition of opera buffa is the avoidance of magic and the supernatural, because these are usually not dramatic elements that effectively contribute to the desired sense of truth, naturalness, and simplicity that Enlightenment aesthetics demanded. Therefore, the fairy godmother and her magic pumpkin-coach had to be dropped from the story. Standing in for the magic fairy godmother, we have the Prince's tutor, a dignified, elderly gentleman who likes Cinderella's kindness, and therefore functions as her entrée to the Prince's ball. Finally, because comic opera had always relied on scenes in which characters traded clothes, this, too, was worked into Rossini's version of the Cinderella story. In this case the Prince, who is out searching for the perfect bride, decides that he can better assess each candidate's motives by trading roles (and clothes) with his valet, Dandini. Thus, when Cinderella falls in love with the servant (the Prince in disguise), the Prince knows for sure that her heart is pure. Dandini functions, therefore, as the common *buffa* servant who trades places with his master and enjoys every moment of it, like Leporello in Mozart's *Don Giovanni*.

A more detailed examination of the first act of *La Cenerentola* will demonstrate how all of these general modifications to the standard Cinderella story come together to make this opera work. A traditional opera buffa usually opened with either a chorus or more often a small ensemble. For this opera, Rossini chose the latter—a duet between Cinderella's two stepsisters. As the curtain goes up, Clorinda is practicing dance steps while her sister Tisbe is decorating herself with flowers. Their little duet sets the tone of female vanity in a lighthearted comic vein. While the sisters are thus occupied in their frivolity, Cinderella sits off in a corner tending to a fire so she can make coffee for her sisters. She interrupts their merriment with a little canzona (a simple song) about a king who chooses innocence and goodness over pomp and beauty in the woman he decides to marry—a song obviously related to the subject of Cinderella's present circumstances.

Strangely for a comic opera, this number is written in the minor mode with all its suggestion of gloom and despair. There is a serious sentimentality about this little piece that subtly suggests right from the start that Cinderella is more than the usual *buffa* servant character.

Next the Prince's tutor, Alidoro, arrives disguised as a beggar seeking alms. His goal seems to be to identify the good souls who might be potential marriage partners for his Prince. Of course, the sisters send him away—they have no interest in humanitarian actions—but Cinderella offers him bread and coffee. When the sisters realize what Cinderella is doing, they attack her in front of Alidoro, who tries to break up the altercation. This entire interaction among the four characters is expressed musically in a little quartet, which reminds us that the use of such ensembles marked one of the fundamental differences between serious and comic opera in the previous century. Ensembles were simply not heard in opera seria (with the exception of an occasional duet), and their use in comic opera represented a breakthrough in the development of musical action—a subject to which we will return later.

Another element of the new opera buffa that Rossini brought to prominence was the chorus, little used in the works of Mozart. In the next scene of *La Cenerentola*, a chorus of courtiers appears to announce the arrival of the Prince himself, who will invite the sisters to a fancy ball. Such choruses have dramatic value principally as contrast for the other musical numbers that feature solo singing. But the chorus suffered a diminishing importance in Italian opera after Monteverdi's *Orfeo* of 1607. Rossini's inspiration for the inclusion of choruses in his comic operas was surely the French operatic tradition, in which choruses had always played a prominent role. Because Italian opera had never relied much on choral singing before the nineteenth century, there was a dearth of professional choral singers to employ for this purpose. The result was that weak and often untrained singers were pressed into service as choristers, and composers were therefore forced to write fairly simple music for these groups. This explains why the choral writing in Rossini's operas is so simple in comparison to the style of the arias and ensemble numbers. A careful listening to any of the choruses in *La Cenerentola* will reveal a music that frequently consists of only one melodic line doubled in all the voice parts (a kind of group aria). Then when the music does break into harmony, the individual parts (soprano, alto, tenor, and bass) all continue singing the same rhythm, suggesting, perhaps, a fear on the composer's part that four rhythmically independent parts would only confuse his choral singers. Clearly Rossini saw safety in uniformity.

This scene, in which everyone anxiously prepares for the arrival of the

Prince, ends in a wonderful number that combines the quartet (Alidoro, the sisters, and Cinderella) with the chorus in a madcap musical climax. The sisters get all excited about the ball and start ordering Cinderella to help them get ready, while Alidoro and the chorus comment on their vanity and the potential excitement of the party. In this ensemble we find the common *buffa* vocal technique of *patter*. This is a tongue-twistingly rapid delivery of text usually on one repeated note. Ex. 2-1 gives some idea of the kind of vocal dexterity needed to execute the patter style of singing. Notice, especially, the speed at which the basic unit of musical time (the half note) passes: 120 beats/second. That equals one beat every half-second. At that speed the number of words the singer must squeeze into every beat becomes especially difficult—and even more so when some of the eighth notes carry elided syllables, as seen on the fourth note of the second line, where the syllables *lo*, *ho*, and *un* all have to be sung on one fleeting note.

Example 2-1. Excerpts from act 1 Quartet with chorus.

Finally Don Magnifico makes his entrance, having been awakened from a wonderful dream by all the commotion. His aria begins in a mock serious style but then soon falls into the more common *buffo* bass style with lots of rapid repeated notes (more patter). A look at the text for this aria will show that it is partly the libretto that is responsible for this comic style. Unlike the texts for opera seria arias, which usually have no more than two stanzas of four lines each, *buffo* arias are often set to a long, unbroken string of lines that causes the composer to have to find a way of setting all those words as efficiently as possible. These rambling texts, therefore, result in aria forms never seen in serious opera: forms that involved more themes, more contrasting sections, and new rondo-like designs that could accommodate large amounts of text.

Magnifico's patter aria.

Miei rampolli femminini	My female offspring,
Vi ripudio; mi vergogno!	I disown you; I'm ashamed!
Un magnifico mio sogno	You came and interrupted

Mi veniste a sconcertar.	A splendid dream of mine.
(Come son mortificate!)	(How vexed they are!)
Degne figlie d'un barone!	Worthy daughters of a baron!
Via, silenzio, ed attenzione.	Come now, be quiet and pay attention.
State il sogno a meditar.	Just think about my dream.
Mi sognai fra il fosco e il chiaro	I dreamt, part clearly and part foggily,
Un bellissimo somaro;	Of a most beautiful donkey;
Un somaro, ma solenne.	A donkey, but an impressive one.
Quando a un tratto, oh che portento!	When suddenly—oh what a wonder—
Sulle spalle a cento a centoon	On its shoulders hundreds
Gli spuntarono le penne,	Of feathers grew
Ed in aria, sciù, volò!	And up into the air it flew!
Ed in cima a un campanile	And on top of a steeple
Come in trono si fermò.	As if upon a throne it came to rest.
Si sentiano per di sotto	Below could be heard
Le campane a dindonar, din, don,	The bells chiming—ding, dong,
Col cì cì ciù ciù di botto	With your cheep cheep suddenly
Mi veniste a risvegliar.	You came and woke me up.
Ma d'un sogno sì intralciato.	But here is an explanation of the symbols
Ecco il simbolo spiegato.	In such a tangled dream.
Etc., etc.	Etc., etc.

Up to this point in the opera we have not heard a lot of the virtuoso style of singing for which Rossini's operas are so famous. But that changes as Prince Ramiro enters (in disguise as his own valet). This is the scene in which the Prince and Cinderella first meet and become attracted to each other. One might justifiably expect the Prince to sing in this virtuoso style, as that was the style in which all of the aristocratic characters in opera seria expressed themselves. But hearing the peasant girl, Cinderella, sing in this same virtuosic style is what makes Rossini's comic operas different from those of the previous generation of Italian composers. Of course, there is a dramatic justification for her singing in this vocally ornate style: the music thereby identifies Cinderella as an aristocrat, despite the torn and tattered clothes she wears and menial chores she is forced to perform.

After Prince Ramiro and Cinderella have gotten to know each other, Dandini (dressed as the Prince) enters with much pomp. His first aria is a marvelous parody of the opera seria style. The text shows that he is comparing himself to a bee who buzzes from flower to flower in search of the sweetest nectar.

Dandini's aria.

Come un'ape ne' giorni d'aprile	As a bee on an April day
Va volando leggera e scherzosa;	Flies lightly and playfully

Corre al giglio, poi salta alla rosa	First to the lily, then to the rose
Dolce un fiore a cercare per sè:	Seeking a sweet blossom for itself,
Fra le belle m'aggiro e rimiro:	So I go roaming and look among the fair maids
Ne ho vedute già tante e poi tante:	I've already seen so many;
Ma non trovo un giudizio, un sembiante,	But I can't find wisdom or a face,
Un boccone squisito per me.	A delicious mouthful for me.

In eighteenth-century opera seria, this kind of aria was commonly known as a "simile" aria. Here Ramiro's valet, all puffed up with the importance of his pretend role, strikes a comic note as Rossini parodies this well-known operatic convention. The scene works especially well if the singer overdoes the grandiosity of the whole thing and exaggerates the musical gestures to make the parody obvious. This technique of borrowing musical styles from opera seria for the purpose of parody in opera buffa dates back at least as far as Mozart, and formed the cornerstone of much of the comic effect in many of his operas, especially those of the *dramma giocoso* type. (For a more detailed discussion, see the chapter on *Don Giovanni*.)

This brings us to the famous quintet at the end of act 1. At this point we can begin to see why the musical form of the ensemble was so useful to composers of comic opera. The opera buffa ensemble was an important invention that allowed these composers to incorporate dramatic action into musical numbers. The usual process by which an opera at this time unfolded was for its texts to be divided into two different categories according to their function in the drama: either narrative or reflective. The narrative texts, which included all of the dialogue between characters, was set as recitative. This allowed for the easiest comprehension of the words, so that the audience could understand what was happening onstage. Then at points in this unfolding dramatic action, the librettist would pause for a moment of reflection in which a character would express how he or she was feeling about a particular dramatic situation. These reflective texts were set to music of a more lyrical nature and thus took shape as the arias and duets of the opera, which are usually referred to as the "set pieces." But comic opera composers discovered that by incorporating some of the action of narrative texts into the music of the ensemble numbers, they could reduce the amount of boring recitative needed to advance the plot. For this purpose composers reintroduced the kind of semimelodic vocal style that had been characteristic of the earliest seventeenth-century operas. The term for this semimelodic vocal style is *arioso*. In terms of its tunefulness, this style lies somewhere between the speechlike quality of recitative and the fully lyrical melodies of an aria. Thus dramatic action set by the composer as arioso leads to dramatic reflection set in fully lyrical music. In the quintet at the end of act 1, the sisters have just departed for the ball, leaving Ramiro, Don Magnifico, and Cinderella behind. Then Dandini returns to see why his master has been delayed. Cinderella begs her stepfather to allow her to go to the ball, but he refuses and threatens her with physical punishment, at which point Ramiro and Dandini step in to prevent this. Then suddenly the Prince's tutor, Alidoro, arrives (now without his beggar's disguise) with a proclamation stating that it is known that Magnifico has three daughters, not two, and that they all must attend the ball. Cinderella gets excited, but Magnifico claims that the third daughter is dead, and that Cinderella is nothing but a servant girl. This rather complex unfolding of action is all treated musically in arioso, allowing Rossini to guarantee that his audience will catch the important unfolding of the dramatic action among all of his characters in music that projects the words clearly.

As the drama comes to a critical moment, when Magnifico announces that his third daughter is dead, the action stops and the music moves into the lyrical section of the quintet in which each character reacts to the situation, mostly in asides to the audience. This alternation of action in arioso with reaction in fully lyrical music was one of Rossini's most important innovations in his remaking of Italian comic opera in the early nineteenth century. Prior to this, such ensemble numbers had always been written in a continuously lyrical style, as in the works of Mozart, where the apprehension of the text was often sacrificed to the beauty of multiple interweaving melodic lines. This new division of texts into narrative and reflective types, with the corresponding division of the music into semimelodic and fully lyrical sections, became the standard technique for building ensembles in both comic and serious Italian opera for the next fifty years.

In any opera, the most important ensemble was the finale that brought each act to a close. In Mozart's hands, the ensemble finale took shape as a string of smaller ensembles arranged usually to begin as a duet, and then to add more and more characters, moving through a trio, to a quartet, and perhaps finally to a quintet with the chorus added at the end. Such an arrangement produced a dramatic crescendo of activity that was matched by the growing complexity, excitement, and volume of the music. Mozart's technique had been to treat the discrete sections of the finale like movements in a symphony, with each in its own tempo, meter, and key. The music unfolded continuously, with no use of recitative, for up to twenty minutes—an achievement about which Mozart was extremely proud. In the nineteenth century, Rossini continued this basic technique of building finales in sections of increasing activity, but did so with the addition of arioso for the setting of those texts that contained action. The finale to act 1 in *La Cenerentola* depicts the ball at the Prince's palace. It begins with a duet between Ramiro and Dandini, as they try to figure out which of the sisters Alidoro thought was the right one for the prince to marry. Then the sisters enter vying for Dandini's attention (still thinking he is the real prince). This makes the duet into a quartet, and here we can see the kind of slightly less lyrical music (arioso) that Rossini uses for conversational texts. Only at the very end, when the text begins to comment on the action that has unfolded up to this point (the Prince has offered to allow his valet to marry the sister he doesn't choose, and neither lady is happy with the prospect of becoming a servant's wife), do all the voices come together for true lyrical ensemble singing.

End of quartet in act 1 finale (reflective ensemble).

RAMIRO: *[playing Dandini]*
Sarò docile, amoroso,
Tenerissimo di cuore.

RAMIRO:
I'll be obedient, loving,
Most tender-hearted.

CLORINDA:
Un scudiero! No signore.
Un scudiero! Questo no.
Con un'anima plebea!

CLORINDA:
A servant! No, sir!
A servant! This no.
With a plebian soul!

TISBE:
Un scudiero! No signore.
Un scudiero! Questo no.
Con un'aria dozzinale!

TISBE:
A servant! No, sir!
A servant! This no.
With such vulgar ways!

BOTH:
Mi fa male, mi fa male
Solamente a immaginar.

BOTH:
It makes me ill
Just to imagine.

DANDINI, RAMIRO:
La scenetta è originale.
Veramente da contar.

DANDINI, RAMIRO:
The scene is original.
Truly to be cherished.

Next, Rossini adds the chorus and Alidoro to the mix, with the latter announcing the arrival at the ball of a mysterious veiled woman, about whom everyone is extremely curious. This interchange is set to more arioso before moving gradually into a full quintet for the text in which each character expresses either their jealousy or their eager anticipation.

The first act finale ends with the entrance of Don Magnifico, who is astonished to see Cinderella, or someone who he thinks looks like her.

Having never seen her in fancy clothing, he cannot quite be sure of her identity. His opening arioso leads eventually to the concluding ensemble in which everyone takes part. Composers of both comic and serious opera in the early nineteenth century always cast this closing section of the finale in a fast tempo to guarantee an exciting conclusion as the curtain came down. And many, like Rossini, also added a large crescendo to the music to drive the scene to an even more powerful climax. The fact that this formal technique of increasing tempo and volume was employed in both the serious and comic operas of Rossini is itself telling of the direction in which Italian opera was headed at this time. The old musical distinctions between the ornate opera seria and the simpler opera buffa were beginning to fall away, as comic opera gradually adopted more and more of the style of serious opera, making these old arch rivals now virtually indistinguishable from a musical point of view.

Beyond the first act lie many musical numbers that duplicate much of the style and compositional techniques found in act 1. There is no need to survey all of these, but some special musical-dramatic moments deserve mention. The first of these is the marvelous *buffo* bass aria that Magnifico sings near the beginning of the second act. In this classic patter aria, which, like all such arias, derives its comic effect from the rapid delivery of the text, we see Magnifico imagining himself in a new position of authority after one of his daughters becomes Princess. While this style of tongue-twisting singing had long been standard fare in comic bass roles, its retention by Rossini may also have been his way of allowing the bass voice to participate in the display of virtuosity that in other roles took the form of vocal dexterity in intricate passagework (scales and arpeggios that sound more like technical etudes for flute or clarinet than arias for voice). Bass voices were, because of their low pitch range, simply less agile than higher voices. So elaborate decorative melodies of the kind that sopranos and tenors sang, were really not possible for such low voice types. In place of that, composers tended to rely on the impressive ability of most basses to enunciate a string of words at surprisingly rapid tempos.

One of the most unusual moments in act 2 is the instrumental interlude labeled "storm music" in the orchestral score. This is a short programmatic orchestral number (without voices) that begins immediately after Don Magnifico and his daughters return home from the Prince's ball. The Don has finally learned that Dandini is not really the Prince, and this little deception has put him into a towering rage. It is late at night, and everyone retires to bed, leaving the stage clear for the storm that follows. Dramatically, this instrumental music was meant to represent the Prince's late-night ride to find Cinderella, and just as surely, his anxiety at the thought of losing her. But why is he trying to find Cinderella? Since there is no stroke of midnight deadline in this opera as there is in the fairy tale, Cinderella did not have to make a hasty exit from the palace, dropping her slipper on the way. In the opera, the Prince tells Cinderella that he loves her, and from that moment the story has to go in a somewhat different direction than the fairy tale everyone knows. To get Cinderella out of the palace so the Prince can go chasing after her, Rossini's librettist decided that she should reject the Prince's immediate declaration of love, and impose on him a test of his sincerity—an unfortunate complication of the operatic plot. She will leave, and he must hunt for her—essentially a totally silly and illogical game of hide-and-seek. But opera librettos often make even less sense than fairy tales, so rarely has this particular artificial obstacle to true love been the source of critical objections from either scholars or audiences.

Without the aid of a sung text for the scene in which Ramiro charges through the countryside to locate his beloved, Rossini was forced to come up with some purely instrumental music. The idea to make that orchestral interlude represent a storm was undoubtedly one of Rossini's best inspirations in the opera. Instrumental depictions of storms were by no means new to opera in Rossini's day. They appear in many eighteenth-century works, both Italian and French. What is unusual about Rossini's storm scene is that he included it in a comic opera, whereas heretofore, such scenes were restricted to serious opera, in which they became musical metaphors for the subconscious, turbulent passions of the characters caught up in emotionally wrenching circumstances. In adopting this technique for his comic opera, Rossini took yet another step toward reducing the musical differences between comic and serious styles in opera—ultimately one of his greatest achievements in the history of this genre. Eventually, thanks to his work, comic opera was able to achieve a status equal to that of serious opera, and to serve as a vehicle for masterpieces such as Verdi's *Falstaff* and Wagner's *Die Meistersinger*—operas whose musical sophistication clearly demonstrated that the humble origins of opera buffa had been fully transcended.

One final and most important example of this rapprochement of comic and serious styles in Rossini's *buffa* operas can be found in his portrayal of the heroine throughout the opera. First of all, she is a contralto, a voice type that was rarely used in comic opera before Rossini, but one that he borrowed from his own serious operas, where such voices began to replace the outdated castrati of the past. Furthermore, Cinderella is no ordinary *buffa* heroine. Her character evolves considerably from her opening little folk song in act

1 to the level of musical and personal maturity demonstrated in the final ensemble, where she dominates the stage with her elaborate vocal *fioriture* (decorative singing). The virtuosity of her part in this finale, along with its prominence over those of her singing partners, creates the dramatic effect of a complete character transformation from demure stepsister to munificent aristocratic princess. Herein lies the beauty and power of opera: that music can underline and add new levels of understanding to dramatic situations. In this instance, Cinderella moves from rags to riches, and this transformation is projected through her music—both its style and its relationship to other music around it. With this final scene, the transformation of Cinderella is complete; in her final form she seems to anticipate many of the famous sentimental heroines of later nineteenth-century bel canto opera. On the broadest metaphoric level, Rossini's musical depiction of this rags-to-riches heroine symbolizes his transformation of Italian comic opera from its simple, unsophisticated eighteenth-century musical roots to its new iteration as a musical-dramatic genre able to compete for the same audiences with the best serious operas of the time.

While Rossini's *La Cenerentola* is still popular today because of its charming music that provides abundant opportunity to hear great singing, this is ultimately an opera of immense historical importance as well. In it (as well as in his other comic operas), Rossini managed to grapple with the problem of how to move beyond Mozart, of how to find a way to write comic opera without duplicating the style and techniques of his famous predecessor. Unlike opera seria, which was in desperate need of rescue from imminent sociological irrelevance, comic opera really needed no such remaking at the turn of the nineteenth century. It was only by virtue of Rossini's genius that he was able to find a way of making a place for himself as a composer of opera buffa after Mozart. There was not to be another major rethinking of Italian comic opera until the very end of the century, when Verdi accomplished yet another major transformation of this genre with the writing of *Falstaff*.

Chapter 3

Verdi's *Falstaff*: The Final Frontier

W ith the birth of opera buffa in the early eighteenth century, the world of Italian musical theater gained an alternative to the artificialities of older opera seria. The new comic genre distinguished itself through the adoption of the popular, French *style galant*, consisting of transparent, homophonic textures; syllabic text setting; rapid tempos; major modes; and a concomitant rejection of the vocal melismas and elaborate improvisation characteristic of the bel canto style of serious opera. Both the simple musical style and the new subject matter—based on romantic intrigues that glorified the newly influential middle class—made opera buffa a form of musical entertainment that catered to the changes percolating in eighteenth-century society. But this new, socially vital opera underwent some major changes of its own in the early years of the nineteenth century, when Rossini initiated the major revolution discussed in the previous chapter. With that revolution, he remade the musical language of comic opera by abandoning the simple, almost folklike style of the past, replacing it with the same ornate decorative vocal melody that had always characterized serious opera. In addition, he revolutionized serious opera by replacing the old aristocratic subjects drawn from ancient history, with new, contemporary subjects, designed to appeal to the increasingly bourgeois audiences that had always been drawn to comic opera. In making these changes, Rossini caused comic and serious opera to become more alike, and much of the rationale for the former, as an alternative to the latter, faded as the nineteenth century wore on. If the composers who followed Rossini can be taken as an indication of a trend from about 1830 on, we see a marked decrease in the number of comic operas written in Italy, accompanied by a shift of interest toward serious and semiserious librettos. Taking Donizetti as an example, we discover that a full third of his works are comic. But moving on to the next generation of composers, including Saverio Mercadante and Giuseppe Verdi, it becomes apparent how little attention was suddenly being paid to comic works at midcentury. Mercadante's abundant output of approximately sixty operas includes only five that are comic; and of Verdi's twenty-six works, only two are comic.

At the far end of the nineteenth century stands one of those by-then-rare Italian comic operas: Verdi's *Falstaff* (1893). Coming nearly eighty years after

Rossini's revolutionary transformation of Italian comic opera, *Falstaff* represents the second modernization of this genre to take place in the nineteenth century. Like Rossini, Verdi chose not to distinguish between comic and serious opera in terms of singing style and operatic form. His approach to writing comic opera at the end of the century was to bring it into alignment with the many revolutionary changes he himself had brought to serious opera throughout his many years of work in that genre. An understanding of *Falstaff*, then, depends in part upon an understanding of Verdi's transformation of Italian serious opera from the 1840s through the 1880s (essentially from *Macbeth* to *Otello*). Aspects of this evolution are treated in other chapters of this book, but a summary will nonetheless be useful here.

Giuseppe Verdi (1813–1901) stood at the forefront of Italian opera for over fifty years, from the debut of his first opera at La Scala in1839 to the premiere of *Falstaff* at that same theater in1893. Verdi, no less than his German rival Wagner, was caught up in an operatic revolution intent upon creating a new more realistic kind of music drama that unfolded with the same continuity found in a spoken stage drama. But Wagner is always given credit for bringing this revolution to fruition with his almost draconian redefinition of the very concept of opera. Verdi, on the other hand, worked more quietly, in a more evolutionary way, toward the same goal of dramatic realism. For many listeners, especially in his own day, Verdi's last operas represented his final capitulation to the principles of symphonic opera that Wagner had propounded since the premiere of his *Ring* cycle in 1876. But for those less blinded by the histrionics of Wagner's so-called music of the future, Verdi's *Falstaff* stood firmly as a beacon of compromise between the formulas of traditional opera and the ideals of the new symphonic opera as espoused by his German rival. One of the goals of this chapter is to elucidate this central theory about Verdi's late works: that he identified and tackled the very same problems confronting all composers of opera after 1850, but in the process, arrived at a solution to those problems that was uniquely Italian. (See also the chapter on Verdi's *Otello*.)

These problems were many, but the largest and perhaps most fundamental—one faced by both Wagner and Verdi after 1850—was that the drama of a traditional opera unfolded in a series of closed musical numbers (set pieces such as arias, duets, choruses, and ensembles) linked together by sections of speechlike recitative. The recitative accommodated the dialogue necessary for characters to interact and for the plot to progress, while the musical numbers (i.e., the set pieces) allowed for the expression of feelings associated with particularly intense moments in the drama. In this manner, opera became a theatrical event in which the dramatic development continually alternated between action couched in recitative, and reaction (or dramatic stasis) expounded in set pieces that allowed for emotional reflection. (See the chapters on Rossini's *La Cenerentola* and *Semiramide* for details.) This start-and-stop quality was further exacerbated by the fact that audiences regularly interrupted performances to applaud their favorite singers at the end of every aria and duet, thus further holding up the progress of the drama to allow the principal singers to come out of character to acknowledge the adulation of their fans. Additional delays resulted when audience applause was so great that singers were "forced" to repeat the entire number before moving on with the opera.

Furthermore, all early nineteenth-century Italian opera was bound by strict forms, mostly derived from the works of Rossini, which governed the structure of both the libretto and the music. (See chapter 4 for details.) These musical forms, and seemingly everything else about Italian opera, were motivated by the need to allow audiences to satisfy their desire to hear great singing. If the dramatic action of a particular plot did not naturally fit the preordained musical structures, then it had to be twisted and pounded into shape until it did. Italian opera of this era was a form of musical entertainment that was not so much about good drama as it was about good singing: a style of opera in which the needs of the drama were regularly sacrificed to the needs of the music. Singing and singers ruled supreme in the opera houses of Italy until about 1850, when Verdi began rethinking the priorities of music drama.

The story of Verdi's career is that of a composer who began at an early age to question the values of Italian opera of the 1830s. Because he, more than any of his immediate predecessors, was concerned with the question of dramatic effectiveness in opera, Verdi looked for ways to remain faithful to the literary sources he chose to set to music. In trying to create a better balance between the dramatic and musical elements in opera, he was forced to renounce all of those compositional practices that had served merely to glorify the human voice. Old forms had to be abandoned when they no longer suited the disposition of the action, and ways had to be discovered to keep the drama moving ahead, without the continual interruption of final cadences that cued lengthy rounds of applause from enthusiastic audiences. Along the path from *Macbeth* to *Rigoletto* and on to *Otello*, Verdi refined his technique for creating a more realistic dramatic flow in opera. (See chapter 7 for a full explanation of how he did this.)

As Verdi's last opera, *Falstaff* represents the application of these new techniques to the genre of comic opera in the closing years of the century. In this case, the idea for another opera based on Shakespeare came from

Verdi's librettist, Arrigo Boito, who was looking for ways to coax the old master out of retirement after the success of his previous opera, *Otello*. Boito suggested that Verdi should end his career with a comic opera, something that would surprise audiences and at the same time give him a chance to refute his reputation as a composer who could only write serious opera—a reputation earned when his only other comic work, *Un giorno di regno*, failed miserably at its premiere in 1840. Upon receipt of the new libretto in 1889, Verdi's first reaction took shape as a positive proclamation that he had been dreaming for years of writing another comic opera, but had never been able to find a libretto that satisfied his need to avoid the outdated conventions of the genre. Thanks to Boito, the fading embers of a seventy-six year-old composer's art were fanned to life with a Shakespearean libretto that would inspire him to revolutionize comic opera one last time. Despite his initial enthusiasm, however, Verdi began to demur, telling Boito he was too old to write another opera, and that work on such an opera would interfere with Boito's own compositional activities. But the librettist easily saw through all these excuses, and demanded that work on their *Falstaff* commence immediately.

For the most part, Boito adapted Shakespeare's *The Merry Wives of Windsor* in making the libretto for this opera. But the character of Falstaff, which is so central to that play, also appears in Shakespeare's *Henry IV*, Parts I and II, where he is first seen in the role of confidant to the wayward Prince Harry. In addition, Shakespeare also presents Falstaff as a common highwayman and opportunist who makes his living stealing from wealthy travelers. But at the same time he is a man of considerable wit, good cheer, and self-confidence, who enjoys life to the fullest in a totally unembarrassed, hedonistic manner. This depiction of Falstaff, supported by specific scenes and lines borrowed from *Henry IV*, is carried over into Boito's portrayal of the jolly, fat hero of Verdi's opera.

In bringing the Falstaff plays to the operatic stage, Verdi was again concerned, as he had been throughout his career, with fidelity to his sources, as well as with creating an opera that unfolded with a continuity more like that of a stage play. To achieve these goals, he drastically reduced his reliance on lyrical set pieces such as arias and duets, because the symmetrical, repetitive melodic patterns of these musical numbers induced composers to repeat much of the libretto's text to fill up the number of measures required to create a full set piece. This text repetition led to characters in the drama expressing their ideas in a manner that bore no relation to the real world. As if dramatic characters communicating through singing weren't unrealistic enough (one of the most basic objections leveled at the genre of opera), the fact that they did so by continually repeating themselves further compounded the sense of theatrical artificiality in the opera house of Verdi's youth. Thus, in an aria or duet audiences might regularly expect to hear a composer turn two lines of text into something far more repetitive, as follows:

> With pain and anguish in my heart,
> I return to her from afar.

Musical setting:

> With pain and anguish in my heart
> With pain and anguish, pain and anguish,
> I return to her from afar,
> Return from afar, from afar.

This is exactly the kind of stylized expression that could only be avoided by replacing the symmetrical phrase structures and closed repetitive musical forms of operatic set pieces with open-ended, nonrepeating musical structures based on short orchestral motifs, which could be continually sequenced while the vocal text unfolded over top of them in an arioso style. As a style of operatic melody, arioso is not especially interesting in and of itself, but composers compensated for this by making sure the accompanying orchestral motifs had a memorable melodic profile of their own. In essence, the melodic interest in an arioso texture shifts from the voice to the orchestra.

The opening of *Falstaff* is a marvelous demonstration of this arioso technique. Before exploring this scene, however, we must take note of the fact that Verdi did not begin his opera with the conventional (one might even say de rigueur) introductory chorus. Had this been an opera written by Rossini or Donizetti, the first scene of Shakespeare's play, which contains only a handful of characters, would had to have been modified to create an excuse for a chorus at the beginning of act 1. In such a hypothetical opera, the scene in the Garter Inn, which Shakespeare populates only with Falstaff, a couple of his friends, and Dr. Caius, would have required augmentation by a large crowd of drinkers who could function as a chorus. This chorus would then have sung an introductory number, perhaps about the lazy life of highwaymen and the pleasure of wine, before Dr. Caius could break in to complain about Falstaff. But part of Verdi's revolution was to eliminate these dramatic conventions that distorted the literary sources on which operas were so often based. Therefore, *Falstaff* begins instead with only a few characters onstage (as in Shakespeare) singing to one another in arioso.

Although designed to accommodate a continual, nonrepeating delivery of text, and to avoid the symmetrical patterning and sectional division of closed musical forms like the aria (i.e., those with a clear beginning and end), arioso was also not without a musical form of its own, especially in the hands of great composers like Verdi. The opening scene of the opera depicts Sir John Falstaff holding court in the Garter Inn, where Dr. Caius has come to complain that Falstaff has beaten his servants and "violated" his house. He also accuses Falstaff's companions, Bardolph and Pistol, of robbing him while he was drinking at the inn the night before. This scene involves rather complex dialogue, as the characters trade insults in rapid-fire exchanges. Verdi began by setting Dr. Caius's complaints to a quick, almost frantic, staccato motif in the orchestra (see Ex. 3-1).

Example 3-1. Opening of act 1, sc. 1—orchestral motif.

At the point where Falstaff begins his unperturbed response to these accusations, the mood of the music changes, and Verdi launches his hero with a slower tempo and a new motif. This new motif (Ex. 3-2) is rhythmically related to the one that opened the scene, but its melodic shape now involves conjunct (i.e., stepwise) motion and a more legato and lyrical style of performance, which perfectly communicates Falstaff's relaxed demeanor.

Example 3-2. Orchestral motif accompanying Falstaff's response.

As soon as Falstaff finishes his "response" to the doctor's accusations, the music returns to the motif heard at the beginning. In this way Verdi managed to bring the same sense of large-scale formal symmetry (in this case ABA form) to lengthy passages of arioso as had always applied to the closed musical forms like the aria. Considering that for two hundred years prior to this, opera had had no musical form other than that which was found in its individual set pieces, we can safely conclude that Verdi's efforts at establishing a formal structure for his arioso passages represented an attempt to solve this long-standing compositional problem by freeing the musical-dramatic narrative of opera from the worn-out musical formulas of the past.

The opening scene of *Falstaff* demonstrates that the principal use of arioso in Verdi's day was as a replacement for recitative in the setting of dialogue. In such circumstances, it allowed composers to move through large sections of conversational text without repeating words, while providing those texts with greater musical value or interest than they would have had if set to recitative. Beyond this advantage, the substitution of arioso for recitative also eliminated the disruptive contrast between speechlike music and fully lyrical vocal writing that one finds in earlier Italian opera. The semimelodic style of arioso brings the dialogue and narrative texts closer in melodic style to the sound of the fully lyrical set pieces, thus lending to opera something more like the dramatic continuity one finds in a spoken stage play.

Although arioso can safely be thought of as a semimelodic vocal style, there are nonetheless moments in Verdi's use of this technique where he allowed the voice to briefly adopt the lyricism and symmetry of an aria. In this opening scene, after Dr. Caius leaves the inn, Falstaff complains to his comrades that keeping them around costs him a lot of money, which he doesn't have. He says to Bardolph,

So che se andiam, la notte,
    di taverna in taverna,
Quel tuo naso ardentissimo mi
    serve da lanterna!
Ma quell risparmio d'olio tu
    lo consumi in vino.
	I know that if we go from
	    tavern to tavern at night,
	That fiery nose of yours serves me
	    as a lantern!
	But what I save on oil,
	    you consume in wine.

Example 3-3. A lyrical moment in the arioso of act 1, sc. 1.

Example 3-3 *(continued)*

na - so   ar - den - tis - si - mo   mi   ser - ve da lan-ter   -   na!   Ma quel ri - spar-mio

d'o - lio   tu   lo   con - su - mi in   vi - no

Ex. 3-3 illustrates the far more lyrical music Verdi wrote for these few lines. Notice that this section of music falls into a phrase pattern of AABA'C, which temporarily relieves the frenetic forward motion of the music heard up to this point in the scene.

Toward the end of his career, Verdi's use of arioso led many critics to accuse him of having adopted the symphonic style of Wagner, whose entire operatic technique was founded upon the principle of vocal *Sprechgesang* (literally, "speechsong") supported by a dominant orchestral background of leitmotifs. Verdi, of course, was deeply wounded by these accusations of stylistic plagiarism, strongly insisting that it was not *his* style but that of the younger Italian generation, which leaned in the direction of the "symphony." In a letter of 1884 he warned against this tendency in modern Italian opera, saying, "Opera is opera, and symphony is symphony,"[1] as if to make clear the roots of his own compositional technique in the tradition of good singing and the beauty of the human voice. Verdi was simply not ready to follow Wagner's lead in completely rejecting the lyrical set pieces that had served as the backbone of the Italian operatic tradition for over two hundred years.

The measure of Verdi's adherence to this Italian tradition can be found in part 2 of act 1, where the opera's heroines, Alice and Meg, discover Falstaff's plan to seduce each of them, and Alice's husband is independently warned of the situation by Bardolf and Pistol. Most of this part of the act is given over to extensive ensemble singing clearly reminiscent of an older tradition of Italian comic opera. The scene is laid in the garden of Alice Ford's house. It begins with a quartet for the ladies (Alice, Meg, Dame Quickly, and Nannetta) who express their disgust over Falstaff's indecent proposal to both Alice and Meg. The style of this quartet recalls many of the great ensembles in the comic operas of Mozart and Rossini—fast-paced, staccato singing in rhythmic unison. Its sprightly style communicates the appropriate comic effect

---

1. Osborne, 1971, 225.

even if the actual text seems fairly serious. As the ladies finish their ensemble and exit the stage, Dr. Caius, Bardolph, Pistol, and Fenton all enter in conversation with Ford (Alice's husband). Unknown to the ladies, Bardolph and Pistol have come to warn Ford of the impending seduction of his wife. In an animated quintet, they continue the comic style of the ladies' preceding quartet. Eventually the five men and four women find themselves onstage together (in separate groups), which allows Verdi to combine all nine voices in a marvelous, large ensemble that brings the act to a close. In terms of its overall structure, this second part of act 1 is clearly modeled on the complex ensemble finales of earlier Italian opera buffa, in which a growing number of characters on stage and a corresponding crescendo of musical activity bring the act to a dramatic climax. These ensembles of solo characters had long been a part of the Italian comic opera tradition, and mark *Falstaff* as something different from Verdi's serious operas, in which end-of-act ensembles usually involve at least one section of slow moving music, and almost always include a much larger role for the chorus. The ensemble at the end of act 1 recaptures the older principles of comic opera construction not just in its musical style, but also in its dramatic effect of combining unfolding action with occasional points of dramatic repose that allow for a moment of multiple points of reflection on a particular turn of events. Verdi's *Falstaff* can therefore best be understood as a compromise between the traditional techniques and style of Italian comic opera, and the more modern technique of arioso-based continuous opera that Verdi had forged over the years in his serious operas. (See the chapters on *Rigoletto* and *Otello* for further details.)

Other parts of the libretto of act 1, part 2 also call up a more lyrical, and therefore more old-fashioned, style of melodic writing. The duet between the young lovers, Nannetta and Fenton, which intervenes between the opening ensembles (the quartet and the quintet) and the final nonet, is one such moment. Here Verdi abandoned the old duet form in which each character was given a long, solo section to sing before moving into the true duet. In this particular duet Fenton and Nannetta never sing together. Instead, Verdi adopted the new "conversational" style of duet writing he had developed in his later years for use in serious operas. In this new style, singers take turns "speaking" to each other exactly as they would in a stage play. The resulting music (see Ex. 3-4) sounds something like an aria in which two singers share the melodic line in alternation.

Example 3-4. Fenton-Nannetta duet, act 1, part 2.

Verdi's new conversational style of duet writing enabled him to adhere to the underlying operatic principle of minimal text repetition that motivated his overall approach to modernizing Italian opera at the end of the nineteenth century. But in the case of the duet between Nannetta and Fenton, he also found a way of accommodating this conversational style within the framework of traditionally lyrical vocal melodies, thus giving his audience the best of both worlds.

It becomes clear then, after only a cursory hearing of parts of *Falstaff*, that Verdi's goal in modernizing Italian comic opera was to combine the element of ensemble singing (originally one of the main differentiating factors between serious and comic opera in the eighteenth century) with the more modern technique of continuous opera based on the use of arioso. But although Verdi was content to retain the traditional ensemble finales that so clearly defined comic opera of the past, he was less motivated to continue writing arias of the kind that had once formed the centerpieces of both comic and serious Italian opera. Although this opera contains a few brief moments of solo singing for which Verdi wrote some lovely melodic vocal lines, these sections are never extensive enough to qualify as real arias. Nor do they have the patterned formal structure of the independent arias of earlier Italian opera. Perhaps Verdi came to realize (as did Debussy ten years later in his *Pelléas et Mélisande*) that song was simply too blunt a tool for the musical depiction of the intricate subtleties of human emotions. Such is the case with Falstaff's famous soliloquy at the close of the first scene of act 1. This speech on the futility of honor was borrowed by Boito from Shakespeare's *Henry IV*, Part I, where Falstaff torpedoes the value of honor as defined by the nobles with whom his friend Prince Harry is usually associated. In setting this paraphrase of Shakespeare's lines, Verdi again wanted to avoid, for the sake of reality, the necessity of text repetition that grows out of the use of patterned musical forms like the aria. He therefore resorted to the use of arioso to produce the illusion of opera that unfolds more continuously rather than as a set of unrelated lyrical numbers sandwiched between stretches of dialogue in recitative.

Similarly, a complex emotional outpouring such as we hear from Master Ford in act 2, when he learns that his wife has made an illicit assignation with Falstaff, is also handled by Verdi in the more flexible arioso style, with little recourse to true melody until the very end of the number. While Ford's solo here doesn't sound like an aria, it still retains many of the usual earmarks of that old form: a lengthy uninterrupted expression of a single character's feelings at a particularly intense moment in the drama. As such it is reminiscent of the arias of older Italian opera, complete, in this case, with full musical closure at the end. But Verdi, ever mindful of the need to create a continuous flow to his new operas, cleverly built an orchestral bridge between the point of this closure (where Ford stops singing) and the section that follows, where Falstaff returns to usher him out of the inn. Such bridges serve to glue together, into one long uninterrupted flow, those few sections of music that do come to a full cadential close, thus preventing audiences from jumping in and stopping the drama with applause. They effectively lend the illusion of a dramatic continuum similar to that found in the works of Wagner. Little wonder so many critics were fooled into thinking that Verdi had become an Italian convert to the symphonic style and technique of his northern rival.

Allusions to the comic operas of Mozart continue at the end of act 2 of *Falstaff*, where Verdi again writes a large ensemble finale. Here Falstaff has come to his romantic rendezvous with Mistress Ford, but is interrupted by the arrival of her husband and his friends who plan to catch him in the act of seducing a married woman. The action is typical of the usual Italian end-of-act finale: a large group of people onstage, much confusion among all the characters, and lots of activity in which everyone has something different to say about the situation. Even a cursory hearing of this ensemble finale will remind listeners of the tremendous confusion generated by Mozart in the ensemble finales of his greatest Viennese operas such as *Le nozze de Figaro*.

In 1893 Verdi knew, of course, that *Falstaff* was to be his last opera, his farewell to the world of musical theater. And like so many composers before him, he came to the end of his career with a need to make a grand summarizing musical statement. We can see this urge to return to the past, to remaster the fundamentals of the craft of composition, in the late works of nearly every famous composer. For Bach this creative urge resulted in his colossal *Art of the Fugue*, for Mozart it resulted in the extravagant counterpoint of his Requiem, for Beethoven the need to demonstrate his craftsmanship led to the intricacies of the late quartets and in his study of Palestrina, for Schubert it found expression in the study of Bach. Verdi was no exception in this regard. As he composed the final pages of *Falstaff,* he too must have been aware that this was his final word on the art of dramatic composition. This may well be the reason we find two examples of vocal fugues in this opera. Mastery of the technique of fugal composition had, since the days of Bach, been the focus of musical training for all aspiring composers—a true measure of one's technical skill. Verdi himself had begun his musical education with just such training long before he entered the operatic world. Then for years, his writing of opera required little in the way of such musical pedantry, focused as it was on the production of beautiful solo vocal lines and orchestral accompaniments. Fugue is not usually seen as a dramatic form of music, and has never really had a place in the world of opera. Why then does it appear so prominently in *Falstaff?* Did Verdi perhaps come to the end of his career with the same classicizing spirit that obsessed so many great composers before him? Did he, like Mozart and Beethoven, need to leave some artistic mark of his prodigious musical talent in a form that had always defined the craft of musical composition?

Even before beginning work on *Falstaff,* Verdi wrote to Boito saying he had written a comic little fugue that he hoped could be worked into their new opera. Indeed, Boito did just that at the end of act 3. But well before that, in act 1, at the point where Falstaff ironically directs Dr. Caius to "go in peace" (the last words of the traditional Catholic Mass), Verdi has his henchmen, Bardolph and Pistol, start to sing a mock Amen fugue. This little fugue hardly gets started before Falstaff angrily cuts it off. But the joke is well played here—a mock sacred fugue in a comic opera.

Returning to the fugue Verdi composed before starting work on the opera, we see that the point chosen for the insertion of this academic contrapuntal exercise was the last ensemble finale that served as a moralizing summary for the whole opera. "Tutto nel mondo è burla" (Everything in the world is a farce), writes Boito at the head of a double quatrain of lines that again recalls eighteenth-century comic opera, where such moralizing ensembles were know as "vaudeville" finales. Mozart's *Don Giovanni* contains perhaps the best-known example of such a finale among operas in the currently active repertoire. But whereas Boito's libretto makes dramatic reference to a past convention in comic opera, Verdi's music references instead the music of Bach and Handel. The fugue (Ex. 3-5), written in authentic late baroque style, involves all eight of the opera's main characters along with an accompaniment of a chorus of townsfolk who have assembled for this final public humiliation of Falstaff.

Example 3-5. Final fugue.

This ensemble is to Verdi's operas what Beethoven's *Grosse Fuge* is to the literature of the string quartet: a final apotheosis of artistic achievement from the mind of a revered artist at the end of his career. We can only marvel at the way Verdi summarizes 150 years of musical tradition in one exciting finale, bringing not only his opera and his career, but also a whole era of Italian musical theater, to a grand culmination.

The birth of comic opera in the early eighteenth century resulted from a need to create a new, simpler, and more natural style of opera at a time when audiences were becoming more bourgeois and opera seria was becoming ever more artificial and formulaic. Rossini and Verdi, working at opposite ends of the nineteenth century, each transformed the ideals of Mozart's opera buffa, adapting them to the needs of new audiences and changing aesthetics in the Romantic era. Verdi's reformation of Italian comic opera was one that brought the genre into alignment with the trend toward more continuous opera, as advocated by Wagner. But he did so by keeping in focus many of the operatic ideals that had always distinguished Italian opera from that of its northern neighbor. As a result, *Falstaff* brings to the world of comic opera an appreciation for greater realism in the musical unfolding of the drama, accomplished through the use of arioso in place of the closed musical set pieces of Rossini's operas. Where opera was once the showcase for great virtuoso singers, the prima donnas and primo uomos of a bygone era, it was, by century's end, the home of a new musical-dramatic aesthetic—one that better balanced the art of singing with the needs of the drama. *Falstaff*, Verdi's final masterpiece, completes the long evolution of comic opera from eighteenth-century simplicity to late-nineteenth-century sophistication, without sacrificing those ideals that had always made opera buffa a uniquely Italian experience.

PART II
Bel Canto and Beyond

CHAPTER 4

The long line of famous nineteenth-century Italian composers of serious opera begins with Gioachino Rossini, who was part of a far-reaching revolution that literally saved this kind of opera from near extinction at the end of the previous century. This rebirth of Italian opera seria grew out of the major currents of social change that swept through eighteenth-century politics, economics, and the arts—a change born out of the forces of Enlightenment thinking about human liberties, social justice, equality, and political self-determination. The Enlightenment, as manifested in the writings of such social philosophers as John Locke and Jean-Jacques Rousseau, demanded equality and new human rights for the middle class, which eventually led to the destruction of a system of aristocratic privilege that had ruled European life for centuries. In music, such revolutionary thinking resulted in several important changes in eighteenth-century styles, forms, and genres. Of these, one of the most important was the creation of a new operatic genre known in Italy as opera buffa. The raison d'être of this new kind of opera was social satire, carried out in plots depicting servant characters who regularly outwitted their aristocratic masters, and taught them, in the process, basic lessons in human dignity and equality. Opera buffa appeared as early as 1733, when Pergolesi wrote his little two-act "intermezzo," *La serva padrona*, but the genre came to an apex of perfection in the Viennese operas of Mozart, especially those based on the Figaro trilogy of the French playwright Beaumarchais, whose *Le mariage de Figaro*, had been banned from production in both Paris and Vienna because of its outrageously inflammatory and insulting depiction of the French aristocracy. The heroes of this kind of opera were, quite obviously, members of the lower classes of society—usually the servant characters. Accordingly, comic opera adopted a new simpler musical style, one more in keeping with the needs of new "blue-collar" audiences to which these works were meant to appeal.

The meteoric rise in the popularity of opera buffa explains why there are so few serious operas written in the late eighteenth century, and why those that were written have not remained active in the repertoire today. In its heyday, Italian opera seria had been very much an aristocratic form of entertainment, even if, as was the case, the opera houses of Europe were open to general admission of the lower classes. Everything about opera seria was designed to cater to and flatter a well-heeled audience. The subject matter that formed the basis of the plots in these operas was regularly derived from either mythology or, more commonly, ancient history—subjects with which most well-educated, well-read European aristocrats were thoroughly familiar. In addition eighteenth-century opera seria always ended happily, partly because opera had been, from the time of its invention around 1600, intended as an after-dinner courtly entertainment in which tragic endings would have been inappropriate, and also because these happy endings nearly always resulted from the magnanimous intercession of an aristocratic character in the drama who was intended by the librettist to reflect the values of the real-life aristocrats in the audience. But as the tides of social change began to shift in the late eighteenth century, interest in this kind of opera waned rapidly. Its style was by then judged to be artificial and stilted, like the aristocrats to whom it appealed. The new simplicity and naturalness of the Enlightenment failed to find expression in these operas, in which everything from the entrance and exit of characters to the number of arias each was allowed to sing was controlled by a strict set of seemingly arbitrary operatic traditions and expectations. Furthermore, the artificiality of these operas was compounded by the fact that the lead male roles were nearly always sung by soprano castrati: men who had been castrated before puberty to retain their high voices. The castrati relied on highly developed technical virtuosity, dazzling improvisational skills, and beautifully spun-out legato phrases to win the adulation of audiences throughout the eighteenth century. But hearing the great heroes of antiquity singing in soprano voices was not something that any objective listener could claim was either natural or simple. In addition, the principal musical vehicle for the demonstration of the castrato's vocal technique was the da capo aria, itself a highly formalized and artificial musical form consisting of a long orchestral introduction followed by two contrasting sections of vocal music (A and B) set to two stanzas of poetry. The first section (A) was always repeated at the end (the da capo) to allow the singer to freely ornament the melodic line on its second presentation. Despite the dramatic lack of logic in returning to the opening textual material at the end of the aria, no one objected to this formal procedure because audiences loved hearing their favorite singers improvise extravagantly ornamented melodic lines for the purpose of demonstrating their technical and musical prowess. Arias of this type easily lasted between six and eight minutes each, and with demands for encores, regularly resulted in operas that ran up to four hours in performance. As the social climate of Europe shifted toward the values of the common man; however, the highly stylized and artificial opera seria came gradually to signify all that was wrong with the ancien régime, and as a result, found itself without an audience and in danger of extinction.

This is where Rossini enters the picture as part of a new generation of composers who realized that if the declining fortunes of opera seria were to be reversed, they were going to have to find a way of adapting this aristocratic genre to the changing social climate of post-Revolutionary Europe. The first step in this direction, clearly exemplified in the works of Rossini, was to find new operatic subjects with which middle-class audiences might be more familiar. Thus the standard opera seria subjects drawn from ancient history gradually faded away in favor of more relevant and realistic subjects drawn from modern history or contemporary literature. Of course, those terms *modern* and *contemporary* must be understood from the point of view of a composer working around 1810 to mean anything occurring or written within the previous 200 years. Contemporary literature, by this standard, included such writers as Shakespeare, and modern history meant anything occurring as far back as the reign of Queen Elizabeth of England. A perusal of the titles of Rossini's serious operas clearly illustrates the trend toward these new subjects without completely rejecting the old:

Ancient history	Modern history/ Contemporary literature
Tancredi (1813)	*Elisabetta, regina d'Inghilterra* (1815)
Armida (1817)	*Otello* (1816)
Mosè in Egitto (1818)	*La donna del lago* (1819)
Ermione (1819)	*Guillaume Tell* (1829)
Semiramide (1823)	

In addition, the traditional happy endings of earlier opere serie began to be replaced by tragic endings of the kind we know from later nineteenth-century opera. Rossini was among the first to try to wean audiences from their expectation of a happy ending, but he was only partly successful in doing so.

Italian serious opera of the eighteenth century had been devoted almost entirely to the art of great solo singing. Its form, therefore, was essentially nothing but a string of da capo arias linked by secco recitatives. *Secco* means "dry," or speechlike in terms of melodic style; that is, totally devoid of any melodic interest. The inherent contrast between this kind of recitative (designed for the rapid and easily perceptible delivery of dialogue) and the far more melodic arias, must have troubled such composers as Rossini, who felt perhaps that the stylistic juxtaposition of two such highly contrasted styles of singing damaged the musical flow of the opera as a whole. Whereas arias were always accompanied by the orchestra, recitatives were accompanied only by the harpsichord and a solo cello, thus resulting in a severe contrast between the two kinds of music, and effectively isolating the arias as stand-alone concert pieces instead of as lyrical moments in a continuously unfolding musical drama. Rossini's solution to this problem was to borrow the style of "accompanied" recitative used extensively in the French operas of Gluck at the end of the previous century. Because this kind of recitative employed the orchestra instead of the harpsichord as accompaniment, it lessened the inherent discontinuity between the arias and the recitatives. In addition, the French also wrote recitatives in a more melodic style than did their Italian counterparts, further reducing the drastic contrast between recitative and aria in their operas and creating a greater sense of musical continuity. The first of Rossini's operas to adopt this new style of accompanied recitative was *Elisabetta* in 1815.

The unrelenting dependence of the old opera seria on the aria as the essential formal vehicle for the delivery of the drama led to a stupefying sameness in musical structure scene after scene, and act after act. Rossini and his early nineteenth-century colleagues again looked elsewhere for hints as to how this boredom might be relieved.

As before, the solution was an eclectic one based on borrowing successful elements from other operatic traditions. For one, Rossini recognized that French composers had long made effective use of the chorus in their operas. But because Italian opera had always been focused on solo singing, the possibility of choral singing had never really been seriously considered. As the new century dawned, however, Italian composers came to see choral singing as a valuable technique for bringing much needed variety into the tired old opera seria tradition.

Rossini rounded out the restructuring of serious opera with one last borrowing, not this time from French opera, but from the world of Italian opera buffa. There, he found the ensemble—groups of two or more solo singers—that had never been utilized in serious opera because of its concentration on virtuosic solo singing. An occasional duet was really the only ensemble singing that one could generally hear in a serious Italian opera before Rossini; but comic opera featured ensembles of many kinds, including duets, trios, quartets, and the large "ensemble finale" that usually brought each act to a climactic close with all the main characters singing together, often accompanied by a small chorus. So ensembles, along with the change of subject matter, the use of the chorus and accompanied recitative, all quickly became staples of Rossini's newly redesigned serious opera in the nineteenth century.

Considering how important Rossini was in the establishment of a new form of Italian serious opera, it may seem ironic that the Italian portion of his career spanned only thirteen years, from 1810 when he wrote *La cambiale di matrimonio* for the Teatro San Moisè in Venice, to 1823 when he wrote *Semiramide* for the same theater. Shortly thereafter, he moved to Paris to take up writing French opera, including his greatest work, *Guillaume Tell*, with which he ended his career in 1829. Out of the ten years during which Rossini worked in Italy, eight were spent in Naples where he produced seven operas for the Teatro San Carlo. Naples was at the time the most cosmopolitan center of opera in all of Italy, and one of the few cities in which Italians could hear performances of German and French opera, along with contemporary Italian works. It was, in fact, the heavy influence of French opera in Naples that pushed Rossini into adopting aspects of that style in the remaking of nineteenth-century Italian opera. His use of accompanied recitative along with the dependence on choral singing are important aspects of the new Italian style that he might never have thought of using had he worked elsewhere in these critical years.

Taken as a whole, Rossini's Italian serious operas show him to have been a transitional composer whose works look both back into the grand era of bel canto singing of the eighteenth century and ahead to the new melodramas of Verdi. This mixture of new and old can best be seen in an opera like *Semiramide* (1823), his last written in Italy. The subject, drawn from a play by Voltaire, tells of the ancient Babylonian queen, Semiramide, who murdered her husband, King Nino, with the aid of her lover, Prince Assur, and then exiled her infant son, Arsace. As the story opens, twenty years or so have passed since the death of the king, and the people of Assyria demand that the queen take a new husband, who will become their new king as well. Like most of the other serious operas of Rossini, this one opens with an introductory section of music built around the chorus, which sings in a celebratory fashion while the main characters in the drama state their individual positions: Prince Idreno wants to marry Princess Azema, Prince Assur wants to become the next king, and the high priest Oroe is reluctant for any of this to happen because he knows the rightful heir to the throne is still alive. The choral writing around which much of this opening section of music is built is decidedly simple. Although the chorus had been borrowed from French opera, the more complex style of French choral writing was not possible in Italian opera, most likely because trained choral singers were not in abundance in a country where solo singing had long been the only important element in opera. As a result, any kind of choral writing in which there was significant independence of parts would have resulted in sure disaster as these untrained singers were tempted to follow the person singing next to them. For this reason Rossini's choral writing is always in rhythmic unison (homophonic rather than polyphonic) and often in melodic unison as well. The resulting texture is something more like a group aria than a true chorus. (See Ex. 4-1.)

Example 4-1. Act 1, opening chorus of Babylonian people.

Just as Semiramide is about to accede to the wishes of her people and announce the name of the new king, the fire on the sacred altar of the temple of Baal mysteriously goes out—an event that everyone interprets as a sign of the displeasure of the gods. The ceremony is suspended amid confusion, consternation, and incriminations.

After this introduction, the hero of the opera finally makes his entrance to sing his first aria. Here we see Rossini holding firmly to past opera seria traditions by casting this character, Arsace, as a mezzo-soprano voice. In the previous century, this would have meant a castrato, but now that these artificial male sopranos were shunned in the new climate of naturalness and realism in opera, Rossini's hero takes form as a female mezzo *en travesti* (dressed as a man). This kind of cross-dressing had long been a part of Italian comic opera, where women frequently played the part of teenage boys who were almost men. Cherubino in Mozart's *Le nozze di Figaro* is a prime example of this kind of "trouser role." But the idea of an opera's hero being played and sung by a woman was clearly a makeshift solution to the question of how to hold on to the sound of the great castrati of the past once they had begun to disappear from the stage.

Arsace is a commander in the queen's army, and has been called back to the royal court, unknown to him, so that Semiramide can announce him as her new husband. The aria he sings upon his entrance explains to the audience that he is in love, not with the queen, but with the Princess Azema, whom he looks forward to seeing. The aria that Arsace sings here is written in a new form that Rossini began to employ as a replacement for the old da capo form of the past. The problem with the da capo aria was that it embraced a dramatically illogical progress caused by the repetition of the opening lines of its text at the end of the form, as explained earlier. Thus, to accommodate a satisfying rounded musical form (ABA), opera librettos of the time were forced to inflict a degree of dramatic redundancy on the unfolding of the action. To avoid this, Rossini began employing a new aria form that served the same purpose of repeating some of the music in the aria, to allow a singer to improvise, but at the same time avoided the problem of the illogical dramatic recapitulation of the opening text. This new aria form, known as the cavatina-cabaletta, also contained two stanzas of text, A and B, but it was now the B stanza that was repeated at the end to form a structure that became ABB in performance. In this new aria form, the composer would usually begin with an opening recitative that led to the first section of the aria, the cavatina. This was a section of slow, lyrical music embellished with numerous melodic decorations known as *fioriture* (flowers). These are little decorative "blossoms" on the main melodic line that take the form of turns; trills; mordents; short, rapid scale patterns; and more—all aimed at making the melodic line more florid. The cavatina usually ends with an unaccompanied cadenza, in which the orchestra comes to a stop and the singer improvises a short section of highly decorative music before the final closing cadence, exactly as though the aria were a kind of vocal concerto. In the cavatina that Arsace sings (Ex. 4-2), we can see these decorative *fioriture* that add so much gracefulness to the melodic line in a bel canto aria.

Example 4-2. Act I, Arsace's cavatina, "Ah, quel giorno."

Following this opening slow section, the aria moves into its second half, the cabaletta. This portion is faster in tempo, and is usually far more difficult in terms of vocal technique. Rapid scales and arpeggios give the cabaletta the style and effect of an instrumental etude, in which notes must be delivered with impeccable accuracy as they fly by with incredible speed. Audiences thrilled at this kind of singing, and waited with nervous excitement for the repeat of the entire cabaletta in which the singer would improvise additional ornaments that made the music even more difficult. Ex. 4-3 illustrates how Rossini's original melodic line in this cabaletta might have been further decorated in performance.

Example 4-3. Act 1, Arsace's cabaletta, "Oh, come da quel dì."

For most singers this improvised decoration of a melodic line was more than just a matter of adding trills and turns, and filling melodic skips with scale passages. Often the melodic line itself was subjected to alterations that substantially reshaped it, at least partly obscuring the original in the process.

Eventually the use of female mezzo-sopranos to play the part of great military heroes gave way to the more modern practice of casting these roles as tenors. The fact that Rossini's last Italian opera reverts to this old-fashioned tradition of the female-voiced hero after he had already written several operas with leading roles for tenors is indicative of the fact that progress toward the modernization of Italian serious opera was not made in a straight line. Rossini's tenors were, of course, required to sing in the same bel canto style as were their female predecessors, and to display the same kind of vocal agility. Often the tenor roles Rossini created cover extremely large ranges of well over two octaves, sometimes from as low as an octave below middle C (c) to a high C, two octaves above middle C (c^2). These extremely wide-ranging parts present modern tenors with serious problems in performance. Today a high C is understood to be a high note in a tenor's range, and one by which the merit of a singer is sometimes measured. To expect a modern tenor to sing the even higher notes Rossini and other composers of the early nineteenth century so often wrote, is to expect the impossible. The explanation for the difficulty that contemporary singers face when performing these bel canto operas is not that today's tenors are less well trained than those in Rossini's day; rather, that in the early nineteenth century, all tenors sang in a falsetto voice everything written beyond about a G above middle C. This tradition of using a falsetto sound to take the high notes was done away with in 1837, when the famous French tenor Gilbert Duprez sang the role of Arnold in a production of Rossini's *Guillaume Tell*, and sang all the high notes in full chest voice. Since then tenors have always resorted to this full voiced, heroic approach to singing notes in the upper register, but as a result have been forced to compromise somewhat when faced with the extremely high parts found in some of Rossini's operas (both serious and comic).

The cavatina-cabaletta was not the only new form employed by Rossini in his serious operas. Ensembles, particularly those that closed each act, occupied a large portion of these new works. In the comic operas of Mozart, the ensemble finale assumed an unparalleled importance in the formal design of each act. Here Mozart incorporated continuously unfolding dramatic action in nonstop music (i.e., with no recitative), building the number of characters and the musical momentum right to the final curtain. In borrowing the idea of such large ensembles from comic opera,

Rossini seems to have recognized that the dramatic and musical crescendo of tension found in Mozart's ensemble finales suited the hectic confusion of the plots he usually dealt with in his comic operas, but that this formal design was less well suited to the often more stately pacing of the plot in his new serious operas. A new formal design therefore had to be found; and this new form consisted of alternating sections of recitative/arioso with sections of lyrical ensemble singing, often employing the chorus as an important musical-dramatic element. As with the aria, the ensemble finale opened with a long section of music in a slow tempo. An introductory chorus often leads to an initial section of dialogue between some of the characters set as arioso (semimelodic writing) with some occasional lyrical solo singing (included probably to make up for the reduced number of arias in these operas). In these sections, the dramatic action moves forward until a dramatic point of crisis is reached. At this point the action comes to a halt to give all the singers an opportunity to react emotionally to what just happened. These sections of emotional reaction are set as fully lyrical numbers for the main characters—quartets, quintets, sextets—often with the chorus accompanying. The opening slow section of the ensemble finale might have one or two of these lyrical ensembles in which the characters on stage plant their feet, face the audience, and sing away at full throttle (what singers usually refer to as the "park and bark" technique). Eventually the finale moves into a fast section called the *stretta*, where more dialogue in arioso between characters leads to a final ensemble with chorus to make a rousing conclusion. The use of the ensemble finale was critical in the formation of Rossini's new serious operas. Appearing at the close of most acts, these ensembles brought together all the main characters along with the chorus in an arrangement of musical numbers that alternated sections of dialogue that propelled the drama forward, with sections of lyrical ensemble singing in which the action came to a halt to give characters a chance to react emotionally to an important dramatic event. The large-scale structure of these finales, like that of the aria, involved two parts, one slow, the other fast. The overall form could be diagramed as in the following schematic.

Schematic of an ensemble finale.
Part 1—slow tempo

Section	chorus	recitative or arioso	ensemble #1	arioso	ensemble #2 (with chorus)
Function	sets mood	dialogue	group emotions	dialogue	group emotions
Momentum	inaction	action	inaction	action	inaction

Part 2—stretta (fast tempo)

Section	arioso	final ensemble
Function	dialogue	group emotions
Momentum	action	inaction

Such an ensemble finale appears at the end of act 1 in *Semiramide*, when the queen is ready to announce to her assembled court and populace her choice for husband and new king. This finale begins, as most do, with a general chorus of rejoicing, as usual, written in a simple homophonic style with rhythmic unison. There follows a section in which Semiramide makes everyone swear to honor and obey the new king, whoever he may be. This oath of allegiance is set as a beautiful quintet of the major characters—the first ensemble—in which for a moment the action ceases while we get this general group reaction to Semiramide's command. Next, she announces that Arsace is her choice, and everyone, including the crowd has something to say about this selection. All of this unfolds in a melodic style that moves freely between arioso and something a bit more interesting melodically. Suddenly the earth shakes and the tomb of the dead king opens to reveal the ghost of King Nino. Again the action stops as everyone reacts with fright to this new development in an ensemble that includes five main characters plus the chorus; this is the second ensemble. Next, Semiramide and some of the others engage the ghost in conversation trying to discover what he wants. He responds that Arsace will indeed reign as the new king, but that there are old crimes that must be avenged before this can happen. This dialogue moves the finale into another section of arioso that leads to the arrival of part 2 and the new faster tempo. This is a short stretta in which everyone onstage reacts to the situation with the line, "Alas, the eternal order of nature is convulsed on this day!" Ironically the music Rossini wrote for this closing ensemble doesn't quite seem to fit the mood implied in the text. The music is in C major, and has a dancelike triple meter that gives it a buoyancy that seems at odds with the words, "a wrathful god unlocks hell." (See Ex. 4-4.)

Example 4-4. Act 1, stretta of the finale.

Example 4-4 *(continued)*

Nu - me — i - ra - to — di-
schiu - de — l'a - ver - no sor - gon l'om - bre — dal ne -
ro — sog - gior - no

Although somewhat shocking to modern audiences, this apparent lack of attention to matching musical style to the mood of the text would not have raised an eyebrow in Rossini's day. Bel canto opera meant beautiful singing and beautiful music, no matter what. Even the most violent actions unfolded in music that was at times disarmingly "pretty" and even joyous, as is the case here at the end of act 1 in *Semiramide*. The accurate depiction in music of the emotions and moods of a particular text was simply not a priority for composers or audiences in the early nineteenth century. Furthermore, this kind of apparent mismatch of music and text in Rossini's operas frequently resulted from the fact that he often borrowed music from earlier operas when he was pressed for time by a deadline for a new work. This kind of self-borrowing was possible because many of his earlier operas had limited performance runs in far distant cities, making it most unlikely that anyone listening to the new opera would have heard the earlier one from which he could have borrowed a large section of music. In making these borrowings, Rossini was not at all concerned with whether the text of the new opera expressed the same mood as that of the old opera from which he wanted to steal some music. He cared only about whether the libretto of each opera was written in the same poetic meter. If it was, then the music written for the words in the earlier work would also fit the words for the new opera, and the transposition of music from one to the other would have been seamless.

Although the large ensemble finales were extremely important in Rossini's new serious operas, he also made effective use of the smallest ensemble, the duet. Rossini employed a specific musical form for his duets that one finds repeated with almost formulaic regularity in many of his serious works. Like the cavatina-cabaletta and the ensemble finale, the tempo pattern of the duet moved from slow at the beginning to fast at the conclusion. Ahead of the opening slow section, some introductory recitative, in which the characters engage in a dialogue, set the dramatic situation. This new duet form seems ironically to have been designed to offer the opportunity for more solo singing by giving each character a chance to be heard alone before joining with his or her partner in a true duet style. These solos, which always appear near the beginning of the duet, are like miniature arias, sometimes even including a short cadenza at the end. The second half of the duet changes to a faster tempo, and like the cabaletta of the aria form, shows off the technical ability of the singers with exciting vocal writing for each of them. The entire form can be diagrammed as follows:

PART 1, slow tempo:

Recitative (two characters in conversation)

Solo for character 1 (statement of feelings to lyrical music)

Solo for character 2 (statement of different feelings to the same music)

Arioso (more conversation)

Duet with cadenza at the end

PART 2, fast tempo:

Arioso (conversation)

Duet (final resolution of dramatic dilemma)

Duet repeated (to enable ornamentation for vocal display)

At the end of *Semiramide* we encounter a duet of this kind that will serve to illustrate the form. At this point in the drama, Arsace has already been apprised by the high priest of the fact that Assur and Semiramide conspired in the murder of King Nino, and that Arsace himself is the long-lost son of the king. (Semiramide is thus inadvertently planning to marry her own son.) In this duet he confronts his mother with his true identity, and with the fact that he knows of her part in the murder of his father. All of this takes place in an opening recitative that leads to the first musical section of the duet in a slow tempo. This section, known as the *primo tempo*, begins with the usual solos for each character. Interestingly enough, the music for these solos is identical despite the fact that the two characters involved are expressing completely contradictory points of view on the subject at hand. Thus, in this case, Semiramide suggests that Arsace should kill her to avenge his father, while Arsace, in his solo, flatly rejects the idea that he could ever murder his own mother regardless of the provocation. Except for the opening four measures, the melodies for these contrasting sentiments are identical, as Ex. 4-5 illustrates.

Example 4-5a. Opening solo for Semiramide.

Example 4-5b. Parallel opening solo for Arsace.

Example 4-5b *(continued)*

The logic of writing the same music for both solos seems unexplainable from a dramatic point of view; however, in this kind of opera, a musical logic justifies the practice. Because Italian opera was still very much a showcase for great singing, and because audiences had their favorite singers much the way sports fans today have their favorite players, the writing of two identical solos allowed for the easy comparison of one singer against the other, effectively turning duets like this one into a singing competition.

Once these solos are finished, this slow section of the duet closes with a lengthy section in which the singers are featured in ensemble. Here, too, the dramatic logic of two conflicting points of view is ignored as both singers move in parallel motion through the same music. (See Ex. 4-6.)

Example 4-6. Act 2, end of *primo tempo* in duet.

The duet now moves into its second half, the stretta, which like the cabaletta in an aria, is in a fast tempo. It, too, often features some solo singing that allows each singer to show off his or her technique, before ending with both characters singing together in a true duet style. Also like a cabaletta is the repetition of this fast section to allow for further melodic improvisation. In this particular duet from the end of *Semiramide*, the text for each singer, as in the opening slow section, again represents their opposing points of view on the dramatic situation confronting them:

SEMIRAMIDE:
Ah, a cruel presentiment of some danger unknown to me chills my blood.

ARSACE:
Smooth your brow, mother, and calm your fears.

Nonetheless, this final section of the duet is constructed of a series of similar phrases that alternate between the two characters. Because they are so similar, and in some cases actually identical, the audience is again allowed the opportunity to compare dueling virtuosos. (See Ex. 4-7.) Notice that the first eight measures of each solo are rhythmically parallel but melodically different. But beginning with m. 9, both solos take up exactly the same music, giving the audience the chance to compare each singer's rendition of the same musical material.

Example 4-7. Act 2 duet stretta.

Despite the fact that *Semiramide* is an opera written at least partly in the old style (especially in terms of singers and subject matter), it ends with a nod toward the modernization of Italian serious opera by adopting the tragic ending exactly as set out in Voltaire's drama on which the libretto is based. Arsace descends into his father's tomb in search of Assur, whom he knows he has to kill. Semiramide also enters the tomb in an attempt to protect her son from Assur. In the darkness, Arsace strikes at an obscure figure, thinking it to be Assur, when in fact it is his own mother whom he has attacked and killed. With this more modern ending, *Semiramide*, like Rossini's career as a whole, seems to straddle the fence between old and new stylistic priorities in Italian serious opera. The new aria form of the cavatina-cabaletta allowed the composer to adapt the Italian preference for beautiful singing to a new more realistic form, while the incorporation of the duet and ensemble relieved the monotony of a continual barrage of solo arias as found in earlier opera seria. Yet at the same time Rossini's insistence on keeping the female voice in the part of his opera's hero, along with his selection of a subject drawn from ancient history, speak to the power of older traditions still active well into the new century.

The importance of Rossini as a composer of serious opera has long been outshone by his popularity as a composer of comic opera. Although his works in this latter genre, such as *Il barbiere di Siviglia* or *La Cenerentola*, are masterpieces of comic writing, the genre of opera buffa was itself not in need of salvation. It was, in fact, the dominant operatic genre in Italy at the turn of the nineteenth century. Serious opera, on the other hand, needed someone like Rossini to resurrect it after the debacle brought on by the social revolution of the late eighteenth century. In finding a way to make Italian opera relevant for a new audience in a new era, Rossini became a hero for all time. The formal patterns he established in his new serious operas became the basis of all Italian opera for the rest of the century. His work in serious opera earned him the well deserved reputation of one of the most important innovators in the history of opera, despite the fact that the works on which this reputation rests have yet to become mainstream repertoire in opera houses around the world.

CHAPTER 5

BELLINI'S *I PURITANI*: HYBRID OPERA

I Puritani represents a highly specialized kind of "singers'" opera, which owes its existence to a particular historical era, a particular operatic place, and a particular operatic aesthetic. The appreciation of a work like this depends, perhaps even more so than is the case with other less specialized works, on an understanding of the social and artistic milieu in which it was written. In the case of *I Puritani*, the operatic aesthetic is that of the Italian bel canto, but the milieu was Paris in the 1830s. It is this clash of styles and environments that makes Bellini's opera something unique. The decade of the 1830s was perhaps the greatest in the artistic prominence of Paris, a city that became an artistic mecca for artists of many types and nationalities. It was home to the literary avant-garde, led by writers such as Victor Hugo and Alexandre Dumas fils, as well as to revolutionary artists such as Delacroix, who spearheaded the new romantic movement in painting. Lastly, Paris was the city to which musicians flocked from near and far to make their reputations in what was then the artistic capital of Europe. Liszt and Chopin were lionized in the piano world, Paganini's violin playing took the city by storm, and Italian opera composers and singers introduced Parisians to a new style of singing known as *bel canto*. Paris was truly a city of international expatriates, in which the only native French musician of any merit was Hector Berlioz, who shocked Paris with his audacious program symphonies.

Vincenzo Bellini was one of several such Italian expatriates who came to make Paris his home, at least for a short while, in the 1830s. Born in Italy in 1801, Bellini received his musical education in a small conservatory in Naples, where he wrote his first opera as a student in 1825. This work was so well received at a school production that he was immediately asked to produce a new work for the city's professional opera house. After the success of that work, he moved on to write about one opera a year until his untimely death in 1835. He was not, obviously, a prolific composer in the mold of Rossini or Donizetti; rather, a slower and more careful writer. Through the late 1820s and early 1830s he built a remarkably successful career with works in which singers and audiences alike found a particularly beautiful melodic inspiration and a unique musical voice.

In 1833 Bellini left Italy to produce some of his operas in London. From there he visited Paris, where he was immediately asked to write a new work for the Théâtre-Italien, the city's most important "alternative" opera house. The main musical theater in town was the Paris Opéra, which, by 1830 was staging almost nothing but serious French grand opera. The Théâtre-Italien, on the other hand, was the foreign opera house in Paris, staging both serious and comic works by Italian composers. From the 1820s on, this meant the operas of Rossini, Donizetti, and then in 1833, Bellini. The Théâtre-Italien and its all-Italian repertoire brought into distinct relief the differences between French and Italian opera of the early nineteenth century. These differences hinged primarily on contrasting attitudes about the role of drama and music (i.e., of acting and singing) in opera. The French had always valued a dramatically coherent libretto, treating it with the respect usually accorded a stage play by one of their great dramatists, such as Corneille or Racine. The fact that these dramas were to be sung rather than spoken, apparently made little difference to how most Frenchmen valued such literary works. By contrast, Italian audiences seemed not to care much about dramatic logic or construction in their opera librettos, as long as they supplied ample opportunity for beautiful singing. Italian opera was criticized by the French as sounding more like a concert in costume than a drama in music. And from the Italian point of view, French opera productions were infamous for the shrieking on stage that passed for singing. Even the young Mozart commented on the wretched state of singing in France when he visited Paris in 1778 and wrote home to his father: "If only the French sopranos wouldn't sing Italian arias; I would forgive them their screeching in French, but to ruin good music [Italian music]—it's unbearable."[1] Generally speaking, French composers, in their attempt to emphasize the importance of the libretto, had never developed the kind of decorative tunefulness in their music for which Italian composers seem to have had such a natural gift. Consequently French singing never developed the same priorities as found in Italian singing. So the Théâtre-Italien succeeded in Paris partly because French audiences, starved for a good tune in the operas of Gluck, Spontini, Cherubini, and Lesueur, responded favorably to the musical attractiveness of the Italian bel canto style. Apart form this melodic attractiveness, however, one might wonder how a foreign style, so diametrically opposed to the native French aesthetic of opera, could possibly succeed in Paris. The answer may be

---

1. Spaething, 148.

exactly because it was foreign, and would have appealed to snobbish Parisians who valued the appreciation of any foreign art form as a sign of good breeding and education. If so, the popularity of the Théâtre-Italien could be attributed to its appeal to the cultural elite of Paris, ever cognizant of the social cachet associated with attending productions at this foreign venue.

In 1833 Bellini was flattered to be asked to write for a major theater such as this. The opera he wrote, *I Puritani* (1835), proved to be his last, but more important, it also proved to be different from his earlier purely Italian works (i.e., those works written for production in Italy). To begin with, Bellini was unable to work with his usual librettist, Felice Romani, who had written the text for nearly every one of his earlier operas. The two of them had a severe falling out over Romani's long delays in supplying Bellini with verses for their last collaboration, *Beatrice di Tenda*. Each man accused the other of deliberately trying to sabotage the work, and neither forgave the other for the disastrous outcome. As a result, Bellini had to find a new librettist with whom to collaborate. The person he chose was a fellow Italian expatriate, Count Carlo Pepoli, a writer with no previous operatic experience. Interestingly, the libretto that Pepoli produced for Bellini took the composer down a path that seemed to lead to a stylistic rapprochement between French and Italian opera. *I Puritani* is clearly an Italian opera in every sense of the word, but it also demonstrates many links to the style of native French grand opera that was becoming increasingly popular at this time. One of the goals of this chapter, then, is to demonstrate how this opera is modeled after the typical French grand opera of the 1830s while also managing to retain the most important aspects of the Italian bel canto style.

To explain this stylistic synthesis, a short review of French grand opera will be useful here. (Also refer to the chapters on grand opera in part VIII for more details.) Most of the time, the term *grand opera* is used far too loosely and inaccurately to describe any big, serious opera of the nineteenth century.[2] In actuality, grand opera is a specifically French invention of the early nineteenth century. It sprang into being shortly after the French Revolution (1789), when Napoleon came to understand that grandiose opera could be used to glorify the new empire, and operatic audiences suddenly became less aristocratic, and more bourgeois. To suit

---

2. For instance, the musical comedienne Anna Russell, in speaking about Wagner's *Ring* cycle, quipped that "that's the beauty of grand opera: you can do anything as long as you sing it." Nowhere did she make note of the fact that the *Ring* cycle is not an example of grand opera.

the needs of this new middle-class audience, composers of opera dropped their old mythological and allegorical subjects in favor of new subjects drawn mostly from modern history. More specifically, these historical subjects usually featured two large groups of people at war with one another (the empire in action). The large bodies of people provided an excuse for large choruses, something that had long been very popular in French opera but had rarely been included in Italian opera, where solo singing was far more important. Against the political background of the large warring factions, these new operatic subjects set the personal story of two star-crossed lovers, one from each warring group. This is what might be called the "Romeo and Juliet theme" in French grand opera: a player from one side of the conflict is in love with a member of the enemy party, thus setting up a love vs. duty dilemma that motivates the entire drama. Along with the large choruses in grand opera, went a concentration on the most elaborate, spectacular scenery imaginable. This scenic element was so important that the French actually thought of the dramatic shape of an opera as the product of a series of changing scenes that formed a collection of *tableaux*, or pictures. Because of the large crowds of choristers and the overwhelming scenery, French opera tended to be more static than Italian opera. Compounding this sense of slow motion in the drama was the French use of lengthy ballets in their operas, something else for which the Italians had no patience.

When it came time for Bellini to select a subject for his new opera in 1833, he turned to a contemporary French play titled *Têtes rondes et Cavaliers* (*The Roundheads and the Cavaliers*) by Jacques-François Ancelot and Joseph Xavier Saintine, which concerned itself with the seventeenth-century English Civil War between the monarchy and Cromwell's Puritans. This is exactly the kind of drama that would have made a wonderful grand opera libretto for Meyerbeer—the two opposing political forces present ample opportunity for grand opera choruses, while a private love story between a royalist sympathizer and a Puritan girl supplies the necessary individual love intrigue against which the large-scale political struggle can be played out. Although this kind of grand opera–like libretto is not completely unheard of in Italy (Bellini's own *Norma* is one such) it seems far too coincidental that such a libretto for an Italian opera was produced in Paris in 1835. Perhaps Bellini and his librettist intuitively responded to the kinds of dramatic subjects that floated around Paris in those days, or perhaps they made a conscious decision to model their opera more closely after what was popular at the Opéra. Yet while much of *I Puritani* takes on the characteristics of French grand opera, Bellini clung tenaciously to his native Italian style, thus combining what he hoped Parisians would find to be the best of both worlds.

The opera opens at a castle in southern England where Puritan forces are in control. A chorus of soldiers sings about their readiness to fight the royalists. Nearly every nineteenth-century serious opera, both French and Italian, opens with a chorus. But what is unusual for an Italian opera is the way this chorus is divided between onstage and offstage groups. The use of offstage music to expand the space of the stage and thereby create the illusion of distance in the theater was a specifically French technique that was used by composers of large-scale grand opera to bring to the theater a more three-dimensional experience. The opening scene of *I Puritani* presents a wonderful example of this French influence at work in an Italian bel canto opera. It begins with an offstage chorus of soldiers singing about the dawning day. This chorus is contrasted with an onstage group of soldiers who pick up the theme of the waking soldier marching off to battle. This whole section then concludes with a small offstage quartet singing a morning hymn to the glory of God. All together this choral opening occupies about nine minutes of stage time, during which essentially nothing happens—a typically French tableau-oriented approach to music drama. Similarly, the chorus that opens act 2 is equally as long. In addition, it should be noted here that it is not just the length of these choruses, but also their prevalence throughout the opera that indicates a French approach to the construction of *I Puritani*. Few other Italian operas from the early nineteenth century rely so heavily on the use of the chorus.

Interestingly, the style in which Bellini wrote his choruses was not French, but rather typically Italian, meaning that they were written in a style that choristers in Italy could sing. Because the regular use of the chorus was new in Italy after 1800 (Rossini having been one of the first to introduce it into serious opera), there were relatively few good, well-trained singers available for this kind of work. Most Italian singers devoted themselves exclusively to solo work. Thus, Italian choristers were likely to have been less well trained and were perhaps easily confused when someone standing next to them sang a part that was different from theirs. Realizing this, composers of Italian opera tended to write fairly simple choruses. This often meant music in which everyone sang the same tune in unison (like a group aria), or if multiple parts were required it meant keeping the harmony as simple as possible and the rhythm the same in all parts. Ex. 5-1 illustrates this kind of choral writing drawn from the opening onstage chorus of soldiers in act 1.

Example 5-1. Typically Italian choral style in *I Puritani*.

While all choral writing—French and Italian—features a predominance of simple homophonic textures (all parts singing the same rhythm), the choruses one finds in many French operas seem more often to depart from this chordal style and to involve a greater independence of part writing that makes them more difficult to sing. Whether the Théâtre-Italien did not have access to the same singers who worked in the chorus at the Opéra, or whether Italian composers were afraid to abandon their own comfortable choral style is not exactly clear. But whatever the reason, Bellini's choruses are, for the most part, conveniently simplistic from the singers' point of view.

One of the perennially attractive aspects of *I Puritani* is Bellini's solo and duet writing in the early nineteenth-century bel canto style. Bel canto originated in the previous century with the work of the great castrati. These highly artificial soprano- and mezzo-soprano-voiced men were specifically trained to produce a beautiful tone; a long, smooth legato; unbelievable technical agility; and improvised decorative ornaments. The use of these castrati in early nineteenth-century opera gradually died out (mostly for sociological reasons explained in chapter 4), but the style of singing that they had practiced was handed on to and kept alive by the singers, both men and women, of the new romantic era.

In the next scene of act 1, Bellini introduces his audience to Riccardo, a Puritan nobleman who is in love with and was promised the hand of Elvira. But Elvira's father has now consented to her marrying the man she really loves, Arturo, despite the fact that he is a royalist sympathizer.

In this aria, the jilted Riccardo pours out his grief in what is a beautiful example of Bellini's bel canto style. The aria is a typical Italian cavatina-cabaletta (see the full definition in chapter 4), which means it has two parts, the first slow and decoratively lyrical, and second fast, florid, and technically difficult. The second part was then repeated to allow the singer the opportunity to add even more difficult improvised ornaments to the composer's original melodic line. The Italian word *fioriture* (flowers) is applied to the kind of decoration that bel canto composers like Bellini wrote into their slow lyrical lines. In this aria we can hear a fine example of such writing in the third phrase of the opening melody. Ex. 5-2a extracts from this phrase the basic (unadorned) melodic contour that underlies Bellini's tune.

Example 5-2a. Cavatina, "Ah! per sempre io ti perdei," basic shape of third phrase.

The actual decorated line as written by Bellini is far more ornate, as can be seen in Ex. 5-2b.

Example 5-2b. Third phrase as written by Bellini.

The cavatina closes with an extended unaccompanied cadenza, which was written out by the composer as in Ex. 5-3a, but was, in Bellini's day, always further ornamented or otherwise changed in performance to suit the voice of an individual singer. Ex. 5-3b suggests a possible alteration of the cadenza that would suit a baritone with an especially strong high register. Today, singers generally ignore this tradition of altering or extending the cadenza with newly improvised passagework, choosing instead to sing only the bare framework indicated by the printed music.

Example 5-3a. "Ah! per sempre io ti perdei" cadenza as written.

Example 5-3b. Possible ornamented version of the cadenza.

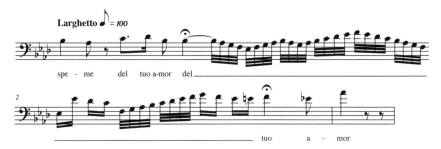

The second half of the aria, the cabaletta, is traditionally the faster and technically more difficult part. By the 1830s, however, cabalettas in male parts had begun to lose some of their speed and to shed much of the vocal display that characterized the earlier bel canto style. Composers such as Bellini began to replace the vocal pyrotechnics (at least in the men's parts) with a simpler, slower lyricism, while still trying to maintain the high level of excitement that was characteristic of the traditional cabaletta. Much of Riccardo's cabaletta is indeed fairly simple, as can be seen in Ex. 5-4.

Example 5-4. Beginning of cabaletta.

But the very end of this cabaletta returns briefly to the vocal virtuosity of the past, bringing with it a particular set of difficulties for singers (and record producers) of the twentieth century. In the 1830s baritones, like sopranos and tenors, were trained to sing these technically difficult passages with dexterity and precision. Bel canto technique was not limited to soprano and tenor roles in those days. But over the intervening years, this light, almost pristine style was sacrificed to the development of a larger, heavier sound that was necessary to fill new, larger opera houses and be heard over the larger orchestras found in the late nineteenth century. The training required to sing these larger, heavier roles has resulted over the years in the creation of generations of singers who have little exposure to, or training in, the old bel canto style, and consequently have tremendous difficulty managing the intricacies of this style in performance. Some singers (or conductors) solve this problem in performance by making cuts of the most difficult music. Thus Rolando Panerai, in a 1953 recording of this opera with Maria Callas, made a cut from the easy opening of the cabaletta directly to the final cadence, completely eliminating the extremely difficult passage work.

The next scene introduces us to Elvira and her uncle, Giorgio. In a lengthy duet (Ex. 5-5) she begins by lamenting the fact that if she is going to have to marry someone her father has picked for her, she will die of a broken heart. Here is a fine example of why the bel canto style was so reviled by reform-minded composers such as Richard Wagner later in the century. Elvira's ebullient music, with its elaborate warbling coloratura, seems somehow unsuited to the gloomy text that she sings: "If I am forced to the altar, desperate in that instant, I will die of grief."

Example 5-5. Elvira-Giorgio duet, act 1, sc. 2.

As explained in chapter 4, this apparent mismatch of musical style and text was simply a nonissue to Italian composers for whom the creation of beautiful vocal melody was the preeminent concern of opera. But for modern listeners, this may be one of those times when opera doesn't work as well dramatically as one might hope.

Fortunately for Elvira, her uncle then informs her that he has managed to change her father's mind, and that she can now marry her true love, Arturo. This and most of the other duets in the opera all have a somewhat looser form than do those found in most Italian operas of this time. The usual form for a duet (outlined in detail in chapter 4) begins with an opening slow section (equivalent to the cavatina in an aria) that includes a solo for each character leading to a duet for both of them together. The second part (equivalent to the cabaletta of an aria) is in a much faster tempo, with some dialogue between the characters leading to a fast, excited duet to close the number. As is the case with the cabaletta in an aria, this fast section is usually repeated (i.e., written out twice in the score). The duet between Elvira and her uncle follows this standard form fairly closely, but includes one extra, unexpected solo for Giorgio (the uncle) in the slow opening section. This suggests that Bellini's librettist, Carlo Pepoli, did not feel obliged to slavishly follow the standard Italian form for duet writing, but took the rather freer French approach of allowing the needs of the drama to dictate the form of the libretto.

It has always been remarked about Bellini (especially in CD liner notes) that his melodic style was a major influence on the piano writing of Frédéric Chopin. The third scene of act 1, in which we first meet the character of Arturo, gives us a chance to test the validity of this hypothesis. Musically speaking, Arturo is introduced here as part of a choral scene in which he has an embedded solo line.[3] That solo has all the usual earmarks of the Bellini style: delicate, graceful, and decorative. That Chopin was a great admirer of bel canto opera, and that he modeled much of his delicately filigreed piano melodies after specific melodic prototypes found in Bellini's music can be seen in Ex. 5-6a, which illustrates a small portion of Arturo's solo at the opening of act 1, scene 3, where everyone is rejoicing over the fact that he is going to be allowed to marry Elvira. Example 5-6a is followed by two short examples of passages (Ex. 5-6b1 and 5-6b2) drawn from the piano music of Chopin, both of which show a remarkable similarity to the melodic shape of the Bellini sample. Notice especially the characteristic pattern of the sixteenth notes in each sample.

---

3. This interweaving of soloist and chorus is yet another example of a characteristic of French grand opera that Bellini's librettist copied in *I Puritani.*

Example 5-6a. Arturo's solo in the quartet, act 1, sc. 3.

Example 5-6b1. Chopin Nocturne, Op. 27, No. 2.

Example 5-6b2. Chopin Nocturne, Op. 9, No. 2.

In the finale of act 1 we meet a new character, Henrietta, the Stuart queen, who is a prisoner of the Puritans and who is to be sent back to Cromwell's parliament for execution. Despite his impending marriage to Elvira, Arturo decides to save the queen by running off with her disguised as his bride. Of course, when Elvira finds out that Arturo has escaped with the prisoner, she mistakenly assumes he has abandoned her for another woman on the day of their wedding. The pain associated with this grief causes her to lose her mind toward the end of the finale. The first signs of her mental distress take place within the overall context of the style of choral-ensemble writing that characterizes all such finales in Italian opera. While the text Elvira sings clearly shows her to have lost touch with reality in this scene, her music actually contains little that would indicate madness on the part of the soprano. The true "mad scene" occurs, rather, in the next act. Having been shocked out of her senses at the end of act 1 when Arturo apparently abandoned her for another woman, Elvira now suffers from periodic mental aberrations. Here in act 2 she has a large aria (actually another cavatina-cabaletta) in which the audience experiences the full extent of her deranged mental state. Mad scenes like this were not new to nineteenth-century opera, but they did become more numerous after 1800. Perhaps the most famous example is the mad scene in Donizetti's *Lucia di Lammermoor*, written in 1835. Bellini also contributed his share: in *Il pirata* (1827) and *La sonnambula* (1831). This particular "mad" aria is the centerpiece of the entire opera, and the soprano's delivery of the beauties and intricacies of Bellini's music will either make or break the show. I have seen productions in which an enthusiastically appreciative audience simply would not stop applauding and yelling until the soprano finally came out of character and took a bow before moving on to the next scene.

The challenge for any composer of such scenes was to find a way of indicating madness in music. That is, he must make his audience recognize that a character is mad just by listening to what he or she sings. Over the years, composers have tried several different solutions to creating musical madness. Generally they all begin by assuming that the music, like the character's mind, must be somehow aberrant; that is, must depart in some way from normalcy. Therefore if a normal aria style can be defined, then an aberrant one can be created. In most cases composers chose to depict madness by abandoning the musical periodicity and melodic continuity that were characteristic of the "normal" aria style. Donizetti, for example, composed Lucia's mad scene aria with a melody consisting of short disjunct phrases of little or no tunefulness—just the opposite of his usual style. This technique creates a melody that continually breaks off its direction, interrupts itself, and, essentially, has no continuity, like the irrational thoughts of a character gone mad. In the process of moving between lyrical and arioso type phrases, Donizetti also obscured the usual cavatina-cabaletta form, making it difficult to even determine exactly where the introductory recitative leaves off and the real cavatina begins. A somewhat similar approach can be seen in *I Puritani*, where the madness of the aria can be calculated more from its irregular form than from any particular melodic irregularities. Bellini constructed the entire aria in the style of an Italian *scena*: a scene involving several characters in conversation, the music for which usually consisted of both lyrical melodies (in an aria-like style) and sections of less tuneful arioso designed to deal with the dialogue between the characters. In this "aria," Elvira interacts with her uncle, Giorgio, and her rejected lover, Riccardo. As the scene unfolds, it becomes clear from their dialogue that Elvira does not recognize either of them, believing instead that she is speaking with her fiancé, Arturo. In the context of this *scena*, the usual solo aria becomes vastly extended with unexpected sections of arioso dialogue and music marked by surprising tempo changes. The cavatina opens with a text in which Elvira laments her abandonment by Arturo, set to a lovely melody in the typical Bellini style.

Example 5-7. Act 2, sc. 1, opening of Elvira's cavatina "Qui la voce sua soave."

But this cavatina is followed by a new section of music in which Elvira, thinking Giorgio is Arturo, asks if he has come to take her to the wedding festivities. Here the music changes tempo and assumes a partylike mood, completely foreign to the usual cavatina style and form. To close out the cavatina, Bellini returns to the slow music of the opening, but now with the melody being shared in alternation by all three characters as Elvira again falls into a lamentation about lost love. Finally the tempo changes again, this time signaling the arrival of the cabaletta, which, however, is preceded by a fairly lengthy section of introductory arioso dialogue among the characters. At last the real cabaletta takes shape in the expected solo for Elvira, which somewhat surprisingly shows no signs of any irregularity of vocal style or form. It's effectiveness as a piece of "mad" music is, rather, dependent upon the soprano's ability to improvise truly elaborate ornaments in the repeat of the cabaletta that will make it seem somehow extravagantly deranged, bordering on being out of control, and fully indicative that the singer has, in a musical sense, gone mad.

Act 3 opens with storm music. Like operatic mad scenes, storm scenes date far back into the history of opera. Bellini's most immediate models were surely the operas of Rossini, especially *La Cenerentola*, which contains a marvelous example of this kind of music (see chapter 2). In most cases music that represents a storm in opera serves metaphorically to depict the turmoil of the human psyche. Today's equivalent of these operatic storm scenes is the almost clichéd used in Hollywood films of heavy rain to accompany powerful emotional moments in a drama. How many times have we seen a pair of lovers in a film fighting about some aspect of their relationship all the while standing (without umbrellas, of course) in the middle of a rainstorm. So in the world of filmmaking, the act of becoming soaked in a rain storm is a metaphor for the emotional intensity of whatever is taking place between the characters who are getting soaked. Similarly, nineteenth-century opera composers used storm music to accompany scenes of high dramatic intensity. In this case the dramatic moment is the return of Arturo, whom everyone believes to be a traitor, and who has narrowly escaped the Puritan troops who are chasing him. Although Italian composers wrote numerous storm scenes throughout their operas, they tended not to exploit the full dramatic potential of these purely instrumental pieces because, for the most part, they firmly believed that the role of the orchestra was to quietly and unobtrusively accompany the star singers, not to draw attention to itself. As a result, Italian storm scenes usually seem like gentle April showers next the hurricanes one encounters in French and German opera.

Once Arturo has safely eluded his predators, he signals his arrival to Elvira by singing a love song, actually a ballad, which she recognizes as his. Their reunion, of course, is cause for a rather excited duet. Here again we see a French influence at work in the formal freedom of this piece, suggesting a deliberate avoidance of the formulaic approach to duet writing that nearly every other Italian composer since Rossini clung to almost religiously. In this duet, the standard two-part (slow-fast) Italian pattern is obscured, and a looser French form is adopted in which interspersed throughout the opening slow section are many more solo sections in a faster tempo. And the big slow duet at the end of the first half of the piece is missing entirely. But more important than the French formal freedom of this duet is its musical impact. The success of this duet, and of the whole opera, for that matter, rests almost entirely on Bellini's inspired vocal writing. Like his most successful compatriots, Bellini knew the singing voice and knew how to use it effectively. But the danger of operas that are so dependent on great vocal writing is that they are therefore dependent on great singers. In 1835 Bellini had at his disposal some of the best singers in all of Italy. Notice here that because the Théâtre-Italien did not hire French singers, for reasons having to do with vocal style, Bellini was able to use Giulia Grisi to sing the role of Elvira and the tenor Giovanni Rubini for Arturo. Along with two great Italian baritones, this cast literally brought the house down. Reviewers mentioned the electricity of the performance on opening night. Today more than ever, this need for great singers like those for whom Bellini wrote the opera is paramount for a successful production. In understanding the performance problems in an opera such as this, it may be worth pointing out that Rubini was a tenor famous for his high register, and consequently Bellini tailored the part of Arturo to Rubini's strengths by writing several high Ds into his part (one note beyond c^2) in addition to a high F (f^2) in the finale of act 3. This last note, however, is rarely sung by tenors today, and is always lowered to a more manageable D-flat instead. One of the few tenors in recent memory to try singing the high F was Gregory Kunde, who appeared in the role of Arturo in a Metropolitan Opera production in 2006. He was reported to have tried out the high F in rehearsals, but then to have wisely decided in performance to take the usual route of lowering the note to a D-flat. In defense of this alteration, made by most of today's tenors, we must remember that in Bellini's day all tenors sang their highest notes in a pure falsetto voice, making such incredibly high parts far easier. In this modern era, however, when tenors are expected to sing even the highest notes of their parts in a full chest voice, such extremes of register become unrealistic in performance.

While *I Puritani* is clearly a bel canto opera (with all the strengths and weaknesses associated with that genre), it clearly stands apart from most examples of that genre. As an Italian opera that emerged in Paris in the 1830s, against a background of the newly popular French grand opera, *I Puritani* crosses over fixed generic boundaries by adopting a broad historical subject that lends itself to the inclusion of some favorite French characteristics, such as large choruses and offstage music. The opera, therefore, takes on a certain French largeness of conception even though the musical style and forms are mostly—and one might say thankfully—still very Italian.

CHAPTER 6

VERDI'S NABUCCO: THE BEGINNING OF THE END

O nly a handful of Verdi's twenty-six operas are active in the repertoire of major opera companies around the world. If this fact tempts you to say, "That's a shame," you might want to consider that this is just the way the business of opera ought to work, because for a large part of his career, Verdi turned out new operas at the rate of more than one a year—not a schedule conducive to the production of carefully crafted, thoughtfully written works. Verdi himself referred to these years—the mid-1840s—as his "years in the galley," by which he meant working conditions bordering on slavery, designed to fulfill the demands of the business (not the art) of Italian opera.

This distinction between the business and the art of opera is a subject of sufficient importance to warrant a closer look at exactly what was going on in Italian opera houses of the early nineteenth century. Today, of course, we tend to think of opera as a form of high art—some would even say too high, implying that it is simply "elitist." But that is not how Verdi's audiences understood this musical genre. Nor is it the way composers themselves thought of opera in the early nineteenth century. Composers of that era never held as their goal the creation of great works of art. In Italy, especially, opera was first and foremost a popular form of entertainment, something more like the movies of our time. If an opera was occasionally thought-provoking, insightful, or profound, that was fine as long as it was also enjoyable and attractive to middle-class audiences who demanded little more than some great tunes, exciting scenery, and splendid costumes. If the music was memorable, nearly everything else about an opera might be excused or overlooked, especially the element of drama. And if the singers were great, sometimes even the most uninspired, dull music would be forgiven as well. Above all, Italian audiences loved their singers and their singing. In the eighteenth century, this love of singing was manifested in the public idolatry of operatic castrati, those male singers with soprano or mezzo-soprano voices who played the roles of military heroes, magnanimous monarchs, or mythological gods, all the while sounding unnaturally like women dressed in male clothing. These castrati ushered in the era of bel canto (the style of beautiful singing described in earlier chapters) that depended for its effectiveness on purity of sound (beautiful tone), vocal agility as demonstrated in the ability to sing incredibly difficult passage work (scales and arpeggios), and the ability to add improvised ornamentation to already ornate arias and duets. High dramatic art meant little to audiences obsessed with the vocal acrobatics practiced by the castrati of this era.

This then was the world of Italian opera into which Giuseppe Verdi stepped around 1840. Granted, the castrato had already disappeared from Italian opera by the early 1830s, the victim of a change in audiences that reflected the move away from aristocratic patronage toward new middle-class audiences, for whom such artificialities were unpleasant reminders of the evils of aristocratic class and privilege. But Verdi's immediate predecessors in Italian opera, Donizetti and Bellini, managed to keep alive the tradition of bel canto in soprano roles and in the voices of the new heroic tenors. In general, Verdi's early operas are all the product of a need to pander to the operatic taste of the time. As such, many of these works have rightfully fallen out of the repertoire. At best, works such as *Alzira*, *Attila*, and *Stiffelio* have some limited historical interest. But here and there among these early works of Verdi are some true operatic gems—works that presage the unique genius of the composer who, along with Wagner, was eventually to dominate and revolutionize nineteenth-century opera. One of these great early works is *Nabucco*.

The genesis of this, Verdi's third opera, is fascinating and helps to explain its special position among his early works. In the late 1830s, Verdi held a secure position as *maestro di musica* in his hometown of Busseto. But in his heart he knew he wanted only one thing: to become a great composer of opera. So he took a bold step and resigned his provincial position in order to move with his young wife and second child (the first had died in infancy) to Milan to try to make a career in the world of opera. Some years earlier, he had studied composition in Milan, and before leaving the city to take the church job in Busseto, he procured a libretto to set to music. It was this opera, *Oberto*, which Verdi took back with him to Milan in 1839 in an attempt to secure a first performance. After months of fruitless interviews and attempts at making connections in the Milanese opera world, Verdi suffered a personal tragedy: his second child died. Left now with no children, he pushed bravely on, finally getting the break he so desperately needed. His music was brought to the attention of the famous soprano, Giuseppina Strepponi, who in turn recommended it to Bartolomeo Mirelli, the impresario at La Scala. The opera was put into production and performances were well received—not exactly a triumph, but a moderate success for the unknown composer from the provinces. Best of all, Mirelli immediately contracted Verdi for three more operas.

As was the practice in those days, it was the impresario who determined which librettos were going to be set by which composers. Mirelli therefore handed Verdi a libretto for a comic opera, because that was what he needed for the following season. Verdi, however, was not by character a comic type (far from it) and he had no real interest in setting such an opera. But what was he to do? While he was trudging along with the composition of this new opera, his wife suddenly fell ill and died. His whole family now wiped out within a few short years, Verdi became depressed. Now in even less of a mood to write a comic opera, he pushed himself to finish the work. Not surprisingly, the premiere was a fiasco at which the audience booed so loudly that all further performances had to be canceled. Verdi vowed then and there to give up composition altogether.

A year went by, during which Verdi supervised productions of *Oberto*, both in Milan and Genoa, but was otherwise unable to work. He had in his possession another libretto from Mirelli, but had written not a note of music for it. Then a chance encounter with the impresario on the streets of Milan brought about the resurrection of Verdi's career. Mirelli had never lost faith in the young composer despite the failure of his comic opera. So when he discovered that Verdi had not written a note of his next opera and had even quit composing altogether, Mirelli decided to offer him something different. He brought Verdi to his office at La Scala and took back the libretto he had originally given him, forcing upon the reluctant composer in its place a libretto based on the Biblical story of the Jews enslaved by the Babylonians. Verdi recalled many years later how he went home with no intention of setting this libretto, when suddenly the book dropped out of his coat pocket and fell open to a page on which appeared a lament of the Hebrew slaves in captivity drawn directly from the Biblical lamentations of Jeremiah, which Verdi had set as a choral work years earlier in Busseto. He was struck by the power of the text and the pathos of the dramatic situation. Perhaps feeling homeless himself, caught in a hostile land and betrayed by fate, Verdi's interest was piqued. Despite his vows not to write another note of music, he found himself unable to resist the appeal of this libretto. Soon *Nabucco* was finished and scheduled for production.

What the audience heard and saw on the fateful night of that premiere was something quite new in Italian opera. Almost instantly, Verdi was recognized as a revolutionary new voice in the musical theater. Yes, there were still elements of Donizetti to be found here and there in the score, but the feel of the music was somehow different: more dynamic, more dramatic, more exciting than anything ever heard at La Scala before. As uneducated musicians, the members of that opening night audience were in no position to analyze what they were experiencing. All they knew was that it was different, and they liked it. One aspect of Verdi's new musical style that struck audiences immediately was his use of the orchestra. To this point in the history of Italian opera, the role of the orchestra had always been to accompany singers in an unobtrusive fashion that would not draw attention away from their great voices and beautiful singing. Simple harmonic support was all that was called for. But Verdi seems to have subscribed to a different philosophy: that the orchestra might be used as a powerful tool in the creation of dramatic moods. Its range and variety of instrumental color, volume, and rhythmic patterning could all be called upon to augment the emotional intensity of the music.

The first sign of this new approach to the orchestra occurs even before the curtain goes up. The overture to the opera is a declaration of independence from the predominant sound of string instruments that Italian audiences had come to expect. The brass, rarely used to great effect in Italian opera before 1840, were suddenly everywhere apparent in Verdi's score. Admittedly, the actual source of all this brass writing may have been more of a happy accident than a real conviction on Verdi's part that Italian opera orchestras could be more dramatically expressive. Given the fact that part of Verdi's boyhood musical education included directing and writing arrangements for the Busseto town band, his use of brass instruments may have grown naturally out of the experiences of his early years as a town musician. Much of *Nabucco* is, in fact, colored by the style of military music with which Verdi had become so familiar.

The overture is then followed by more music dominated by the sound of brass instruments as the curtain goes up on the opening chorus of Hebrews lamenting the wrath of God. Throughout the opera, Verdi continues to return to this sound, often at moments of peak dramatic intensity. The unusual reliance on the power of brass instruments in Verdi's orchestration was especially noted by critics in Paris, where *Nabucco* was produced some years later. In a typically clever French pun on the opera's full title (*Nabucodonosor*), one newspaper complained about Verdi's use of the orchestra with the following quip: "The playbill is wrong. We were promised a Nabucodonos-or [literally, in French, a Nabucco of gold], but all we got was a Nabucodonos-cuivre [a Nabucco of brass]."[1]

Verdi's use of brass timbres in this opera is only the beginning of a growing sensitivity to the dramatic potential of orchestral sound that sets his music apart from that of his immediate predecessors. Another aspect of his operatic style in which audiences noticed something new and different appeared in his ensemble finales. Usually in Italian opera, the end of each act brought the dramatic action to a climax in which all the main characters appear on stage with the chorus. These finales had for years been cast in a predictable musical form handed down from Rossini to Donizetti and then to Verdi. (See chapter 4 for a schematic diagram.) That form comprised an alternating pattern of action via dialogue (in recitative or arioso) and dramatic stasis via emotional reaction (in musical ensemble numbers), through two large sections, the first slow, the second fast. While Verdi adhered closely to this standard formula, his music exuded a new dynamism and energy that pitched the level of musical excitement higher than ever imagined by Italian opera audiences.

A synopsis of the opera's action in the first act will serve to clarify this point. The heroine, Abigail, is the illegitimate daughter of King Nebuchadnezzar; and because she has been raised from birth as part of his family, she is thought by everyone to be a royal princess. The "seconda donna" in this opera is Fenena, the King's legitimate daughter. In act 1, Jerusalem is under attack by the Babylonians and the defeat of the Hebrews appears inevitable. Their one hope for salvation lies in the fact that they have captured Fenena and are holding her prisoner. Fenena, we learn, is in love with the Hebrew prince Ismael. Their love duet near the beginning of the opera is interrupted by the unexpected entrance of Abigail, leading a troop of Babylonian warriors. In the ensuing trio, she announces that she, too, loves Ismael, and that she can save his life (and the lives of his countrymen) if he will renounce her "sister" and devote his love to her (Abigail). Ismael, of course, would rather die. The finale then begins with the arrival of Nabucco at the head of his attacking troops. He demands the surrender of the Hebrews. But the Hebrew high priest, Zechariah, threatens to murder Fenena, who is still held captive. This action sets up the first slow ensemble in the finale, in which everyone reacts to this dramatic standoff between Nabucco and Zechariah. In this ensemble Abigail has an important, soloistic part that must be projected above the rest of the singers. (See Ex. 6-1.) The vocal power needed to bring this part to the foreground

---

1. Osborne, 1979, 51.

of the concerted ensemble hints at the direction in which Verdi's new vocal style was headed.

Example 6-1. Excerpt from end of the slow ensemble in act 1.

Then just as Zechariah is about to stab Fenena, Ismael grabs his knife and sets her free. In so doing, of course, he betrays his own country to save his true love. This sets up the final ensemble (the fast one) that closes the act with the defeat and capture of the Hebrews. What must have struck audiences in Verdi's day as extraordinary about this final ensemble is its presto tempo and its rhythmic drive, both of which contribute noticeably to a heightened sense of dramatic energy and a level of excitement unlike anything ever heard before in Italian opera.

Verdi's relationship to the highly popular singing style of bel canto was also new around 1840. As heard in the operas of Rossini, Bellini, and Donizetti, bel canto was a highly florid, decorative vocal style that required singers to have a beautiful tone and superb technical agility. Both high and low voices were expected to demonstrate the essential elements of the style, along with the ability to improvise additional ornaments to show off their vocal technique (and to send audiences into paroxysms of enthusiasm). It was Verdi who almost single-handedly destroyed bel canto singing (along, I might add, with the voices of some very fine singers such as his future wife, Giuseppina Strepponi). While retaining many of its essential features in his early operas (especially in soprano roles), he began to write melodies that demanded a much more forceful and dramatic style of delivery. This new, heavier style required larger voices than did the pure bel canto style—voices capable of producing more volume throughout a larger range. Gradually the lighter more agile voices of the past were displaced by the bigger operatic voices we know today.

The beginning of the end of bel canto might be traced to the role of Abigail in *Nabucco* (originally sung by Giuseppina Strepponi). At the opening of part 2 ("The Unbeliever"), Abigail has an important aria in which elements of Verdi's new style are easy to hear. At this point in the opera, the Hebrews are slaves in Babylon. Nabucco is off somewhere continuing his conquests, and Fenena has been installed as temporary monarch. Abigail is simply furious about everything: her love of Ismael has been rejected and she was not appointed ruler in her father's absence. In the recitative that precedes her cavatina, we hear the voice of an angry woman. In her very first phrase, she must sing, loudly and forcefully, a melodic line that descends to middle C, generally a weak register for a bel canto soprano. Thereafter, this recitative pushes the soprano through extremes of vocal range and frequent, large, dramatic skips, all to be done with lots of volume. (See. Ex. 6-2.)

Example 6-2. Excerpts from Abigail's recitative.

The cavatina that follows (Ex. 6-3) is considerably softer, in the usual bel canto style of florid legato vocal writing. Here, as Abigail laments her lost days of joy and happiness, we can see the last vestiges of the old decorative style hanging on and coexisting with Verdi's new, more dramatic style as heard in the preceding recitative. In general, soprano parts like this were the last to abandon bel canto decorativeness, while male parts, even in the operas of Donizetti, had already made the move to a simpler lyricism. Ex. 6-3 illustrates the tell-tale signs of decorative writing in the several short melismas where one syllable of text is set to several notes to make a melodic turn, mordent, or roulade of some kind.

Example 6-3. Cavatina, "Anch'io dischiuso."

Between the cavatina and the following cabaletta, Verdi interjected some new dramatic information. The high priest enters to report that Fenena is setting the Hebrew prisoners free, and that the crowd is calling for Abigail to assume power in her stead. This change of mood motivates the new faster tempo of the cabaletta. In a style something like a military march—very angular and rhythmic—Abigail looks forward to seizing power and seeking revenge on her sister, who is the only rightful heir to the throne. Here, in Ex. 6-4, Verdi's vocal style looks somewhat simpler, but is still characterized by small vocal melismas and rapid scale passages that were the hallmark of bel canto singing.

Example 6-4. Abigail's cabaletta.

Example 6-4 *(continued)*

na - to; ben sa-prà la mia ven - det - ta____ da__ quel__ seg - gio ful-mi-

nar

As might be expected in an opera that lay so close to the height of bel canto fanaticism, the usual rules of performance apply to this aria. Thus, the traditional repeat of the cabaletta is supplied by Verdi in his score, thereby offering the soprano the requisite opportunity to embellish the melody on the second run-through, something that Italian audiences always eagerly anticipated.

Duets were also an important part of nineteenth-century Italian opera, and were mostly composed to a standard two-part (slow-fast) form that imitated the structure of the cavatina-cabaletta. (See full explanation in chapter 4.) The most important in *Nabucco* is the one that appears in part 3 ("The Prophecy"). Nabucco has been struck mad at the end of part 2 after declaring himself the Hebrews' new god. Abigail places him under house arrest and forces the deranged old man to sign the death warrant for the Hebrews. Without realizing that his daughter Fenena has converted to Judaism, he approves the mass execution of the Jews, including his daughter—exactly what Abigail wanted. In this duet Verdi demonstrated that he had little use for the traditional duet form that audiences had come to expect. His new compositional principle seems to have been that if the dramatic situation did not fit the old musical form, then the form had to be altered to fit the new dramatic situation. Here, Verdi wanted to create a real dialogue of contradictory moods, so he wrote a duet in which the traditional lyrical solo sections are limited to Nabucco's pleadings to save Fenena. Abigail, whom one might expect to have a corresponding solo has nothing slow and lyrical to sing at all. Instead, she sings only fragmented angry retorts to Nabucco in a style marked by lots of repeated notes and dramatic octave leaps. In fact, the duet contains a total of eighteen octave jumps in Abigail's part, nearly all in the downward direction. But her part, while heavy and dramatic, also makes passing reference to the old bel canto style. Ex. 6-5 illustrates a small excerpt from Abigail's part that contains elements of both the old and new style of singing in this opera. The beginning of the example is marked by loud repeated notes and octave skips that suggest the mood an angry woman, while the end of the excerpt introduces trills and melismas that pay homage to the old decorative style of singing.

Example 6-5. Abigail's part from duet with Nabucco in part 3.

To maintain the psychological distance between these characters Verdi also violated the tradition that brought both voices together in rhythmic unison and parallel melodic motion at the end of this first half of the duet. Instead his music for each character remains independent, suggesting the dramatic difference in their respective points of view. Verdi also abandoned the tempo scheme of the standard Italian duet (slow-fast), opting instead for an arrangement of tempi that better suited the mood of each character as he or she sings. Atypically, the opening of the duet is marked "allegro vivo" (see Ex. 6-5) and doesn't assume the usual slow tempo until Nabucco's first solo. Then, after the expected turn to a faster tempo for the second half, the duet veers off course yet again, as Nabucco makes a further appeal, in a surprising slow tempo, to Abigail to save Fenena from execution along with all the rest of the Hebrews. This willingness to place dramatic requirements above the traditional formal structures and musical style of bel canto opera was the basis of Verdi's operatic revolution, and lies at the root of his importance as the initiator of a new approach to Italian opera that gradually moved away from its old reliance solely on beautiful decorative singing, into a new world of meaningful music drama.

To appreciate how potent the effect of *Nabucco* was on audiences in Milan in 1842, we must understand the symbolism that was read into the opera by Italians who were especially receptive to political messages, and all too ready to interpret the work as a metaphor for the oppressive situation that their country was then enduring. For most of the nineteenth century,

"Italy" was nothing more than a collection of independent duchies, each with its own government and even (surprisingly) language. During most of Verdi's early career, these duchies were occupied by foreign troops, first Napoleon's armies, then the Austrians. Not surprisingly, Italians seethed under the rule of Austria, and underground freedom militias, organized and directed by political liberals, were active everywhere. This movement toward independence and political unification was known as the Risorgimento. The years of its greatest activity, the 1830s and '40s, were also the years in which Verdi was most concerned with getting his career off the ground, and his total absorption in music prevented him from taking an active part in politics of any kind. His goal was simply to become a famous composer of opera. The Biblical story of the enslavement of the Hebrews by the Babylonians, which he was setting to music, was for him a story of star-crossed lovers from opposite nationalities eventually triumphing over obstacles of all kinds. But Milanese audiences saw the Hebrews as a symbol for the Italians themselves, and the Babylonians as a symbol for the Austrians who enslaved them. The famous choral text that first drew Verdi's attention to this libretto, in fact, became a tune that moved out of the opera house and into the streets, where it took on the function of a battle song for independence-minded patriots. This is the chorus of Hebrew slaves (Ex. 6), in which the Jews lament their lost homeland in vivid poetic imagery:

Va, pensiero, sull' ali dorate;	Go, thoughts, on golden wings
Va, ti posa sui clivi, sui colli,	Go, rest on the hills, the mountains
Ove olezzano tepide e molli	Where, soft and warm, the sweet breezes
L'aure dolci del suolo natal!	Of our native land are fragrant!
. . . .	. . . .
Oh, mia patria sì bella e perduta!	Oh, my country so beautiful and lost!

Example 6-6. Chorus, "Va pensiero."

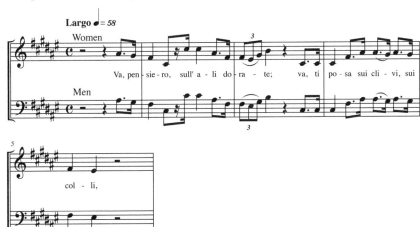

Historians, looking for evidence that Verdi was an active Italian nationalist who used his music to whip up patriotic feeling among opera-goers, have made much of the fact that this tune is written in choral unison. It is, they say, not really a chorus of multiple parts at all; it is a single melodic line sung by the entire chorus—a kind of group aria. In addition, the melody lies in a narrow vocal range that sits well for nearly every kind of voice, even the untrained voices of the audience. Those who believe that Verdi was an active Italian patriot point out that he must have known, or at least hoped, that this tune would be picked up by Italian patriots and sung everywhere with a conspiratorial wink of the eye. In fact, audiences did recognize the allegorical message in the text, and did indeed sing the tune, right along with the chorus onstage.

But was political provocation really Verdi's intention? A couple of additional facts may help clarify the issue. First, the chorus is written in unison because, as Verdi himself observed, Italian opera choristers were terrible. As explained in earlier chapters, choral singers were not as well trained as the soloists who sang the lead roles in these operas. As a result, they were far more likely to become confused by complex choral writing with independent parts. So naturally a chorus in which everyone sings the same tune in the same rhythm makes sense simply from a practical point of view. The same logic explains why the tune lies in a range that is easy for everyone to sing. What then looks like a calculated attempt by a budding political nationalist to invite the audience to identify with and even to sing along with the enslaved Hebrews, may have been nothing more than a result of the exigencies of Italian opera production in 1842.

Verdi actually seems to have been shocked by the political success of his new opera, and surprised that shortly after its premiere, he began receiving invitations to attend some of the important salons and soirées of the Milanese political intelligentsia, where he was first drawn into discussions of Italian independence and made aware of the power of music in effecting political change. Eventually Verdi did become an active force in the movement for freedom, but in *Nabucco* we have a fortuitous accident more than a calculated incitement to revolution. Regardless of the composer's intentions, audiences responded to what they saw as the hidden political message of the opera, and recognized in Verdi a powerful new voice of the Risorgimento as well as of Italian opera.

In part 4 ("The Shattered Idol") the mad king, seeing his daughter about to be executed, pleads for mercy from the God of the Hebrews. He accepts their God as his own, and is instantly restored to sanity. The final scene of the opera is the rescue of Fenena and the saving of the condemned Hebrews by Nabucco. It opens with a funeral procession of the Jews being led to execution, a number in which we again get a sample of Verdi's unique brass-dominated orchestration, here utilizing unusual soft dynamics to create a mournful effect. In the nick of time, Nabucco rides in to save the day. He orders the pagan idols destroyed and the Hebrews set free. He commands all to bow and worship the one true God. In a wonderful ensemble of soloists and chorus everyone does so. But here Verdi employed the special choral device of a cappella singing. Since so much of the rest of the opera had been marked by the sound of heavy brass, this section makes a powerful contrast by its total omission of all instrumental accompaniment. One might say that Verdi's growing awareness of the value of instrumental timbre in opera also included the use of its exact inverse. One last demonstration of his special sensitivity to the power of instrumental color comes in the final scene where Abigail appears after having taken poison in an extreme act of repentance. She presents herself in this sacrificial mode to the unusual accompaniment of a solo viola and English horn, a remarkably evocative orchestral timbre that perfectly captures the dark, mournful mood of this scene.

Nabucco marks what might be described as the beginning of the end of Italian bel canto opera. Although the overall impression this opera makes in performance is one of a bel canto work, its greater dramatic intensity, and its many incitements to use the utmost force in the voice points in the new direction of later nineteenth-century melodrama. For such a young, unknown, unproven composer, Verdi certainly took chances in the writing of *Nabucco*. He had a vision of Italian opera that ran against the currently popular tradition of beautiful singing. Here for the first time in Italy, we can see a composer driven by a need to place dramatic truthfulness before musical convention, and to be guided by the axiom that music must mould itself to the drama in order for opera to succeed. After *Nabucco* it would become harder and harder for composers to justify the use of ornate melodies to capture the dramatic affect of an entire opera, simply insisting, as it were, that if the melodies were attractive and the singing dazzling, nothing else mattered. Through the best of Verdi's early works, audiences saw the dawn of a new era in Italian opera, one in which the music was going to exist because of the drama, not in spite of it.

PART III
Italian Opera in Revolution

CHAPTER 7

VERDI'S *RIGOLETTO*: NEW DIRECTIONS IN ITALIAN OPERA

Rigoletto is one of those works of art that speaks to audiences on two different levels simultaneously. As a popular opera that nearly everyone can enjoy on the most immediate level, there is much to recommend it. Its plot is shocking and moving, its characters are genuinely human and sympathetic, and its music is exciting and tuneful. But *Rigoletto* is more than just popular; it is also a masterpiece of music drama with levels of sophistication that lie hidden beneath its superficial attractiveness. It is this deeper level of musical-dramatic sophistication that I want to explore here. In so doing, my hope is to trace the source of this new sophistication in Verdi's growing need to reform several of the most fundamental traditions of Italian opera of the early nineteenth century.

Before undertaking this survey of Verdi's new approach to writing opera in the middle of his career (1850s), we must first backtrack to circa 1840 to examine the state of Italian opera at the point when he began his career. In the years leading up to the composition of *Rigoletto* in 1851, Italian opera had been a booming entertainment business not unlike that which can be found in Hollywood today. As explained in the previous chapter, this business was based upon the principle of giving people what they wanted, of playing to the lowest common denominator, and ultimately, of achieving widespread popularity. Our present-day view of opera as an elitist form of high art would never have occurred to an Italian composer of the early nineteenth century. The opera world of those days was ruled by singers and impresarios, not by composers (who, incidentally, were actually one of the least important cogs in the wheel of operatic fortune). As late as the third decade of the nineteenth century, opera production was still a business in which an impresario leased a theater, hired a roster of the most popular singers he could find, and then assigned librettos to composers he thought could satisfy the demands of audiences for brilliant vocal display. Composers, even as late as the middle of Verdi's career, were expected to write music especially suited to the strengths of the particular singers on staff at the opera house where the new work was to be given. And if the singers objected to anything the composer had written, he was expected to make changes to suit their whims. Composers were also usually expected to direct the first three performances of any new work, after which (i.e., after the composer left town) singers were free to make whatever changes they thought necessary to improve the music, thus wreaking havoc on what the composer had left behind by frequently transposing, rewriting, cutting, and even making substitutions in parts they didn't like. Under these circumstances, composers were essentially powerless to control the overall effectiveness of the music drama. They understood their role in the production of an opera, and tended not to question it.

This lopsided balance of power in the world of opera began to shift gradually during Verdi's career; and it was he who was largely responsible for the emergence of the composer as the controlling artistic force in Italian musical theater after 1850. Because the immense success of his early operas led to a demand among impresarios for his services, Verdi was able to cater to his own dramatic instincts and to insist on doing things his way. He began by curtailing the abuses of singers, demanding that they no longer make wholesale substitutions in their parts. He also moved the style of singing away from one involving elaborate vocal display to one of simpler, more direct dramatic expression. And perhaps most difficult of all, he trained singers to be willing to sacrifice their need for public adulation to the greater need of musical-dramatic truthfulness. By 1850 it was Verdi, not an impresario, who decided what subjects he would set to music; it was Verdi, not his librettist, who sketched out the overall structure of the dramatic action and who decided what the characters were going to say; and it was Verdi, not the singers, who dictated the kind of vocal effect demanded by the drama, even if that meant something other than the traditionally beautiful vocal production of the past. In the middle years of his career, Verdi was thus poised to move into new worlds of operatic reform that would allow a more sophisticated depiction of the subtleties of character; and he did just that with *Rigoletto*.

After having begun his career following the model of Italian opera inherited from Donizetti and Bellini, Verdi eventually became dissatisfied with what his predecessors had done. By the early 1850s he had identified what he thought were several problems with traditional Italian opera, and in *Rigoletto* he addressed each of them with bold new solutions. Although these "problems" are interrelated, a discussion that separates them into two large categories will aid in understanding the issues Verdi faced at the time.

PROBLEM 1—THE LACK OF MUSICAL CONTINUITY

Italian opera had always consisted of a collection of individual musical numbers (hence the term *number opera*)—arias, duets, and ensembles classified as set pieces—strung together on a thread of recitative. Until the middle of the nineteenth century, this recitative had always been an untuneful, speechlike vocal style that composers used to deliver most of an opera's dialogue. It had the advantage of allowing the easy comprehension of words as well as the rapid traversal of large amounts of text. The problem with Italian opera at this time was that the continual alternation of recitative and more lyrical set pieces created a violent disruption of both musical style and dramatic momentum. This was especially true when (as they so often did in the early nineteenth century) singers insisted on coming out of character to accept audience applause after each aria or duet, before resuming the roles they were playing in the drama.

Verdi, like his German contemporary Wagner, wanted to create an opera in which applause did not interrupt the flow of the drama, and in which the musical style did not continually shift so violently. He began attacking this problem early in his career by taking the traditional introductory chorus, with which nearly all operas of that time opened, and expanding it into a large complex dramatic scene (a *gran scena*). This expansion was accomplished by attaching the chorus to other kinds of musical numbers in a way that produced one long uninterrupted musical unit comprised of smaller pieces welded together without pause. In *Rigoletto*, we can see this new larger musical unit built up through the fusion of smaller parts at the opening of act 1. The scene opens with some dialogue between the Duke and one of his aristocratic courtiers, followed by a miniature aria for the Duke, a little duet for the Duke and the Countess Ceprano, more dialogue, and finally a large ensemble of soloists with chorus. The way Verdi managed to weld all these musical sections together is through the use of arioso, a vocal style used only sparingly in the previous century, but brought into prominence in the nineteenth century as a replacement for traditional recitative. Because arioso lies halfway between the speechlike quality of recitative and the fully melodic style of set pieces, it is not especially interesting—only slightly more lyrical than recitative. But in any section of arioso the lack of melodic interest in the vocal parts is usually compensated for by the orchestra, which offers a real melodic counterpoint to what the singers are doing, thus giving the whole texture some genuine musical interest.

In the opening scene of *Rigoletto*, we find the Duke of Mantua in the midst of an orgiastic party, as he surveys the women around him and talks with fellow courtiers about the possible new conquest of an unidentified young woman he has seen at church, unaware that this woman is the daughter of his own hunchback court jester, Rigoletto. This dialogue is presented in vocal arioso cleverly accompanied by an orchestral melody that represents some dance music being played in the background at the party by an onstage band and string orchestra. This dance music forms a continuous melodic background against which the singers weave their semimelodic lines (the arioso) to deliver the necessary dialogue and narration. The dance music even accompanies some of the sections that are more like traditional set pieces: the little duet between the Duke and the Countess, for example. Because the dance music permeates the whole opening scene, it acts like musical glue providing unity and tying everything together. Enhancing this unity is the additional fact that the musical cadences that usually bring sections to a close are here elided with the beginnings of the following musical sections in a way that discourages any interruption with applause and keeps the music moving forward.

Extended musical-dramatic arches such as this reflect Verdi's concern with the creation of long-range continuity in this opera. Scene 2 of the first act demonstrates this same concern in a different way. This scene is made up primarily of duets augmented with a short solo for Rigoletto and Gilda's famous aria "Caro nome." A diagram illustrates the large dramatic arch of this scene beginning and ending with Rigoletto in ensemble with one or more other characters. The next smaller arch in the scene is formed by the respective solos for Rigoletto (at the beginning) and Gilda (at the end). Inside this arch is a still smaller, central one consisting of two important duets, the first for Gilda and Rigoletto, the second for Gilda and the Duke.

Act 1, scene 2 dramatic arch.

Sparafucile-Rigoletto / Rigoletto / Rigoletto-Gilda / Gilda-Duke / Gilda / Courtiers-Rigoletto

Within this large archlike dramatic structure, Verdi tried to create further musical/dramatic continuity through the use of the anticipatory appearance in the two central musical numbers of a character or characters who play an important role in the set piece that follows immediately after. Verdi began by inserting the Duke into the duet that Gilda sings with her father. This happens at the point where Rigoletto is warning Gilda never to go out and always to keep the door locked. Suddenly the Duke slips into the courtyard where Rigoletto and Gilda are having this conversation.

There he overhears their exchange and learns for the first time that Gilda, the object of his most recent amorous overtures, is actually Rigoletto's daughter. The Duke's intrusion here (including the couple of short lines he sings) is meant to link this duet to the next, between him and Gilda. His anticipatory appearance in the first duet serves as a prelude to the larger role he plays in that following duet. Symbolically, his role in the first duet is to represent a wedge that will drive Gilda and her father apart so he can replace Rigoletto both musically (in the following duet) and dramatically (as the man in her life).

In the next duet (between the Duke and Gilda), Verdi continues this technique of interjecting foreign characters. This time the interjection consists of a chorus of courtiers who have come to Rigoletto's house to avenge themselves on the court jester by abducting Gilda, whom they believe to be his mistress. As Gilda and the Duke are finishing their duet, they arrive in the street outside Rigoletto's house. At this point they sing only a couple of short lines. But their appearance in the midst of the duet serves the same bridging function between set pieces as did the Duke's appearance in the previous duet. In this case the courtiers' role is gradually expanded in Gilda's aria ("Caro nome") that follows her duet with the Duke. And when that aria is finished, these same courtiers become the principal characters in the ensemble finale that closes the first act. Thus, the whole scene is not so much a series of discrete duets and solos (as it might have been had someone such as Donizetti written it), but rather a larger musical unit in which the various parts are dramatically, if not musically, connected to their immediate neighbors. Verdi thus took the first step here in the opening scenes of act 1 toward creating a dramatic trajectory that crosses the boundaries between individual musical numbers, and in which audience applause at those traditional junctures is discouraged.

Yet another example of Verdi's concern with musical-dramatic continuity appears near the end of the opera in act 3, where the scene is laid on the outskirts of town, at a ramshackle inn run by Sparafucile, a hired assassin. Rigoletto has brought Gilda here because he knows the Duke frequents the inn for the purpose of visiting Sparafucile's attractive sister, Maddalena. Rigoletto's plan is to expose Gilda to the Duke's true licentious character, and to prove to her that he is not the "nice guy" whom she thinks is truly in love with her. After forcing her to watch the Duke's attempted seduction of Maddalena (which takes place in a famous quartet), Rigoletto orders Gilda to go home, change into male attire, and prepare to leave town. In a recitative, he makes arrangements with Sparafucile for the Duke's murder, but this plan is forestalled when Maddalena pleads with her brother to spare the Duke's life, as she, too, has been smitten with him. This leads to a trio in which Gilda overhears the plan made by Sparafucile and his sister to trick Rigoletto by substituting for the Duke's body that of any other person who might visit the inn that same night. It does not take Gilda long to decide to become that "other person," the sacrifice of whose life will save her lover. Normally the lengthy dialogue at the beginning of a scene such as this (starting after the quartet) would have been set as an extended section of recitative, which, in turn, would have led to the trio. As at the beginning of act 1, Verdi again set himself the goal of somehow creating an overarching musical unit that would weld the recitative and the trio into one unified whole to keep both the action and the music moving in an uninterrupted crescendo to a point of climax. This he accomplished by using the orchestra to depict a growing storm that underlies this entire scene.[1] As the quartet finishes and the recitative commences in the new scene, Verdi allows a few motifs of storm music to intrude into the orchestral accompaniment. This includes some flashes of flute and piccolo sounds (depicting lightning), a plaintive oboe, and a wordless chorus humming a chromatic line, (evoking the moaning of the wind).

Example 7-1. Act 3 storm music.

---

1. As discussed in chapter 2, storms are common fare in nineteenth-century opera, where they serve to express metaphorically the turmoil of the human soul.

Example 7-1 *(continued)*

These interjections gradually become more and more prominent in the music until the full storm breaks out exactly at the point when Gilda walks through the door of the inn and is stabbed to death by Sparafucile. Gradually the storm subsides as Gilda's lifeless body is dragged away and thrown into a sack for delivery to Rigoletto. The musical-dramatic timing here is perfect. First, the storm music provides continuity between the recitative/arioso with which the scene begins and the dramatic trio with which it ends, again creating a larger musical-dramatic unit than was common in Italian opera of the mid-nineteenth century. Furthermore, the storm music gradually intensifies to the point where its climax coincides exactly with the most dramatic moment of the action. Nowhere in the middle-period of Verdi career is the use of orchestral music to unify and support the unfolding of the dramatic narrative better managed than in this scene. With the writing of *Rigoletto*, Verdi broke out of the predictable arrangement of discrete musical numbers that had burdened Italian opera with an artificial dramatic structure since the days of Rossini early in the century.

PROBLEM 2—THE INFLEXIBILITY OF
TRADITIONAL MUSICAL FORMS

A large part of the revolutionary quality of *Rigoletto* concerns its arias: not their number (which is fairly average), but their form and style (which is totally new). Taking shape at this point in Verdi's career was a growing desire to reform the overall shape and dramatic effectiveness of Italian opera, as seen in the preceding discussion. After having begun his career by simply adopting the musical forms that he had found in the operas of his predecessors, Verdi was ready by midcentury to strike out in a new direction with a refinement of Italian opera that required a rethinking of the old traditions that audiences had come to love and expect. These traditions included specific musical structures (formal patterns) that had governed all operatic set pieces for decades. Verdi gradually came to understand that the most valuable of these set pieces, for the purposes of dramatic music, was the duet. This, after all, is where the interpersonal conflicts that make opera work are played out. In a letter written in September 1852, he referred to *Rigoletto* as an opera "conceived without arias, without finales, as an unbroken chain of duets."[2] In making the duet the center of musical attention in his new opera, however, Verdi found its standard musical form (inherited from Rossini) far too limiting for the infinite variations of dramatic situations that he wanted to set to music. As conceived by earlier Italian composers, this standard form consisted of two large sections: one slow, the other fast. (See detailed explanation and diagram in chapter 4.) The most important elements of the duet were the solos for each character near the beginning of part 1, and the change of tempo (and mood) for the excited conclusion in part 2. The almost continual application of this formal design to every duet situation found in Italian librettos written between about 1810 and 1840 proved both dramatically constrictive and musically predictable. It worked for some dramatic situations, and not for others. But earlier composers cared little whether the standard duet form suited the drama or not, as long as the formula allowed room for the production of brilliant vocal writing—which it did. Verdi, on the other hand, was driven by the need to remain faithful to his original dramatic sources as he adapted the literature and plays of his day to the operatic stage. His motto might well have been *prima la parola, poi la musica* (first the word, then the music). Or to put it another way, the drama shapes the musical form, not vice versa.

This need to break with the inherited traditions of operatic form shows itself both in Verdi's writing of duets and arias. The second scene of act 1, where Rigoletto returns home from the Duke's party to his daughter, Gilda, is a fine example of how the old operatic duet form could be reshaped to make a special dramatic point. On the way home, Rigoletto is intercepted by the hired assassin Sparafucile, who asks if Rigoletto might be in need of his services. The entire duet that unfolds between them owes nothing

---

2. Kimbell, 1981, 635.

to the traditional formal structure that Verdi knew so well. Instead of the individual solos usually heard at the beginning of a standard Italian duet, which then led to a section of duet singing, this duet is more like a miniature orchestral tone poem over which the voices converse in a realistic dialogue using nothing but arioso-style melody. This is the same kind of arioso Verdi used at the opening of the opera to create a long, over-arching musical unit. Here in the Rigoletto-Sparafucile duet, however, Verdi uses the arioso not as a device for linking smaller lyrical numbers into a single larger unit, but rather as a replacement for the traditionally lyrical number itself. His goal seems to have been to create a more realistic interchange between characters, one in which they never sing at the same time, but rather communicate in strict alternation, as one would expect to find in a stage play. While the voices are engaged in this arioso, the orchestra is busy unfolding the melodic commentary that gives meaning to what the characters are singing. Here Verdi also exercised his emerging sense of orchestral color as a powerful musical-dramatic tool by employing the very unusual instrumental sounds of solo cello and solo double bass playing the orchestral melody that serves as the backdrop for the dramatic action onstage.

Example 7-2. Act 1, Rigoletto-Sparafucile duet.

Two further examples of Verdi's departures from traditional operatic forms serve to illustrate how he was able to use these musical exceptions to make an important dramatic point about a character, in this case the heroine, Gilda. Following the duet between Rigoletto and Sparafucile, Rigoletto enters the courtyard of his home and is greeted by Gilda. There follows a duet, in which we discover much of the background about both of them. Verdi begins by replacing the usual recitative with a continuous melodic line that is split between the two singers, almost like an aria sung in alternating phrases.

Example 7-3a. Act 1, Rigoletto-Gilda duet.

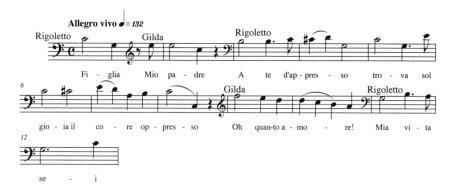

After the duet arrives at Rigoletto's solo section, the audience would have expected (by the conventions of standard Italian operatic form) Gilda to sing her solo, probably to the same music Rigoletto just sang. But Verdi made the bold decision to eliminate Gilda's solo, and to move instead directly into the section in which both characters sing together. Not until the second half of this duet does Verdi allow Gilda to sing alone, and even there what she sings is simply a repeat of the music her father just sang before her, as can be seen in Ex. 7-3b.

Example 7-3b. Continuation of Rigoletto-Gilda duet.

Example 7-3b *(continued)*

me - te, pad - re   mi - - o?   Las - sù in

In cutting her solos and/or forcing her to mimic her father, Verdi leaves us with the impression that Gilda is weak and immature, and has no character of her own. She is, as David Kimbell has observed, "a mere child, passive, submissive and wholly unegocentric,"[3] who is only able to function in a subservient relationship to the men around her, in this case her father.

Now in the very next number, also a duet, we see Gilda with the Duke. Here Verdi does exactly the same thing to the poor girl. As before, a shared melodic line replaces the usual recitative and leads to the first solo section, the Duke's, which then quickly becomes a duet, without Gilda ever getting the solo any prima donna would have expected and demanded. The fact that Verdi did not give Gilda the kind of solo section here that a prima donna would normally expect to see in a duet says something important about her character: first, Gilda is clearly not a usual prima donna, and second, Verdi had gotten to the point in his career where he was able to usurp the power of singers in his quest for dramatic truthfulness.

The first of these points—that Gilda is not an ordinary operatic prima donna—demands elaboration. Verdi intended for us to see Gilda as a woman with no independent personality. She lives and functions only in relation to the men in her life, both the Duke and her father. Her subservient role in the duets she sings with each of them mirrors her subservient role in the drama, at least here at the beginning of the opera. The reason this perception of her character is so important, of course, is that she will undergo a personality transformation later—a transformation that can be made to seem more powerful if one understands what Verdi intended to portray with this character at the outset of the opera. Thus an important facet of Gilda's character is communicated through this avoidance of a traditional operatic formal pattern. But if one has no knowledge of the traditional formal pattern in all other Italian opera of the time, then one will also miss the key dramatic point that Verdi was trying to make about Gilda's personality and its transformation.

This departure from musical norms for the purpose of making dramatic points carries through to some of the arias as well. Again it is Gilda who is most affected by these deviations from traditional practice. It has often been

---

3. Ibid.

observed that her only real solo in the whole opera, the famous "Caro nome" that follows her duet with the Duke (in which he avows his enduring love for her) represents yet another departure from tradition in that it is not the usual large-scale, two-part (slow-fast) cavatina-cabaletta with which prima donnas were usually introduced to the audience. The very fact that Verdi brought Gilda onstage in act 1 in a duet rather than in an aria was, from the start, an insult to the soprano and a comment about Gilda as a person in the drama—that she was not important or strong enough to deserve a bold solo entrance. Then, to add insult to injury, when Verdi finally allowed Gilda to sing alone, he gave her a simple one-part aria in strophic variation form. Strophic form is the simplest kind of song form in music: the same tune repeated again and again for every stanza of text, as in a hymn tune. Although Verdi varies the repetitions of the tune here (Exs. 7-4a–7-4c), the structure is still one of absolute simplicity, as befits Gilda's personality at this point in the drama. (It is worth noting that while the form is simple, the aria itself is actually extremely difficult to sing.)

Ex. 7-4a. Gilda's "Caro nome."

Example 7-4b.

Example 7-4c.

Unlike the heavyweight arias with which Verdi introduced some of his other heroines (Lady Macbeth in *Macbeth* or Abigail in *Nabucco*, for example), Gilda's aria is light and simple and is designed to project the illusion that Gilda is not the kind of ambitious, domineering woman that we frequently encounter in Verdi's other works, the kind of prima donna who demands a large entrance aria to make her presence known to all. Here we have an example of *true* characterization through music, as Verdi used his abandonment of an inherited tradition to create operatic characters of greater complexity and truthfulness.

In the early 1850s when Verdi was working on *Rigoletto*, his motivation for making a reform of Italian opera grew at least partly out of what he saw as the limitations of the cavatina-cabaletta as a musical-dramatic tool. The musical rationale for this kind of aria had always been to show off the singer's purity of tone along with his or her ability to make lovely smooth legato phrases in the opening slow section, and then to demonstrate the skill with which he or she could negotiate various kinds of decorative passages (*fioriture*) in the fast concluding section (the cabaletta). This section was always repeated, at which point the singer added as much improvised ornamentation to an already difficult melodic line as could tastefully be managed. The goal in so doing was really nothing more than to wow the audience with technical virtuosity. In short, the cavatina-cabaletta was unapologetically designed as a showcase for singers' vocal abilities. The form evolved at a time in the history of opera when singing was more important than drama: that is to say in the era of unadulterated bel canto. To the extent that Verdi recognized the limitations of such singer-dominated opera—opera held hostage to the display of vocal gymnastics—he became ever more determined to create a new kind of Italian opera that better balanced the display of singing on the one hand, with the effective portrayal of realistic dramatic situations on the other. His frustration stemming from the need to use one musical aria form or one duet form to satisfy an infinite number of dramatic situations, led to his abandoning the musical forms of traditional Italian opera in favor of inventive alterations and modifications of those forms that allowed him better to serve the drama.

Another significant example of this search for alterations of old forms that could then serve new dramatic purposes can be seen in some of the arias that Verdi wrote for Rigoletto, especially the one that he sings in act 2 after the courtiers have abducted Gilda and brought her to the Duke's bedroom. Suspecting what they have done with his daughter, Rigoletto arrives at the palace in a fit of anger, trying to find her. First, he damns and threatens the nobles, and then, only after realizing that he is powerless to secure her return, does he resort to pleading. To set this scene as an aria, Verdi was forced to turn the usual cavatina-cabaletta around so that the fast, energetic, cabaletta-like section came first to capture Rigoletto's anger, and the slow, lyrical, cavatina-like section then followed at the end for the moment when Rigoletto is reduced to pleading for the return of his daughter. Although the tempo of the opening section is not as fast as what one would expect in a traditional cabaletta (marked quarter note = MM80), the rhythmically animated orchestral accompaniment here, with sextuplets of sixteenth notes on every beat of the measure, lends to this section the furious energy usually associated with the cabaletta.

Example 7-5a. Rigoletto, "Cortigiani" opening agitated section.

The final section, by comparison is even slower (quarter note = MM56), and creates the illusion that this section of the aria functions as the traditional slow, lyrical cavatina.

Example 7-5b. "Cortigiani" slow completion.

This inverted cavatina-cabaletta now works to capture the essence of the dramatic situation. Through the unconventional slow close of this aria, Rigoletto is shown to be a broken man placing himself at the mercy of his sworn enemies. By comparison, the traditional aria form ending with the excited, fast cabaletta would only have made a meaningless mess of the drama in this situation.

Beyond the ever-popular Italian aria lay other new more flexible forms of solo singing, to which Verdi resorted in his search for unusual musical means to capture the psychological complexities of characters such as Rigoletto. In addition to reversing the order of the usual two sections of the standard cavatina-cabaletta as he did for Rigoletto's act 2 aria, Verdi also had recourse to solo arioso as a mode of vocal expression that he could reserve for especially volatile moments in the drama. One such moment occurs in act 1, right after Rigoletto's first meeting with Sparafucile, and before he returns home to Gilda. In an emotionally tormented soliloquy, Rigoletto rails at his fate in life. The text, which begins, "Pari siamo! . . . Io la lingua, egli ha il pugnale" (We are the same . . . I have my tongue, he has his dagger), continues at some length. Its poetic structure suggests that the librettist intended this to be a recitative,[4] but Verdi must have felt that the dramatic situation was too emotional for simple recitative, and thus settled upon the unique solution of setting the entire text as a solo arioso. This gave him the freedom to write something that was more melodically expressive without having to write an aria, which would have been far too songlike and regular in its phrase structure for the volatility of this particular dramatic moment. In the following example, notice how the vocal line falls somewhere between the speechlike quality of recitative on the one hand, and the tunefulness of an aria on the other. Examples of arioso had appeared in operatic solos long before this, but nearly always as a prelude to a real aria. In Verdi's use of this technique, the arioso stands alone as an independent musical number.

Example 7-6. Excerpt from "Pari siamo."

---

4. Italian poetry that mixes unrhymed lines of eleven and seven syllables was referred to as *versi sciolti,* and was always intended for setting as recitative rather than as a lyrical set piece.

Example 7-6 *(continued)*

In light of Verdi's willingness to trade old musical forms for new more flexible ones that meet the demands of the drama, it is worth noting that the only character in this opera who gets to sing a traditional cavatina-cabaletta is the Duke. This is partly because the dramatic situation that accompanies his aria at the beginning of act 2 suits the standard musical form. But there may be more behind Verdi's use of this traditional form for the Duke's aria at this point in the drama. Just as Verdi used new and unusual musical forms to make specific dramatic points about Gilda, he used an old traditional aria form here to make a point about the Duke. At the end of act 1, unaware of his own courtiers' plan to abduct Gilda, the Duke returned to her home (after their duet) only to find her missing. As act 2 opens, we find him back at his palace, where he laments the loss of his "beloved" in an outpouring of emotion.

> I seem to see the tears
> Flowing from those eyes,
> When between doubt and fear
> Of sudden danger,
> Remembering our love,
> She called for her Gualtier.
> He could not help you
> Dearest beloved girl,
> He who with all his soul wants
> To make you happy in this world.
> He who for you would not envy
> The angels in their spheres.

Given the fact that the Duke is an unabashed rake and faithless libertine, there would seem to be something a little out of character in this text. Suddenly this cad wants us to believe that he is truly in love with Gilda, and that he is a transformed man—not a likely change by any stretch of the imagination. In analyzing this alteration in the Duke's behavior, we must understand that it was mostly forced upon Verdi and his librettist by the rules of operatic censorship, which required that royalty never be portrayed onstage as immoral or corrupt. This, in fact, is why Victor Hugo's king in the play *Le roi s'amuse*, from which Verdi borrowed the plot for his opera, became the opera's Duke in the first place, to lessen the censorial offense by reducing the character's level of nobility. Without a doubt, there is something phony, transparently predictable, and artificial about the Duke at this point in the drama. And it is Verdi's use of the cavatina-cabaletta that confirms this suspicion about the Duke, because this aria form had by this time become as artificial, inflexible, and predictable as the Duke himself. But beyond this artificiality lies also the implication of something simplistically formulaic and therefore without depth or complexity. Indeed, when compared with Gilda and Rigoletto, the Duke is a far less interesting, more two-dimensional, predictable, and operatically old-fashioned character. In this particular aria, the cavatina serves as a lament, carried out in a fairly simple two-stanza form with a coda and cadenza.

Example 7-7a. Duke's "Parmi veder le lagrime."

Following the cavatina, the courtiers enter to explain that they have abducted Gilda and brought her to the palace—to the Duke's bedroom, in fact. This news motivates the completely predictable and totally conventional response of joy projected in the cabaletta that follows. In what might be called the usual "excited style," the Duke puffs himself up and struts around stage singing about the "power of love" to make him a slave. If subterfuge and pretense were an important element of his character, this aria might have made sense, as the Duke feigns a caring demeanor. But since the Duke has no reason in this situation to pretend to be what he is not, his attempt to convince the audience of his sincerity is almost comical.

Example 7-7b. Duke's cabaletta "Possente amor."

Verdi's choice of the old-fashioned, artificial cavatina-cabaletta is thus like a musical wink of the eye from composer to audience, as if to say through his music, "We all know this character is as fake and predictable as the musical form in which he is singing."

Rigoletto is surely one of Verdi's most popular operas, and that popularity rests equally on its gripping drama and its tuneful music.[5] But beyond this popularity, lies another whole level of importance in this work. It is in *Rigoletto* that Verdi first began to find a new mature style, which allowed him to reinvent the business of Italian opera as an important art form, to finalize the transfer of power from singers to composers, and lastly, to undertake a reevaluation of the very nature of Italian opera itself and to set the direction in which it was to develop over the next half century.

---

5. Verdi realized, for example, that the Duke's aria "La donna è mobile" was going to be the next great pop tune among Italian citizens, and so wisely decided to withhold it from rehearsals of the opera until the very last minute so that the premiere would not be spoiled by any leaking of the tune to the public ahead of the performance.

PART IV
Opera as Autobiography

CHAPTER 8

BEETHOVEN'S *FIDELIO*: A CASE OF SELF-SALVATION

Envision this scene: a young soprano—a student of voice at a major U.S. conservatory—is rehearsing an aria from *Fidelio* to sing in a class that she is taking on the music of Beethoven. The professor walks into the classroom just as the soprano, frustrated in her attempts to grapple with the difficulties of the music, unleashes an emphatic four-letter expletive: "What the ____ did Beethoven think he was doing?" To which the startled professor responds, "Indeed . . . what do you think Beethoven's response to that question would be if he were here today?"

And thus we come to the perennial question about *Fidelio*: What *was* Beethoven thinking when he wrote this opera, and why is it such a difficult work on so many different levels? Generally hailed as a masterpiece, especially in academic circles, *Fidelio* is at the same time frequently reviled by singers who find it unrewarding, and by audiences who find it hopelessly boring on stage. Because of this, artistic directors of opera houses around the world are often reluctant to mount new productions for fear of losing money on the venture; and as a result the opera gets little public exposure. So why is *Fidelio* such a paradox, and exactly what *are* the problems with this opera that have resulted in this conundrum? Why did a composer like Beethoven, for whom opera was not a major focus, bother writing such a work at all?

The answer to these questions must begin with a review of two of the most persistent myths that have grown up around this opera over the years. The first of these claims that Beethoven had little interest in opera as a genre, and that because he paid much more attention to symphonic and chamber music than to dramatic vocal music, his skills as a composer of opera were limited. Part of this myth is fact: *Fidelio is* Beethoven's only opera, and based on that fact alone, one might conclude that this genre was clearly not of primary interest to him. But we must be careful not to judge Beethoven's interest in opera based solely on the number of such works he actually completed. Although he never really appreciated comic opera (which he usually described as either inane or morally debase), he did like serious opera; and throughout his life, he continued to look for librettos that he felt were worthy of setting to music. In addition to *Fidelio*, he worked earnestly on several other opera projects, including a libretto by Emanuel Schikaneder called *Vestas Feuer* (an ancient Roman subject), Shakespeare's *Macbeth* (for which he left sketches from 1808), and Goethe's *Faust* (discussed and projected with the poet himself in 1812). Beethoven also contributed arias and finales to operas by other composers. In general, all evidence points to the composer's ongoing interest in writing opera. As he wrote in 1811 to one of the directors of the Imperial Opera, "It is very difficult to find a good libretto for an opera. Last year I turned down no less than twelve or more of them."[1]

The second myth about *Fidelio* is that this opera clearly demonstrates that Beethoven had no idea how to write effectively for the voice. Like the first myth, this, too, contains a kernel of truth. Yes, some parts of this opera seem cruelly unidiomatic for the voice, but much of its music, on the other hand, actually proves just the opposite—that Beethoven had the capacity to write lyrically and graciously for the voice. Given the fact, then, that he was interested in opera, and that he could write idiomatically for voice when he wanted to, we must now grapple with the original questions regarding the nature of this work and Beethoven's motivation for writing it. Since he was never able to find another opera libretto that satisfied his needs, one must conclude that there was something special about this opera, something that fulfilled a creative need in the composer, which no other operatic subject was able to do. But what was this personal connection that drew Beethoven so strongly to this work?

On the most mundane level, we cannot discount the possibility that part of Beethoven's desire to undertake this project might have been the lure of potentially large profits. Although generally unsympathetic toward comic opera, he was well aware of just how popular this genre had become since the mid-eighteenth century. He recognized that composers of comic opera (especially in Italy) were making fortunes on the production of their most popular works. Why shouldn't he do the same? To the extent that Beethoven struggled all his life with the need to become rich and famous, opera may well have represented an easy path to his financial goals.

Another important aspect of Beethoven's personal attraction to this opera was surely its French connection. In the summer of 1802, he suffered an emotional breakdown that led to the writing his famous Heiligenstadt Testament, a document in which he struggled with the impact of his growing deafness on his identity as a musician. Following that crisis, he returned to Vienna in a healthier and more productive frame of mind. The years around 1803, when Beethoven was beginning work on *Fidelio*, were

---

1. Anderson, 1961, vol. 1, 325.

marked by great successes in the publication, commissioning, and even the reception of his new works. Despite this apparent success, Beethoven was not happy. Writing to one of his publishers at this time, he said, "Please remember that all of my acquaintances hold appointments and know exactly what they have to live on."[2] By implication he seems to be complaining about the uncertainty of a freelance career. So Beethoven decided, almost on a whim, that after the completion of *Fidelio*, he would relocate to Paris, where he imagined he would be better received and would find a permanent position of some kind. At the same time he decided to title his new third symphony the "Bonaparte" and not to publish it until after his move to Paris. He also dedicated his latest violin sonata to the French violinist Rodolphe Kreutzer, despite the fact that Kreutzer thought the work was a monstrosity and refused to play it. Based on this evidence, can there be any doubt that Beethoven was trying to ingratiate himself with Parisian audiences, musicians, and politicians in 1803? This attempt on Beethoven's part to establish a connection with France is relevant to the composition of *Fidelio* because the libretto for that opera was originally written in French by Jean Nicolas Bouilly, and set to music by the French composer Pierre Gaveaux in 1798. In Beethoven's mind this French libretto may have been just one of several pieces of an elaborate scheme designed to establish a link with Paris that would make him a more sympathetic interloper in the French capital, should that move ever become a reality at this point in his career.

To appreciate the significance of this French connection in Beethoven's life, it will be helpful to make a short digression into the history of the composition of *Fidelio*. It was Emanuel Schikaneder, the librettist for Mozart's *Die Zauberflöte*, who commissioned Beethoven to write this opera. Schikaneder was at the time director of the Theater an der Wien in Vienna, where he had been staging, with considerable success, a series of French rescue operas. This was a special kind of French comic opera (with spoken dialogue) that featured (paradoxically) serious plots based on contemporary post-Revolutionary events in France, where innocent victims were almost daily being thrown into prison (usually illegally) and then frequently rescued by faithful servants or loved ones. A typical example of this kind of opera, and an immensely popular work in Paris in the 1780s, was Grétry's *Richard, coeur de lion*, based on the rescue of the English King Richard from enemy capture during the Crusades. *Fidelio* is just such a rescue opera, originally titled *Léonore, ou l'amour conjugal*. Schikaneder simply took this popular libretto and had it translated into German so Beethoven could set it for his Viennese audiences.

---

2. Solomon, 2001, 169.

Beyond these French connections in this opera lie other personal motivations for the writing of *Fidelio*. One of these was Beethoven's empathy with the ideals of the Enlightenment. Like most European intellectuals, Beethoven embraced the principles of brotherhood, justice, equality, humanity, and freedom that were a part of the new thinking of intellectuals and philosophers in the late eighteenth century. As such, the young composer became a supporter of Emperor Joseph II, one of the most enlightened monarchs in all Europe. When Joseph died in 1790, the twenty-year-old Beethoven composed a commemorative cantata to celebrate his many political and religious reforms. One particularly moving moment in this cantata occurs in a soprano aria that depicts Joseph as the "bringer of light" (in the usual allegorical sense of wisdom and justice). It was the central melody of this aria that Beethoven plagiarized for use fifteen years later in *Fidelio* for the climactic scene in which Leonore unlocks the chains that imprisoned her husband.

Example 8-1a. *Cantata on the Death of Joseph II*, soprano aria.

Example 8-1b. *Fidelio*, Act 2 (end), oboe melody accompanying Leonore's release of her husband.

Underlying both appearances of this melody is the theme of justice and freedom that were central to Beethoven's Enlightenment sympathies.

Emperor Joseph was not the only figure of the Enlightenment to capture Beethoven's admiration. Napoleon Bonaparte also loomed large in his pantheon of heroes, as an example of the power of human aspiration to lift the common man to the highest echelons of nobility. This sympathy with Napoleon's achievements led to Beethoven's decision to title his third symphony the "Bonaparte." But when Napoleon declared himself emperor in 1804, Beethoven became disillusioned with his hero, claiming he had betrayed the ideals of the Revolution. In a fit of rage, he tried to erase the word "Bonaparte" from the title page of his symphony, leaving behind only a hole in the paper where the name had originally appeared. In Beethoven's mind, then, both his third symphony and his opera share a French provenance as well as the Enlightenment themes of heroism and brotherhood.

Beyond Beethoven's devotion to the principles of the Enlightenment, lay a more personal connection between the composer and his opera. On an allegorical level, both he and the hero of the opera, Florestan, shared the similar predicament of imprisonment—Florestan locked in his dungeon cell, and Beethoven trapped in his growing deafness. Symbolically, Florestan is Beethoven, struggling against his unjust adversity, a prisoner of his undeserved fate, alone, cut off from the rest of the world. Recall that this opera was written immediately after Beethoven's emotional collapse in Heiligenstadt in the summer of 1802. In the "testament" he penned that summer, he struggled with depression caused by the onset of his handicap. He wrote about the painful feelings of inadequacy that accompanied the first signs of his deafness, and how he even entertained the possibility of suicide. But Beethoven emerged from that depression with a renewed will to battle the forces of darkness, to grapple with fate, and to emerge in a glorious triumph. In a letter from that time, he wrote, "I will seize Fate by the throat; I will surely not be defeated."[3] Consider then Florestan's struggle in act 2 of the opera. The scene begins in the near total darkness of his underground cell, and culminates in the full sunlight and open air of the prison courtyard where all of the prisoners are released. The journey from imprisonment to freedom through which Florestan moves is the same journey from darkness to light that Beethoven himself experienced immediately following the Heiligenstadt collapse. Florestan and Beethoven are, in this sense, one and the same person, and it is unlikely that Beethoven could have read the libretto for *Fidelio* without recognizing himself in his hero.

The idea of a personal identification between the composer and a fictional character in his opera could partly explain Beethoven's intense interest in this work. But the issues of personal identification run even deeper than Beethoven's connection to Florestan. For Beethoven, the character of Leonore, Florestan's devoted wife and savior, might have had personal meaning as well. Beethoven himself never married, but throughout his life searched desperately (usually in all the wrong places) for a perfect female companion of the kind that Leonore represents. What Beethoven needed was someone to rescue him, not from prison, but from himself— someone to make him a better man. In this regard, it is especially revealing

---

3. Ibid., 149.

that his first candidate for this position of the noble savior (i.e., the role of Leonore in his own life) was a young lady with whom he grew up in Bonn, named, coincidentally, Eleonore von Breuning. Clearly the multiple levels of personal identification between Beethoven and the characters and events in this opera must have powerfully drawn the composer into his work on *Fidelio*. Thus the reason Beethoven wrote only one opera may be partly related to the fact that he was unable to find another libretto that satisfied so many personal needs, that played into so many personal issues and deeply held fantasies, and that allowed him an arena in which to vicariously triumph over his real-life adversity.

Just as circumstances surrounding the composition of *Fidelio* are full of paradoxes and misunderstandings, so too is the music itself. Besides the two myths dealt with at the outset of this chapter, there have arisen, over the years, various other myths about this opera: that Beethoven had no gift for writing comic music (i.e., all the comic moments in the drama sound labored); that *Fidelio* is an uneasy and incongruous mixture of comic and serious elements that don't fit well together; and that this work is just plain boring onstage.

To address some of these additional misunderstandings, we need again to separate fact from fiction. Fact: *Fidelio is* a mixture of serious and comic music and drama that results in a highly contrasting confluence of musical styles. But so too is one of Mozart's greatest operas, *Die Zauberflöte*. And as the success of that work so aptly demonstrates, the lack of stylistic unity alone is not sufficient reason to condemn any particular opera. In Beethoven's case the mixture of comic and serious elements is easily explained by the provenance of the libretto in the French rescue opera tradition. Such works usually included comic situations intermixed with the more serious elements of the drama because their overall form was that of opéra comique. As a result of the structure of the libretto, much comic music stands side by side with some of the opera's most serious scenes and characters. An example of this comic music is the opening duet between Marzelline and Jaquino in act 1. These are two characters who represent the lowest social class in the opera: Marzelline is the jailor's daughter, and Jaquino is her simple-minded boyfriend who is pestering her to become his wife. If this were an opera by Mozart, these characters would be part of the servant class—people like Susanna and Figaro. Such characters are always the ones given *buffa*-style music. This style, cultivated by composers of Italian comic opera in the previous century, is characterized by rapid tempos, major modes, simple melodies built in symmetrical phrases, and simple diatonic harmonies. Beethoven's duet captures all these musical characteristics in a perfect imitation of the *buffa* style of Mozart. Those listeners who insist that this music sounds somehow labored or forced in its comic character may simply be allowing their appreciation of the serious music in *Fidelio* to color their hearing of the comic moments in the score.

On the other hand, this matter of mixing serious and comic music together in one opera, seems to have troubled Beethoven himself, as though he knew that there was something problematic with that combination. Altogether, Beethoven worked on three different versions of this opera, struggling in each case with exactly this issue of how (or whether) to mix serious and comic styles in *Fidelio*. Each version of the opera shows him experimenting with ways to pare down the comic elements in the libretto and to rearrange them so as not to undercut the serious scenes. For example, the earliest (1805) version of the opera included a comic duet for Leonore and Marzelline placed disruptively between the murder duet of Pizarro (the warden of the prison where Florestan is jailed) and Rocco (the head jailor) and the equally serious aria for Leonore in which she sings about the power of wedded love driving her to rescue her poor husband. This duet was cut in the first revision of the opera (1806) as Beethoven tried to grapple with the problem of how and where to place the comic numbers so that they would not completely destroy the credibility of the serious portions of the drama. In its final (but never completely finished) form of 1813, the serious parts of the drama do indeed outweigh the comic, thus causing the comic music to seem less relevant to the overall dramatic progress of the work. This, however, does not mean that Beethoven's comic music is unsuccessful on its own terms.

When singers assert that *Fidelio* is typical of Beethoven's unforgiving, unidiomatic solo vocal writing, they are referring to the fact that some of the music is untuneful (too many repeated notes in a row), and that the syllabic setting of the German text frequently places too many consonants too close together for them to be able to make a beautiful vocal sound. An example of such vocal writing can be found in one of the important arias for Pizarro in act 2.

Example 8-2. Pizarro, "Ha, welch ein Augenblick."

Example 8-2 *(continued)*

In evaluating this kind of vocal writing, one must first recognize that all of Beethoven's melodic writing is not as challenging as this, and when it is, there are always reasons why he wrote the way he did. As a character in this drama, Pizarro functions as the classic villain. Given that role, there is no reason for him to sing beautiful melodies. Both here and elsewhere, Beethoven's melodic writing for this character is perfectly in keeping with his function in the drama.

There is perhaps no better example of the stylistic range of Beethoven's vocal writing than Leonore's famous aria "Komm Hoffnung" in act 1. It begins with an arioso (a highly melodic recitative) in which she responds to having overheard Pizarro's plans to murder her husband. For the lines, "Monster, where are you running? . . . What savage cruelty have you planned?" Beethoven creates a melody full of angularities, sharp rhythms, and repeated notes, all to the accompaniment of an angry motif in the orchestra that sets the violent tone of the scene. In addition, his syllabic text setting again places the consonances close together, as seen in the last line, "Was hast du vor in wilden Grimme?" Such text setting precludes the opportunity for a singer to make a beautiful vocal sound on an uninterrupted open vowel.

Example 8-3. Leonore's arioso, "Abscheulicher!"

Example 8-3 *(continued)*

But for the main body of the aria, Beethoven changes to a far gentler style, and writes the following graceful melody to accompany the line, "Come, Hope, let not your last star be eclipsed in despair."

Example 8-4. Slow section of Leonore's aria, "Komm Hoffnung."

Finally the aria concludes with a fast section to the words "I follow a voice within me, unwavering, and am strengthened by the faith of wedded love." Here Beethoven takes up a more animated style of vocal writing with dramatic leaps motivated by the excitement that Leonore feels at the thought of being able to reach her husband in time to save him.

Example 8-5. Culmination of Leonore's aria.

Although the opening and closing sections of this aria are a response to an anxious situation faced by Leonore, and are therefore not pretty melodies of the kind that are easy to sing or to remember, the middle section gives ample evidence that Beethoven could, when the dramatic situation called for it, write as lovely a melodic line as anyone. The genius of Beethoven, then, lies not in the fact that his music is always beautiful, but rather that his vocal writing is at all times dramatic—unattractive when it needs to be, and gentle when the occasion calls for tenderness.

This quality of Beethoven's music stands in distinct contrast to that of his Italian contemporaries, for whom the primary operatic concern was lyricism and vocal beauty. Even Mozart, an Austrian whose operatic training was mostly Italian, once observed (in a letter to his father) that while operatic music must capture the good and the bad in every character, it must never cease being beautiful music.[4] Beethoven seems not to have fully accepted this dictum, and consequently some of the music in *Fidelio* oversteps that

---

4. Anderson, 1985, 769

boundary between the ugly and the beautiful that Mozart refused to cross. But mostly, the opinion that *Fidelio* is not a singer's opera derives from the fact that Beethoven seemed to believe that expressive music-drama could not be achieved with the limited melodic resources of "tunefulness," and that other means of dramatic expression must lie in the toolbox of every opera composer. For audiences of today, who love Donizetti and Puccini, *Fidelio* can therefore be a difficult evening at the opera, and an example of an opera that just does not seem to "work." Not only are these audiences unable to whistle any great tunes on the trip home from the theater, but they can also become frustrated by the absence of action onstage, which causes this opera to seem stagnant. This particular criticism of Beethoven's opera derives, however, from a confusion about where the real drama in opera takes place. For Beethoven, the source of the drama—in opera as well as instrumental music—lies in the intense internal conflicts that arise out of the juxtaposition of highly contrasted musical materials themselves.

Perhaps the foremost demonstration of this idea is Florestan's aria at the beginning of act 2. The scene opens in a dungeon cell. The stage is in almost total darkness, and because Florestan lies in chains, alone, half dead, little physical action is possible. As the curtain goes up, the orchestra paints a mood of bleak hopelessness with an extended introduction of dark, brooding music. Finally Florestan props himself up to croak out his dying thoughts and feelings in a grand recitative and aria. The first word out of his mouth is a rather dramatic "Gott" sung on a long, G above middle C (not an easy way to begin an aria), as he complains to God about the injustice of his situation. Following this recitative, Beethoven settles into a far more tuneful section in which Florestan relives the contentment of his youth and laments his present situation.

Example 8-6. Florestan, act 2 aria.

Then the mood shifts as the drama (all still in the music) becomes more intense. Florestan is overtaken by a vision: a hallucination in which his wife, Leonore, appears in the guise of an angel come to free him from his earthly bondage and suffering. Here Beethoven captures the intensity of Florestan's emotion in a vocal melody situated relentlessly in the upper part of the tenor's vocal range. This melody then climbs continually higher as the aria progresses. To accompany and augment the strain this rise in pitch produces in the tenor's voice, Beethoven adds an extraordinary oboe obbligato, which itself reaches painfully high into the uppermost register of the instrument (to an F two and a half octaves above middle C). The energy required to play this accompanimental part, along with the resulting pinched tone of the instrument in that register, perfectly complements the strain in the singer's voice and effectively captures the dying man's frenzy in purely musical terms. Of course, because arias in general represent points of emotional reflection in an opera, there is usually not much acting involved, and therefore nothing much actually happens onstage at this point. But what separates Florestan's aria from so many others is that there is a considerable amount of drama unfolding in the music, leaving both the tenor and the audience exhausted in the end.

This concept of drama that resides in the music may work convincingly in theory, but there are occasions when audiences can justifiably become confused about whether certain sections of *Fidelio* contain any drama at all (musical or otherwise), as happens for instance in the quartet for Fidelio, Rocco, Marzelline, and Jaquino in act 1. Here Fidelio (Leonore disguised as a young man who comes to the prison seeking work as a jailor [5]) finds himself (herself) being graciously accepted by the head jailor, Rocco, as a potential mate for his daughter, Marzelline, all while Marzelline's old boyfriend, Jaquino, becomes furiously jealous. But this quartet, in which everyone has a different emotional reaction to the developing situation, receives from Beethoven a most unusual musical setting. His quartet is cast in the form of a four-part canon, in which each character enters the musical texture one after the other singing exactly the same melody. Not only does this contradict the usual rule of operatic ensemble writing, which suggests that each character should express a unique emotion in equally unique music, but the whole quartet unfolds at an almost unbearably slow tempo, stretching out the piece to a duration of five full minutes. One might well ask where the drama is in this scene. While the music is hypnotically beautiful, the apparent lack of correlation between the music and the four characters' different emotions, leaves us hunting for an explanation of what dramatic effect Beethoven was aiming for here. Because there is neither

---

5. Here Beethoven puts to a new serious purpose the old comic opera technique of a character masquerading under an assumed identity through the change of clothing.

drama onstage (in terms of an interaction among characters that results in a progressive action) nor drama in the music (in terms of contrasting and conflicting musical styles), we can safely conclude that Beethoven must not have seen this as a "dramatic moment" in the usual sense of the term. A careful look at the libretto, in fact, makes clear that each character is thinking aloud at this moment, and that there is no confrontation or communication between any of them that would lead to any development of the drama. But of course, this is true of nearly every large-scale operatic ensemble one can think of. So Beethoven's insistence on giving each character exactly the same music to express contrasting emotions must be understood as an attempt on his part to create a dramatic state of suspended animation through complete inaction and musical stasis.

Returning now to the question posed by the frustrated singer in the opening imaginary scenario, we can ask again, "What did Beethoven think he was doing here?" What kind of opera is this? On one level, the answer is extremely simple: as Beethoven began work on *Fidelio*, he most likely imagined he was simply fulfilling a commission from Schikaneder for a rescue opera that might lead to an increase in his popularity and wealth. But a more complex explanation might include the possibility that as his work progressed, his response to the subject matter became skewed by his personal empathy with the characters and events constituting the more serious portions of the drama. Although there is nothing inadequate about Beethoven's comic music in this opera (as is sometimes claimed), his more serious music is so different, so much more intense than his comic style, that the juxtaposition of the two creates what might be described as a series of musical non sequiturs. As mentioned earlier, Mozart's *Die Zauberflöte* is perhaps the only other opera in which such glaring examples of musical non sequiturs manage to coexist without disrupting the dramatic logic of the work (although some experts have claimed that Mozart's comic-serious masterpiece *is* dramatically illogical). Mozart was able to absorb these violent musical contradictions into the general fabric of his opera by virtue of the fact that it is a "magic" opera (in which the impossible is always possible) and because it is actually two operas in one—the story of Papageno/Papagena on the one hand and Tamino/Pamina on the other— neither of which intersects in any meaningful way in the course of the drama. Beethoven worked under more restrictive conditions with his libretto, in which the same characters are involved in both serious and comic scenes, and because of that, he seems to have felt uneasy about the paradoxical confluence of comic and serious elements in this work. Although he spent many years of his career trying to resolve the inherent contradictions in the libretto, he eventually left the work without ever really finding a satisfactory solution. Little wonder that more than two hundred years after its premiere, scholars and audiences alike continue to find *Fidelio* somewhat less than perfectly satisfying—a flawed masterpiece as it were. Despite the fact that Beethoven recognized the problem with which the libretto burdened his work on this opera, there is little reason to believe he ever once considered his music problematic, either for singers or audiences. Aspects of the style of Beethoven's vocal writing that today make the music unattractive for some listeners and difficult for some singers are the very elements that make the music dramatic. The forceful pounding on a single repeated note, the densely packed syllabic setting of the text that leaves no room for singers to expand their sound on open vowels, the wide melodic leaps, the ungrateful tessitura, and the requisite forceful vocal delivery are all musical tools with which Beethoven dredged up and gave expression to our deepest, darkest fears of evil and injustice in the world. Without these emotions, the final victory for freedom, truth, and nobility would be meaningless. Just as Beethoven himself needed to live through the pain of his handicap in order to arrive at his own spiritual emancipation, so the music of *Fidelio* must pass through violence and ugliness in order for the transcendent beauty of the last act finale (the rescue scene) to be most effective. Beethoven's fundamental musical-dramatic aesthetic grew out of his conviction that drama arises out of conflict and tension, and that the human voice is just another musical instrument, another color, in the arsenal of techniques that a composer has at his disposal to create this tension. Throughout his career, Beethoven's music was frequently characterized as "abstract." This usually means that the composer was more concerned with his musical ideas *in the abstract* than he was with ease of performance or audience appreciation. By this standard, Beethoven's music has a life of its own, on the page and in one's head. In his search for expressive music, Beethoven often demanded from instruments and players alike, techniques bordering on the unidiomatic, that went beyond what performers could comfortably accommodate. As a result, much of the music throughout the broad spectrum of his works is difficult and ungratifying to perform and not easy to listen to. A piece like the *Grosse Fuge* (op. 133 string quartet), for example, is a thorny work in which musical beauty plays no part. *Fidelio* may be equally thorny, although for different reasons. Opera was simply another medium in which a composer like Beethoven could create something intensely expressive and dramatic. If we abandon our usual expectations of what an opera is, and embrace this broader concept of drama in music, then we will have come a step closer to understanding *Fidelio*, a masterpiece of deeply felt emotions in which a fundamental human struggle is played out in music on an operatic stage. That struggle was Beethoven's struggle; its hero is Beethoven himself. And if this opera is indeed flawed, like the human spirit that it tries to capture, then it is so mostly because it overreaches, and in so doing, attempts more than it can achieve. This, of course, is the romantic ideal, around which artists like Beethoven built their world of hope. For the nineteenth-century composer, striving was the very essence of greatness, underlying everything that gives meaning to life. From this perspective, *Fidelio* takes on a new meaning as an opera of musical autobiography that fulfilled Beethoven's own subconscious agendas and, in the process, forces us to reevaluate our understanding of exactly what a music drama is, or can be.

CHAPTER 9

BERLIOZ'S *LA DAMNATION DE FAUST*:
WHEN IS OPERA NOT OPERA?

Hector Berlioz, one of the earliest and most radical composers of the nineteenth century, is today remembered mostly as a composer of daringly original instrumental music, including his famous *Symphonie fantastique* (an autobiographical program symphony that took the world by surprise in 1830) and an assortment of programmatic overtures that are also widely performed. Given Berlioz's reputation as a composer for orchestra, it might come as a surprise to learn that he also loved opera, and at first intended to make his career in this genre. But if this were true, why did he write so few operas, and why are those that he did write so rarely done these days? The search for an answer to these important questions leads us into an exploration of the general nature of Berlioz's relationship to the genre of opera as he knew it in early nineteenth-century France, and to a quick overview of his extant operas, which include *Benvenuto Cellini* (a heroic-comic opera written in 1838 and based on the autobiography of the famous Italian Renaissance goldsmith and sculptor by the same name), *Les Troyens* (a large grand opera, written twenty years later in 1858, and based on parts of Virgil's *Aeneid*), and *Béatrice et Bénédict* (a comic opera written toward the end of his life, in 1862, and based on Shakespeare's *Much Ado About Nothing*).

The first of these operas was unique, breaking the mold of standard genres popular in Paris at the time. *Benvenuto Cellini* straddled the fence between serious and comic opera (much like Beethoven's *Fidelio*), creating a genre that left audiences confused about what the composer intended to create. It was an inauspicious beginning to his operatic career, and the debacle surrounding the production of that work froze Berlioz's budding reputation before it could come into full bloom. Twenty years passed before he could work up the courage to try his hand at another opera, this time the five-act *Les Troyens*, cast in the mold of Meyerbeer. But here, too, Berlioz surprised audiences by basing his opera on a subject drawn from ancient history and mythology, the kind of subject that had not been popular in French theaters since the days of Gluck nearly a century earlier. In alienating (or at least dumbfounding) his audience this way, Berlioz assured himself another defeat in the very genre about which he cared so deeply. He had, over the years, cemented a reputation for himself as an iconoclast, a composer of difficult music, who could not be trusted to write in the prevailing popular styles of the day, and on whom no opera company could risk taking a chance with a commission. In short, Berlioz's insistence on writing his own kind of opera sealed his fate with this genre, and resulted in the paucity of works we have today.

In this regard, nothing better illustrates the uniqueness of Berlioz's musical-dramatic mind than his *La damnation de Faust*, a work which is not really an opera at all, but which the New York Metropolitan Opera chose to produce in its 2008–09 season as if it were. As conceived by the composer, *Faust* was something like a concert opera (Berlioz actually called the work a "dramatic legend"), intended for performance without costumes, scenery, or stage action. The closest Berlioz himself ever came to entertaining the possibility of a staged production of his Faust drama was a conversation he had in 1848 with the manager of one of London's theaters about the possibility of revising the work, with Eugène Scribe's help, into an opera. But these discussions never materialized into real work on an opera, and no solution to the many staging difficulties in the "dramatic legend" ever materialized.

The story of Faust was well known throughout Western Europe for centuries, both in oral and written forms. Most of the earliest printed versions, such as Christopher Marlowe's *Dr. Faustus* of 1604, are simple Christian allegories concerning the battle between the forces of heaven and hell. It was not until the nineteenth century that Goethe was able to take the bare outline of the legend and flesh it out into a fully developed drama in which the theme is not so much the battle between good and evil, but rather the dichotomy between human aspiration and achievement. In this regard, Goethe's drama is a quintessential product of the romantic era, an era that saw the development of the individual hero out of the collective common man of the eighteenth century. In Goethe's hands, Faust became this new nineteenth-century hero: a man whose reach exceeds his grasp, whose aspirations outstrip his accomplishments, and whose eternal striving for knowledge and fulfillment proves ultimately unattainable. Goethe depicts Faust as a doctor, scientist, and philosopher, who has reached the end of his life and finds himself still frustrated by his inability to discover the answer to the most elusive of all questions: the meaning of life. In a fit of frustration with the godly life he has lived up to that point, Faust calls on the devil (Mephistopheles), offering him a challenge: "If ever you lure me with your lying flatteries . . . if you bamboozle me with pleasure, then let this be my final day . . . If ever I should tell the moment: oh stay! You are so beautiful! Then you may cast me into chains, then I shall smile upon perdition!" (ll. 1699–1702) In essence, Goethe's Faust is a man who will not be tempted by trivial pleasures; rather, only by the experience of a moment of true beauty, in which he desires time to stand still forever. With this tall order, Faust allows Mephisto to show him his tricks in a dramatic confrontation of conflicting wills and purposes that Goethe plays out over two separate volumes: part 1, finished in 1808, and part 2, in 1832.

Romantic composers found Goethe's depiction of Faust as an eternal striver especially appealing because they were themselves strivers, reaching for new levels of communication through music, hoping in some instances to use their art to create a new kind of personal expression and even to improve society. It was this empathy on the part of romantic composers with the metaphysics of *Faust* that spawned the large number of musical settings of Goethe's drama in the nineteenth century. Adaptations appeared in the form of operas, ballets, piano works, and symphonies. In the world of opera alone, Faust works by Ludwig Spohr, Arrigo Boito, Ferruccio Busoni, and of course Charles Gounod have graced the stage. But for the most part, these adaptations all flattened out and simplified the metaphysical complexities of Goethe's portrayal of Faust, making him into a Don Giovanni–like rake whose main goal in life was simply to enjoy himself. Thus Gretchen, who in Goethe's drama is a means to an end (i.e., the discovery of the meaning of life), becomes in most of the operatic adaptations an end in herself (the fulfillment of corporal lust).

But the truth of the matter is that such oversimplification is almost a necessity in opera, because music is not an art that deals well with metaphysical intellectualization. Music better portrays simple emotions such as love, hate, or jealousy that arise out of the dramatic interaction of characters. Questions about the meaning of life and the eternal striving after philosophical ideals are not subjects that usually make for good arias and rousing ensemble numbers. So most of the operatic Fausts become hedonists whose main goal in life seems to stem from the fairly shallow desire to experience wine, women, and song after years of ascetic scholarship and philosophizing. Berlioz, of course, was not writing an opera, but rather what he called a "dramatic legend," so perhaps there is reason to hope that his Faust might be different from the rest.

Berlioz devoured Goethe's *Faust* in a French translation published in 1827, when he was a student at the Paris Conservatoire. Like other young romantic composers, he was struck by the noble ideals of the hero and his uncompromising passion to understand the world and his place in it.

Berlioz's interest in this work first took shape in a plan to set to music what he referred to as the "poems" in *Faust* (the lyrical moments in the text). He thus produced in 1828 a work titled *Huit scènes de Faust*, a collection of eight different moments in the drama where an individual (or a group) sings a song. These moments include the choral Easter hymn near the beginning, Brander's song of the rat, Gretchen's ballad of the king of Thulé, as well as her famous spinning song. The *Huit scènes* were, to be sure, not an opera, and Berlioz never intended to tell a story with what were no more than a handful of song texts from the play set to music. In addition to this vocal work, other Faust music was brewing in Berlioz's head in these student years. He tried (unsuccessfully) to secure a commission to write a Faust ballet for the Paris Opéra, and he talked about the possibility of writing a programmatic symphony on the subject of Faust. Neither work came to fruition, however.

After completing the collection of songs and choruses that make up the *Huit scènes*, Berlioz seemed to have satisfied his interest in Faust. But then, seventeen years later, he returned to the subject. In 1845 he asked the librettist Almire Gandonnière to draft a text for what was to be a rather unusual, quasi-operatic version of the story that could incorporate the original eight "songs" of 1828. But Gandonnière finished only parts of four scenes in this libretto, forcing Berlioz to take over the task of completing the rest of the text on his own. Up to this point in his life, Berlioz's most successful dramatic music had not been his operas (of which he had completed only one by 1840), but rather his symphonies: the *Fantastique*, *Harold en Italie*, and especially *Roméo et Juliette*. The latter work blended vocal solos, choruses, recitative, and purely instrumental music into one large-scale work for which Berlioz coined the generic descriptor "dramatic symphony." All three of these symphonies contain not just programmatic, but also narrative implications, suggesting that Berlioz seemed most comfortable with music in which he could tell a story by mixing vocal and instrumental sections as the needs of the drama required. His *Faust* is, in many ways, a prime example of this blending of symphonic and operatic elements, which so uniquely defines Berlioz's compositional technique as a music dramatist.

Before getting to the music itself, it may be instructive to speculate about why a composer like Berlioz would revisit the Faust subject in 1845, so many years after his initial infatuation with the drama and the completion of a musical setting of some of its texts. In this regard, the most intriguing possibility is that Berlioz's renewed interest in this subject grew out of the fact that so much of his music is autobiographical. That is to say, the characters in his musical dramas are projections of Berlioz himself. This, of course, is most true of the *Symphonie fantastique*, which relates the story of the composer's obsessive unrequited love for the English actress Harriet Smithson. In this same manner, Berlioz may have used Faust as a projection of his own persona in his concert opera. While he probably identified with Faust on many levels—the genius whose reach exceeded his grasp, the visionary idealist alone in the world—the most important connection between the fictional Faust and Berlioz was that both were great men who abandoned innocent women. If this parallel were one that Berlioz himself recognized (something, of course, that no one can know) then his return to this subject at exactly the time when his marriage to Harriet Smithson was breaking up (1844) would be no accident. The extreme heartbreak and suffering Berlioz experienced over leaving his wife is evident in letters written at this time, in which he says she was not to blame for the breakup, and he is saddened by the "despondence" his "abandoning her" has caused. For Berlioz, the oppressive guilt resulting from this abandonment could only be assuaged through his music, where he and Faust became metaphorically one and the same man, and a cathartic resolution for one (Berlioz) could only be achieved through the punishment of the other (Faust). Thus Faust (the fictional character) had to suffer the just consequences of his action—some kind of calamitous punishment, which in this case takes the form of eternal damnation—so that the Faustian alter-ego (i.e., Berlioz) could move on with his life. Unfortunately, Berlioz did not find in Goethe's drama the specific ending to this story that he needed. Goethe actually left the conclusion of part 1 fairly ambiguous in order to be able to continue the story into part 2, where ultimately Faust's soul is rescued from the devil by the intervention of heaven's angels. So to end his opera, and to punish Faust in the process, Berlioz decided to have his protagonist dragged off to hell. The fact that this solution to terminating the drama represents an outrageous and willful departure from the literary model, which Berlioz otherwise followed quite faithfully, is a clear indication of the significance encoded in this change to Goethe's original text. Had Berlioz not found himself in the particular circumstances of a failed marriage in the mid-1840s, had he not felt guilty about his actions, and had the protagonist of his concert opera not shared that same guilt, one suspects he would have faithfully copied Goethe right to the end of the drama, rather than altering the end of the Faust story to suit his own autobiographical and psychological purposes.

Berlioz allowed himself several other moments of free adaptation in this music drama, most notably at the opening. Scene 1 is set on a plain in

Hungary, a location that Goethe never mentions in his play, and one that would seem to have nothing to do with the Faust story. The first musical number in this scene is a solo for Faust, who is communing with Nature in the typical fashion of a romantic artist who takes sustenance from solitude and separation from the struggles of society. This connection with such an important aspect of the romantic aesthetic was, in and of itself, sufficient motivation for Berlioz to begin his "opera" with a deviation from his source. But this solo is not a standard operatic aria, at least not for voice. As Ex. 9-1 demonstrates, Berlioz created an interesting melody for the orchestra, which he allows Faust to double in selected places. The total effect is one of a voice fading into and out of a continuous orchestral melody.

Example 9-1. Faust's opening solo.

Example 9-1 *(continued)*

More important, in terms of why this solo fails to produce the usual effect of an aria, is the fact that of the more than six minutes the piece occupies, less than three involve the voice. The rest of the music is purely instrumental, like a miniature tone poem. This is one of the principal reasons why Berlioz's *Faust* is not an opera. In the mind of the listener (what might be called the theater of the imagination) Faust can be pictured alone on the Hungarian plain and can then be erased from memory during the long instrumental section that follows the completion of his music. But on an opera stage, Faust is left sitting silent while the orchestra plays on after him. What kind of stage direction is required here? Should Faust be silently musing during the orchestral portion of this scene? Or should he be pacing about the stage? In the original concert version of the work, such questions are immaterial, but onstage where it is especially difficult for a solo character to stand around doing nothing, this is a critical issue.

After a chorus of peasants interrupts Faust's musings, the scene suddenly changes to another part of the plain, where the good doctor encounters an army in full battle dress. This army is accompanied by a popular piece known as the Hungarian March (*Rákóczy March*), which Berlioz was writing at exactly the same time as his work on *Faust*, and then decided to include in his "dramatic legend." The predetermined inclusion of this piece, of course, would seem to explain the necessity for the Hungarian setting of the first scene; but this departure from Goethe's original text may not be as opportunistic as first appears. The inclusion of this scene is more than just a convenient excuse to incorporate a popular march in a new dramatic work; it is, additionally, a way to make a point about an aspect of Faust's personality by showing his extreme indifference to even the most glorious, patriotic inspirations, such as an army marching off to war. Despite the fact that this scene has nothing to do with Goethe, it does have something to do with Berlioz's conception of the heart and soul of Faust.

Example 9-2. Hungarian March.

Act 2 (or part 2, as Berlioz calls it) opens with a scene drawn from Goethe's play: Faust alone in his study, lamenting his boredom and frustration with life in a long solo section. Like Faust's solo at the opening of part 1, this, too, is not an aria, because the essential musical material again lies in the orchestra, while the voice fades in and out of the texture. Its overall effect is that of an orchestra number with a vocal obbligato, an effect that contradicts and detracts from the generally operatic quality of the work.

The next important musical number is the Easter Hymn (one of the original *Huit scènes* of 1828). This is a beautiful piece of music, but it, too, is decidedly unoperatic in its seven minutes and forty seconds of slow choral singing, which in a staged version must be sung from offstage, as Faust must seem to hear this music in the distance. Lovely as it is, this offstage chorus makes for an awkward dramatic moment, because the only character on stage is again doing nothing. Like Faust's two solo ariosos that open each of the first two parts of this "opera," and feature the orchestra so prominently, this is more of a concert piece, clearly not designed with the exigencies of a staged production in mind. It quickly becomes apparent in studying *La damnation de Faust* that generic contradictions such as these determine the fundamental nature of the whole work and suggest that Berlioz's understanding of "music drama" was far from what traditional opera audiences expected to see in the theater.

Once Faust asks the devil to show him his tricks, the real action commences, and the two companions are off on the various adventures that make up the rest of the story. Some of these, such as the scene in Auerbach's tavern, where Mephistopheles first takes Faust to show him a good time, lend themselves to more or less standard operatic treatment. The same is true of Faust's aria at the beginning of part 3, where he finds himself alone in Marguerite's bedroom, overcome by the purity and sanctity of the place. Another scene that demonstrates this traditional operatic configuration is the opening of part 2, scene 2, where Mephistopheles sings a lovely, if also fairly standard, operatic aria, "Voici des roses," most notable for its unusual and colorful orchestral accompaniment of a choir of trombones and a solo trumpet playing in its lowest register.

Mephistopheles's aria is followed immediately by another move into the unoperatic world of the listener's imagination, in which Berlioz's dramatic instincts take form in scenarios more easily realized in the mind's eye than onstage. Here a chorus of gnomes and sylphs is ordered by Mephistopheles to put Faust into a deep sleep in which he will experience a dream vision of Marguerite. Berlioz never expected that this chorus of mythic characters might have to make an onstage appearance in an operatic production. For that reason, he also asked that we imagine them dancing immediately after they finish singing. In a staged production of the work, this "ballet of the sylphs" would have to be danced by a different group of sylphs than the ones who just sang the chorus, because singers and dancers are rarely one and the same people in an opera company. In itself, this presents no great problem for a staged production; but the very fact that Berlioz even imagined such a combination of singing and dancing from one group of characters is a clear indication of how unidiomatic this "opera" can be.

In cataloguing the various elements of this work that remove it from the world of real opera, we must not overlook Berlioz's penchant for the use of the *fantastique* (supernatural). Some fifteen years earlier he had first employed the term in the writing of his first symphony, which was titled *Épisode de la vie d'un artiste: Symphonie fantastique* (1830). In that work, the final movement takes place in hell, where the "artist" of the story (Berlioz) dreams that he has been condemned to eternal damnation for the murder of his beloved. The program for this movement describes ghosts, ghouls, goblins, and monsters of the underworld, all assembled for a Black Mass to celebrate the artist's death. Along similar lines, Berlioz's musical adaptation of Goethe's *Faust* contains numerous scenes of the *fantastique*, and these scenes are what separate this concert opera from all the other real operas on this subject. Of course, any story about devils and conjuration is ripe for such supernatural scenes, and Goethe himself supplied plenty of them in his play. But Berlioz tended to add additional supernatural scenes to Goethe's play wherever he felt they might augment the implicit mood of the drama. We already encountered one such scene in the chorus of singing, dancing gnomes and sylphs in part 2. In part 3 Berlioz added a similar, and far more problematic, scene for the Will of the Wisps that one could say might have been suggested by their incidental inclusion in Goethe's "Walpurgis Nacht" scene near the end of his drama. In Berlioz's adoption of these spirits, he has Mephistopheles call on them to use their singing and dancing to seduce Marguerite into accepting Faust when he finally arrives at her doorstep. Berlioz wrote a charming little minuet for these spirits to dance; but here again a staged version of this work deprives an audience of the use of their inventive imaginations by forcing the Will of the Wisps to take human form. In legend, the Will of the Wisps were thought to be the malevolent flaming spirits of the dead whose goal was to lead unsuspecting travelers into dangerous marshlands. In reality, these flames were probably instances of self-igniting methane gas trapped in marshlike bogs. But in the absence of a coherent scientific explanation for these flames that rose out of the ground, people centuries ago invented the story that they were evil spirits. With this in mind, it might be hard to tolerate any kind of traditional operatic staging that used humans to represent these spirits. Berlioz would not likely have ever written such a scene if he had known that these fiery spirits would have to be embodied in the form of singing/dancing choristers, something that almost guarantees that the magic of the scene will evaporate as quickly as the Will of the Wisps themselves. Here we can see that Berlioz's "theater of the imagination" was in many regards an effective dramatic technique exactly because it didn't have to deal with the limitations inherent in making the *fantastique* real.

Toward the middle of Goethe's play is a scene that has been become famous through the song setting made by Schubert under the title "Gretchen am Spinnrade." What Goethe wrote for this scene in his play is a spinning song in which Gretchen sits alone at her spinning wheel and sings about her abandonment and her anxious hope that her lover will return: "Meine Ruh ist hin, mein Herz ist schwer" (My peace is gone, my heart is heavy). The Gretchen that Schubert depicted in his lied setting of this text is a woman riddled with nervous anxiety. His relentless piano accompaniment (Ex. 9-3) depicts the continual turning of the spinning wheel, while short breathless phrases in the vocal part set the mood of nervous energy that pervades this portrayal of the abandoned heroine.

Example 9-3. "Gretchen am Spinnrade."

Example 9-3 *(continued)*

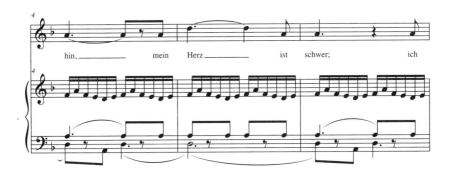

In the two most famous operatic versions of this story, those by Gounod and Berlioz, each composer takes a different approach to this scene. In the first place, neither of them uses Goethe's text exactly as it appears in the play, as did Schubert. Both composers use freely adapted texts that give the same dramatic impression. Like Schubert, Gounod tries to capture the sense of the spinning wheel in his orchestral accompaniment. But the slower tempo along with the smooth lyrical melodic phrases give the whole aria a more relaxed and contemplative quality than what one hears in the Schubert song. Gounod's heroine clearly sounds less panicked about her situation than does Schubert's.

Example 9-4. Marguerite's spinning song from Gounod's *Faust*.

Example 9-4 *(continued)*

Berlioz goes one step further in this regard. He makes no attempt to turn this aria into a spinning song. Instead, a plaintive English horn solo introduces the aria. Both it and the ensuing vocal line, accompanied by pizzicato double basses sounding like a slow pulsing heartbeat, bring to this music an overwhelming sense of sadness. The reason Berlioz's setting of this text is so different from either of the other two, is because he had a powerful personal empathy with the theme of abandonment, which caused him to write an aria more full of grief and sympathy for Marguerite than we find from either Gounod or Schubert. I would further suggest that this is yet again a matter of an autobiographical association at work in Berlioz's music. If Berlioz indeed returned to the Faust subject in the 1840s because it allowed him to live out in a fantasy world the guilt he felt about leaving his wife, then this particular aria would indicate that he had a deep sense of empathy with the sadness that such a personal abandonment produces. He experienced such abandonment both as a child (when his mother disowned him for insisting on taking up a career in music) and in his relationship with Harriet Smithson. These abandonments were hurtful for all parties concerned, and Berlioz's music for this aria is ample demonstration of how a composer can channel his real-life experiences into his music to achieve a cathartic release from personal tragedy.

Example 9-5a. Marguerite's aria, orchestral introduction.

Example 9-5b. Marguerite's aria.

Following this heart-wrenching aria, Berlioz latches onto a scene in Goethe's play that none of the other composers who dealt with this subject bothered to set to music. Goethe labels this section "Forest and Cavern." In the play, this scene actually precedes the spinning song, but Berlioz reversed their order to show Faust's recourse to Nature as a balm for the guilt he seems to suffer over the abandonment of Marguerite. The power of Nature as a life-giving and rejuvenating force was important to romantic artists. However, Goethe's Faust was not a romantic artist; he was a medieval doctor/philosopher. Therefore, the use of this romantic theme of rejuvenation in Nature substantiates the connection that both Goethe and Berlioz felt between certain aspects of Faust's character and qualities of the romantic spirit in general.

Faust's Invocation to Nature.

Croulez, rochers! Torrents précipitez vos ondes!	Crash down rocks! Torrents, hurl your water!
À vos bruits souverains ma voix aime à s'unir.	With your majestic sounds my voice loves to be united.
Forêts, rochers, torrents, je vous adore!	Forests, rocks, torrents, I adore you!
Mondes qui scintillez, vers vous s'élance le désir	Glittering worlds, toward you rushes the desire
D'un coeur trop vaste et d'une âme altérée	Of a heart too vast and a soul thirsty
D'un bonheur qui la fuit.	For a happiness that is fleeting.

This solo number, like so many of Faust's earlier solos, is yet again not an aria. In the usual Berlioz fashion the piece is more of an orchestral tone poem with a semimelodic vocal obbligato. The phrases are irregular in length, and seem to have no particular melodic contour (at least not one that has the memorability of a good tune). The "Invocation to Nature" bears some connection with the new German school of symphonic opera, which had its roots in works such as Carl Maria von Weber's *Der Freischütz* (1821) and was fully to evolve in the music dramas of Wagner. But, as Berlioz's "invocation" demonstrates, the Germans were not the only composers of opera to resort to a symphonic style.

Between the "Invocation to Nature" and the end of Faust's story lies a considerable amount of plot detail in Goethe's play, nearly all of which Berlioz skipped over, probably because he found in it nothing inherently musical. Here is a further demonstration of the difference between Berlioz's "dramatic legend" and a true opera: the latter usually unfolds as a coherent narrative that connects one event to the next, whereas the former stitches together often unconnected dramatic moments while omitting most of the connective narrative. As a musical dramatist, Berlioz was never concerned with plot per se. His was a technique of locating those moments in a drama that were intrinsically musical and then pasting them together in a string of pictures (the French call them *tableaux*), the entirety of which gave an impression of the drama as a whole. In the case of *Faust*, the musical adaptation of some of those moments worked best as traditional vocal numbers, whereas others must have seemed better suited to a treatment in which instruments predominate. For this reason *La damnation de Faust* is like a genetic (or maybe "generic") mutation in the world of traditional opera, one that looks familiar on a superficial level, but which actually consists of numerous alterations of important structural elements or basic building blocks that make up the very substance of the work.

As Berlioz approached the end of his version of the Faust story, he latched onto the dramatic potential of two lines of stage directions in Goethe's play that set the scene: "Faust and Mephistopheles mounted upon black horses in a furious gallop." At this point, Faust has been told that Marguerite is now in prison (for the accidental murder of her mother), and he forces the devil to ride with him to rescue her. This extremely exciting section of music again depends for its effect more on the orchestra than on the voice. Needless to say, Gounod's treatment of this particular scene does not begin to approach the symphonic expansiveness of Berlioz's setting, which he called the "Ride to the Abyss." Berlioz includes some imaginative stage directions here, calling first for a group of women and children to be seen praying at a wayside cross and to be nearly run over by the galloping horses. Then hideous monsters pursue Faust and Mephistopheles. Skeletons appear and dance around them, and finally it begins to rain blood. This is all prime material of the *fantastique*, on which Berlioz depended so much in dramatizing this Faust story, and which is so difficult to bring to a staged version of the work. Little does Faust know, of course, that he is not riding to the prison to save Marguerite but instead to his own damnation.

The "Ride to the Abyss" leads without pause into the finale in hell, where Faust's damnation is assured. For the demons of the underworld, Berlioz invented a nonsense language that augments the sense of the *fantastique* in this scene.

Final scene, language of the damned.

DEMONS AND THE DAMNED:
Ha! Irimiru Karabrao!
Has! Has! Has!
Tradioun marexil fir tru dinxe burnudixe.
Fory my dinkorlitz.

This outcome, of course, directly contradicts Goethe (for reasons already discussed), but the fate of Marguerite, whose soul rises to heaven in a final apotheosis, does not.

The fact that the Metropolitan Opera was able to make a fully staged production of this concert opera in 2008 was mostly the result of the application of advanced computer technology and visual effects of the kind rarely seen on an opera stage. Here for the first time, computers were programmed to work interactively with the singers and to generate much of the scenic background that gave the supernatural effects a believability no normal staging could ever have. Despite the technological wizardry that made the Met production so successful, it is important to remember that *La damnation de Faust* is still not an opera in the usual sense of that word, for all of the following reasons:

1. To a large degree the work is episodic rather than narrative; that is, it presents a collection of isolated dramatic moments without filling in the dialogue and narrative that connects these moments.
2. The work is laced with long stretches of purely instrumental music suggestive of a hybrid genre, part symphonic tone poem and part opera.
3. The element of the *fantastique* found throughout the work makes *Faust* very much a piece that works better in one's imagination than on stage. Any staging, even at the Metropolitan Opera, will surely require some major compromises to be made with Berlioz's original dramatic intentions.
4. Some of the musical numbers in the piece have the slow pacing and extended scope of concert music. Berlioz clearly had little concern with the needs of a stage drama to be continuously moving forward.
5. Nearly all of the minor characters in Goethe's drama are eliminated, leaving only the three major figures of Faust, Marguerite (Gretchen), and Mephistopheles. Not many real operas have so few characters.

Despite all these departures from regular operatic form, *La damnation de Faust* is an effective piece of music drama. One might even venture the theory that it is because of its departures from normal operatic form that this work is so successful. Berlioz's version of the Faust legend embraces so much of the magic and atmosphere found in the original play that it comes closer perhaps to what Goethe intended than does any real opera. Over the years it has been staged many times with varying degrees of success. But only recently has the kind of visual computer technology that one regularly finds in motion pictures been applied to the production of an opera, resulting in a rendition of Berlioz's unique music drama that is at last as satisfying (perhaps even more satisfying) onstage as it is on recordings.

PART V

SHAKESPEAREAN OPERA

CHAPTER 10

The nineteenth century was the era of musical romanticism; and what more romantic tale could there be for music to tell that that of Romeo and Juliet? Above all, this is a story that celebrates the power of raw emotion and physicality over rational thought and action. If the romantic age was a time in which emotion triumphed over intellect, then the story of these two star-crossed lovers was the perfect vehicle for nineteenth-century composers. It touches the part of each of us that wants to believe in love at first sight—the part of us that understands what Shakespeare meant when he penned Romeo's response to the first glimpse of Juliet: "O, she doth teach the torches to burn bright. . . . I ne'er saw true beauty till this night." (1.5.43, 52) For teenagers like Romeo and Juliet, Shakespeare seems to suggest that nothing more is required to assure everlasting happiness—a truly romantic notion if there ever was one. Shakespeare comes under consideration here, of course, because his version of this story was the one most often used by romantic composers as a source for adaptation.[1] It is not by accident that the English bard might be said to have been the perfect poet for the romantic age, because not until the nineteenth century did composers begin setting his works to music on a regular basis. This renewed interest in his works as the source of musical inspiration clearly suggests that Shakespeare's writing struck a sympathetic chord with romantic composers. One very practical reason this renaissance of interest in Shakespeare had to await the dawn of the nineteenth century was that there were few translations of his works into French, German, or Italian before the 1820s, thus limiting his exposure abroad. But this in itself is only symptomatic of a larger problem with the appreciation of Shakespeare. Between the time that he wrote most of his plays (around the year 1600) and the flowering of interest in his works over two hundred years later, there falls the great era of classic drama, spearheaded by French writers such as Corneille and Racine. Their

---

1. Many other versions of the Romeo and Juliet legend preceded Shakespeare's, including some important Italian novellas that date from the late fifteenth century. Although these earlier versions of the story differ in detail, there are certain elements that remain common among all of them: the two warring families, the faked death of Juliet, and the double suicide at the end.

ideas regarding the principles of good drama were based upon the ancient Greek concept of the "unities of time, place, and action." These dramatic precepts proclaimed that a good drama was one that represented an action that unfolded within a single twenty-four-hour period, one that took place in only one location, and one that involved only a single line of dramatic action. Clearly, this is not how Shakespeare's plays work. Most of them take place over many months or even years, involve several changes of location, and often involve multiple intersecting lines of dramatic action. For these reasons Shakespeare was judged by eighteenth-century French writers to be a dramatic barbarian, untutored in the rules of good play writing. But then the eighteenth century gave way to the nineteenth, and the age of reason and intellect was washed away by a new spirit in which rule breaking and the assertion of individuality were valued over all else. Suddenly Shakespeare's works underwent a rediscovery, and Shakespeare, the dramatic barbarian, became Shakespeare the heroic individual, the romantic rule breaker. With the new reverence for his genius came a new awareness of the value of his plays as sources for musical adaptation. Composers as diverse as Verdi, Berlioz, Mendelssohn, Gounod, and Tchaikovsky all used Shakespeare as the source for musical adaptations of different kinds.

Like other dramatic or literary sources treated to operatic adaptation, Shakespeare's plays presented composers with numerous problems in making the move from spoken to sung words. The most obvious of these is that if the large number of words in a spoken play were set to music, the resulting opera would be unendurably long, simply because sung text takes so much longer to deliver than spoken text. So as a rule, large cuts must be made in the text of any play bound for the operatic stage. But in the case of Shakespeare, it is precisely this text—the language in and of itself—that lends such depth to his characters and interest to the drama. In addition, the sheer number of characters and the complexity of their relationships in a Shakespearean play require drastic simplification in order to make the drama manageable on the operatic stage. Lastly, the mixture of comic and serious episodes in nearly all of Shakespeare's works was something that serious opera of the nineteenth century would not tolerate. Therefore, nearly all of the comic buffoonery that defines Elizabethan drama is also cut in operatic adaptations.

When Charles Gounod came to the writing of *Roméo et Juliette* in 1867, he was already an experienced, if not always successful, veteran of Parisian operatic stages. Although he had begun his career as a church organist and a composer of sacred music, a singer friend, Pauline Viardot, convinced him to turn his compositional energies to the theater, where large sums of money and popular reputations were more easily made. His first attempts at this new genre took the form of grand opera in the style of Meyerbeer, the reigning king of serious French opera in the middle of the nineteenth century. But Gounod soon found he had little predilection for this style of opera, so he quickly switched tracks and invented a new kind of opera that relied less on scenic spectacle and massed choral effects, concentrating instead on the musical exploration of individual characters. This new, more personal kind of opera was called opéra lyrique, and its first manifestation was *Faust* in 1859. (See chapter 12.) There followed in this same style *Mireille* (1864) and *Roméo et Juliette* (1867), all three immensely successful during Gounod's lifetime, and extremely popular for years thereafter. These operas were first staged at a new theater in Paris, the Théâtre-Lyrique, designed as a venue that would offer an alternative to both the large-scale serious works at the Paris Opéra and to the lightweight comedies produced at the Opéra-Comique.

As Gounod approached the writing of *Roméo et Juliette* with his librettists Jules Barbier and Michel Carré, he was aware that there were two musical versions of this story that had already appeared within the last thirty years: Bellini's opera *I Capuleti e i Montecchi* (1830) and Berlioz's *Roméo et Juliette* symphony with vocal solos and chorus (1839). In fact these two earlier settings of the Romeo and Juliet story were themselves related; it was Berlioz's dissatisfaction with Bellini's treatment of the subject that led to the creation of his unusual symphonic version. While studying in Italy as the winner of the 1830 Prix de Rome competition, Berlioz encountered Bellini's opera and was outraged by how little it had to do with Shakespeare, an author he revered. In Bellini's defense, however, his opera was not, and did not pretend to be, based on Shakespeare, but rather on the various earlier Italian sources of the story, a fact of which Berlioz was conveniently unaware. Bellini's telling of the Romeo and Juliet tale differs most from Shakespeare in the following ways:

1. Romeo and Juliet have been secret lovers for some time before the story begins.
2. They are never secretly married.
3. When hostilities between their two families come to a boiling point, Romeo tries to convince Juliet to run away with him, but she refuses out of her sense of duty to her family.

We find in Bellini's opera, therefore, much less of the romantic dueting that one might expect from two youngsters just falling in love. Instead we get duets in which the lovers argue about a course of action that will solve their problems. Bellini's opera is also unusual in that the character of Romeo is cast as a mezzo-soprano, thus making it one of the last serious Italian operas to hold on to the by then old-fashioned tradition of the female-voiced hero, i.e., the castrato or female mezzo-soprano. For that reason the opera is also one of the last great bel canto works of the nineteenth century, with numerous rapid scale passages, arpeggios, trills, and mordents highlighting the vocal parts. In this regard, Bellini's opera occupies a far different operatic world from that which Gounod entered over thirty years later.

More relevant to Gounod was the symphony that Berlioz wrote on the same subject in 1839. Although specifically a concert work, this symphony is decidedly dramatic and includes, along with purely instrumental movements, several solo vocal numbers (arias if you will) and extensive choral music. Berlioz called this unusual piece a "dramatic symphony," and explained in the preface to the work that he chose not to write an opera because he felt that certain episodes in the story lent themselves to more faithful musical representation as purely instrumental pieces, whereas others demanded a text to make clear the emotional and dramatic significance of the scenes. In addition, an opera suggests that the composer intends to tell a coherent story, which Berlioz had no mind to do. He preferred instead to extract only those dramatic moments from the play that he felt lent themselves to musical representation; that is, the emotional high points of the drama minus the less interesting dialogue that links them.

Gounod was exactly fifteen years younger than Berlioz. Both had studied with the same teachers at the Paris Conservatoire, both had won the Prix de Rome, and both lived and worked in Paris. Gounod admired the music of his older compatriot, and Berlioz, in turn, supported Gounod with kind words and favorable reviews in the daily papers for which he regularly wrote, even when he privately felt Gounod's music was not especially distinguished or unique. The first evidence we have of Gounod's appreciation of Berlioz and of his homage to the symphonic *Roméo et Juliette* occurs at the very beginning of his opera. It begins, like Berlioz's symphony, with what might be described as a programmatic overture—an overture that musically depicts, through instruments alone, an important dramatic element in the story: the opening street battle in act 1 of Shakespeare's play. In fact, some productions of Gounod's opera actually stage this overture as a pantomimed battle between the Montagues and the Capulets. The Berlioz symphony opens with a depiction of this same scene, but then goes on to include the intervention of the Prince to put a temporary halt to the hostilities.

Beyond the similarity of the overtures lies another far more striking parallel between Gounod's opera and Berlioz's symphony: their inclusion of Shakespeare's Prologue, which includes those famous lines at the very opening of the play:

> Two households both alike in dignity
> (In fair Verona, where we lay our scene)
> From ancient grudge break to new mutiny
> Where civil blood makes civil hands unclean. (prologue.1–4)

With this prologue, Shakespeare wanted to simply tell his audience what the play was going to be about. In 1839 Berlioz vastly expanded the idea and function of this prologue. Rather than just giving his audience a general idea of what the symphony would deal with, he used his prologue to actually narrate a large portion of the story. His opening is a free paraphrase, in French of course, of Shakespeare's prologue. What is unique about this prologue is that Berlioz set it as a choral recitative (i.e., an adaptation of the usual speechlike solo recitative of opera to multiple choral voices), something one never hears in opera, cantata, oratorio, or any other kind of dramatic vocal music.

Example 10-1a. Choral recitative from prologue to Berlioz's *Roméo et Juliette*.

The only other piece of dramatic music (to my knowledge) that also uses this unusual vocal technique is Gounod's *Roméo et Juliette*. The fact that both Berlioz's symphony and Gounod's opera share this unusual vocal technique, and that in both works this device is applied to exactly the same lines from the prologue of Shakespeare's play is a sure sign that Gounod was modeling his opera after techniques he found in the work of his predecessor.

Example 10-1b. Choral recitative from prologue to Gounod's *Roméo et Juliette*.

When faced with the problem of how to make Shakespeare's text into an opera libretto of manageable length, Barbier and Carré were handcuffed by several specific operatic traditions. One of the most common of these dictated that an opera should always begin with a chorus. Fortunately, Shakespeare's play does begin with a crowd scene that could have made a fine choral number: the street fight between the two families. But Gounod's librettists must have felt that there was little of essential dramatic value in this opening scene (or in those that immediately follow), and that to start there would have made necessary some harmful cuts in later scenes that were more important. So they decided to omit the opening scenes of the play and to begin the opera with the next choral opportunity, the Capulets' party. In so doing, however, they skipped over two dramatic moments from the beginning of the play that are actually essential to an understanding of the unfolding action: the important scene in which Lady Capulet talks to Juliet about the possibility of marrying Count Paris, and the wonderful Queen Mab speech that Mercutio makes on the street, as Romeo and his Montague friends make their way to the Capulet party.

In a stroke of adaptational brilliance, Barbier and Carré found a way to lift these important events out of the opening of the play and to reposition them within the party scene. Thus in the opera, the Montagues' arrival at the party causes Romeo to feel ill at ease and to explain that he had a foreboding dream about what might happen if they crash the party. This then leads easily to Mercutio's response, the Queen Mab speech. Gounod casts the role of Mercutio as a baritone, but one who must have a high, light voice capable of creating the necessary airiness associated with Shakespeare's fairy queen. This wonderful aria also recalls Berlioz and his symphony. In that work, the Queen Mab speech appears twice, first as a tenor aria with chorus, then later as a purely instrumental piece. The aria is again remarkably similar to that which Gounod wrote for his opera nearly thirty years later, as both rely less on attractive melody, and more on transparent textures, animated rhythms, and sparkling, high woodwind and string orchestrations.

The other important event that Gounod lost in the decision to start his opera with the Capulet party was the interchange between Juliet and her mother about Count Paris. This scene was cleverly reinstated in the party scene of the opera as a conversation between Juliet and her nurse, who asks what her young charge thinks of the possibility of marrying the count. Repositioning rather than cutting this scene gave Gounod the opportunity to expand musically upon the short conversation Shakespeare wrote for Lady Capulet and Juliet, which in the play takes the following form:

LADY CAPULET:
How stands your disposition to be married:

JULIET:
It is an honor that I dream not of. (1.3.65–66)

LADY CAPULET:
Speak briefly, can you like of Paris's love?

JULIET:
I'll look to like, if looking liking move. (1.3.96–97)

With these lines Shakespeare seems to suggest that Juliet hasn't really thought much about marriage, is neither in favor of nor opposed to the idea, but that she will give it careful consideration. Although there might seem to be little musical potential in this exchange between mother and daughter, Gounod's librettists found in this scene an opportunity to allow music to expand on the spoken text of the original. Here, in short, was an opportunity for a soprano aria—and hopefully a real show-stopper. But because it is so difficult to make an extended aria out of the words, "Okay, I'll think about it" (which is essentially what Juliet is saying to her mother), Barbier and Carré were forced to write a fairly extensive new text that owes little to Shakespeare but instead reminds us more of the character of Marguerite in Gounod's other famous opera, *Faust*. So our operatic Juliet says no to marriage because she wants to live the intoxicating dream of youth a little longer. For this new text, Gounod penned the famous aria "Je veux vivre," a brilliant waltz tune, and one of the most popular arias he ever wrote. And no one seems to care that it's not exactly in keeping with the character of Shakespeare's Juliet.

Example 2. Juliet's "Je veux vivre."

But almost immediately after this aria, Juliet meets Romeo in the middle of the party. Here the opera takes up the wonderful first conversation between the two youngsters, which, as Romeo takes Juliet's hand, is couched by Shakespeare in the cleverest religious imagery:

ROMEO:
If I profane with my unworthiest hand
This holy shrine, the gentle sin is this:
My lips, two blushing pilgrims, ready stand
To smooth that rough touch with a tender kiss.

JULIET:
Good pilgrim, you do wrong your hand too much
For saints have hands that pilgrims' hands do touch,
And palm to palm is holy palmers' kiss. (1.5.92–99)

This is one of the most magical moments in the play: that first awkward moment when a boy wants to introduce himself to a girl who has captured his attention, and wants to have something clever to say to her. Here Gounod's librettists paraphrased Shakespeare as faithfully as possible, and Gounod created the first of several duets between Romeo and Juliet that form the backbone of this opera. But Gounod didn't call this piece a duet; he titled it instead a "madrigal for two voices," implying that it is not a musical number like a true duet, in which two voices blend together, but is instead more like an aria (the word *madrigal* suggests a solo song) sung by two voices in alternation. This idea of a musical conversation rather than an ensemble is strikingly symbolic, in the sense that Romeo and Juliet have not yet gotten together, but are simply testing each other out, with every clever religious metaphor out of one of their mouths provoking an equally clever response that becomes a duel of wits. The music here demonstrates that Gounod's gift for music drama lay largely in his ability to create touchingly simple and innocent melodies.

Example 10-3. Act 1 "madrigal" duet.

After this attractive duet, act 1 closes with a large choral finale in which Tybalt (the most irascible of all Capulet's young men) discovers who the party-crashers are, Romeo discovers that Juliet is the daughter of his enemy, and Juliet discovers the same about Romeo.

Act 2 brings us to the famous balcony scene in Shakespeare's play. Romeo, lingering behind after the party breaks up, jumps the wall of a garden leading to Juliet's bedroom. Hiding in the bushes he sees her preparing to retire and then overhears her private testimony of love. For the famous Shakespearean lines, "But soft, what light through yonder window breaks? It is the east and Juliet is the sun!" (2.2.1–2) Gounod writes a cavatina[2] (little aria) for Romeo, the text of which is an almost exact translation into French of the lines he speaks in the play. "Arise fair sun and kill the envious moon/ Who is already sick and pale with grief/ That thou her maid [Juliet] art far more fair than she."

Example 10-4. Romeo's cavatina.

This then is followed by the actual balcony scene, in which Romeo reveals himself to Juliet, and the two exchange vows of love and fidelity. Here, as in Shakespeare, there are lots of words to get through, none of which Gounod's librettists were willing to cut. As a result most of the opening of this duet is written in a free arioso style (something like an ornate recitative) that allowed Gounod to accommodate the large amount of text he had to put to music. Composers of opera often find lengthy texts like this incompatible with truly lyrical melody. This is why a composer such as Verdi, for one, was constantly telling his librettists to write as few words as possible. And perhaps this is why Gounod didn't attempt a real love duet here until near the end of the scene. After all the dialoguing is finished, and the only thing left to say is "farewell," Gounod finally gives the audience what it surely must have hoped for in this balcony scene: some good romantic dueting.

---

2. The term in French opera has a significantly different meaning than its Italian equivalent.

The balcony scene love duet is one point where Gounod and his nineteenth-century predecessors parted ways. Bellini's Romeo and Juliet opera has no such scene because his libretto was not based on Shakespeare, to whom the balcony scene is unique. And Berlioz, who did follow Shakespeare and recognized the importance of this scene, took the radical approach of setting this love duet as a completely instrumental number in his symphony. His reasoning in defense of this unusual solution was, as he himself said, that he wanted to give his "fantasy a latitude that the exact meaning of sung words would not permit."[3] Whether we agree with Berlioz's thinking in this matter, there is no denying the beauty of his purely instrumental solution. Gounod's duet suffers under the restriction of an expansive conversational text; Berlioz's music cuts directly to the emotional meaning of the situation without becoming entangled in a web of Shakespearean words (poetic and elegant as they might be).

In writing act 3, Gounod's librettists were again forced to compress Shakespeare's more expansive text by moving directly to Friar Laurence's cell for the marriage of Romeo and Juliet. The close of this ceremony brings with it a lovely quartet that includes Friar Laurence, Romeo, Juliet, and her nurse. To the words, "God of goodness! God of mercy! Be Thou blessed by two happy hearts," Gounod created an ecstatic climax, with music that he planned to reuse at the end of the opera. Hereafter I will refer to this important melody as the "ecstasy" theme.

Example 10-5. Quartet "ecstasy" theme.

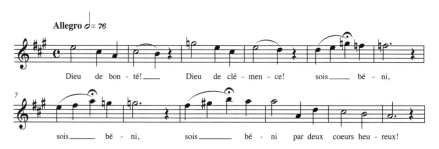

Act 3 then culminates in a large choral finale that includes the duel between Mercutio and Tybalt, followed by Romeo's killing of Tybalt, the intervention of the Prince, and the banishing of Romeo from Verona.

Act 4 brings us to Juliet's bedroom, where she has just spent the night with her new husband, having forgiven him for killing her cousin Tybalt.

---

3. Berlioz, 1839, preface.

This, too, is a love duet: the third in the opera thus far. It commences in 9/8 meter (the only piece in the opera in this meter) and has a gentle rocking quality about it. Both the text, "Night of marriage! Sweet night of love," and the musical style recall a similar duet in Berlioz's opera *Les Troyens*, which had its premiere at the Théâtre-Lyrique just a few years before the production of Gounod's *Roméo et Juliette*. Both duets occupy positions of central importance in their respective operas, both deal with nights of love between a man and a woman. (In Berlioz's *Les Troyens*, it is Dido and Aeneas who have fallen in love and are celebrating that love under the starry sky of a Mediterranean summer night.) And lastly, both duets feature the gentle rocking style of compound meter. Taken together, these parallels constitute evidence of a conscious technique of musical allusion on Gounod's part, acknowledging, as it were, his indebtedness to his older colleague.[4]

Eventually Romeo hears the lark singing and realizes that it is dawn, and that he must depart from the city. As in Shakespeare, Juliet refuses to believe that what he hears is a lark, insisting instead that it is a nightingale.

JULIETTE:
Roméo! Qu'as-tu donc?

ROMÉO:
Écoute, ô Juliette!
L'alouette déjà nous annonce le jour!

JULIETTE:
Non! Non, ce n'est pas le jour.
Ce n'est pas l'alouette
Dont le chant a frappé ton oreille inquiète,
C'est le doux rossignol,
    confident de l'amour!

JULIET:
Romeo! What is it?

ROMEO:
Listen, Juliet!
Already the lark announces daybreak!

JULIET:
No, it's not the day.
It's not the lark
Whose song strikes your anxious ear.
It is the sweet nightingale,
    confidant of love!

These lines of text are set to a vocal melody that returns in the tomb scene at the end of the opera, where Romeo sings Juliet's lines of denial in a final dramatic recall of their earlier love duet. In this way, Gounod created a powerful musical allusion that supports the dramatic flashback, and thereby lends to the opera a unifying device that draws together its various parts through immediately perceivable musical associations. For purposes of later analysis of the final tomb scene, I will refer to this melody as the "lark" theme.

---

4. This connection between Gounod and Berlioz is important, because too little is usually said about how Berlioz influenced French composers in the generation after him. Gounod's several allusions, both direct and more oblique, to his predecessor are ample evidence of a lineage of compositional style in France in the nineteenth century.

Example 10-6. "Lark" theme from the act 4 bedroom duet.

Finally Romeo gives in to Juliet's plea for him to stay a while longer. Here the duet leads to a short orchestral interlude that Gounod also elects to repeat in the tomb scene. This important melody can be labeled the "sacrifice" theme, because it underlies a moment in the drama when Romeo offers to sacrifice his life to stay with his new wife.

Example 10-7. Orchestral "sacrifice" theme.

At this point in the drama, Gounod's librettists began to depart somewhat from Shakespeare. After Romeo leaves, Juliet's father announces his plan for her wedding to Count Paris. In distress, Juliet immediately seeks help from Friar Laurence, who gives her the magical sleeping death potion with which she can escape the dreaded marriage. Although there is no wedding ceremony in Shakespeare, Gounod must have thought that a wedding march with assembled guests would make an appropriate end-of-act choral finale. Modifications such as this to a literary source are common in opera, where composers sometimes have to invent crowd scenes that are not in the original drama just so they can end an act with a traditional large choral finale. Thus, act 4 closes with Juliet collapsing during her wedding ceremony, apparently dead.

The fifth and final act takes place at Juliet's tomb, where Romeo will come to visit what he believes to be his deceased wife and to die at her side. Berlioz also chose this tomb scene for musical depiction in his symphony, and it appears in Bellini's opera as well, because it is common to all the earlier literary versions of the Romeo and Juliet story. Here again Berlioz decided to entrust this important dramatic moment to instrumental music.

He begins with an exciting section that represents Romeo's breathless arrival at the tomb and then proceeds to music that depicts Romeo's grief and his taking of the poison he has brought with him, and finally to his sudden joy as Juliet awakes from her sleep. But this sequence of events is not what Shakespeare wrote. In the play, Romeo arrives at the tomb and finds Juliet dead, takes his poison in despair and dies. Only after he is dead does she awake to find him, and then stabs herself to follow suit. In revising Shakespeare's ending as he did, Berlioz was following the version of the story as he encountered it in both Bellini's *I Capuleti e i Montecchi* and in a popular revision of Shakespeare's play made by the English actor David Garrick, which was produced in Paris throughout the 1830s. These un-Shakespearean versions of the story, themselves based on some of the earliest Italian novellas, add an additional element of pathos to the tragedy by allowing the lovers to share a moment in each other's arms before their inevitable deaths. From an opera composer's point of view, the departure from Shakespeare offered the opportunity to write yet another duet with which the drama could be brought to a close. In Gounod's *Roméo et Juliette*, that duet serves as an emotional and musical recapitulation of some of the key moments of the drama that have led to this catastrophe. Musically it is constructed of alternating sections of arioso and short, aria-like passages. Near the beginning of the duet Romeo laments the death of his wife in a few lines of text that begin, "O ma femme." This lyrical section consists of a new vocal melody laid over an orchestral accompaniment that the audience would recognize from its appearance earlier in the opera: first at the end of the prologue, and then again at the beginning of the act 4 bedroom love duet. This is some of the loveliest music in the opera, featuring an unusual orchestration that begins with solo cellos.

Example 10-8. Tomb scene duet.

The repetition of this theme in the tomb scene, recalls all the earlier scenes in which it played a prominent part—the prologue and the bedroom scene. The tomb scene thus unites all of the opera's dramatic themes through this special music: irrational hatred in the prologue, and transcendent love in the bedroom scene. Through the power of music, these themes of hatred and love are juxtaposed here in the tomb scene with the theme of death in a way that draws connections between all three as only an opera can do. Through Gounod's music, the audience is instructed that love cannot survive in the presence of hatred. Herein lies the beauty and power of opera.

Gounod continues the tomb scene duet with additional examples of musical recall. At the point where Juliet wakes up, she sings, "Dieu, quelle est cette voix . . ." (God, what is that voice?) to the accompaniment of another phrase drawn from the act 4 bedroom duet. This is the "sacrifice" theme, originally heard immediately after the moment when Romeo agreed to risk his own life to stay with Juliet. Now in the tomb scene at the point where this theme reappears, Romeo has just taken the poison, making the ultimate sacrifice to join his wife in death. So again the recall of specific melodic material serves to unify dramatic moments of similar meaning. At the climax of this duet, as the lovers embrace for their brief moment of joy, they repeat this "sacrifice" theme and then move directly into the "ecstasy" theme borrowed from the act 3 wedding quartet. (See Ex. 10-5.) This theme is itself derived from a melody that first appeared in the act 1 love duet (the "madrigal"). In both the act 1 "madrigal" duet and in the wedding quartet the emotion associated with this theme is one of overwhelming joy. In the tomb scene where this borrowed tune reappears yet again, the young lovers experience another moment of supreme joy as Juliet awakes from her sleep to find Romeo at her side—but one that lasts only a moment before she discovers that her husband has poisoned himself. Although this happy reunion, like the one in Berlioz's symphony, is based on both Garrick's bowdlerization of Shakespeare and Bellini's opera, there is no denying that it makes an effective theatrical moment. By uniting the themes of joy, sacrifice, and death in this one tortured moment, Gounod paraphrases the common Romantic understanding of the ecstasy of death, especially death through sacrifice. In this context, the sacrifice of a life produces a joyous release from the pain of an uncomprehending world. Romeo and Juliet are only fully able to realize their shared joy in a shared death that releases them from a world of hate. The opera then draws to a close as Juliet stabs herself to a final repetition of the "sacrifice" theme. Here in the tomb scene, these elaborate musical allusions to other moments in the drama form a complex web of melodic relationships that unify the various dramatic themes of the story in a single tragic denouement. These relationships are summarized in a chart of this scene.

Act 4 Tomb scene

BORROWED FROM THE BEGINNING OF ACT 4 BEDROOM LOVE DUET

ROMÉO:
Ô ma femme! Ô ma bien-aimée!
La mort en aspirant ton haleine
  embaumée
N'a pas altéré ta beauté!
Non, non, cette beauté que j'adore
Sur ton front calme et pur semble
  régner encore
Et sourire à l'éternité!
Pourquoi me la rends-tu
  si belle Ô mort livide?

ROMEO:
O my wife! O my beloved!
Death, while inhaling your embalmed
  breath
Has not altered your beauty!
No, that beauty that I adore
Reigns still on your pure,
  calm face
And smiles to eternity!
Why do you give her back to me
  so beautiful O ghastly death?

....

"SACRIFICE" THEME FROM ACT 4 BEDROOM LOVE DUET

JULIETTE: (awakening)
Dieu! Quelle est cette voix, dont la
douceur m'enchante?

JULIET:
God! What is that sweet voice that
enchants me?

ROMÉO:
C'est moi! C'est ton époux
Qui tremblant de bonheur
Embrasse tes genoux!
Qui ramène à ton coeur
La lumière enivrante
De l'amour et des cieux!

ROMEO:
It is I! It is your spouse
Who, trembling with happiness
Embraces your knees!
Who returns to your heart
The intoxicating light
Of love and heaven!

JULIETTE:
Ah! C'est toi! Ah!

JULIET:
It's you!

REPEAT OF "SACRIFICE" THEME

ROMÉO:
Viens! Viens, fuyons tous deux!

ROMEO:
Come! Come, let's fly together!

JULIETTE:
Ô bonheur!

JULIET:
Oh happiness!

ROMÉO:
Viens! Fuyons au bout du monde!
Viens, soyons heureux

ROMEO:
Come! Let's fly to the end of the earth!
Come, let us be happy

Fuyons tous deux.	Let us flee together
Viens!	Come!

TEXT AND MUSIC FROM ACT 3 WEDDING QUARTET

Dieu de bonté! Dieu de clémence!	God of goodness! God of mercy!
Sois béni par deux coeurs heureux!	Be blessed by two happy hearts!

. . . .

ROMÉO: (in a weaker voice)	ROMEO:
Écoute, ô Juliette!	Listen, Juliet!

TEXT AND "LARK" THEME FROM ACT 4 BEDROOM DUET

L'alouette déjà nous announce le jour!	The lark already announces daybreak!
Non, non, ce n'est pas le jour, ce n'est pas l'alouette!	No, it's not the day, it's not the lark!
C'est le doux rossignol, confident de l'amour.	It's the sweet nightingale, confidant of love.
[He slips from Juliet's arms.]	

JULIETTE: [picking up the flask of poison]	JULIET:
Ah! Cruel époux! De ce poison funeste	Ah! Cruel husband! You have not left me
Tu ne m'as pas laissé ma part.	My share of this poison.
[She throws away the flask and draws out a dagger.]	

Ah! Fortuné poignard,	Ah! Happy dagger
Ton secours me reste!	Your help remains!
[She stabs herself.]	

ROMÉO: [half rising]	ROMEO:
Dieu! Qu'as-tu fait?	God! What have you done?

JULIETTE: [in Romeo's arms]	JULIET:
Va! Ce moment est doux!	Done! This moment is sweet!

"SACRIFICE" THEME FROM ACT 4 BEDROOM DUET

Ô joie infinie et suprême	Oh joy, infinite and supreme
De mourir avec toi! Viens! Un baiser!	To die with you. Come! A kiss!
Je t'aime!	I love you!

JULIETTE AND ROMÉO:	JULIET AND ROMEO:
Seigneur, Seigneur, pardonnez-nous!	God forgive us!
[They die.]	

Everyone knows that Gounod's *Roméo et Juliette* is an opera full of beautiful music. But beyond that beauty lies the elaborate web of thematic recall diagramed in the chart above. Such instances of thematic recall in an opera serve to add deeper layers of meaning to the drama and to bring the whole work to a higher level of musical-dramatic sophistication. *Roméo et Juliette* is therefore an example of how compelling a good opera can be. By uniting music and words in a synergistic fashion, great composers like Gounod can turn opera into a kind of drama whose overall effect transcends that of its individual parts. In recognizing the numerous dramatic themes that run through the Romeo and Juliet story, Gounod astutely called on music to underscore those themes and their connections for his audience. In building the final duet on so much music from earlier in the opera, he created poignant emotional associations that ordinary spoken drama cannot bring to the stage. As Romeo and Juliet die together, we are forced by Gounod's music to recall their first love, as well as the hopeful passion of their marriage and the larger issues of self-sacrifice. So while much of the verbal sophistication of Shakespeare's play has been lost in translation to the operatic medium, music supplies emotional connections that no spoken drama can duplicate. Little wonder that this opera has survived the test of time and remains one of the most popular works in the French repertoire.

CHAPTER 11

VERDI'S OTELLO: ADAPTATION AND FORM
IN LATE-NINETEENTH-CENTURY OPERA

The goal of this chapter is to use Verdi's *Otello* to explore two musical-dramatic issues, both of which will serve to elucidate the genius of this composer at the end of his career. The first of these has to do with the subject of adaptation—that perennial question of how a composer takes a stage drama and turns it into a successful music drama. The other issue (already touched upon in the chapter on *Falstaff*) involves the question of operatic form and the relationship of Verdi's late style to the new symphonic techniques of Wagner.

Despite the fact that there is a plethora of Shakespearean operas in existence, almost none was written before the nineteenth century. As explained in the last chapter on Gounod's *Roméo et Juliette*, this state of affairs had much to do with the scarcity of translations of Shakespeare's plays prior to the early nineteenth century, which would have impeded the creation of opera librettos in French, Italian, or German. But the scarcity of translations was itself a reflection of the disregard with which these works were treated in the preceding century. It took the dawning of the romantic era to awaken an interest in, and appreciation for, the plays of the English bard. Only after this renaissance of popularity, spurred by the romantic aesthetic of creative freedom from restrictive rules and fixed forms, was it possible for composers to begin adapting Shakespeare to the operatic stage on a more regular basis. In Italy there were many examples in the first decades of the nineteenth century of what look like Shakespearean operas, the most famous of which were Rossini's *Otello* (1816) and Bellini's version of the Romeo and Juliet story, titled *I Capuleti e i Montecchi* (1830). But all of these operas shared one characteristic: None of them bore any real relationship to Shakespeare. It was not until Verdi came upon the operatic scene around 1840 that we finally get a composer who cared enough to try to copy in music what Shakespeare had produced in words. During the course of his long career, Verdi worked on four Shakespearean operas: *Macbeth* (1847) early in his career, *Otello* (1887), and *Falstaff* (1893) from his last years, and *Re Lear*, an unfinished project that he continued to dream about far into his old age.

The adaptation of a Shakespearean play to opera presents any composer with often insurmountable hurdles. Not the least of these are the facts that many of the plays take place over vast expanses of both time and place, they often involve intricate plots and subplots with large numbers of characters, and they always depend for much of their theatrical effect on the richness of their language and the beautifully crafted dialogue that brings each of the characters to life. By contrast, opera is an art form that thrives on simple plots with few characters, lots of action, and simple, succinct dialogue. How Verdi guided the efforts of his librettists in overcoming the inherent difficulties of making Shakespeare into opera without losing its very essence is the story of his genius as an adaptor of literature to music. He succeeded where others failed because he was able to find ways of allowing music to compensate for many of the dramatic intricacies of the spoken play, most of which inevitably had to be cut or simplified to make an opera libretto.

One of the greatest demonstrations of Verdi's genius in this regard is *Otello*, the next to last of his twenty-seven operas, premiered in 1887. The libretto for this work was written by Arrigo Boito, one of Italy's greatest poets, and a fine composer in his own right. But had Verdi been left to his own devices, he probably would never have written this opera. After the premiere of *Aida* in 1871, he had decided that except for the occasional supervision of new productions of earlier works, his career was more or less finished. Although he was the most successful and most famous composer of his generation in Italy, Verdi saw himself as having been superceded by a younger generation of composers devoted to the avant-garde principles of symphonic opera as invented by Wagner. He wrote to his friend Clara Maffei in 1878, asking, "For what reason should I write? . . . I would have it said of me all over again that I didn't know how to write, and that I've become a follower of Wagner."[1] In his opinion, it was time to step aside and to take up a new life as a gentleman farmer at Sant' Agata, the large estate he had purchased just outside of Busseto, his old home town in northern Italy. Thus, the difficult task of coaxing Verdi out of retirement fell mostly to his publisher, Giulio Ricordi, and to his wife, Giuseppina Strepponi, both of whom had ulterior motives to see Verdi continue composing—Giuseppina because she hated the prospect of retirement from active musical life in the theater, and Ricordi because he undoubtedly wanted to make more money publishing new operas by Verdi. The bait used by the two of them to lure Verdi away from farming and back to active composing was nothing less than one of his favorite authors, Shakespeare. Ricordi instructed Boito to

---

1. Budden, 1981, 299.

draw up a scenario based on *Othello*, and then cajoled Verdi into looking at it. Once he was able to overcome his distrust of Boito, who had years earlier taken the side of Italy's younger, modern composers in criticizing the old master, Verdi soon found himself composing parts of this new work despite his intention to avoid it altogether.

In looking at the most obvious differences between Shakespeare's play and Verdi's opera, we notice not only that much of the original play has been cut from the opera, but also that there are a few scenes in the opera that cannot be found anywhere in the play. An appreciation of the greatness of *Otello* begins with an understanding of how these additions to Shakespeare balance and compensate for the excisions that had to be made in the process of adapting a complex stage drama to music. Shakespeare's play, unlike the opera, begins in Venice and then continues on the island of Cyprus for acts 2 through 5. It is the opening Venetian act of the play that Boito chose to cut from his libretto. But it is in this first act that Shakespeare introduces and fleshes out the personalities of all the main characters: Othello, the heroic black general of the Venetian army; Iago, his jealous and vengeful ensign; Desdemona, his delicate, cultured, young Caucasian wife; and Cassio, his lieutenant and the source of much of Iago's discontent. In act 1 we discover several extremely important facts about this cast of characters:

- Iago hates Othello because he has been passed over for promotion in favor of Michael Cassio, a longtime friend of Othello; and that because of this, Iago is planning to seek his revenge on both of them.
- Iago uses Othello's race against him, alerting Desdemona's father to the fact that his daughter has eloped with a black man: "Even now an old black ram is tupping your white ewe," (1.1.88–89) is how he indelicately puts it.
- Othello is a true hero who is calm and assured under attack from Brabantio (Desdemona's father) who accuses him of having seduced his daughter with black magic: "That she should run from her guardage to the sooty bosom of such a thing as thou . . . thou hast practiced on her with foul charms." (1.2.70–71, 73) To this accusation, Othello responds eloquently in a speech before the Venetian senate, in which he explains how he and Desdemona fell in love. This speech is critical to the impression of Othello's greatness that Shakespeare wants to impart, and, as a result, is probably the pivotal dramatic moment in the first act of the play.

Because so much of importance to one's understanding of the play and its characters happens in act 1, its elimination by Boito, to make an opera of manageable length, would seem to seriously jeopardize the musical adaptation even before the curtain goes up. Verdi's audience would therefore not have been exposed to the portrayal of Othello's heroism, majesty, and dignity. Nor would they be aware of how and why Desdemona fell in love with Othello, the full motivation for Iago's villainy, or the racial motif that forms the basis of Othello's tragic insecurities later in the drama. Having given up all this important dramatic background and characterization, Verdi was forced somehow to find other means by which to make his operatic audience aware of everything that the play's first act supplies—especially the impression of Othello as a great hero. But how was this to be accomplished?

Shakespeare's act 2 and Verdi's opera begin in Cyprus, where a huge storm threatens to demolish Othello's fleet and army as they battle an invasion of Turks. One by one, the Venetian ships begin to put into port during the height of the storm: First Cassio arrives safely, then Iago in the company of Desdemona and Emilia, and then finally Othello. The general's first lines as he disembarks are to his wife, who has been anxiously awaiting his arrival. He goes directly up to her and engages her in the following dialogue:

OTHELLO:
O my fair warrior!

DESDEMONA:
My dear Othello!

OTHELLO:
It gives me wonder great as my content
To see you here before me. O my soul's joy!
If after every tempest come such calmness,
May the winds blow till they have wakened death!
And let the laboring bark climb hills of seas ...
If it were now to die,
'Twere now to be most happy; for I fear
My soul hath her content so absolute
That not another comfort like to this succeeds in unknown fate.

DESDEMONA:
The heavens forbid
But that our loves and comforts should increase
Even as our days do grow!

OTHELLO:
Amen to that, sweet powers!
I cannot speak enough of this content;
It stops me here; it is too much of joy.
And this, and this, the greatest discord be [*they kiss*]
That e'er our hearts shall make! (2.1.182–98)

Shakespeare, having already established Othello's heroism in act 1, obviously felt free to explore here another more tender side of his hero. But because Verdi cut Shakespeare's first act, it was imperative for him to present his operatic Otello[2] in a heroic light right from the outset. This, after all, is the most essential ingredient of his personality. To begin the opera with Shakespeare's scene of tenderness would have misrepresented to Verdi's Italian audience the true heroic stature of the playwright's protagonist. So this scene of tender reunion had to be eliminated, or more accurately, postponed, so that Verdi could demonstrate Otello's greatness instead. This he did by pruning away all the extraneous entrances of the secondary characters at the beginning of the opening scene and starting the opera *after* they had all arrived safely through the storm. Only Otello is left at sea with the risk of being shipwrecked, and all that remains is for him to make a dramatic solo entrance at the beginning of the opera, having defeated both the Turks and the elements of nature. When he does arrive, his first lines are not to Desdemona (who is nowhere to be found in Verdi's opening scene) but to the general populace—words of victory after the defeat of the Turkish fleet. Thus Shakespeare's opening dialogue between Othello and Desdemona is cut and reused by Verdi in a big love duet at the very end of the act. In its place, Verdi and Boito had to create a far more dramatic entrance for their operatic hero. But what was this going to be?

Having cleared the stage of the entrance of extraneous characters, the way was now open for Verdi and Boito to arrange the bold solo entrance that would draw the audience's attention directly to Otello. But this clever bit of stage chicanery would only be completely effective if Verdi could find a musical device that would accompany the visual gesture and communicate instantly the same heroism that Shakespeare had so carefully constructed in his first act. Boito's idea was to write a lengthy monologue for Otello, some kind of heroic speech, in which the opera audience would immediately perceive his greatness; but Verdi vetoed that plan, insisting instead that Otello be given as few words as possible at this important moment to allow

2. When referring to Verdi's opera or its hero, I use the Italian spelling "Otello," but will retain the English spelling of "Othello" when referring to Shakespeare's play or its protagonist.

music to make the point about his heroism more directly. His idea was to use the chaos of the storm that opens the opera as a vehicle for the demonstration of Otello's power. This storm is presented in Shakespeare's play only obliquely. Without the benefit of scenic effects, Elizabethan theater had at its disposal only the lines spoken by each actor onstage. In this case, a conversation between Montano and a "gentleman" suggests that they are standing in the midst of a raging storm that threatens to destroy the Venetian fleet.

> MONTANO:
> What from the cape can you discern at sea?
>
> GENTLEMAN:
> Nothing at all, it is a high-wrought flood; I cannot 'twixt the heaven and the main descry a sail.
>
> MONTANO:
> Methinks the wind hath spoke aloud at land; A fuller blast ne'er shook our battlements. If it hath ruffianed so upon the sea, what ribs of oak, when mountains melt on them, can hold the mortise? What shall we hear of this? (2.1.1–9)

Working with the advantage of music to create the same effect, Verdi took Shakespeare's storm and turned it into a scene of musical chaos: a huge choral/orchestral prelude that functions somewhat like an overture for the entire opera. Verdi's storm is chaotic for two reasons: its dissonance and its lack of a key center. The dissonance is supplied by an unusual organ part written in the pedals only. This part consists of nothing but a three-note tone cluster (C, C-sharp, D) that is heard continuously under the chorus and orchestra during the entire storm scene. Augmenting this rumbling dissonance at the bottom of the orchestra are bold, chromatic harmonies that prevent the storm from settling into any one key. Much like the storm movement in Beethoven's "Pastoral" Symphony, this entire section is basically without a clear tonal center. Otello's arrival is thus preceded by this musical depiction of a storm that far outstrips in its raw power that which Shakespeare was able to suggest with words alone. The musical pandemonium that Verdi created here serves the sole purpose of paving the way for Otello's heroic entrance. After several minutes of musical chaos, Otello arrives onstage, and everything in the music changes. Although the dissonant organ pedal continues until the storm has totally subsided, the modulating tonality settles quite audibly into the stable key of E major. Metaphorically speaking, Otello produces order out of chaos, as only a great hero could. Having thus worked this miracle by the force of his presence,

René Pape as Leporello and Thomas Hampson in the title role of Mozart's *Don Giovanni* at the New York Metropolitan Opera, March 1, 2004. (Photo © Marty Sohl/Metropolitan Opera)

Jean-Paul Fouchécourt as Bardolph, Bryn Terfel in the title role, and Mikhail Petrenko as Pistol in Verdi's *Falstaff* at the New York Metropolitan Opera, September 23, 2005. (Photo © Ken Howard/Metropolitan Opera)

Anna Netrebko as Gilda and Carlo Guelfi in the title role of Verdi's *Rigoletto* at the New York Metropolitan Opera, December 1, 2005. (Photo © Ken Howard/Metropolitan Opera)

John Relyea as Mephistopheles and Marcello Giordani as Faust in Berlioz's *La damnation de Faust* at the New York Metropolitan Opera, November 7, 2008. (Photo © Ken Howard/ Metropolitan Opera)

Anna Netrebko as Juliet and Roberto Alagna as Romeo in the tomb scene from Gounod's *Roméo et Juliette* at the New York Metropolitan Opera, September 25, 2005. (Photo © Ken Howard/Metropolitan Opera)

Deborah Voigt as Cassandra in a scene from act 1 of Berlioz's *Les Troyens* at the New York Metropolitan Opera, February 10, 2003. (Photo © Marty Sohl/Metropolitan Opera)

Roberto Alagna as Don José and Elina Garanča in the title role of Bizet's *Carmen* at the New York Metropolitan Opera, December 31, 2009. (Photo © Ken Howard/Metropolitan Opera)

Marcelo Alvarez as Cavaradossi and Karita Mattila in the title role of Puccini's *Tosca* at the New York Metropolitan Opera, September 21, 2009. (Photo © Ken Howard/Metropolitan Opera)

Maria Guleghina in the title role and Salvatore Licitra as Calaf in Puccini's *Turandot* at the New York Metropolitan Opera, January 4, 2010. (Photo © Ken Howard/Metropolitan Opera)

Logan W. Erickson (far left) as the apprentice, Anthony Dean Griffey in the title role, and Patricia Racette as Ellen Orford in Britten's *Peter Grimes* at the New York Metropolitan Opera, February 28, 2008. (Photo © Ken Howard/Metropolitan Opera)

there is little need for him to say much at all. No long-winded speech was necessary, nor could any such speech ever have accomplished what Verdi was able to show about Otello's power through the metaphoric meaning of his music. Otello's lines are thus reduced to a bare minimum to allow the music to make its point uninhibited:

Esultate! L'orgoglio musulmano	Rejoice! The Muslim pride
Sepolto è in mar.	Is buried in the deep.
Nostra e del ciel è gloria.	The glory is ours and heaven's.
Dopo l'armi lo vinse l'uragano.	After our arms, the storm has conquered him.

The remainder of Verdi's act 1 follows Shakespeare fairly closely. Verdi borrowed some lines from the first act of the play to let audiences know that Iago was passed over for promotion and is now angry about it. Then Iago schemes to get Cassio drunk, a brawl ensues, and Otello must again bring peace. Cassio is disgraced and demoted, and Iago becomes Otello's new confidant. Not until the end of the act did Verdi decide to bring Desdemona onstage for the first time. The resulting duet between her and Otello is essentially the love scene transplanted from the beginning of Shakespeare's act 2, where Othello steps off his ship and greets his wife with tender affection. An important element of Shakespeare's version of this encounter between Othello and Desdemona is a line that Iago speaks in an aside to the audience: "O you are well tuned now! But I'll set down the pegs that make this music, as honest as I am." (2.1.199–201) Here Shakespeare clearly wanted to remind his audience that Iago was about to set out on a scheme of villainous revenge against Othello. Boito wanted to include this important line in the love duet, somehow having Iago lurking in the background singing behind the two lovers. But again Verdi overruled his librettist, saying that Iago's intrusion in that manner would be too clumsy and too obvious. So the duet focuses exclusively on Otello and Desdemona, and Iago's presence, as we will see shortly, is only a musical one. As always, Verdi tried to find musical solutions to problems of dramatic adaptation such as this. Some years ago, the Verdi scholar David Lawton postulated the fascinating and provocative theory that Verdi's solution for how to interject Iago into this duet was to incorporate into the most critical moments of that number the two tonalities (C major and F major) in which Iago sings throughout the first act of the opera, to suggest that the beauty of the love between Otello and Desdemona might be poisoned or undermined by his wickedness.[3] Lawton pointed out that Iago's keys are foreign to the central

---

3. Lawton, 1978

tonality of E major in which the kiss between the lovers takes place, and in which Otello is first presented so heroically at the opening of the act. The keys of C and F metaphorically throw the key of E major off track, much as Iago's scheming throws Otello off his course of love for Desdemona. In fact, the music that accompanies the kiss itself, the so-called *bacio* theme (Ex. 11-1), is nothing more than an extended cadence in E major, which is momentarily interrupted by the interjection of a C major chord in the last couple of measures.

Example 11-1. "*Bacio*" theme.

If Verdi had consciously organized his duet in this fashion, around tonalities that had specific dramatic meaning, he would have been one of the first Italian composers to work in this manner. In analyzing the score, there is no denying that the love duet is at important moments characterized by the very colorful and surprising juxtaposition of the unrelated keys of E major and C major. But one has to question what kind of meaning this use of keys could have had for Verdi's average listeners. To recognize that C and F are keys associated with Iago throughout the first act, one would have to be able to recognize and remember these keys when they were being sung. But for anyone without perfect pitch (which is almost everyone), pitch memory lasts no more than a few minutes at best. So it would be impossible for the average listener to recognize that Otello kissed Desdemona in E major, the same key in which he made his heroic entrance thirty minutes earlier, and that the keys of C and F major represent Iago by virtue of their use in his part for a few brief moments in an earlier scene. Thus the meaning of these keys would have no relevance for a listener's perception of the drama of this love duet at the end of the first act unless he or she had first analyzed the score and become aware of the key relationships with which Verdi was working. Lawton is right to point to the symbolic use of these keys throughout Act I in general and in this duet in particular, but only in so far as they might have functioned as tools used by the composer to organize the musical-dramatic construction of the duet. In essence, these key relationships allowed Verdi to claim that he had brought Iago into the conversation between Otello and Desdemona through musical means alone, as he said he wanted to do. But surely he deluded himself if he thought this technique of assigning meaning to specific tonal centers would have the same effect on his audience as does Shakespeare's unequivocal use of a spoken aside from Iago.

The elimination of the first act of Shakespeare's play presented Verdi and Boito with some severe adaptational challenges in the organization of the first act of their opera; in addition, the second act of the opera also rearranges and adds to Shakespeare's act 3, on which it is based. The structure of this act sheds some interesting light on Verdi's formal procedures at the end of his career. The act consists almost entirely of traditional kinds of Italian operatic numbers: duets, an aria, a quartet, and a chorus. But there is nothing traditional about the way Verdi assembled these set pieces. Like his German colleague Richard Wagner, Verdi had been moving throughout his career toward an operatic form that focused on continuity through the elimination of discrete set pieces that had always encouraged Italian audiences to interrupt the drama with endless rounds of applause at each final high note and closing cadence. Both Wagner and Verdi wanted to create the kind of continuity that one finds in a stage play, where characters speak in alternation, not together, where characters do not repeat themselves endlessly, and where the proportion of action to reflection (i.e., dialogue to soliloquy) in the text heavily favors action that moves the drama forward. To accomplish this, Wagner created a new symphonic technique that featured the elimination of independent set pieces, such as arias and ensemble numbers. Where Wagner's librettos call for an interchange between two characters, these characters sing one after the other rather than together as in a traditional operatic duet. Although Verdi had also moved in this direction with some of his operas after *Rigoletto* (1851), especially in his duet writing, he was nonetheless steeped in an Italian tradition that had long celebrated the hegemony of the voice in opera. It was this tradition that forced him to find an alternate route to the same goal of producing dramatic continuity in his operas. Reluctant to abandon the old set pieces altogether, he looked for ways of disguising the seams between them, as well as ways of making the set pieces themselves sound less continuously lyrical, less song-like. Working under the influence of his exposure to French opera, obtained through work on *Les vêpres siciliennes* (1855) and *Don Carlos* (1867), Verdi developed at the end of his career a new more flexible kind of melodic writing. Gone from this new late style were the lyrical lines based on predictable, symmetrical phrase lengths that characterize his early vocal writing. In their place arose a new more through-composed melody that was supple and irregular, like the French language that inspired it. Because French poetry did not always rely on lines of equal length, or of fixed accentuation patterns, Verdi's melodies written to French words became far more fluid and unpredictable than his old Italian melodies. Yet this new melodic style, by virtue of its irregularity, was also less memorable in terms of its tunefulness than were the melodies of Verdi's early years. By applying his new melodic style to Boito's new more realistic libretto, which kept text repetition to a minimum, Verdi was able to capture the same sense of continual renewal in the unfolding of his melodic lines that Wagner had achieved with his famous *Sprechgesang*. Both styles are what could be described as semi-melodic and more speech-like in their contour, and thus more realistic in their avoidance of "song" in the strictest sense of the word.

Act 2 of *Otello* opens with just such a flexible melodic moment, as Iago counsels Cassio as to how he might be restored to his former position as Otello's captain. Technically, this exchange between them would be called a duet, but one written in Verdi's new style, wherein the two characters never sing together, but converse in the more realistic fashion of Wagner. Also Wagnerian is the orchestral motif that underlies the entire duet. This motif is repeated and developed in a symphonic fashion, resulting in continually evolving variations of the basic idea. (See Ex. 11-2.)

Example 11-2. Act 2 duet, Iago and Cassio, orchestral motif with developed variations.

Example 11-2 *(continued)*

This orchestral motif is then used to create a bridge between the end of the duet and the beginning of Iago's "Credo" aria that follows, seamlessly blending one number into the next. In this manner, Verdi created the illusion that his set pieces were part of a large unbroken continuity that flows seamlessly from one number to the next.

As Verdi's career progressed over the years, he seemed to make it a point to gradually decrease the number of arias in his operas. These old-fashioned moments of individual reflection, encapsulated in a pattern of repeating and contrasting melodic phrases with considerable text repetition, had long been seen for what they so often were: shameless displays of virtuoso singing that were more about the beauty of the voice than about the effectiveness of the drama. As a result, Iago's aria that follows the opening duet avoids most of what Verdi no longer liked about arias: It has no discernable form, no double quatrain of poetry set to patterned two-measure phrases for each line of text, and no big cadenza at the end. The new style of this aria features a through-composed form and Verdi's new flexible melodic style. This irregular and unpredictable melodic style is itself a response to changes in poetic form that were also appearing late in the nineteenth century. Much of Boito's poetry for the *Otello* libretto rejects the classical Italian form that required each line of poetry to have the same number of syllables. His new poetic style embraces irregularity of line lengths, and, as a result produces far fewer regular patterns of accentuation (of stressed and unstressed syllables) than one encounters in most of Verdi's earlier works. Because the poetry is irregular in its accentuation patterns, Verdi's melodies are likewise irregular, without the singsong quality that one usually associates with an Italian opera aria.

Iago's "Credo" aria represents Verdi's more modern approach to the use of traditional operatic set pieces. At the same time, it also affords us another opportunity to see how the composer dealt with problems of adaptation, as he was continually forced to rethink Shakespeare's drama in musical terms. Whereas nearly all of Verdi's act 2 is drawn directly from Shakespeare's act 3, this moment of solo reflection on Iago's part is nowhere to be found in the play. Verdi and Boito must have felt the need for this textual interpolation in order to compensate for something they lost in the cutting of Shakespeare's first act. It was there that Iago explained to the audience his motivation for seeking revenge on Othello. Without this explanation, Iago's later behavior would make little sense, and the action of the drama would seem contrived at best. But even Shakespeare seems to have struggled with making a case for why Iago should be so outraged that he needed to completely destroy Othello's happiness, because on the surface, the fact that he was passed over for a promotion would seem to be insufficient justification for his rage. Shakespeare therefore took great pains to detail as much of the relationship between Iago and Cassio as possible, including the fact that Iago feels his rival is nothing but a bookish warrior who "never set a squadron in the field" and whose "soldiership" is "mere prattle without practice" (1.2.22–27). Othello's promotion of Cassio becomes then more than a matter of preferment; it becomes an injustice that cannot be tolerated. But even with all this information, Shakespeare must still have felt that he needed something more convincing. As a result, he added at the very end of the act, one more perceived insult on Iago's part: he believes that Othello has been sleeping with his wife, Emilia. As he explains to Roderigo at the end of act 1, "I hate the Moor, and it is thought abroad, that 'twixt my sheets he's done my office" (1.3.384–86). For his part, Verdi must have felt the same uneasiness over the issue of Iago's motivation. But unlike Shakespeare, he did not have the luxury of being able to drop hints of his motivation over the course of an entire act. Music needs to move swiftly and decisively in the communication of emotions like those that plague Iago. Verdi decided, therefore, that a direct statement of Iago's motivation was the only way to make his actions seem justified in the context of an opera. The "Credo" aria serves that purpose by reducing the explanation for Iago's villainous behavior to a simple statement that he is born evil and believes in an evil god.

Iago's "Credo" aria.

> I believe in a cruel god
> Who created me in his image,
> And who, in fury, I name.
> From the very vileness of a germ
> Or an atom, I was born wicked.
> I am a villain because I am a man,
> And I feel within me the primeval slime.

This text encapsulates in the most succinct manner possible all the reasons that Iago is such a wicked character. Has Boito captured in this text all the subtleties that make Shakespeare's character so enigmatic? No.

Indeed one might argue that this Iago is a mere shadow of Shakespeare's more complex character. But Boito's text explains to an opera audience, in one concise dramatic gesture, exactly why Iago is so evil. For the purposes of a music drama, this serves as an elegant solution to a thorny problem of adaptation.

The process of adapting a play to music always stumbles over the issue of finding ways of allowing characters to sing together, when in a play no one ever speaks at the same time as someone else. Operatic ensembles had long occupied a position of importance in Italian opera of the nineteenth century, wherein duets, trios, and larger group numbers offered some musical contrast to the solo arias. But from a dramatic point of view, these ensemble numbers forced librettists to create completely unrealistic situations in which multiple characters simultaneously express their feelings about a single dramatic event. Any composer who was intent upon reforming nineteenth-century opera, as was Wagner for instance, would probably have given up writing ensembles altogether, exactly because they violated the demand for realism that invaded opera late in the century. But the ensemble had been such an important part of Italian opera through the ages that a composer like Verdi found himself straddling the fence between the need to eliminate set pieces involving ensemble singing and the need to make room for these fundamentally Italian musical forms even as he radically modernized the operatic tradition from which they sprang. Verdi's dilemma was therefore not whether to write trios and quartets, but how to create opportunities for such ensembles without sacrificing the dramatic integrity of his original source.

In act 2 of *Otello*, Verdi created a marvelous quartet for Otello, Desdemona, Iago, and Emilia by cleverly overlapping two parts of one scene that occur sequentially in Shakespeare's play. Act 3, scene 3 of the play contains two dramatic events, each involving two characters. First, Othello insistently rejects Desdemona's suit in support of the disgraced Cassio. Suddenly he feels the onset of a severe headache, prompting his wife to offer her handkerchief to bind his brow. He angrily throws the handkerchief on the ground and abruptly leaves with her at his side. Next, Emilia enters, finds the handkerchief, and then gives it to Iago, who had long been asking her to steal it for him. Out of these two conversations, Verdi created a quartet by having Otello and Desdemona remain onstage while Iago and Emilia have their exchange. In doing so, Boito was forced to invent something for the first two characters to do and say while the second pair begins speaking. As a rule, of course, Verdi and Boito invented as little as possible in making this opera, preferring, wherever they could, to borrow relevant lines from Shakespeare. In this quartet, the lines sung by Otello were borrowed from a conversation he had elsewhere in the play with Iago, who tried to suggest to the insecure general that his wife may have been happier with a man of her own age and race.

Act 2 Quartet.

> DESDEMONA:
> If in ignorance I have offended you, my husband
> O say the sweet and happy word of pardon.
> Your loving bride am I,
> Humble and submissive . . .
>
> OTELLO:
> Haply because I am not practiced
> In the deceitful arts of love . . .
> Or because I am declined
> Into the vale of years,
> Or that my complexion
> Is of this dusky hue . . .
>
> IAGO:
> Give me that handkerchief
> You picked up just now!
> You resist in vain
> When I command!
>
> EMILIA:
> What mischief is in your mind?
> I can read your face.
> Your wicked envy
> Well I know.

In this quartet Verdi plumbed the depths of emotion that underlie each character's words. Desdemona's earnest sweetness, Otello's weakening self-confidence, Iago's menacing demeanor, and Emilia's indignation and suspicion are all communicated in the different kinds of music each of them is given to sing. While most of Boito's libretto consists of lines like these, cleverly translated or paraphrased from Shakespeare, it is Verdi's music that heightens the emotional meaning implied in these lines. Because music functions as a direct, non-verbal communication of emotions, capable of elucidating that which only lies implicit in spoken words, opera has the power to bring to words (even the most poetic words) a new level of meaning and interpretive elucidation.

At the end of act 2 Verdi created yet another such dramatic moment in which music serves to clarify the meaning of words. By this point in the drama, Iago has planted the seed of suspicion of Desdemona's infidelity in Otello's feeble brain. In a lengthy duet between the two of them (which is again written in a thoroughly conversational style), Otello becomes convinced of his wife's guilt, and works himself into a jealous frenzy. He kneels to swear an oath of revenge, but before he can rise, Iago kneels beside him to join the oath taking as a brother in arms against treachery. The irony of Otello's unwitting acceptance of help from this false friend is painful to watch in the play, but even more painful to hear in Verdi's opera. We want Otello to know what we know about Iago. In the opera this discrepancy between what Otello feels and what the audience feels is magnified by the music. The score is heavily weighted with brass instruments, lending a sense of raw power to Otello's anger. The melodic shapes well up like waves of seething fury, and the rhythms have a stately grandeur that gives the scene a false sense of self-righteous pomp. In short, Verdi's music makes real the emotions that Otello feels, and in the process helps clarify his tragic mistake by providing a visceral dichotomy between the reality of the situation and Otello's firm but errant perception of it. The overwhelming effectiveness of this scene is at least partly the result of an addition that Boito made to Shakespeare's dialogue. At the end of the duet, Verdi abandoned the modern style of conversational duet writing, based on Shakespeare, to allow Otello and Iago to sing together in the manner of a traditional Italian duet. The powerful moment when they kneel to swear revenge on Desdemona, is nowhere to be found in the play, but was needed in the opera just so that Verdi could arrange for the two men to sing together like this. In fact, duets of this type between a tenor and a baritone are seen elsewhere in Verdi's operas, often in a scene like this one in which two characters are forging an alliance of friendship. Verdi's *Don Carlos* offers a fine example of this typical "friendship" duet between the opera's hero and his most loyal and trusted friend. In *Otello*, Verdi played upon this tradition for ironic effect, as Otello joins forces not with a friend, but with an unrecognized enemy.

Verdi's act 3 includes the famous scene in which Otello overhears Iago and Cassio talking about the handkerchief that Desdemona lost. Otello wrongly believes that she has given it to Cassio as a token of her love, which leads him to firmly commit to killing both of them for this suspected adultery. The act then ends with the arrival of Lodovico and representatives from Venice, who bring orders for Otello to return home, leaving Cassio in charge of Cyprus. As in Shakespeare, Otello becomes angry with Desdemona as she explains to Lodovico that she plans to fix the rift between her husband and Cassio. He strikes her in a fit of anger, and everyone reacts with horror. Here Verdi steps back from his Shakespearean model to do something thoroughly operatic. In the play, Lodovico confronts Otello on his outrageous behavior, and Otello stalks out in a huff. But in the opera, Verdi takes this opportunity to write a large ensemble finale—a long, grandiose, musical number for chorus and all soloists singing together—of the kind that traditionally brought an act of an Italian opera to a climatic close. In such scenes, a crowd of people gathered along with all the principal characters experiences some kind of pivotally dramatic event. The action then comes to a complete halt while everyone concerned reacts to this event on an emotional level. The chorus and soloists plant their feet, face the audience, watch the conductor, and sing away. By the last quarter of the nineteenth century, however, these large choral-solo numbers were becoming a thing of the past as composers followed the lead of Wagner in moving toward a more realistic kind of opera in which the drama was not forced to stop while a group of singers collectively reacted to some dramatic situation. Such collective musical reactions were often referred to in the musical score with the term *concertato*, which itself implies the inherent problem with this musical-dramatic form: that it was more a concert in costume than a real drama of action in music. The fact that Verdi clung to this aging tradition in the face of modern trends in opera at the end of the century is a measure of his own personal operatic dilemma of being pulled by the opposing forces of modernization and retrenchment at the end of his career. In Shakespeare it is only Lodovico who reacts to Otello's striking his wife. But in the opera, the old Italian manner gets the upper hand, and everyone voices a reaction to this unprovoked attack on an innocent woman.

Otello ends, as does Shakespeare's play, with the murder of Desdemona. Otello bids his wife retire for the evening, saying he will come to her shortly. As she prepares for bed, she speaks with Emilia about a girl she knew long ago, who had been betrayed in love. This girl used to sing a song, which Desdemona calls the "Willow Song." Here at the beginning of act 4, she sings this song for Emilia. Such songs within an opera (i.e., moments when we are made to understand that a character is singing rather than speaking) are often used to comment obliquely on the action that is unfolding before us. Here, the poor maid, Barbara, has suffered the same fate that Desdemona is about to experience. Her song, written with folklike modal inflections, strikes a mood of wistful melancholy that establishes the calm before the storm in this last act.

Example 11-3. Desdemona's "Willow Song."

Next, Desdemona sings a prayer, an Ave Maria, before retiring to bed. Although there is no such prayer in Shakespeare, this musical number is surely derived from Othello's question to Desdemona in the next scene, "Did you pray tonight?" Its purpose is to further develop the mood of tranquility before the horror of the murder to come, and to remind the audience of Desdemona's innocence. The Ave Maria is, in effect, a musical counterpoise to the tumultuous murder scene that follows it—an almost extraneous device for setting up musical contrast and dramatic effect. It is also one of the most beautiful musical moments in the opera.

Example 11-4. Desdemona's "Ave Maria."

Finally, Otello enters while Desdemona sleeps. Without saying a word, he sneaks up to her bed, accompanied by music for double basses alone that is at once both stealthy and brimming with pent-up hostility. As in Shakespeare, he bends over the sleeping Desdemona and kisses her three times. But here Verdi does something Shakespeare could not: his orchestral accompaniment repeats the "kiss" motif (*bacio* theme) from the love duet at the end of act 1. This is the same music that accompanied Otello's lines in that duet, which were drawn directly from the play. We are thus devastatingly reminded of the irony of this dramatic moment in which the kiss of love has now become the kiss of death. Such emotional connections are only possible through the power of music to augment and/or clarify the meaning of words and actions in a play.

Only after Otello has snuffed out his wife's life, does Emilia make him aware of the error of his action. As in Shakespeare, Otello kills himself when he realizes what he has done. But again, music adds an extra dimension to our understanding of the drama at the moment when Otello dies with the words:

> I kissed thee ere I killed thee, no way but this,
> Killing myself, to die upon a kiss.

Here Verdi again repeats the kiss motif with potent effect as a final poignant reminder of what could have been, were it not for Otello's tragic flaw.

At the end of his career, Verdi was caught on the horns of an aesthetic dilemma searching for a way to modernize opera without giving up those musical principles that Italians had held dear for so many centuries. His heritage was based on an axiomatic acceptance of opera as an expression of emotions encapsulated and made manifest in a series of lyrical musical numbers. As the composer matured, he came to realize that these closed musical forms of high lyricism were not compatible with every kind of text in every dramatic situation, and that their repeating musical forms were artificial and unrealistic from a dramatic point of view. But he was loath to follow the path of Wagner and to give up altogether on operatic set pieces such as the aria, duet, and concerted ensemble. *Otello* then, is Verdi's answer to Wagner. It is an opera in which lyricism is reserved for only those dramatic moments that truly call for it, an opera in which Verdi's new semimelodic style bears a large burden of carrying the drama, an opera in which the orchestra plays an integral role in building the dramatic effect, but at the same time, an opera that adheres to the traditional Italian principle of music drama as a collection of lyrical moments. Was Verdi, as he feared, hopelessly old-fashioned by 1887? Undoubtedly so. But is *Otello* nonetheless a masterpiece of lyric drama that refines and modernizes a tattered tradition without renouncing that which always made Italian opera so popular? Yes, even more so.

PART VI

FROM LITERATURE TO OPERA

CHAPTER 12

GOUNOD'S *FAUST*: A HERO'S TRANSFORMATION

T he immense popularity of Gounod's *Faust* over the 150 years since its premiere can be measured not only in the countless performances and recordings it has received over the years, but also in the fact that this was the work with which the Metropolitan Opera chose to inaugurate its old opera house in 1883. Further evidence of the high esteem in which Gounod was held at that time could be seen boldly emblazoned on the decorative proscenium arch over the stage of that grand old opera house, where his name stood side by side those of the greatest composers of opera, such as Mozart, Verdi, and Wagner.[1] Today Gounod's reputation has fallen into partial eclipse, and if the new Metropolitan Opera house (at Lincoln Center) had such a decorative frieze, one would not expect to see his name so prominently displayed among those of the greatest heroes of opera. But at the end of the nineteenth century, Gounod's popularity was unparalleled among opera-goers, and performances of *Faust* outnumbered those of almost every other opera in the repertoire through the middle of the twentieth century. Although this work may no longer amass the astounding number of performances it once did, it is nonetheless still an important part of the basic repertoire of most major opera houses throughout the world, and therefore an important work with which to become familiar.

Faust is not only a great piece of music drama, but also an opera of some historical importance—one that presents audiences with an eclectic mix of different musical styles and generic types that cut across the national boundaries and rigid categorizations that were common in mid-nineteenth-century opera. In Paris in the 1850s, one could hear serious historical French grand opera, opéra comique, Italian opera, and other kinds of lightweight theatrical entertainments. Each of these had a musical profile all its own. But when Gounod's *Faust* was produced in 1859, it surprised audiences by ignoring these generic distinctions, offering instead a unique blend of techniques drawn from several current operatic styles. In its initial form, this opera combined the spoken dialogue of opéra comique, with the serious

---

1. This arch was actually the product of a redecoration of the original theater that took place after a fire in 1892.

plot commonly found in French grand opera, and a new less grandiose style of production found in contemporary Italian opera.

An understanding of how Gounod came to write this unusual opera requires a brief look at his background. Born into an artistic family in 1818 (his mother was a pianist and his father was a painter), Gounod quickly showed a talent for both art and music, with the latter eventually winning his serious attention. He studied both piano and voice as a boy, but was most interested in his harmony and counterpoint lessons with the famous Paris Conservatoire teacher, Anton Reicha. Eventually Gounod went on to study composition at the Conservatoire and to win the coveted Prix de Rome in 1839. This allowed him to travel to Rome to study for two years. Like Berlioz, who won the Prix de Rome almost a decade earlier, Gounod found nothing of value in the study of contemporary Italian opera. But he reveled in the discovery of the great religious music of past centuries, particularly that of Palestrina. His newfound interest in sacred music accounts for Gounod's growing association with the Church at this point in his life (especially with a new branch of progressive, socially liberal Catholicism), and his composition of some early masses and other sacred genres.

When he finally returned to Paris, Gounod allowed his interest in the Church to lead him directly into taking a position as an organist and church music director in 1843. Then in 1847, he enrolled as a student at the St. Sulpice seminary to pursue his goal of becoming a priest. This career track, however, was cut short by a life-changing event: his introduction to the famous soprano Pauline Viardot, who convinced the young composer that a career in the church was a waste of his talents, and that far greater fame and glory awaited him in the world of opera. To back up this advice, she arranged for Gounod to receive a commission from the Paris Opéra for a new work titled *Sapho*, a lyric tragedy in three acts on an antique subject of the kind that had not been popular since the early years of the century. Despite weak prospects of success, Gounod felt this was an opportunity he could not turn down. But the composer proved to have no gift for this kind of serious opera, and both this and his next work, the grand opera *La nonne sanglante* (The Bloody Nun), failed dismally and forced him to reexamine his newly chosen career path.

At that point Gounod decided to try his hand at something different: a musical setting of Goethe's *Faust*. Although the projected opera was turned down by the Opéra, Léon Carvalho, director of the new Théâtre-Lyrique, offered to stage the work in 1856 (although the actual production was delayed until 1859). This alternative theater had made a reputation for its staging of opéras comiques, foreign operas in French translation, and new works by young, less experienced composers. Most important, in terms of the impact on the kind of opera a composer could write for this theater, was its size—at that time, only a little over half the capacity of the Paris Opéra—and Carvalho's limited resources. Large choruses and spectacular scenery of the kind one encountered at the Opéra were difficult to accommodate in this theater, and as a result, Gounod was forced to adapt his musical style and form to the more intimate venue in which he was now working. This adaptation primarily involved writing an opera that would concentrate more on the development of individual characters and their interactions, and less on the large-scale scenic and choral effects found in grand opera. Through this theater, a new kind of French opera was born: one that we know today as opéra lyrique.

Gounod's familiarity with the Faust subject came through two sources: the French translation of Goethe's play made by Gérard de Nerval (which Gounod had read during his student days in Rome), and a French play by Michel Carré titled *Faust et Marguerite*. But long before these two works, the tale of Faust was known throughout Europe in various popular forms, including collections of folk tales, and other dramatic representations such as the 1604 *Dr. Faustus* of Christopher Marlowe. Despite the fact that dramatizations of the Faust legend date back hundreds of years, musical treatments of it were not common until the nineteenth century, after Goethe, in his two-part dramatization of the legend (1808 and 1832), transformed the story into something more than a simple moralizing, cautionary tale. Of the more than thirty-five versions of the Faust legend that composers have set to music over the years, only four predate Goethe's writing of his part 1. (See also the discussion of this drama in the chapter on Berlioz's *La damnation de Faust*.) In Goethe's hands, Faust became an archetypal romantic hero, the striving idealist of the new era, the man whose reach exceeds his grasp (both intellectually and emotionally). It was therefore his specific reshaping of the character of Faust into a symbol of romantic striving to which nineteenth-century composers so often responded.

For Gounod, the attraction of Faust as a struggling intellectual may have gone beyond a generalized romantic idealism and soul-searching to include a more personal identification with Goethe's hero. In the play, Faust refers to himself as a man with "two souls trapped within one breast" (1112), an admission that he is driven by both spiritual and corporal desires, a man struggling to balance these contradictory human urges. Gounod was similarly a man of two spirits, both very opposite. As a man of the church, he was a spiritual being, but as a man of the theater, he inhabited a world of the flesh, a world which throughout history had always been thought of by the church as the devil's playground, and all its people as lost souls. For Gounod, Faust was therefore a kind of literary projection of himself as a contradictory duality.

While Gounod's operatic setting of the Faust story was based in part on Carré's play, mentioned above, the libretto by Jules Barbier and Carré himself relied mostly on Goethe's *Faust* part 1 for much of the plot of the opera. Of course, one of the greatest difficulties facing any librettist-composer team is that of adapting a great piece of literature to the operatic stage. This is nowhere truer than in the case of Goethe's *Faust*. As is usual with such pieces of literature, the original is a subtle, nuanced work that deals with complex intellectual concepts. Opera, on the other hand, as Verdi always suggested, seems to live in a world of action and emotion, where convoluted ideas and verbosity are uneasy bedfellows with the expression of musical feeling. Thus, a successful musical adaptation of a drama such as *Faust* will necessarily have to pare away much of the subtlety of conceptualization found in the original, and boil what was originally an extremely complex work down to something far simpler, something that deals with raw emotion. The process of making a musical adaptation of a literary masterpiece is not, then, purely one of translation, but rather one of reimagining the essence of the original in terms of the techniques and artistic essence of the new medium. Gounod's reinterpretation of Goethe's *Faust* is, in this regard, a model of various problems that confront composers who try to make such transfers from one artistic medium to another, and of the possible solutions that can be found to those problems. What follows here is an exploration of only those aspects of Gounod's opera relating directly to this matter of adaptation: how it was carried out, and what effect it had on the final musical product.

The operatic Faust is himself a fine example of how much reshaping was required to bring this character to life onstage. In Goethe's play he is a doctor, philosopher, scientist, and teacher, who had devoted his life to the acquisition of knowledge, but now feels cheated because all of this knowledge has brought him no closer to finding the true meaning of life. As he says at the outset, "Mysterious even in the light of day, Nature keeps her veil intact; whatever she refuses to reveal, you cannot wrench from her with screws and levers" (672–75). And then shortly thereafter, "What we don't know is really what we need, and what we know is of no use to us whatever" (1066–67). Out of frustration, he turns to necromancy and, as he does, articulates what he feels he has been missing these many years:

Therefore I have turned to magic,
so that by the Spirit's might and main
I might yet learn some secret lore;
that I need no longer sweat and toil
and dress my ignorance in empty words;
that I might behold the warp and woof
of the world's inmost fabric . . . (377–83)

Such lines would seem to suggest that Faust was searching for some universal truth, some understanding of how and why things are the way they are. This, he decides, is knowledge that cannot be found in books, or acquired through study. But such metaphysical abstractions as the meaning of life are exactly the kinds of subjects with which music does not deal well. Thus Goethe's Faust, in all his abstract complexity, is not the kind of character who could easily be projected on the operatic stage. So Gounod and his librettists were forced to scrap the literary hero and to invent one of their own, while retaining as much of the action and setting of the original drama as possible. Accordingly, the setting of the opening scene of the opera follows Goethe's play almost exactly, with Faust alone in his study lamenting the fact that he knows nothing after all these years of disciplined study. He contemplates suicide (as in Goethe) but is dissuaded by an offstage chorus of young girls and harvesters (also similar to Goethe). But Gounod's Faust then begins to diverge from his literary counterpart, as he curses the irrelevance of these happy people to his life and calls for the devil to appear. Although the motivation for this sudden call to hell is not completely clear, this direct appeal to the devil at least circumvents the far more convoluted manner in which Faust actually encounters the devil in Goethe's play.

Once they meet face to face, Mephistopheles is able to offer Faust the deal of a lifetime: Faust's soul in the afterlife in trade for whatever he wants here and now. In Goethe, of course, the devil offers to show Faust the good life, which Faust superciliously dismisses with the following lines:

If you should ever find me lolling on a bed of ease,
Let me be done for on the spot!
If you ever lure me with your lying flatteries,
and I find satisfaction in myself,
if you bamboozle me with pleasure,
then let this be my final day!
This bet I offer you! (1692–98)

Clearly this literary version of Faust is looking for something far subtler than pleasure. But operatically speaking, his desire for the intangible is too abstract to be made clear in music. So in Gounod's hands, Faust becomes not an idealistic searcher for truth and the meaning of life in the universe, but rather a simple, crude hedonist, who can think to ask the devil for nothing more than youth and pleasure, and who is all too willing to take him up on his offer, no strings attached. Little wonder that Richard Wagner, among many German artists at the time, decried Gounod's opera as a desecration of one of the greatest masterpieces of German literature. But such criticisms miss the point of what adaptation from literature to music is all about. Gounod's simplification of his main character is no mistake, but rather the product of a transposition across genres that forces the composer to evaluate which aspects of his characters will survive the translation into a new medium—one with an inherently different set of communicative strengths—and which will not. Opera audiences simply have to accept that the musical Faust is not the same character as the one known from Goethe's drama.

In 1859 Gounod's new opera marked a sharp departure from the kinds of theatrical musical entertainments that were prominent in Paris at that time. After his early failures with grand opera, Gounod tried something entirely new with his adaptation of *Faust*. Instead of the usual broad historical drama that pitted one nation or ethnic/religious group against another, supported with spectacular scenery, grand processions, pantomimes, and elaborate ballets, *Faust* is an opera of human interest, cast on a much more intimate scale. As premiered in 1859, the opera actually contained spoken dialogue as in an opéra comique. Only later, in 1860 did Gounod redress *Faust* in full serious attire by adding sung recitatives for productions abroad, and later, in 1869, further bulking up the work with a ballet for the Paris Opéra. But all along he felt unconstrained by the various operatic traditions of serious French opera. The first of these conventions to be abandoned was that of the opening chorus. In fact, it was not just French grand opera, but nearly every Italian and German serious opera as well, that began with a de rigueur chorus, leading directly to an "entrance aria" for one of the main characters. Gounod's elimination of the traditional opening chorus in *Faust* was, to be sure, the result of the fact that Goethe's play presents a choral opportunity not at the very beginning, but slightly later, after Faust has introduced himself and pronounced his various complaints about life. In following that sequence of events, Gounod arrived at a musical structure for his opening scene that he described as a *scène et choeur* (a scene leading to a chorus). This terminology usually implies a musical number in a flexible arioso style. But in keeping with a French tradition of vocal writing dating all the way back to Lully (seventeenth century), the arioso style frequently leads to short sections of more melodic vocal writing that sound like an excerpt from an aria. This flexible arioso at the beginning of the scene eventually leads to the chorus that everyone would have expected. The whole scene might be diagramed as follows:

Opening *scène et choeur.*

ARIOSO
Rien! En vain j'interroge en mon
  ardente veille
La nature et le Créateur;
Pas une voix ne glisse à mon oreille
Un mot consolateur!

ARIOSO
Nothing! In vain I question, in my
  sleeplessness
Nature and the Creator;
No voice mummers in my ear
A word of consolation!

MELODY
J'ai langui triste, et solitaire,
Sans pouvoir brisser le lien
Qui m'attache encore à la terre!
Je ne vois rien! Je ne sais rien!

MELODY
I have pined, sad and lonely
Unable to break the shackles
That bind me still to the earth!
I see nothing! I know nothing!

ARIOSO
Le ciel pâlit! Devant l'aube
  nouvelle
La sombre nuit s'évanouit!
Encore un jour! Encore un jour
  qui luit!
O mort, quand viendras-tu
M'abriter sous ton aile?
Eh bien! Puisque la mort me fuit,
Pourquoi n'irais-je pas vers elle?

ARIOSO
The sky lightens! Before the
  new dawn
The dark night disappears!
Another day! Another day
  brightens!
O death, when will you come
To shelter me under your wing?
Well then! If death avoids me,
Why should I not go to it?

MELODY
Salut, ô mon dernier matin!
J'arrive sans terreur
Au terme du voyage;
Et je suis, avec ce breuvage,
Le seul maître de mon destin!

MELODY
Hail, o my last morning!
I arrive without terror
At the end of my journey;
And, with this drink, I am
The sole master of my destiny!

CHORUS OF YOUNG GIRLS
Ah! Paresseuse fille
Qui sommeille encor!
Déjà le jour brille
Sous son manteau d'or.

CHORUS OF YOUNG GIRLS
Ah! Lazy girl
Who still sleeps
Already day breaks
Under its cloak of gold.

This alternation of arioso and lyrical melody in Faust's part is clearly audible and easy to see in the score.

Example 12-1. Faust's opening solo.

The process of musical adaptation, which Gounod undertook in this opera, often resulted in the rearrangement of the order of events from Goethe's drama. One such alteration of the original sequence of events occurs here at the beginning of the opera, where Mephistopheles conjures up a vision of Marguerite to seduce Faust into signing away his soul. This mirage is part of a later scene in Goethe's play, but is dramatically well placed here in a duet between Faust and Mephistopheles, where, in the absence of the more complex and abstract reasons set out in Goethe's play, it helps to establish a concrete and simple motivation for Faust's rash decision to sell his soul to the devil. The duet ends with both characters singing about the expectation of pleasure that Mephistopheles has promised Faust. This kind of duet, in which two male characters (usually a tenor and a baritone) bond in an alliance of mutual support, is usually known as a "friendship duet." Such duets appear frequently in nineteenth-century opera. But this one is unusual in its ironic implications, as Mephistopheles is operating here as a false friend of Faust, despite what the music might be trying to suggest. Here the process of adaptation results in the creation of a new level of dramatic understanding, as Gounod's music brings to the situation new shades of insight into the agreement that Faust is about to conclude with the devil. As usual, music takes us beyond the literal meaning of printed or spoken words, into a world of emotional connotation.

Act 2 begins the series of adventures on which Mephistopheles takes Faust. It is at this point in the drama that Gounod introduces Valentin (Marguerite's brother), a character drawn directly from the play. But his introduction into the opera at this very early stage of the drama constitutes a reworking of the play, in which he is not seen until much later, when he confronts Faust as the villain who has ruined his sister's reputation. His far earlier placement in the opera is a clever restructuring of the play that allowed Gounod to use music to develop the relationship between brother and sister by giving Valentin an aria ("Avant de quitter ces lieux") in which he announces that he is abandoning Marguerite to go off to war, but calls on God to defend her in his absence.

Example 12-2. Valentin, "Avant de quitter ces lieux."

Gounod originally planned for the part of Valentin to be much larger, including a duet with Marguerite and an additional aria.[2] But even in its reduced form, this *comprimario* role represents an emotional expansion of a character who in the play functions in an almost completely subservient capacity. Such deviations from the original source material usually arise from the differing needs of spoken and sung media. In the world of opera, a composer may find a potentially musical moment in one of the minor characters of the drama, thus allowing himself the freedom to express emotions not necessarily found in the original spoken drama. In this way, the adaptation becomes a work with an identity all its own, rather than just a musical version of the original model.

Act 3 contains some of the opera's greatest and most famous musical numbers—four of them in close proximity. All of these are arias, and all serve to underline the manner in which music can be used easily to bring to our collective consciousness the real emotions that underlie the dramatic events of a spoken play. The scene begins with Siebel, a teenage boy enamored of Marguerite, showing up at her house with a bouquet of flowers. As he does, he sings the famous aria "Faites lui mes aveux." In Goethe's play, Siebel appears only as part of the scene in Auerbach's tavern. Gounod's librettists have given him an entirely new role in the opera, one

---

2. Giroud, 2010, 177.

that presents Faust with a rival lover, and in the process, intensifies the drama. Musically, Siebel is interesting because his role is sung by a woman, continuing the eighteenth-century tradition of casting very young men as "trouser roles" for mezzo-sopranos.

The next characters to appear in this scene are Faust and Mephistopheles, who have come for essentially the same purpose as Siebel: to leave a little gift—only theirs is a box of jewels. As he stands outside Marguerite's cottage (while she is not at home), Faust sings his show-stopping aria, "Salut demeure chaste et pure," giving expression to his reverence for the simple purity and sanctity of the place she calls home. This particular aria exemplifies one of the major differences between French and Italian opera in the mid-nineteenth century. Italian composers, long devoted to the art of beautiful, decorative singing, preferred to structure their arias in a form they called the cavatina-cabaletta, an aria type that included a slow, lyrical opening section of music followed by a fast, florid conclusion. (See chapter 4 for details.) In this formula, the second section was always repeated to allow the singer opportunity to ornament the vocal line and thereby to show off his or her technique, an essential part of Italian bel canto singing. The new French style of Gounod's opéra lyrique is far simpler, with melodies that are less ornate, almost folklike in style, and with no dramatically irrelevant improvisation. This simplicity is at least partly responsible for the broad appeal and lasting popularity of *Faust*. Gounod's melodies have a powerful, immediate attractiveness and a simple expressivity that differ from the ornate decorativeness of the Italian bel canto style that had been popular in Paris ever since the 1820s, when Rossini's operas were first produced at the Théâtre-Italien. Gounod's melodies call less attention to the singers, and more attention to the music itself.

Example 12-3. Faust's aria, "Salut! demeure chaste et pure."

When Marguerite returns, she sings two memorable solo numbers. The first, taken directly from Goethe's text, is her "Ballad of the King of Thulé," sung as she muses over the strange young man (Faust) whom she met earlier in the day. In the context of his play, Goethe actually intended this text to be sung, but to what kind of music we do not know. It thus functions as a song within a play, and gives a composer of opera a wonderful opportunity to make real what the reader of Goethe's play can only imagine. Here in Gounod's adaptation, this same text now becomes a song within an opera, which is to say, a song within a song. Scenes in which characters sing something that is meant to be a *song* are fairly common in opera, the most usual being some kind of serenade sung under the bedroom window of a young lady. Usually these "embedded songs" are of pivotal importance to an opera's plot. While this particular song is a lovely little ballad, its importance lies in the fact that it is a wonderful instance of musical/dramatic irony. The ballad is about a king who remains true to the memory of his beloved right to his grave. Such fidelity, of course, is not what Marguerite is going to experience with Faust; and the contrast between her life and her song provides a poignant effect.

Finally Marguerite discovers the box of jewels left by Faust and Mephistopheles, and is overcome with excitement. As she tries them on, she sings her famous "Jewel Song." This is as close to an Italianate vocal display piece as Gounod ever gets in this opera, and it perfectly captures the giddy, bubbling enthusiasm of a young girl who just can't control her desire to be decked out in all this finery.

Example 12-4. Marguerite's "Jewel Song."

Gounod sticks close to his literary model with the next scene in which Mephistopheles and Faust meet up with Marguerite and her neighbor Martha. In Goethe's telling of the story, Mephistopheles distracts Martha long enough for Faust to engage Marguerite in a tender conversation. In keeping with Goethe, Gounod breaks this scene into an alternating pair of conversations, or in musical terms, two duets: Mephistopheles and Martha on one side, Faust and Marguerite on the other. In the opera, as one might expect, Gounod eventually allows the four characters to sing together as a quartet, before leading into a final love duet between Faust and Marguerite. The big difference between Gounod's version of this scene and Goethe's again comes down to a matter of simplification. In the opera, the scene ends with Faust having completely captivated Marguerite, and the curtain falling on the two of them in a passionate embrace that suggests the possibility of love making to follow. Again, the play is far less directly suggestive, ending this scene with the lovers simply parting company and promising to meet again. In this way, Goethe is even less clear than Gounod about the exact moment when Faust and Marguerite finally consummate their love. A hint, perhaps, occurs in the very next scene of the play where we see Faust in a vast wooded cavern communing with Nature to sooth his troubled soul. As he speaks to God, we discover the source of his problem:

> And busily he fans within my bosom
> A seething fire for that radiant image.
> I stagger from desire to enjoyment,
> And in its throes I starve for more desire. (3247–50)

Mephistopheles enters and ridicules Faust's weakness, and by suggestion the reader is given to understand that Faust has not seen Marguerite since their passion peaked and then cooled. Mephistopheles says:

> At first your passion rose and overflowed
> As when a brook will swell from melting snow;
> You poured it all into her bosom,
> And now the brook runs dry again. (3307–10)

By implication much has happened that Goethe hasn't told or shown his audience. In an opera, where direct raw emotional expression is essential, such ambiguity courts disaster. So Gounod's revision, in which he shows his audience (or at least suggests to them) the fateful moment of sexual union, makes perfect sense. But one advantage to Goethe's original should not be overlooked: in this cavern scene (which, by the way, Gounod did not set to music), not only are we told directly that Faust has lost interest in Marguerite, but we are also told why, something the opera never makes clear. In this scene Faust says to Mephistopheles,

> Do I not every moment feel her woe? . . .
> It was her life, her peace I had to ruin.
> You, Satan, claimed this sacrifice! (3347, 3360–61)

There it is: Faust is ashamed of his behavior (behavior to which we were never privy) and of the fact that he no longer desires Marguerite, and he avoids her to assuage this guilt, mistakenly thinking that he is doing a good deed for the sake of her reputation.

The omission of this important "cavern scene" from the opera creates a bit of a problem as Gounod moves on to the next scene, Marguerite's famous spinning song. Here at the beginning of the opera's fourth act, she sits alone in her room at her spinning wheel, lamenting the fact that Faust has not returned. In the play, we already know that he has abandoned her, and we know why; but here in the opera, his absence takes us by surprise. One wants to stop the show and ask, "Wait, what happened? Weren't they in love just before the last intermission?" This is the unfortunate result of the kind of drastic pruning necessary to transfer literature to the operatic stage, where singing takes more time than speaking, and details in the original have to be sacrificed to keep the opera to a manageable duration.

Gounod's decision not to include the cavern scene, in which the answer to this question is revealed, highlights another danger of making huge cuts when adapting great literature to the operatic stage. Without our knowing why Faust abandoned Marguerite, the operatic hero now seems to have taken on an altered character—one with the less appealing demeanor of a cad or a rake who has taken advantage of an innocent young woman. He looks like a remorseless villain, and as a result the audience is less likely to have much sympathy for him. Of course this could be good or bad, depending on what the composer wants his audience to feel about Faust as a person. In Gounod's case, this alteration may have been as much a deliberate calculation as it was an adaptational necessity—a theory to which I will return later.

Marguerite's spinning song, like her ballad of the king of Thulé, is adapted almost literally from Goethe's play. As a musical text, these words were already well known from the setting Schubert gave them some forty years earlier in his lied "Gretchen am Spinnrade," an unsurpassed model of musical anxiety. (See Example 9-3, page 144.) Its hypnotically repeating piano accompaniment circles continually around one note, clearly representing the ever turning spinning wheel, while the short breathless melodic phrases of the vocal part capture the nervous expectation and emotional anguish in Gretchen's heart.

In many ways, Gounod's aria, written on a text that was adapted from Goethe's words, attempts to communicate the same idea of a spinning wheel, especially in its orchestral accompaniment. (See Example 9-4, page 145.) But overall, the mood of Gounod's aria feels more subdued, as though the heroine were less panicked about her situation. The melody makes a longer phrase and flows more smoothly than does Schubert's song.

At this point in the drama, the play and opera again diverge. In the opera, the audience has already seen Faust and Marguerite come together, and now learns of his abandonment of her. By act 4, everything points to the complete and irreversible absence of Faust. Gounod's next scene then brings Siebel back to the stage to comfort Marguerite and to swear to avenge the wrongs done to her by her absent lover. Even though this reappearance of Siebel is nowhere to be found in Goethe, it makes sense for this particular operatic adaptation in that it keeps Faust in an unsympathetic position with the audience—an intentional gesture by Gounod, the motivation for which will become clear shortly. But the original play is quite different. After the spinning song, Goethe immediately brings Faust back for another meeting with Marguerite. It is here that the play further confuses an audience on the question of whether Faust and Marguerite have yet consummated their love. Faust says to Marguerite:

> Oh, shall I never hang upon your bosom one short hour,
> Pressing breast on breast, my soul into your soul? (3502–4)

To which she responds:

> Oh, if I only slept alone,
> I should gladly leave the door unlatched tonight,
> But mother's slumber is not deep,
> And if she ever found us there together,
> I should die in terror on the spot. (3505–9)

This makes it seem as though the moment of consummation has perhaps not yet occurred, but Faust's communion with Nature in the earlier cavern scene hinted at just the opposite. Such ambiguity about the connection between Faust and Marguerite that we find in the play would never work on an operatic stage, where dramatic ambiguity is a formula for confusion, and confusion can be the cause of failed productions.

At this point in the play, Faust gives Marguerite a sleeping potion with which to put her mother to sleep so that he may return later for their romantic tryst. As a result of Faust's return to Marguerite, one might see Goethe's version of this character as less of a callous cad than the same character in Gounod's opera. According to Goethe, Faust and

Mephistopheles return to Marguerite's house for their romantic tryst, but as they do, they are intercepted by Marguerite's brother, Valentin, who has returned home from the war (his first appearance in the play). He challenges Faust to a duel, and is mortally wounded in the fight that ensues. Faust runs off, and Valentin dies in his sister's arms, but not before he curses her for the shame she has brought on herself and their family. Faced with this tragedy, Marguerite runs to church, where she seeks absolution. But there an evil spirit confronts her with threats of eternal damnation, on top of which a choir is heard singing parts of the requiem Mass, "And when the judge shall sit, whatsoever is hidden shall be manifest, and naught shall remain unavenged." Little wonder the poor girl faints straightaway.

Gounod, like Goethe, also brings Faust back to visit Marguerite, but delays his arrival along with the murder of Valentin until after her episode in church. Thus, in the opera, her reason for being in church seems to be just to seek forgiveness for her sexual transgressions. Only after this does she watch her brother die, and then really have something for which to ask forgiveness. This perplexing reversal of the order of events as found in Goethe's play was not part of Gounod's original plan for the opera, but arose out of revisions that were made in 1862 for an Italian production at La Scala. Although the reversal of these scenes may seem dramatically wrong-headed, this revision does serve the operatic purpose of delaying the return of Faust to Marguerite, which in turn continues to make him a less sympathetic character than Goethe's Faust.

The end of both opera and play comes with the Walpurgis Night scene, which then leads to the final scene in prison. In folk legend, Walpurgis Night was the night when witches gathered on Mount Brocken (the highest peak in the German Harz mountains) to hold an orgy of evil spirits. This is where Mephistopheles brings Faust, in an attempt to help him forget Marguerite. Here Gounod added the large scenic ballet that was required for any production at the Opéra. The inclusion of such a ballet in the original version of the opera would have been out of keeping with Gounod's intent to prune the size of grand opera and make it more personal, and incompatible with his original use of spoken dialogue in the opera. Somewhere in the middle of this ballet orgy, Faust sees a vision of Marguerite in prison, is suddenly struck with guilt, and demands that Mephistopheles help save her from execution. Accordingly, they mount two horses and charge off to the rescue, with Gounod's music for the frenetic flight of the horses striking just the right mood of fear and anxiety. The breakneck tempo, along with the repeated triplets, captures the feeling of furiously galloping horses.

Example 12-5. The ride to prison.

Faust and Mephistopheles arrive at the prison to find Marguerite jailed for having accidentally caused the death of her mother with repeated ministrations of the sleeping potion that Faust suggested she use to keep the old lady out of the way while they made love. This final prison scene is an example of Gounod's drama-making at its best. Here we see how music can clarify the emotions implicit in a text. By the time Faust finds Marguerite in her prison cell, she has already lost her mind. Such mad scenes are common in opera of the nineteenth century, where their dramatic raison d'être always seems to be to elicit sympathy for the heroine who has been mistreated and consequently lost touch with reality. Gounod's portrayal of Marguerite's madness is extremely effective. Her first response to the voice of Faust is excitement leading to a sweet melody that implies a happy ending.

Example 12-6. Marguerite, prison scene.

But Marguerite, who clearly does not understand why Faust is there and what his intentions are, fails to seize the opportunity to flee. Finally, Mephistopheles intervenes to move things along, but Marguerite recognizes him as the agent of evil, and commends her soul to heaven. This final trio has a magical fervor about it, a sense of triumph in the music as Marguerite sings the lines "Pure and radiant angels carry my soul to heaven." Gounod has her repeat this melodic phrase three times, always one step higher in pitch and slightly louder in dynamics. The urgency of this rising sequence and the nobility of the melodic line combine to create a feeling of radiant triumph as Marguerite "falls lifeless" (as the libretto says) and her soul is transported to heaven.

Example 12-7. Trio finale.

Despite what most nineteenth-century Germans, such as Wagner, thought about Gounod's recasting of Goethe's *Faust*, the opera is actually one of the most successful musical adaptations of a literary masterpiece. In typical operatic fashion, Gounod seems to have been most concerned with the fate of his heroine, not his hero. This adaptational shift of emphasis is most likely the result of the fact that sopranos have always been the favored voices in opera ever since its inception over 400 years ago, and, as a result, a musical version of a stage drama will often focus most of its attention (i.e., the great arias) on the prima donna. Like so many other nineteenth-century operatic heroines, Marguerite is a sacrificial victim whose death is necessary for the hero to live on and to be redeemed in some manner (although in *Faust* this is not immediately apparent because his association with the devil carries on into Goethe's part 2). To shift the dramatic weight of the work to his heroine, Gounod and his librettists were forced to give prominence to some of the minor characters around her—Siebel and Valentin—thereby adding depth to Marguerite's character. The other primary change from Goethe's original play involves Gounod's early withdrawal of Faust from contact with Marguerite. This abandonment (which is not nearly so severe in the play) is another way in which the composer was able to shift sympathy toward his heroine, by making the hero seem more callous than Goethe perhaps intended. So it is possible that in Gounod's adaptation of this great piece of German literature, most of the changes to the original source were made not just to produce the textual excisions necessary to simplify a complex drama of ideas into an opera of feelings (i.e., to suit a spoken drama to the strengths of a new sung medium), but were also motivated by the conventional need of opera in the nineteenth century to feature the sacrificial heroine and to elicit audience sympathy for her plight. Composers as disparate as Berlioz, Verdi, Wagner, Gounod, and Bizet all created operas in which their heroines expire for the purpose of effecting a necessary emotional catharsis (or at least a symbolic release of responsibility) in their male counterparts. (See the chapter on Verdi's *Rigoletto* and Massenet's *Manon* for a further discussion of this theme of the sacrificial female in opera.)

All operatic adaptations of literature recast the original in various ways in order to make the expression of the underlying dramatic theme of the work transmittable to a musical medium. Vast amounts of text, complex ideas of an abstract nature, dramatic ambiguity, and convoluted plots are all incompatible with the direct expression of operatic emotions associated with individual human contacts and confrontations. It would be a great mistake to judge Gounod's *Faust*, or any other such literary adaptation, on the basis of its fidelity to the original drama. Instead, the success of a musical version of a stage play or other piece of dramatic literature must be based on an evaluation of the music's ability to capture the emotional essence of the original without regard to the retention of details of plot and characters. By this measure, Gounod's *Faust* is as much a success in its own terms as is Goethe's drama.

CHAPTER 13

Theoretically speaking, Massenet's *Manon* is a comic opera, conceived for and premiered at the Paris Opéra-Comique. This simple fact helps to explain some of the opera's peculiarities, but also demands further exploration, since there is clearly little that is comic about this opera.

From the very beginning of the history of French opera in the early seventeenth century, there had always been two distinctly different kinds of opera, one serious, the other comic. In the nineteenth century these two types were distinguished partly on the basis of subject matter and partly on the basis of other technical features. By the time Massenet came to write *Manon* (first performed in 1884), many of the features that had traditionally distinguished serious from comic opera in France had been abandoned, thanks mostly to Bizet's *Carmen*, which revolutionized the Opéra-Comique in 1875. By that time, only the use of spoken dialogue continued as a basic unalterable tradition of comic opera in France. As a result, even an opera as untraditional as *Carmen* originally appeared at this theater with the requisite spoken dialogue.

By the time Massenet began composing *Manon*, the use of spoken dialogue at the Opéra-Comique had finally become more an option than a requirement, thus leaving the door open to its elimination in favor of a full musical setting for this new opera. Such a setting would have avoided the jarring disruption caused by the continual alternation between speaking and singing found in earlier opéra comique. But for unknown reasons, Massenet settled on a clever compromise in deciding how to handle the libretto's dialogue: he retained the spoken dialogue, but set it over an orchestral accompaniment. This combination of speech and instrumental music was known in France as *mélodrame*, a technique that had already been used as a special vocal style in many earlier nineteenth-century opéras comiques, and even in Beethoven's *Fidelio*. The use of *mélodrame* lends the opera the impression of greater musical continuity demanded by contemporary operatic aesthetics. Other deviations from the traditional opéra comique model include Massenet's borrowing of techniques from French grand opera, including the use of large choruses to depict crowd scenes, and the use of a decorative ballet, both of which play an important role in *Manon*. In short, we might say that *Manon* is the product of several new trends in French opera at the end of the century, blending the intimacy of comic opera with the tragedy and realism of serious opera.

Many of the operas that make up the what we know today as the "basic repertoire" began life as some form of literature (usually either a play or a novel) that was then adapted for use as a sung libretto. The art of making an opera out of a novel is similar to the art of making a movie out of a novel. Each genre is vastly different, and the process of adaptation is always an imperfect one requiring alterations and compromises. Such is the case with *Manon*, based on a novel by the Abbé Prévost (1697–1763) which originally appeared under the title *Histoire du Chevalier Des Grieux et de Manon Lescaut* (itself the seventh volume of an extended work titled *Mémoires d'un homme de qualité*). It was clearly intended, as can be deduced from the title, to be about the relationship between its two principal characters. In this original version, Manon is a young girl who loves the good life, meets a young gentleman (Des Grieux) who falls in love with her but cannot afford to keep her in the style she so desperately desires, so she abandons him. He in turn remains endlessly faithful, if also eternally dejected, right to the bitter end, at which point we find the heroine arrested and deported as a "*fille perdue*" to Louisiana, where she dies. The story is told from the point of view of the hero who is, according to Prévost, an ambiguous character who manifests a mixture of virtues and vices over which he has no control. This perspective causes the author to lavish much more attention on building a complex psychological image of Des Grieux than he does of Manon.

As is well known, the nineteenth century saw the production of one other famous opera on this story, Puccini's *Manon Lescaut* of 1893, and one less well-known opera with the same title written in 1856 by Daniel-François-Esprit Auber.[1] Because the Auber opera is not one that readers might encounter in the active repertoire, this chapter focuses only on the two better-known versions of Prévost's story, both of which can still be found in production and recordings. These operas (Massenet's and Puccini's) follow the general outline of Prévost's novel fairly closely. But

---

1. In 1894 Massenet wrote a one-act sequel to *Manon* called *Le portrait de Manon*. This little opera has never achieved any success, and has nothing to do with Prévost's novel on which the other Manon operas are based. And in 1952, Grete Weil adapted Prévost's story for a one-act opera by Hans Werner Henze titled *Boulevard Solitude*.

both composers' musical adaptations make some important changes in the original, the nature of which determines the measure of success that each of these works has achieved over the years. First among these was the simplification, for operatic purposes, of the title of Prévost's novel to *Manon* or *Manon Lescaut* (for Massenet and Puccini, respectively). Granted, the original title was too long for an opera, but the change of title also suggests a shift of emphasis designed to focus attention on the heroine at the expense of the hero (although this is less true of Puccini's opera than Massenet's). Some critics charge that in making this change, both composers (Massenet, especially) created for themselves some immense problems that undermined the potential success of their works by focusing attention on a character for whom there can be little sympathy, simply because she is a superficial, amoral, manipulative, narcissist whose ultimate demise seems well deserved. They argue that because the death of such a character would never arouse a great deal of sympathy with audiences, any opera focused primarily on this heroine would suffer accordingly. On the other hand, those who understood the business of opera might claim just the opposite: that in concentrating so heavily on Manon, Massenet made a brilliant adaptational choice by correctly recognizing that opera audiences were much more interested in ambiguous female characters than in ambiguous male characters, and that his musical portrayal of Manon captures the essence of the conflicts she suffers as a heroine of "mixed virtues and vices" (to borrow Prévost's description of Des Grieux). When Massenet wrote *Manon*, he had already begun, with the part of Salomé in *Hérodiade* (1881), what was to become a full gallery of provocative female portraits in music. Manon is just another in a long line of women who are partly good and partly bad, who are both innocent and worldly, and who (as the French composer Vincent D'Indy observed) are marked by a "pseudo-religious eroticism." In the hands of either composer, Manon had the potential, if given the right music, to become a character who could draw tears from an audience that might choose to see her as yet another example of nineteenth-century opera's "sacrificial female" (the victimized woman whose fate is to die).

To better understand the problems that Massenet and Puccini created for themselves in choosing to concentrate the opera on Manon, we need to examine the difference between their opera librettos and the novel on which they were based. For this purpose the chart on the following pages sketches the plot of Prévost's novel in comparison with the action of these two most famous Manon operas.

COMPARISON OF PRÉVOST'S NOVEL WITH OPERAS OF MASSENET AND PUCCINI

PRÉVOST	MASSENET	PUCCINI
	ACT I	ACT I
Des Grieux (DG) meets Manon (M) on her way to a convent. He falls in love and convinces her to run off to Paris with him.	Manon's coach arrives and she is accosted by the wealthy old Guillot who has designs on her. She then meets Des Grieux, who falls in love and convinces M to run off with him to avoid the convent.	Manon's coach arrives. She is admired by the wealthy old Geronte who plans to abduct her. Des Grieux sees her and falls in love. He learns of the abduction plan and convinces M to run off with him to save herself from Geronte.
	ACT II	
While living with DG, M is beguiled into accepting an older suitor to help pay her extravagant bills. (Little is said about how she feels here.)	M is living with DG when she is told that DG will be abducted. If she warns him he will be disinherited, but if she stays quiet a rich lover will be hers.	
	ACT III	ACT II
DG's father abducts him and tells him about the other lover. DG prepares to enter the priesthood in an attempt to forget M.	M begins living with Brétigny, but is totally bored. She meets DG's father and hears that DG is taking holy orders and has forgotten her by now.	M is now living with Geronte after having left DG. She is totally bored and longs for news of DG.
M hears about his new life and comes to get him back. She is repentant. He is won over and abandons the Church for M.	Incensed by the thought that she could be forgotten, M goes to St. Sulpice to seduce DG, who quickly abandons his vows.	M's brother tells DG that M is asking about him. He goes to Geronte's home to get her back.
	ACT IV	
They begin living together again. But the need for money to support M leads DG to take up cheating at cards.	In order to support their new lifestyle, M coaxes DG into gambling. Guillot accuses DG of cheating, and then calls the police to have M and DG arrested. DG is released quickly, but M is ordered deported to Louisiana.	Before making their escape together, M gathers up all of Geronte's jewels. She is caught by Geronte and arrested and sentenced to deportation to Louisiana.
They are financially ruined when servants steal all they have saved.		
M's brother suggests she take another lover to make back their fortune. She agrees. DG follows after her and convinces her to steal her lover's money and return home with him. But the old man has them arrested.		

DG escapes and then rescues M from jail. They begin living together again.		
The son of M's older suitor falls in love with her. She and DG plan to cheat him, but DG is devastated when M chooses to stay with the new lover.		
DG goes to get her back. She agrees to steal what they can before leaving with DG.		
Their plan is discovered and they are arrested again. DG's father gets him out of jail, but M is ordered deported to Louisana.		
	ACT V	**ACT III**
DG plans a rescue attack on the deportation convoy, but his men lose heart and flee. He decides to board ship and follow M to America.	DG bribes a soldier who is escorting M to deportation, but he finds her near death. M dies begging forgiveness, remembering happier days of love.	DG plans to rescue M from jail. When this fails, he pleads to be allowed to follow M to America.
Pretending to be married (so that they can remain together), M and DG begin a new respectable life in New Orleans. DG ingratiates himself with the governor and is appointed to a minor civil job.		
DG decides to formalize their relationship by admitting to the governor that he and M are not really married, but want to be.		
		ACT IV
The governor claims the right to give M away to whomever he decides, just as he did with all the other deportees. He awards her to his nephew, who has long been attracted to M.		Now living in New Orleans, M and DG have to get out of town (because of the duel not shown).
DG and the nephew duel. The nephew falls lifeless, and DG realizes he and M must get out of town.		
They escape into the vast wilderness fearful of the savages, wild beasts, barren plains, and forbidding mountains. M becomes truly remorseful about the suffering she has caused and how unworthy she is of DG's love. She dies. He buries her and waits for death himself.		They cross an arid plain. M is weak and close to death. DG goes off to look for help. While he is gone, M laments her fate. When DG returns, M reminds him of her love. She dies in his arms.
The nephew turns out not to have died. So a search party is mounted to find DG and M. He is rescued close to death.		

This chart demonstrates that the Manon of Prévost's novel allows her greed to undermine nearly every opportunity she has to either stay with, or return to, Des Grieux. Despite her continual avowals of true love, her selfishness causes her eagerly to trade Des Grieux for anyone with greater wealth, without giving her betrayal a second thought. He, however, is no less pitiful. Despite continual abandonment, he never ceases to want Manon and to take her back. He suffers from a blind, desperate love, for which he sacrifices honor, decency, and reputation. Like the classic victim of spousal abuse, Des Grieux is powerless to escape the bonds that hold him to this woman. Only at the end of the novel do we see a transformed Manon who, in the final scenes in Louisiana, is depicted as completely reformed. She renounces the "good life" to live simply with her eternally faithful lover in New Orleans. Before she dies, she appears truly remorseful, not for her own bitter situation, but for the injury she has brought upon Des Grieux. She impresses us with a sincere expression of her unworthiness of his undying love, and her death in this light feels truly tragic and emotionally moving.

As is also clear in the chart, both the operas of Massenet and Puccini contain only a small portion of the events from the novel. We therefore get a much more circumscribed view of Manon in the opera house than in the pages of Prévost's novel. One might think this a boon for the opera, since most of what we see of her in the novel is totally unpleasant. The author builds a portrait of a thoughtless, careless, callous, amoral hedonist whom almost no one could like. In reality, however, it is the power of this unattractive image that makes Manon's final transformation at the end of the novel so effective. In being forced to cut so much of her literary depiction to make an opera of acceptable length, the librettists for both composers seriously jeopardized the success of their musical adaptations. Neither Puccini nor Massenet could lavish such extreme detail on the heroine, so their depictions of her amoral qualities suffer from this lack of accumulating detail and its resulting dramatic weakness. Consequently the final transformation of character necessary to make the drama effective has less to play against, and thus less chance to overwhelm us with its tragic significance. Operas always suffer from this lack of detail when adapting great literature to the sung stage, but what makes opera succeed in these circumstances, and against these odds, is always the power of music to define character, to add another dimension to our understanding of human personalities. The better the composer is at building character through music, the greater the chance that his operatic adaptation will succeed on its own terms.

Beginning from this premise, a closer examination of both operas will reveal how these two different composers struggled with the difficulties of making Prévost's novel into an effective piece of musical drama. The question with which we want to grapple is how a librettist-composer team facing the need to compress considerable narrative detail into a few essential scenes can still manage to capture the essence of a tragic chain of events that will draw from an audience a genuine sense of sympathy for the fate of a central victim. Act 1 in each of these operas is similar: the arrival of the coach carrying Manon, her encounter with a wealthy older admirer, her first meeting with Des Grieux, and her decision to run off with him. But the disposition of the musical numbers in these two operas is markedly different, reflecting completely opposite approaches to adapting Prévost's novel. The focus of Massenet's act 1 is solely on Manon. She has two arias and a big duet with Des Grieux in which important aspects of her personality are depicted. Her first aria ("Je suis encore tout étourdie") introduces us to a timid ingenue. Its musical style is melodically tentative and harmonically simple, as befits this aspect of her character. But a little further on we encounter a second aria ("Voyons, Manon, plus de chimères") that explores another side of Manon's character: the conflict she experiences between her impending life in a convent and her hedonistic love of the good life. Both of these arias are examples of ingenious musical inference drawn by reading between the lines of Prévost's novel. In telling his story from Des Grieux's point of view, Prévost actually gives the reader very little insight into Manon's character, at least here at the beginning of his story. Of course, as a novelist, he can afford to be leisurely about this; he has, after all, 250 pages in which to develop these insights. Composers have much less time in which to draw characters on the operatic stage.

Puccini's opera, on the other hand, follows Prévost's novel more closely in focusing the main attention (at least here at the beginning) on Des Grieux rather than on Manon. In act 1, the hero is the first one to sing an aria: one in which he mocks his own inability to find true love. Manon, by contrast, is introduced only in the context of the following duet with Des Grieux, a musical number that allows her little room for self-revelation. Then Des Grieux has another aria in which he reacts to his meeting with Manon; "I never met a woman like this before," he says. Although these arias communicate a good sense of the hero, Manon remains something of a mystery at the outset of Puccini's opera.

Moving to Massenet's act 2, we hear another important aria for Manon, "Adieu notre petite table," which she sings after being informed that if she does not leave Des Grieux, his father will disinherit him and they will havenothing to live on. Whether she agrees to this separation because she is genuinely concerned about being the cause of Des Grieux's loss of fortune, or whether she is actually coaxed away by her own fear of poverty, is not entirely clear from the libretto. This is one of those operatic situations where only the composer's music can help clarify the meaning of a dramatic moment. For this occasion Massenet wrote an aria of hymnlike simplicity, almost a prayer that suggests some kind of religious sacrifice on Manon's part (Ex. 13-1).

Example 13-1. Manon's "Adieu, notre petite table."

Massenet's music builds some sympathy for Manon by suggesting a genuine regret on her part for the fact that she must leave Des Grieux. Here again these sentiments are the invention of the librettists and the composer, not of Prévost, who gives us no insight into any possible conflicts Manon might have felt over choosing to leave Des Grieux.

In Puccini's version of this story, there is no scene in which we see Manon and Des Grieux living together. Puccini moves instead directly to a scene in the home of her new wealthy "patron," Geronte, where Manon is now living in splendor after having abandoned Des Grieux. In a duet with her brother,[2] we learn that she is totally bored with her majestic lifestyle and

---

2. In Massenet's opera, this character of Manon's male relative is a cousin, not a brother.

is eager for news of her former lover. Part of this duet is given over to a large solo section for Manon (one of her most significant solos in the opera), in which she expresses regret over having left a true love for meaningless riches. Although we are not privy to why she left Des Grieux, this solo (some analysts call it an aria) does lead us by implication to believe that whatever the reason, it must have been something beyond her control, for now she seems only to miss him.

In Massenet's opera this scene of Manon living the bored but elegant life with the older lover appears at the beginning of act 3. Her entrance here is marked by another major solo number, "Je marche sur tous les chemins," which exposes yet another unattractive aspect of her character: that of the self-centered narcissist. Lines such as, "I consent, seeing that I'm so good, to allow you to admire my charming person" and "People bow, they kiss my hand, because I am a queen by my beauty," betray a personality of total self-absorption and unhappiness. This aria might well remind listeners of Marguerite's famous "Jewel Song" in Gounod's *Faust*. It is self-consciously brilliant, full of sparkling orchestration and vocal roulades and *fioriture* that seem to say, "Look at me—I'm beautiful" (Ex. 13-2).

Example 13-2. Manon's "Je marche sur tous les chemins."

This is Manon at her superficial worst. Unlike the innocent Marguerite who seems almost embarrassed by the attractiveness of the jewels she has found, Manon sounds genuinely impressed with herself—"Par la beauté je suis reine," she sings. While the music is attractive, her character is not.

Next in Massenet's version of the story, Manon encounters Des Grieux's father and discovers that his son is about to take holy orders in the aftermath of her departure. Manon becomes obsessed with the fear that she has been forgotten, something her narcissistic personality cannot tolerate. So she sets out to ensnare the hapless chevalier once again. In the wonderful scene set at the church of St. Sulpice, Manon tracks down Des Grieux in an attempt to dissuade him from the rash action he is about to undertake. The duet between them contains a major soloistic part in which she sings in a style full of seduction, recalling that great French operatic femme fatale, Carmen. With this irresistible music, (the theme of which will return at the tragic conclusion of the opera) she completely dominates her victim and lures him away from the church, much as Carmen lures Don José away from his duties and responsibilities in the army. By now Massenet has succeeded in painting a completely well rounded musical picture of the heroine in all her inglorious self-indulgences. The difference between Massenet's heroine and Prévost's is that the literary version of this shallow young woman wins back Des Grieux simply by repenting her infidelity and abandonment of him. Prévost does not have her resort to seduction. That trick, invented by Massenet's librettists, suggests that they must have wanted to invent as many unattractive aspects of Manon's character as they possibly could. But the purpose of this altered portrayal remains unclear at this point in the opera, except that it gave Massenet yet another unattractive aspect of Manon's character to explore in music.

In Puccini's opera, this scene of reunion and reconciliation takes a different form—one, again, that says more about Des Grieux than it does about Manon. Rather than Manon seeking out her former lover, as in Massenet, it is now Des Grieux who has tracked down Manon and come to get her back. We learn that he has always loved her, and she, happy to hear this, begs forgiveness. All is well until Manon insists on taking most of Geronte's jewels before she abandons him in favor of Des Grieux. This lapse into greediness causes Des Grieux to launch into another of his important arias—this one lamenting his addiction to a female such as this. But again Puccini's adaptation misses the opportunity to flesh out the portrait of Manon, concentrating instead on the hero. Nevertheless, Manon's greed results in a delay in their escape that allows the police time to arrive and arrest her.

Massenet omits this scene in which the lovers are caught stealing the old man's jewels. In his opera, the arrest of Manon and Des Grieux takes place at the Hotel Transylvania where everyone has gathered for fun and gambling and where Des Grieux is accused of cheating at cards. This scene effectively summarizes the vast amount of material excised from the novel by showing the audience both the degradation of Des Grieux and the hedonistic superficiality of Manon that caused him to sink so low. Again Massenet's librettists provide the composer with an aria text designed to clarify Manon's love of the carnal aspects of life. Her aria "À nous les amours" expresses a "carpe diem" sentiment. "Who knows if we will be alive tomorrow," she sings. The most fascinating aspect of this aria is its musical association with both the Habanera and the Seguidilla in Bizet's *Carmen*. (See Ex. 13-3a–c.) Specifically, the little melodic figure that takes the form of a sixteenth-note triplet recalls the style, and therefore also the personality, of Carmen, another woman devoted primarily to pleasure, sexual freedom, and amorality.

Example 13-3a. "À nous les amours."

Example 13-3b. Bizet, *Carmen*, "Habanera."

Example 13-3c. Bizet, *Carmen*, "Seguidilla."

Up to this point in both operas, we have completely different impressions of the title character. In Massenet, Manon is seen in turn as innocent, religious, conflicted over her attraction to riches and pleasure, narcissistic, seductive, and hedonistically superficial: a complex and ambiguous mixture of personality traits. Puccini's Manon is much less clearly drawn. We never see her happily in love with Des Grieux, so we have no way to measure the sincerity of her devotion to him. Her one big solo in the duet with her brother in act 2 leads us to believe that she was at one time in love, but is now just bored with the emptiness of her new life of riches, and eager to reclaim the benefits of love. How and why she got to this new life we are not shown or told, nor do we know whether she truly misses Des Grieux or simply longs for more affection than Geronte can give her. In leaving so many questions unanswered, Puccini presented us with a somewhat ambiguous heroine, in an opera whose title suggests that she should be the central character.

Now we come to both composers' biggest challenge: how to make the audience sympathize with the tragic outcome of the love between Des Grieux and Manon. Here Prévost had a distinct advantage over his operatic adapters. The end of his novel is strikingly compelling because the author had the narrative leisure to show us a completely transformed Manon, through a very detailed depiction of her life in Louisiana. She accepts the love of Des Grieux, she renounces all need for riches and glamour, she becomes (with Des Grieux) a model citizen respected throughout the community, she devotes herself to doing good for others (the opposite of her former narcissistic self), and she is at last genuinely happy with herself. Now the tragic conclusion can rend a reader's heart. Out of true happiness they decide to marry, but the revelation of the fact that they were not married all this time leads to the triumph of an evil character devoted to having Manon for himself. It is Des Grieux's mistaken perception that he has killed this rival in a duel that leads to his unnecessary escape with Manon into the desert where she dies.[3] These twists of fate, not brought about by, and not within the control of the hero and heroine, are what devastate the happiness it took them so long to find, and constitute the real tragedy of the drama.

Neither Puccini nor Massenet could devote this much time to a portrayal of life in Louisiana. Puccini at least made an attempt to include some part of this important element of the story. His need to cut much of Prévost's earlier material from his adaptation (especially the scene in which the lovers are first seen living happily together) may, in fact, have been motivated by a recognition that time had to be set aside for the Louisiana scene at the end. In any case, Puccini fell victim to his own musical-dramatic carelessness. Having not taken the trouble to clearly develop Manon's character in the first three acts, he now found himself at a loss to be able to show us a meaningful transformation of that character. Instead, Puccini lapsed into his greatest operatic fault—one that plagues many of his works—the expression of self-pity. Just prior to her biggest and most important aria, Manon sends Des Grieux off to look for help as they recognize that she cannot take another step through the arid plains that must be traversed to escape New Orleans. While Des Grieux is gone, Manon launches into the most passionate expression of feeling we have heard her make anywhere in the opera. But who is this for? Des Grieux is not present, so it cannot be meant for him, as some kind of intimate exchange of heartfelt emotions. As is so often the case in Puccini's operas, this aria is designed only for the audience. The "deserted

---

3. Prévost's knowledge of New World geography seems to have been limited, since his opera makes reference to both deserts and mountains in Louisiana!

woman" who is a victim of her own "*beltà funesta*" (fatal beauty) doesn't want to die, and Puccini would have us cry over this. But one wonders at this point in the opera if even his best heart-throbbing music would be sufficient to evoke the degree of sympathy that would make us care.

Massenet took a different approach to solving this problem of eliciting sympathy and creating a real tragedy out of the story. Unlike Puccini, he made no attempt even to get his characters to Louisiana. His story ends on the way to Le Havre (the point of embarkation), where des Grieux makes his effort to save Manon from deportation by bribing her guards. By the time he gets to her, however, she is half dead, and there is only time for a final duet. But here, at least, we see a truly repentant Manon full of self-recriminations and remorse. She dies in his arms as they remember happier days.

Even for Massenet, who was more explicit than Puccini in his depiction of Manon's character, the absence of the part of her life that takes place in the New World seriously hampered the composer's ability to produce a truly tragic outcome for the opera. The success of Massenet's final scene, and of the entire opera, rests then directly on the music. Only through his music did Massenet have a chance to elicit our sympathy for the characters in the absence of all the dramatic detail that Prevost supplies for this purpose. Fortunately, Massenet was fully up to the task, relying primarily on the technique of thematic recall, taking us back musically to earlier moments in the opera to juxtapose the former Manon with the present Manon. The final duet (Ex. 13-4b) begins with an orchestral accompaniment that alludes to the vocal melody of her first aria (Ex. 13-4a), the one in which she presented herself as a simple ingénue. Both numbers are in the same key, B-flat major, and share the same short, tentative, broken phrases. Furthermore, their aural association for listeners is based on a similar melodic contour that includes a diatonic motion between F and B-flat, followed by a skip up to the end of the phrase on the notes G–F.

Example 13-4a. Manon's first aria, "Je suis encore."

Example 13-4b. Act 5 duet.

Massenet repeats and develops this theme throughout the duet, leading to the final section that begins with an orchestral passage based on a final repetition of this same theme. The theme is then used as the instrumental background for a moment of spoken dialogue and finally for the sung portion of the duet leading to the final kiss. The opera ends with Massenet repeating another important theme in the orchestra, that of the seduction scene at St. Sulpice. (Compare Ex. 13-5a and -5b.)

Example 13-5a. Manon's seduction theme, act 3, "N'est-ce plus ma main."

Example 13-5b. Closing measures of opera.

Here I think we are meant to recall the powerfully seductive Manon of before in the light of her present frailty and vulnerability. Such juxtaposition would naturally tend to highlight for the audience the transformation of character that must be felt for a heart-wrenching sympathy to develop for this poor woman.

Judging from the titles of these two operas, both Puccini and Massenet opted to refocus Prévost's narrative on the heroine, but only Massenet is really successful at doing so. Throughout five acts, he builds a wide-ranging musical portrait of a confusing and confused young woman. He then contrasts (with his music) aspects of her earlier character with the remorseful and broken woman we see in the final scene. Does all of this make a true musical tragedy? Is Manon a victim of anything other than herself? Do we feel that her death is somehow the product of a mistake that could have been avoided if only . . . ? How audiences answer these questions will determine how they react to this opera. But clearly, the exigencies of adapting literature to music (i.e., the drastic simplification of dramatic detail necessary to accommodate the slower pace at which music unfolds and develops) can sometimes overwhelm the best efforts of even the greatest composers. These two "Manons" are a case in point. While the music in each opera brings to the literary original a new dimension of dramatic meaning and understanding, the time required for this kind of emotional elaboration of personalities necessitated huge cuts in the original literary source that maim both operatic adaptations. Realistically speaking, there are occasions like these, when one might have to admit that opera—even good opera—doesn't always work as well as one might hope.

PART VII
SYMPHONIC OPERA

CHAPTER 14

U ntil recently, one of the universal truths of all Western art music was that, like the visual arts, it has some kind of form. Everything, from the sonatas of Beethoven to the symphonies of Mahler and the piano preludes of Debussy, is, according to this axiom, organized around specific structural principles. Form has long been thought to be essential to the understanding and appreciation of music because it gives shape to an art that exists only in time. Music without form simply presents a continual unfolding of new sounds: unrelated, unrepetitive, and unpatterned. Because music is a temporal art, patterns of melodic repetition and of tonal motion away from and back to a home key have for centuries supplied listeners with the perception (or the illusion) of shape in a nonvisual world.

In the literature that deals with the history of opera, one finds much less discussion of musical form than one does in the history of other genres. This is probably because opera deals with drama, and dramatic form is usually assumed to be narrative in nature, which is to say the structure of the drama is nothing more than the sum of the events that make up the plot. Nevertheless, because opera is "drama in music," nearly every composer who ever wrote one has had to deal with the problem of what kind of *musical* form every new work was going to have. Over the years, changes in the principles that govern operatic form have been at least partly responsible for the evolution of its style, as well as for national differences in the very nature of the genre.

Opera began life in Italy around the year 1600, invented by a group of writers, musicians, and other intellectuals who gathered to discuss how music and drama might be combined using principles borrowed from the ancient Greeks. They theorized that the great stage plays of the Greeks were not spoken but sung in a semimelodic style that used pitch to imitate the natural rise and fall of the spoken voice, and used rhythm to capture its dramatic pacing. The extremely simple, minimal music that the inventors of opera first imagined was meant, therefore, only to heighten the effectiveness and emotion of the dramatic text. The music was so closely tied to the narrative structure of the drama that it had little formal shape of its own. This style was known as *recitative*, a sample of which can be seen in an excerpt from act 2 of Monteverdi's *Orfeo* (1607), where a messenger first announces to Orfeo the death of his bride, Euridice (Ex. 14-1). The "recitative" style of these early operas, which has a modicum of melodic interest, is not to be confused with the more speechlike recitative familiar in later eighteenth-century Italian opera.

Example 14-1. *Orfeo*, act 1.

Composers of early opera struggled with the fact that this style of music, as it was applied to the dramatic texts of early operas, lacked the kind of formal coherence found in other vocal and instrumental genres. Recitative flowed forward in a through-composed fashion, rarely repeating rhythmic or melodic patterns. But because repetition is such a fundamental aspect of musical form, any opera based primarily on the use of recitative risked giving the impression of musical incoherence. To guard against this possibility, composers of early opera inserted into their dramatic works numerous short musical pieces such as choruses (which were dropped from Italian opera before the end of the seventeenth century), dances, and instrumental interludes, all of which were designed to relieve the monotony of the musically uninteresting and formless recitative by contrasting it with other kinds of melodically more satisfying music with recognizable formal shapes.

As the seventeenth century wore on, composers of opera continued to grapple with this problem of musical form. After the earliest operas, in which all texts were set to semimelodic recitative, composers began to differentiate the emotional, reflective texts in the drama (basically the soliloquies) from the dialogue texts by turning the former into fully lyrical arias—elaborate musical numbers with an obvious harmonic-melodic design and tuneful melodies—and leaving the latter to be sung as recitative, which had by the end of the century devolved from a semimelodic to a nonmelodic, speechlike style. This new recitative was known as *secco* (dry) *recitative*. The overall structure of late seventeenth-century opera was thus the product of a sequence of lyrical musical numbers (arias and a few duets mostly) with a clear musical form, strung together on a thread of speechlike secco recitative. However, the long-range form of an opera of this type was still little more than the collective pattern of its constituent musical numbers, which, because they had no relation to one another, produced no long-range musical form at all. This kind of opera became known in the eighteenth century as *number opera*, because it consisted of a string of independent musical numbers or *set pieces*. All eighteenth-century opera, from Handel to Mozart, was written using this loose, localized structural principle.

Gradually, the inherent problem with number opera became apparent: Each of the various set pieces from which it was built had the character of a discrete, independent musical unit with a clear beginning and a full stop at the end (often marked by a vocal cadenza). These stops invited audiences to applaud and even to demand encores, both of which broke the flow of the drama as singers actually came out of character to take a few bows in front of their adoring fans. When the drama was finally ready to resume, it did so by shifting style to a secco recitative that was accompanied by the harpsichord. This change from the orchestrally accompanied lyricism of the set piece to the keyboard-accompanied speech-melody of the recitative only further exacerbated the musical discontinuity inherent in number opera.

Gradually composers began searching for solutions to the lack of form and continuity in opera. First Gluck and then Rossini started to address the problem of the stylistic discontinuity between recitative and aria by introducing a new kind of recitative accompanied by the orchestra. This had the advantage of eliminating the continuous, jolting contrast between the sound of the orchestra and the sound of the harpsichord—a small step in the right direction, to be sure. But the introduction of orchestrally accompanied recitative into opera of the late-eighteenth and early-nineteenth centuries still left the genre without a satisfying musical form like that one might encounter in any instrumental music of the time. Operatic form was still nothing more than an irregular pattern of individual unrelated pieces strung together on a thread of recitatives. In Italy, this unsolved problem was first addressed by Verdi, whose *Rigoletto* (1851) was one of the first works in which an Italian composer tried eliding the end of one set piece with the beginning of the next to create the illusion that opera was not continually starting and stopping as it moved from one set piece to the next; rather, it was, as Verdi himself said, "one large piece." Verdi further added to this sense of a more continuous form by substituting arioso (semimelodic writing) for recitative, thus minimizing the melodic disjunction found between aria and recitative in older opera. In most arioso passages, the lack of lyricism in the vocal parts is compensated by a melodic motif in the orchestral accompaniment, which effectively diverts the listener's attention temporarily from the vocal parts onstage to the increased melodic activity in the pit. What is important about this arioso texture is the prominence given the orchestra. In focusing the listener's attention on a melody in the instrumental accompaniment, composers created the first hints of a new orchestra-centered opera that eventually metamorphosed into what we now refer to as *symphonic opera.*

The development of symphonic opera, however, did not take place in Italy, where composers and audiences alike were far too fond of the beauties of the human voice and loved singing too much to relinquish the hegemony of the voice to a group of instruments. Instead, Germany, a country with a rich history of great instrumental music, was where symphonic opera developed and flourished. As far back as the era of Beethoven and Carl Maria von Weber at the beginning of the nineteenth century, German opera had been different from Italian opera in terms of its greater reliance on the orchestra to establish dramatic moods with more than simple unobtrusive harmonic support for the voices. The opening of act 2 of Beethoven's *Fidelio* illustrates this special German characteristic. The hero, Florestan, lies in a prison cell deep in the bowels of the state prison. Chained to the wall, half dead from starvation, he laments his fate in an important aria. Preceding the aria is a lengthy instrumental introduction in which Beethoven effectively uses the orchestra to paint the mood of darkness and hopelessness in Florestan's situation with violent brass and woodwind chords that rip through the lugubrious sound of the strings. In the opening slow section of the aria, Florestan complains that his ironic reward for speaking the truth was to be imprisoned by his enemy. This lyrical section is then followed by an excited fast section in which he imagines he sees an angel in the form of his wife, Leonore, come to comfort him in his hour of suffering. This final part of the aria is accompanied by an oboe obbligato in the orchestra, which in its gradual ascent to an F above high C (f^3), reaches into the most strained and painful register of the instrument at the very moment when the tenor himself reaches the highest tessitura of the aria and holds on to this register with a desperation that matches the intensity of his hallucination. Here, more than in any Italian or French opera of the time, the composer utilized the orchestra to underscore the drama implicit in the libretto, without worrying about whether the instrumental accompaniment would obscure the beauty of the solo voice.

A truly symphonic style of opera involves much more than a bold use of the orchestra, however; it represents an entirely new way of thinking about how music and drama can or should be synthesized. Not until the coming of Richard Wagner did this rethinking take place. Wagner seemed poised from birth to achieve greatness in the opera house. The last of nine children in a family of actors and opera singers, he developed an interest in the theater at an early age. Only the discovery of the music of Beethoven kept young Richard from making his way onstage like the rest of his family. From that fateful discovery of Beethoven, his life's work was determined; he would be a composer of opera. The details of Wagner's early career need not concern us here, except to note that audience misunderstandings surrounding performances of some of his early works led him to dream of a different kind of society in which his work (so he imagined) would be better received. His involvement in an uprising against the German government in Dresden in 1849 led to the issuing of a warrant for his arrest, but with the aid of his friend Franz Liszt, he escaped to Switzerland, where he started to put on paper some of his new ideas about opera, art, society, and revolution. Immediately thereafter, Wagner moved on to put his theorizing into effect with the writing of the librettos for the series of operas known as *Der Ring des Nibelungen*. This cycle of four operas based mostly on native German mythology included, in its finished form, *Das Rheingold*, *Die Walküre*, *Siegfried*, and *Götterdämmerung*—works that have over the years cemented Wagner's reputation in the history of music as one of the most significant and influential composers of all time. The *Ring* cycle generated for its composer an almost reverent idolatry that has elevated Wagner to the status of a musical Messiah ready to lead opera into salvation.

The essence of the Wagner revolution in opera is complex both in theory (as set out in his numerous treatises) and in practice (as manifested in the music itself). Most important, Wagner was the first composer to substitute a new large-scale formal unity for the accidental localized form produced by the series of small-scale musical numbers that made up earlier opera. The resulting works differed so drastically from anything written before, that he chose to refer to them not as "operas" but as "music dramas." The implication of that term is that the narrative flow and pacing of these new operas came closer to that of a spoken stage drama by eliminating the individual set pieces of earlier opera and substituting in their place a continuously unfolding melodic line (an "infinite" or "endless" melody, as Wagner described it). This new melody was designed to be less tuneful than the melody one would encounter in a typical lyrical set piece, because the composer realized that tuneful melody, constructed of predictably symmetrical phrases, led to the writing of "songs" (i.e., arias), which he wanted to avoid. His new melody took the form of a *Sprechgesang* (speech-song) that sounded something like the old Italian arioso: a semimelodic vocal writing that was more interesting than recitative, but less symmetrical and less tuneful than a fully lyrical aria. *Sprechgesang* actually embraced a range of lyricism, including everything from fairly speechlike singing that sounds similar to Italian recitative, to something that almost approaches the sound of an aria. But Wagner studiously avoided the kind of predictable, tuneful lyricism characteristic of Italian opera.

In eliminating the "songs" of traditional opera, Wagner was left with a nonrepetitive melodic line that simply followed the moment-to-moment action of the drama. To this extent, at least a part of the Wagner revolution could be said to have taken its inspiration from the same classical aesthetic that inspired the earliest operas of Monteverdi. Through his theorizing about the synthesis of music and drama, Wagner had brought himself directly back to the same problem that the earliest composers of opera had faced when they invented the genre in the seventeenth century: how to find a form for music that did not conflict with the dramatic narrative of the text. It was here that Wagner hit upon a solution that was not open to the inventors of opera in the year 1600. Perhaps taking the Italian arioso texture as his hint, he decided to infuse his orchestra with a collection of melodic motifs that had specific dramatic connections or associations with characters, events, or things in the story. These melodic bits are today referred to as *leitmotifs*. They are, to use the definition of the famous musical comedienne Anna Russell, really nothing more than a series of "signature tunes."[1] The formal potential of these motifs lay in the way Wagner deployed and used them: like themes in an instrumental symphony. More specifically, his technique was to create an orchestral texture that imitated the style of a development section in a standard symphonic sonata form. In such a development section, a composer takes the two or three themes that he introduced at the beginning of the movement and repeats them in a semirandom order while also shortening, combining, or transforming them into new but related material. The composer thus "develops" his melodic material by exploring its potential to grow and metamorphose. A sample of the technique drawn from the development section of the first movement of Beethoven's Fifth Symphony (Ex. 14-2) shows how the process works. Beginning with the famous motif of a descending third (G to E-flat) arranged as three short notes leading to a longer one, Beethoven launches into variations of this rhythmic-melodic idea that gradually lead him into a complete metamorphosis of the original idea.

---

1. See the recording of her hilarious 1953 lecture-performance on the *Ring* cycle on Sony Classical MDK 47252.

Example 14-2 Beethoven, Symphony No. 5, 1, development technique.

Wagner's idea was therefore that the musical form of his operas could function like the development section of a symphony, and that the constant return to, and transformation of, his leitmotifs would produce a musical unity across the full four or five hour length of his operas. The creation of a musical form through the introduction and repeated transformation of themes was, by the time Wagner was writing his *Ring* cycle, already a very popular compositional technique among symphonic composers of the nineteenth century. The technique, which had originated in the development sections of sonata-form pieces by classical composers, had been expanded in the romantic era to encompass the entire length of a symphonic composition. First Berlioz, in his *Symphonie fantastique* of 1830, and then Liszt, in many of his orchestral tone poems written in the 1850s, created whole works based on the principle of the continuous repetition, development, and transformation of motifs. By adopting this process for use in opera, Wagner created a symphonic music drama in which the order of the appearance of the themes was determined not by purely musical considerations (as in a real symphony), but rather by the characters and events in the drama. But this analogy with the symphony can be stretched too far (as I believe Wagner himself did). The repetition and development of orchestral motifs works well as an organizational principle in a tone poem that lasts thirty or forty minutes, but works less well in an opera that lasts three or four hours, in which the basic motifs may be absent from the musical texture for long stretches of time. As in a Beethoven symphony, then, the leitmotifs in a Wagner opera relate to one another as members of large family groups. Slight changes in one result in the birth of another, and such musical relationships always correlate with dramatic connections between the characters and events that each theme signifies. Ex. 14-3 demonstrates how in act 1 of *Die Walküre*, the leitmotif for the "Rheingold" is simply transposed to the minor mode to make the motif for the earth goddess, "Erda," and is then finally inverted to create the motif associated with the "Dusk of the gods."

Example 14-3a. Motivic transformation in *Die Walküre*.

Example 14-3b.

Example 14-3c.

The invention of symphonic opera brought with it a new relationship between voices and the orchestra. No longer did the orchestra simply accompany the singers with unobtrusive harmonic support. Now the orchestra, because it presents and controls most of the leitmotifs, had become the central element in the audience's perception of the drama. In symphonic opera, the voices seem somehow to be subsumed into the sound of the orchestra, as though they were simply additional instruments in the total musical texture. This idea that the music drama is a fusion of elements of completely equal importance underlies the concept of the *Gesamtkunstwerk* (total artwork) as Wagner first defined it in his treatise *Oper und Drama* in 1851. Much as he supported a political revolution aimed at the establishment of a socialized society, his musical aesthetics leaned in the same direction, toward a total equality of all constituent parts in opera. The *Gesamtkunstwerk* was an expression of a fundamental belief on Wagner's part that the era of vocal dominance in opera, as previously seen in the Italian bel canto style, was dead. Symphonic opera would shift the balance of power away from the voice by elevating the role of the orchestra to that of a significant partner in the making of the overall dramatic effect. In addition, the new importance Wagner gave to the orchestra came with a vast expansion of its size. Along with a larger string section, the number of wind, brass, and percussion players more or less doubled. The need to accommodate such a massive group of instrumentalists led, in part, to the construction of the Festspielhaus (Festival Playhouse) at Bayreuth, where a special tiered pit housed this overly large orchestra in the space under the stage. But size and power alone were not Wagner's only goal with his remaking of the opera orchestra; color was an equally important consideration. New instruments such as the infamous Wagner tuba (treacherously difficult to play in tune) were added to the orchestra to create sounds that opera audiences had never heard before.

The last element in the creation of Wagner's new operatic style concerns the subject of harmony. As anyone who has ever studied the theory of music knows, Wagner was almost single-handedly responsible for the advancement of chromatic harmony in the late nineteenth century. To those unfamiliar with the technicalities of harmony and harmonic progressions in music, chromatic harmony can simply be understood as the result of music that continually employs harmonies that lie outside the key in which the music is fundamentally written. These "foreign" chords bring some startling sounds to the music—sounds that can be used to highlight special dramatic moments. When used on a continual basis, as in Wagner's orchestrations, chromatic harmony creates an unsettled feeling that derives from the fact that the music never has a chance to settle into one key for more than a fleeting moment. But on the largest structural level, Wagner's chromatic harmony is part of his new system of formal organization that allowed the vast prolongation of the symphonic structure, stretching relentlessly over three or four hours. The continual shifting of tonal centers (keys) prevents the music from coming back to rest in the home key too soon, thus prolonging the sense of harmonic suspense that postpones the arrival of the tonic key and the end of the opera. Therefore the largeness of a Wagner opera is not found only in the expanded orchestra, or in the vast scope of the mythological settings, or even in the size of the voices on stage. Rather, these music dramas are "large" in terms of their total elapsed time, and more specifically in the pace at which that time unfolds. They are dramatic megaliths driven by a slow-paced symphonic development that seems to draw us into another world where time unfolds without relation to reality.

In summary, symphonic opera (the music drama) as established by Wagner exhibits the following characteristics:

- The elimination of independent set pieces (arias, duets, etc.)
- An uninterrupted flow of the vocal and instrumental texture, with no places for applause
- A new relationship between the voice and the orchestra that brings the latter into much greater prominence
- Formal unification through the appearance and manipulation of melodic motifs
- An arioso vocal style (*Sprechgesang*) derived from the melodic style of the earliest Italian opera composers.
- An intensely chromatic harmonic vocabulary that aids the vast prolongation of the time frame of the drama

This operatic ideal remained a hallmark of the German style well into the twentieth century, when Richard Strauss became one of the primary disciples of the Wagnerian principles of operatic construction in the generation following the master's death in 1883. Strauss's *Salome*, written in 1905, is a fine example of the symphonic technique carried forward into the so-called expressionist style of the early twentieth century. Expressionism first emerged in the world of painting at the end of the nineteenth century, most prominently in the work of Edvard Munch, a Norwegian artist whose painting *The Scream* in 1893 established the fundamental characteristics of this new style.

Most important, expressionism is a style of art that delves into the subconscious. It might be described as "Freudian art" that seeks to strip away the false pretense of the conscious world to expose the often twisted and distorted emotions of the subconscious. In music, Strauss's *Salome* represents an early example of expressionist tendencies in the world of opera. The title character, Salome, Princess of Judea, develops an intense fascination for the prophet John the Baptist, who lies imprisoned in the palace of Herod, Tetrarch of Judea. When John spurns her advances, Salome becomes even more obsessed with the desire to possess this holy man. In the opera's final scene, after she tricks Herod into executing John, Salome takes his severed head, presented to her on a platter, and fondles, kisses, and otherwise makes love to it in a long solo section. This scene, although a solo, is not an aria. It is rather a miniature symphonic poem based on several motifs that have been associated with Salome throughout the one-act opera, and are here gathered in a grand summation leading to the catastrophic conclusion of the drama.

Example 14-4. Strauss, *Salome*, motifs in final scene.

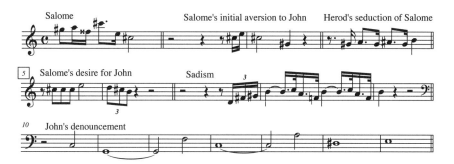

While *Salome* continued the general style of Wagner's symphonic operas, it also propelled that tradition into a twentieth-century style. As with Wagner, the voices and the orchestra are welded into a single entity in which one rarely has the sense that there is any significant vocal melody to which the orchestra is supplying an accompaniment. But Strauss's vocal writing is far more angular (which is to say full of skips in the melodic line) than was Wagner's, giving the melodies a more tortured affect characteristic of the expressionist style in music. Ex. 14-5 illustrates a typical vocal line drawn from the moment when Salome anxiously awaits the arrival of the head of John the Baptist.

Example 14-5. Salome's melody.

While the musical structure of this opera, heavily dependent as it is on a succession of leitmotifs that develop and return along with their attached dramatic meanings, is as symphonic as any of Wagner's works, the textures of *Salome* seem far more complex, as though more instruments are playing more contrapuntal lines all at the same time. Strauss was a far more dissonant composer than Wagner. He blended large amounts of familiar-sounding late-nineteenth-century chromaticism with potent doses of violent dissonance that frequently push the harmonic vocabulary of the opera into full-blown atonality (the complete absence of an audible tonal center). Ex. 14-6 illustrates the end of the opera where Herod sings about how disgusting he finds Salome's actions. Here, a chromatic line in the bass is placed against the dissonant dyad F–G in the upper parts of the orchestra. Then in the second measure, this same whole-tone dyad is counterpointed against a descending whole tone scale again making a dissonant combination. Finally the even more dissonant half-step dyad D–E-flat is introduced against an accompaniment in E-flat minor. This small sample illustrates Strauss's modern twentieth-century harmonic vocabulary, which moved far beyond the more timid use of dissonance in Wagner's operas.

Example 14-6. *Salome* end.

Example 14-6 *(continued)*

The basic style of symphonic opera, then, is one that emerged in Germany early in the nineteenth century. It represented an alternative to the highly ornate vocalism of Italian bel canto opera, and presented a new operatic aesthetic rooted in the dominant tradition of instrumental music in northern Europe. These early tendencies toward an operatic style that favored the orchestra over the voice, as seen in Beethoven's *Fidelio*, then blossomed into the music dramas of Wagner. His style, in turn, impacted opera all over Europe late in the century, when composers as diverse as Puccini and Chabrier fell under the powerful influence of his innovations. Even Verdi was accused at the end of his career of having become an imitator of Wagner. The potency of Wagner's influence throughout the nineteenth century, even in far-flung places, is testimony to the importance of its artistic implications not just for opera, but for all modern music. Wagner attracted attention because he addressed the most fundamental problem that faced all composers of opera since the dawn of the genre in the early seventeenth century: the problem of musical form. Whether other composers agreed with him or not, his bold and innovative ideas demanded attention, thought, rebuttal, and exploration. Few composers in the history of music can claim to have initiated such a significant revolution or to have had such a lasting impact on the development of musical styles in the nineteenth century and beyond.

PART VIII
FRENCH GRAND OPERA

CHAPTER 15

VERDI'S *DON CARLOS*: A FOREIGNER'S VIEW

These days one does not encounter much French grand opera in live productions. The major works of Giacomo Meyerbeer, the veritable king of grand opera for over thirty years in the mid-nineteenth century, are now available only on a handful of recordings. In its purest form, this genre, once so popular in Paris, has all but disappeared from the active repertoire of most major opera houses. What remains today, and what this chapter will explore, are mostly the traces of Meyerbeer's influence on other major composers such as Verdi, whose *Don Carlos* and *Aida* are both examples of this distinctly French genre reinterpreted and adapted by a foreigner.

The term *grand opera* signifies a particular kind of nineteenth-century French serious opera based on plots drawn from modern history. The essential ingredients of grand opera lie deeply rooted in the earliest history of French opera, which emerged in the middle of the seventeenth century as a new genre with musical and dramatic characteristics that differed radically from those found in Italian opera of the same period. In France, a strong national passion for ballet, spoken drama, and choral singing led to the invention of opera that included all of these art forms as essential ingredients of the new genre. What the French omitted from this operatic formula, however, was any concern with virtuosic solo singing, which was, of course, exactly what Italians found most attractive about this new genre. As a result, French opera began life with a concentration on the dramatic element of the genre somewhat at the expense of beautiful singing. It was based on the aesthetic principle that the music in an opera supported great drama, not that the drama supported great music.

Expanding from this basic principle of music drama, French composers in the early nineteenth century (actually Italian expatriates living in Paris[1]) added several new elements to the traditional French style, thereby creating a new kind of opera that came to be known as *grand opera*. One of the earliest of these new operas was Gaspare Spontini's *Fernand Cortez* (1809), an opera about the Spanish conquest of the Mexican Aztecs in

---

1. Even Jean-Baptiste Lully, the founder of French opera in the seventeenth century, was not a native Frenchman.

the sixteenth century. This was followed some years later by Gioachino Rossini's *Guillaume Tell* (1829), which took up the subject of the Swiss revolution against their Austrian oppressors in the fourteenth century. What these two early samples of grand opera have in common is not just a subject matter based on modern history, but more specifically, stories featuring conflicts of a religious or political nature between two large groups of people. The inclusion of large groups at war with one another enabled composers and their librettists to continue to employ the choruses that had long been standard in earlier French opera. Also, because of the expansive nature of the plots in these early grand operas, the scenery that supported the drama needed to be equally large-scale, with spectacular, lavish sets, and breathtaking staging. This scenic grandeur included the use of processions (essentially elaborate parades of characters moving on and off stage like mobile human scenery), pantomime scenes (dramatic action acted out to an orchestral accompaniment without singing), and, of course, the ballet. The last of these constituted a part of what the French referred to as the *divertissement* (the diversion) in opera—essentially a scene in which a character or a group of people give a performance for the entertainment of other characters onstage. Besides the ballet, the divertissement might include various kinds of solo singing that could also serve as entertainment for someone else in the opera. Lastly, grand opera was large-scale not only in terms of the number of singers onstage at any given time and the magnificent scenic spectacle, but also in terms of its scope, which usually included five acts lasting at least four hours or more in performance. Clearly, this kind of opera was not something that theaters with limited resources in small provincial French cities could easily put on, although they frequently tried mounting cut-down versions, for better or worse. In France there was essentially only one theater equipped to produce grand opera in the manner for which it was designed: the Académie Royale de Musique, otherwise know simply as the Paris Opéra. Unlike Italy, where nearly every city had its own major opera company, France was a country in which one city and one theater dominated the production of grand opera.

The history of Giuseppe Verdi's relationship with France and French opera makes a long and fascinating story, which can only be sketched here. Although his grand opera *Don Carlos* (1867) was only the second (and also the last) opera he wrote on an original French libretto, Verdi's experience with Paris and its theaters actually extended back almost to the beginning of his career. Most of his early operas, such as *Nabucco* and *Ernani,* received performances in the mid-1840s at the Théâtre-Italien, a theater that had been responsible for productions of Italian opera in Paris for many years, including the works of Rossini, who had served as its director in the 1820s. Perhaps recognizing the immense popularity of Verdi's early Italian operas with French audiences, the director of the Paris Opéra commissioned him to make a French version of his *I lombardi* for production at that theater in 1847. Its success, under the new title *Jérusalem*, led to Verdi's being offered in 1850 the opportunity to write an original French work based on a play by Friedrich Schiller entitled *Don Carlos*. The idea was rejected at the time, but Verdi remained open to the possibility of working in Paris again in the future. Thus, five years later, when the Opéra again offered him an original French libretto, this time for *Les vêpres siciliennes*, Verdi accepted the commission. This new libretto was by Eugène Scribe, the author whose name, more than any other, was associated with the greatest examples of grand opera, and most important, with the extremely popular works of Giacomo Meyerbeer. With this invitation, Verdi stepped into a foreign world of opera with which he had no previous experience, but which would soon change the course of his whole career.

After *Les vêpres*, the Opéra asked Verdi to make another French translation, this time of his popular *Il trovatore*, which was performed under the title *Le trouvère* in 1857, with several changes, including the addition of a large ballet necessary to make the work more like a French grand opera. Following this association with the Opéra, Verdi returned to writing Italian opera, the next three of which all show a strong influence of the French style he had come to know so well. *Simon Boccanegra* (1857) and *La forza del destino* (1862) both feature the expansiveness of French grand opera, and *Un ballo in maschera* (1859) is based on a translation of Scribe's libretto for Auber's grand opera *Gustave III*. Clearly, Verdi had entered a new international phase of his career, the style of which took its cue from Paris.

Several years passed before the Paris Opéra again approached Verdi, in 1864, with a commission. This time their suggestion was for an opera on the subject of either *King Lear* or Cleopatra (author unspecified), the first of which intrigued Verdi, while the latter sparked little interest. As Verdi mulled over the idea of another Shakespearean opera (*Macbeth* had been his first), the director of the Opéra added Schiller's *Don Carlos* to the list of possible subjects for consideration. After having rejected this subject years earlier, Verdi now found it the most "workable" of his present choices.

The libretto for *Don Carlos* was written by the team of Joseph Méry and Camille du Locle (French librettos were often the product of such teamwork), by freely adapting Schiller's play, itself loosely based on historical fact. Their libretto presents the character of King Philip II in a slightly fictionalized version of the real-life son of Emperor Charles V, the Spanish king who founded the Habsburg dynasty in 1519 and became head of the Holy Roman Empire. Philip was elected emperor in 1556 when Charles abdicated. He married four times, the first of which resulted in a son named Carlos (b. 1545). Between the ages of six and fourteen, Carlos witnessed the last of several wars between Spain and France. This war was eventually settled with the arranged marriage of Prince Carlos to the French Princess Elizabeth of Valois, who was also fourteen years old at the time. But the arrangement was abrogated at the last minute by Philip's decision to marry her himself. That this was the motivation for Carlos's hatred of his father (as the opera suggests) is historically doubtful; the fact that there was such animosity between father and son, however, is incontrovertible. It eventually led to the latter being held under house arrest for most of his life, the excuse for which was that the boy was mentally deranged. Nine years after Philip's marriage to Elizabeth in 1559, Carlos plotted his father's murder and tried to escape from Spain to aid the cause of a group of revolutionaries in the Netherlands (the Flemish revolt alluded to in the opera). Shortly after this failed plot, Carlos died of mysterious causes at age twenty-three.

Like most French grand operas, *Don Carlos* presents a plot based on large-scale conflict, which in this case occurs on several different levels simultaneously. The war between Spain and France is the most fundamental of these conflicts, leading to the arranged marriage of Elizabeth and Carlos. But the librettists added further conflict by transposing the uprising in Flanders (which actually occurred almost a decade after the end of the war with France) into the time frame of the opera. Lastly, the opera offers a third conflict: that between Church and State, or more specifically between their representatives, the grand inquisitor and the king. These conflicts provide the justification for the usual large choruses and scenic spectacle that make grand opera so distinct.

Verdi's approach to writing a grand opera was that of an outsider, an Italian, who was determined to bring to this kind of opera a new intimacy that French composers had so often neglected. In most of the operas of Mererbeer, Halévy, and Auber, the only human interest in the drama usually arose from the fact that a character on one side of the underlying conflict finds him- or herself in love with someone from the other side—the enemy, as it were—thus setting up the classic dilemma of love vs. duty. But in most French grand operas, this personal crisis gets swallowed up in the panoply and pageantry of the larger political, ethnic, or religious conflict, and the individual characters of the drama never receive a full musical depiction as unique, multidimensional personalities. Verdi's Italian operas, on the other hand, had always delved into the interpersonal relationships of its principal characters, presenting penetrating musical portraits that brought these characters to life as real people with whom an audience could sympathize. Fortunately for Verdi, the strong interpersonal relationships that made up Schiller's play allowed Méry and du Locle (with Verdi's continual prodding) to produced a libretto that included, along with the usual large choral scenes, plenty of opportunities for the exploration of individual personalities and their interactions. The resulting confluence of personal and public crises in the drama makes this grand opera somewhat unusual in the French repertoire, and far more interesting than most.

The public conflict in the opera takes place within the large choral numbers, and the personal conflicts unfold in the numerous duets around which the plot is primarily arranged. The interaction of the public and private aspects of *Don Carlos* can be seen as soon as the curtain goes up on act 1. As Verdi originally composed this scene (i.e., before he was forced to make a drastic cut for the premiere), it contained all the essential ingredients on which the public side of grand opera depended. An orchestral introduction sets a lugubrious tone before the entrance of a chorus of peasant woodsmen who lament the long war between France and Spain and the hardships it has brought them and their families. The scene is laid in a forest outside Fontainebleau palace, where a delegation of Spaniards has come to conclude final negotiations for a settlement of the war. Suddenly the opening choral lament of the woodsmen and their wives is interrupted by the contrasting sound of an offstage chorus of royal hunters who ride by singing about the joys of the chase. French composers frequently juxtaposed contrasting music simultaneously heard both onstage and off, to create a three-dimensional effect that augmented the scope of the staging by creating the illusion of distance in the theater. The fact that the onstage and offstage music contrasted with each other simply maximized the effect of the two different planes of musical activity, one close at hand, the other coming from a distance. After this choral opening, Princess Elizabeth enters on horseback and tries to comfort and reassure her people that the war is nearly over and better times lie ahead. The scene then closes with more choral music from the woodsmen onstage and the huntsmen offstage. This fairly elaborate scene was drastically cut before opening night in order to shorten the running time of the entire opera. In the shortened version that replaced it at the premiere, the orchestral introduction and the onstage chorus were eliminated, leaving the offstage huntsmen singing alone. Elizabeth's appearance was reduced to a pantomime, in which she enters distributing alms to her poor, suffering subjects. Much of the choral music traditionally heard at the beginning of a French grand opera, especially the conflict of on- and off-stage music, was thus lost in Verdi's shortened version of this first scene.

That which follows the introduction moves the opera into the realm of personal dilemmas. Don Carlos, who secretly accompanied the Spanish retinue to France, hoping to get a look at the princess to whom he is betrothed, comes out of hiding after Elizabeth has ridden offstage. When she and her page reenter, having lost their way back to the castle, Carlos greets them and falls immediately in love with Elizabeth. Their ensuing duet is constructed in a multisectional, mostly conversational style, consisting of melodic lines alternating between the two characters without any chance for them to actually sing together until the very end, when they declare their mutual love. This personal moment of happiness is short-lived, however, as Carlos and Elizabeth are interrupted by the arrival of a crowd of Frenchmen and dignitaries (in procession of course) from the palace. They have come to announce that peace has been settled, and that instead of marrying Don Carlos, Elizabeth will now marry King Philip, thus becoming the new Queen of Spain. Despite her newfound love for Carlos, Elizabeth has no choice but to accede to this unexpected turn of events, and as a chorus of Frenchmen offstage rejoice at the news of peace, the young lovers sing (onstage) of their heartbreak at being separated even before they were officially united. Thus begins the first of many personal relationships that make up the drama in this opera.

While much of the personal tone of *Don Carlos* unfolds in duets like this one, the relationships among all the principal characters actually take the form of triangular connections. Carlos and Elizabeth are both related to Philip, she as his reluctant wife, and he as a rival lover. Likewise other relationships in the opera develop as triangles: Carlos's closest ally, Rodrigo, Marquis of Posa, is torn between his friendship with the prince and his allegiance to the king, who pursues him as a source of information on the suspicious relationship between Elizabeth and Carlos. Similarly, Rodrigo is also caught up in a triangle between the king, who needs him as a confidante, and the grand inquisitor who sees him as a heretic and a traitor. The number and variety of these triangular relationships are astonishing, and give the opera a depth of character and intricacy of plot that enriches the drama immeasurably. At the base of all these triangles, lies the duet, the musical form through which Verdi differentiated this grand opera from all those written before him, and through which he made a uniquely French genre his own.

These duets are of such importance that they deserve a closer look. Two aspects are worth special scrutiny: form and melodic style. In the second half of his career, Verdi often spoke of the need to avoid the usual musical forms in opera. In a letter to the librettist of *Il trovatore* he wrote, "If only in opera there could be no cavatinas, no duets, no trios, no choruses, no finales, etc.; if only the whole opera could be, so to speak, all one number, I should find that sensible and right."[2] Verdi was expressing here his fear that the string of standard set pieces one usually finds in operas of the time created the effect of a concert in costume more than a drama in music. In criticizing the structure of Italian opera like this, he was subscribing to some of the operatic theories of Wagner (see chapter 14), and his solution to the perceived problem led audiences to attack him as a disciple of his German colleague, and to further assert that Verdi no longer knew how to write for voices. Indeed, we can see in his later operas the gradual disappearance of the standard Italian duet form inherited from Rossini (the form in which two similar solos led to a section of duet singing, all in a slow tempo, after which the tempo increased for an exciting cabaletta-like conclusion). In place of this old formula, Verdi had, as early as 1851 in *Rigoletto*, begun to adopt a more conversational style of duet writing. In that opera, the famous duet between Rigoletto and Sparafucile in act 1 is a prime example of a duet in which there is almost no simultaneous singing, but in which, rather, the voices alternate as they would in a dialogue in a spoken drama. Verdi's goal, then, would appear to have been the creation of greater dramatic realism, and *Don Carlos* represents a major step forward toward this dramatic goal.

After their duet in act 1, Carlos and Elizabeth meet again in the second tableau of act 2. This second duet clearly demonstrates the direction in which Verdi was heading with this important operatic form. In this scene, Carlos has come to the queen to ask a favor: he wants her to intercede on his behalf with the king, to convince him to send Carlos as a Spanish governor to Flanders, where insurrection is breeding. Of the 185 measures in this duet, only seven contain music in which the characters sing together. Instead, the vast majority of the duet is constructed of fairly short alternating sections in which each character responds to what the other has just said. Despite the fact that Verdi adopted this more realistic conversational approach to duet writing here, he also clung to at least one

---

2. Quoted in Budden, 1978, 61.

aspect of the old duet form: its tempo scheme of slow leading to fast. Here the opening section is marked *andante*, and the furious conclusion, brought about by Carlos's admission that he loves Elizabeth, is marked *allegro agitato*. So despite the fact that the singers rarely sing together as in a traditional duet, the whole number retains a familiar Italian feeling to the overall progress of the music.

Within these alternating solo sections of the duet, we see another aspect of Verdi's grand opera style that is less familiar to ears accustomed to his earlier Italian operas: their melodic design. Partly, this new melodic style is the product of Verdi's working with a French, rather than an Italian, libretto. Because opera librettos in the nineteenth century were traditionally written in poetry, the rules of poetic scansion (meters) apply to their musical setting. In this duet, one of the important solos given to Elizabeth is constructed of a quatrain of eight-syllable lines:[3]

Prince, si le Roi veut se rendre	Prince, if the King will accede
À ma prière . . . pour la Flandre	To my wishes . . . for Flanders,
Par lui remise en votre main,	Placed by him in your hands,
Vous pourrez partir dès demain!	You can leave tomorrow!

If this were Italian poetry, these lines would all be in the same poetic meter, and therefore all have the same pattern of accentuation.[4] This uniformity of poetic meter then results in the composer being able to set each line of poetry as rhythmically parallel phrases, usually of two measures each, thus producing an overall melodic pattern with a high degree of symmetry: an eight-measure period comprised of four two-measure phrases (one for each poetic line) in the pattern AABA, or ABAC. French librettos, on the other hand, are written according to French, not Italian, poetic rules. This means first that each line does not necessarily contain the same number of syllables. So a quatrain might have a syllable pattern of 8, 6, 8, 6, or some similarly varied arrangement. Even when a quatrain does consist of lines of equal syllables (as above), French poetic rules do not require the pattern of metric accentuation be the same throughout. In French poetry, the placement of accents is determined not by fixed rules, but by the grammatical structure of the language. To illustrate: A quatrain of Italian eight-syllable lines (called *ottonario* poetry) would always have an

---

3. In French poetry, one does not count the last syllable of a line if it ends with a mute *e*. In addition, certain vowels within and between words (in both French and Italian) are elided to create one large poetic foot.

4. In Italian poetry, this uniformity of poetic stress applies only to lines containing an even number of syllables.

accent on the third and seventh syllables of each line, as these three lines from *Rigoletto* demonstrate:[5]

(Capital letters indicate stressed syllables.)
Quanto—afFETto! . . . quali COre!
Che teMEte, padre MIo?
Lassù—in CIElo, presso DIo,

But the eight-syllable poetic lines that Elizabeth sings in *Don Carlos* have an irregular meter based on the grammatical structure of the language. Her lines thus have the following pattern of accentuation:

PRINce, si le ROI veut se RENdre (accents on syllables 1, 5, 8)
à ma priERe . . . pour la FLANdre (4, 8)
par lui reMISE en votre MAIN (4, 8)
Vous pourrez parTIR dès deMAIN! (5, 8)

This irregularity of accentuation pattern in French poetry makes the symmetrical melodic setting, so familiar from Verdi's Italian operas, less likely, if not impossible, in *Don Carlos*. Verdi's setting of these lines shows how inventive he could be working in French. Rather than the usual Italian approach of making each line of poetry into a two-measure phrase, Verdi decided on the unusual solution of making the first line and a half into a three-measure phrase, and then eliding that phrase with an identical repetition for the setting of the remaining line and a half. (See Ex. 1.) Thus, this elision of phrases (something rarely if ever seen in his earlier Italian operas) allows the last measure of the first phrase to function also as the first measure of the second phrase, making a complete melodic unit of five measures. The last line of poetry is then set to a single three-measure phrase by resorting to some text repetition and the stretching of one note at the end of the phrase to make it last longer than it really needed to.

Example 15-1. Act 2, Elizabeth-Carlos duet.

5. Syllable counting in Italian poetry differs somewhat from that in French poetry. Here, unaccented syllables at the ends of lines are counted as syllables. And as in French poetry, certain adjacent vowels, both within and between words, elide into a single syllable.

Example 15-1 *(continued)*

Ironically the whole period comprises what seems to be a regular number of measures (eight), but that eight-measure structure is built out of the most unusual combination of a five- plus a three-measure phrase. Such three- and five-measure phrases are rare in Verdi's Italian operas, and give *Don Carlos* the immediate feeling that Verdi's French grand opera style is something completely new and different. In addition to the odd phrase lengths, another unusual feature of Verdi's new French style is the abundant use of triplets in the melody, as seen in Ex. 15-1. These triplets are most likely another of Verdi's responses to writing music for French texts, which, unlike Italian, can have long stretches of unaccented syllables. Triplets offer a composer more unaccented notes within a single measure of music with which to accommodate the particular accentuation patterns of the French language.

On a larger organizational level, *Don Carlos* contains scene after scene seemingly built around duets of this sort. Following the Carlos-Elizabeth duet comes another between Rodrigo and Philip that brings act 2 to a close. This, too, is almost entirely in a conversational style, built out of alternating solos that continuously change tempo (although like the Carlos-Elizabeth duet that precedes it, the fastest tempo is saved, as in a typical Italian duet, for the very last section). Here, Philip asks Rodrigo if he needs a favor, to which the marquis responds it is not he, but the people of Flanders, who need help. After the confrontation that ensues from this bold response, the duet moves into a second half, in which Philip tells Rodrigo that he suspects Carlos of being in love with the queen, and gives the marquis free access to Elizabeth in the hope of discovering the truth of the matter. In this second half of the duet, we see examples of yet another aspect of Verdi's new duet style: the mixing of lyrical and nonlyrical melody. Verdi's music balances lyrical phrases of irregular length with contrasting phrases in a style far closer to recitative or arioso, as seen in Ex. 15-2, where Philip sings a lyrical opening three-measure phrase followed by a complementary four-measure phrase typical of Verdi's new unbalanced French style. This lack of balance is caused, again, by the irregularity of the poetry, the first line of which contains twelve syllables, the next ten, and the third only eight. In his setting, Verdi makes the first long twelve-syllable line into the opening three-measure phrase (see Ex. 15-2). He then combines the shorter second and third lines into one melodic phrase of four measures, thus unbalancing the opening period. But the lyricism of these opening phrases quickly gives way at the *poco più mosso* in m. 8 to a few measures of recitative-like writing, before returning to a lyrical phrase in the last four measures. The ease with which Verdi moves in and out of a lyrical style, along with the asymmetry of his phrases, creates a vocal style marked by far greater flexibility, irregularity, and unpredictability than what one is used to hearing in his Italian operas.

Example 15-2. Act 2, Rodrigo-Philip duet.

PHILIPPE:	PHILIP:
Votre regard hardi s'est levé sur mon trône,	Your daring gaze has been raised to my throne,
Mais de ce front où pèse la couronne	But on this brow where the crown weighs heavy
Sachez les tourments et le deuil.	Learn the torments and the grief.

Perhaps the most famous duet in the entire opera is that between Philip and the Grand Inquisitor near the beginning of act 4. At this point in the drama, the king asks the priest if he is justified in sacrificing his traitorous son, Carlos. After having consented to a plan to arrest Carlos, the Inquisitor then asks the king to hand over the other traitor, Rodrigo. Predictably, Philip refuses on the grounds that he needs the friendship and service of this trusted man. This duet, more than any other in the opera, is modeled on the style first set out in the Rigoletto-Sparafucile duet in *Rigoletto* some seventeen years earlier. It consists of a prominent orchestral part over which the voices declaim their lines in the recitative-arioso style, without ever really embracing anything truly melodic. This is the closest Verdi ever comes to adopting Wagner's *Sprechgesang*, in which vocal melody seems to take a subordinate role to the orchestral accompaniment. Ex. 15-3 illustrates a part of the opening interchange between the characters in which this lack of melody is readily apparent when the vocal parts are stripped of their supporting orchestral background.

Example 15-3. Act 4, Philip-Inquisitor duet.

Don Carlos contains a handful of arias in addition to the many important duets. These, too, are not in Verdi's Italian style, and show little resemblance to the old cavatina-cabaletta forms found in his early works. One particularly beautiful and characteristic example of this new aria style appears at the beginning of act 4, where Philip sits alone in his study, lamenting the fact that Elizabeth never really loved him and that his life is about to end unfulfilled. This aria reminds one of a similar aria sung twenty-three years earlier by the other Don Carlos in Verdi's *Ernani*.[6] The dramatic situation is similar: an aging monarch grieves over his lack of youth, and ponders the meaning of power and glory in an otherwise unfulfilled life. But the musical form Verdi employed for his later opera is far less conventional than what he wrote so much early in his career in Italy. The most common aria form found in French grand opera had always been the simple ternary ABA pattern, which Verdi employed here. (See the A and B themes in Ex. 15-4.)

---

6. Historically, the Don Carlos of *Ernani* is the grandfather of the Don Carlos in this opera.

Example 15-4. Act 4, Carlos's aria.

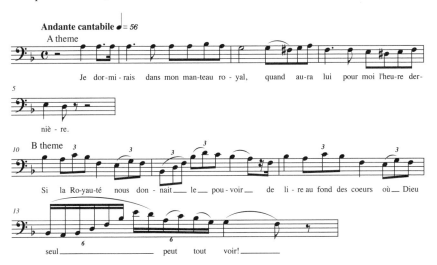

Verdi then extended that ABA form with an additional final statement of the B theme played in the orchestra while Philip finishes his vocal part in an arioso counterpoint. The final structure then becomes A B A B-orch.

The unusual arias and duets of *Don Carlos* are, of course, played off against many of the standard elements of French grand opera, including some wonderful scenes of sheer pageantry and divertissement. The second tableau of act 2 contains a superb example of a scene designed purely for its entertainment value. The queen is visiting the monastery of St. Yuste. While she is inside, her ladies in waiting remain outside, reclining on a grassy knoll. To pass the time, Princess Eboli offers to sing them a song. This famous little piece, the "Chanson du voile" (Song of the Veil) is meant to be understood as a song that a character in the opera "sings" for the purpose of entertaining other characters in the opera. Such songs often appear in opera when a character sings to him- or herself, or perhaps tries to serenade another character. But here the song is meant to entertain a large group of people. Inevitably, too, the subject of the song is a metaphor for something that is about to happen in the opera itself. Eboli sings about a king who grew tired of his queen and tried to seduce a mysterious veiled woman, whom he found sitting alone at night in a garden of the palace, only to discover her to be his own wife. This very same situation nearly ruins Don Carlos later in the opera when he mistakes Princess Eboli for the queen, and in the process betrays his illicit love for Elizabeth to her most jealous rival (Eboli).

One of the opera's largest scenes of pure spectacle also encapsulates a dramatic turning point in the drama. This is the second tableau (finale) of act 3, in which the entire royal court along with the populace at large has gathered to watch the burning at the stake of the heretics condemned by the Inquisition. Such a gathering, of course, calls for a grand procession, or in this case, two. First, a group of monks parade the condemned prisoners across the stage as they sing about the "day of wrath." This is followed by the procession of the entire royal court out of the palace and into the public square, all accompanied by suitably large choruses and grandiose orchestral music. Suddenly in the midst of this gathering of dignitaries, Carlos appears at the head of a delegation from Flanders, come to ask the king for relief from their sufferings. The king immediately declares them all traitors, including Carlos, who has demanded to be given rule over Flanders. He threatens Philip at sword-point, and as the king calls on someone to stop him, only Rodrigo, Carlos's closest friend, steps forward to disarm the prince (poignantly accompanied by the theme from their earlier "friendship" duet). Thus in typical grand opera fashion, the public conflict (the Inquisition and the revolution in Flanders) intersects with one of the major private conflicts (between Philip and Carlos) in one especially large, climactic scene. Once Carlos is disarmed, the celebration of the burning of the heretics can continue. The king and queen parade offstage accompanied by the large choruses of courtiers and the general population, the monks, and the prisoners, all singing together with an additional offstage part that the libretto labels as a "voice on high," leaving Don Carlos and his Flemish deputies alone onstage.

Like Berlioz's *Les Troyens*, written nearly ten years earlier, *Don Carlos* is an atypical grand opera. In the midst of several decades of dominance of this particular form of opera by Meyerbeer, and to a lesser extent Halévy and Auber, it may seem somewhat ironic that the two longest surviving examples of French grand opera are those by an outcast Frenchman (Berlioz) and an Italian. Nevertheless, it is through the very personal approaches both Berlioz and Verdi brought to this genre, that they were able to elevate grand opera to something more than musical pomp and scenic spectacle. Verdi especially, brought to grand opera an Italian sense of dramatic intimacy that imbued its characters with personalities to which an audience could relate, and sufferings with which they could empathize. At the same time, however, Verdi's Italian style was forever impacted by his work with a French libretto. The new suppleness of melodic style (its asymmetries and irregularities), the contrasting levels of melodic lyricism, and Verdi's use of new formal arrangements in the disposition of his musical numbers, all pointed in the direction of his very last masterpieces that lay twenty years in the future.

CHAPTER 16

BERLIOZ'S *LES TROYENS*: A MISJUDGED MASTERPIECE

In 2003 the opera world celebrated the two-hundredth anniversary of the birth of Hector Berlioz with productions of his three rarely heard operas. Although Berlioz may well have been the most important French composer of the nineteenth century, today his fame rests on his programmatic orchestral works, not on his operas. But as is the case with other famous composers who wrote very few operas (Beethoven and Debussy come immediately to mind), Berlioz's failure to gain a foothold in Parisian musical theaters must be understood not as apathy on his part toward the genre, but rather, as the result of a set of personal circumstances that defined both his unique artistic personality and his role in the world of professional music in Paris. Born into a well-to-do family in a small town near Grenoble, where his father was a country doctor and an amateur musician, young Hector was surrounded by a culture of great literature (found in his father's extensive library) and music making. Not surprisingly, he developed a passion for both, especially music composition, at which he tried his hand despite a lack of formal training. But Dr. Berlioz always intended for his son to follow in the family business, regardless of the fact that he showed no interest in becoming a doctor. Only parental coercion and bribery managed to get Hector to agree to enter medical school in Paris. But his love of music quickly overwhelmed his promise to study medicine, and Berlioz eventually abandoned the latter for the study of composition at the Conservatoire. Unfortunately, this was a field for which his lack of formal musical instruction as a boy left him ill-prepared.

At the Conservatoire, Berlioz was an especially difficult student, challenging everything he was taught and refusing to follow the "rules" of composition as espoused by the mostly conservative members of the school's faculty. By the time he graduated in 1830, he boldly announced in a letter to a friend, "I am an Attila come to ravage the musical world."[1] Little wonder the rest of his career was so troubled, or that opera producers looked upon him with a suspect eye. As a result of such self-sabotage, we have only three extant operas from Berlioz's pen: *Benvenuto Cellini*, *Les Troyens*, and *Béatrice*

---

1. Berlioz, 1972, 34.

et Bénédict. Despite this meager output, opera had been something that excited Berlioz since his boyhood days, when he pored over scores of the works of Gluck, discovered in his father's library. By the time he moved to Paris to study composition at the Conservatoire, he had become an avid disciple of that composer's classical musical-dramatic style—a style that was later to have a major influence on his own *Les Troyens.* In addition, Berlioz maintained his connection to the world of opera during these early years by working as a music critic for several Parisian papers, by writing two operas of his own (*Estelle et Némorin* and *Les francs-juges,* both now lost), and by entering the Prix de Rome competition five years in a row, for which he was forced to compose a dramatic cantata for solo voice and orchestra each year.[2]

Berlioz came to maturity in Paris at a time when opera was king. Because the public cared little about symphonic music, and even less about chamber music, a composer wanting to make a successful career, would most likely have had to turn to opera. But Berlioz's desire to follow this career path was continually thwarted by official antipathy for him and his revolutionary musical style. His reputation as an iconoclast (an "Attila") with a bizarre musical style, strangely old-fashioned ideals about drama in music, and impossibly high standards for operatic production, made it impossible for him to secure a commission for an opera. During these youthful years, he struggled to break into the business:

> For four years I have knocked at every door, but none has opened. I cannot
> obtain a libretto to set, nor secure the production of the one with which I
> have been entrusted [*Les francs-juges*].[3]

His only good luck came in 1838, when the Paris Opéra agreed to stage his *Benvenuto Cellini.* Predictably, the production was a complete fiasco, and his reputation as a poor risk in the theater was permanently cemented. So for years, Berlioz expressed his innate dramatic instincts in other genres, of which the "dramatic symphony" (his own invention) is probably the best example. Works such as *Symphonie fantastique* and *Roméo et Juliette* are symphonies that are dramatic not only by virtue of their programs, but more so by their inclusion of operatic styles and devices within what had always been exclusively an instrumental concert genre.[4] *La damnation de Faust* is

---

2. In the first year he entered, Berlioz failed to get past the preliminary round, and so wrote no cantata that year.

3. Berlioz, 1972, 185.

4. Beethoven's Ninth Symphony is the only exception to this rule prior to Berlioz.

another example of this mixture of symphonic and operatic techniques, producing something that might be called a "semi-opera." To this day no one knows exactly what genre this piece best fits into; Berlioz himself called it a "dramatic legend," but it is commonly thought of simply as a concert opera. In any case, Berlioz's desire to write a real stage work could not be sublimated forever. Twenty years after the failure of *Benvenuto Cellini,* he began dreaming of a new opera, to be based on Virgil's *Aeneid,* a work he knew and loved from his boyhood Latin lessons. Writing in his *Memoirs* many years later, Berlioz recalled how he broke down in tears while reading aloud, in one of these lessons, the scene of the death of Dido.

By the time Berlioz came to this idea for a new opera, Paris was deep into its passion for grand opera, best represented at mid-century by the works of Giacomo Meyerbeer. The characteristics of this particularly French kind of opera were first established in the early years of the nineteenth century, in works by composers such as Spontini, Cherubini, and later Rossini (whose *Guillaume Tell* is a prime example). By the mid-1850s, when Berlioz began writing his *Les Troyens,* these characteristics had devolved into a more or less predictable formula that resulted in a kind of opera much different from that being written in both Italy and Germany at the same time. The elements of French grand opera include:[5]

- Five acts
- Elaborate, spectacular scenery
- Historical plots that pitted one country or religious faction against another
- Nearly continual use of the chorus
- Extensive use of ballet (especially in the 3rd act)
- Reliance on processions or parades for scenic effect
- Pantomime scenes

Into this well-established tradition stepped Berlioz in the mid-1850s, with an idea for an opera on a mythological subject. Right from the start, he realized he was in trouble just with the subject itself. His valiant struggle not to write this opera makes almost comical reading in his *Memoirs* and his letters from these years. In the *Memoirs,* for instance, he wrote in 1854:

> For the last three years I have been tormented by the idea for a vast opera,
> for which I would write the words and the music. . . . I am resisting the

---

5. See the more detailed description of the elements of grand opera in chapter 15.

temptation to carry out this project, and shall, I trust, resist to the end. To me the subject seems magnificent and deeply moving—sure proof that Parisians would think it flat and tedious. Even if I were wrong, where would I find a woman of the necessary intelligence and dedication, capable of interpreting the chief role—a role which demands beauty, a great voice, true dramatic ability, impeccable musicianship, and a heart and soul of fire? Still less could I be sure of all the other various resources which I would have to have absolutely at my disposal, without interference from anyone. My blood boils at the very thought of encountering the senseless obstacles that I have had to face in the past. A clash of wills would be exceedingly dangerous, for I feel capable of anything where they are concerned; I would kill them like dogs.[6]

Thanks mostly to his friend the Russian Princess Caroline Sayn-Wittgenstein, Berlioz was persuaded to lay aside these silly reservations and to complete his grand opera. By 1858 the work was finished but, not surprisingly, the Opéra showed no interest in producing it. So by 1863, Berlioz was forced to accept an offer from his friend Léon Carvalho, director of the Théâtre-Lyrique, to stage the work. The only problem was that Carvalho's theater, where Gounod's *Faust* had just made its debut, was considerably smaller than the Opéra. And for a work such as *Les Troyens*, conceived on · a grand scale, this meant having to accept debilitating adaptations and concessions of all kinds. The most important of these had to do with the opera's length. Lacking the resources to stage all five acts, Carvalho forced Berlioz to divide the work in half and agree to a production of the last three acts only (under the title *Les Troyens à Carthage*). Many of the opera's ballets, processions, and other numbers had to be cut, and worst of all, the famous pantomime scene, "The Royal Hunt and Storm" (in act 4), was so butchered in performance that Berlioz himself begged for its elimination. To its credit though, the opera ran for twenty-one performances even in such a mutilated state.

Les Troyens is, then, a work in which Berlioz tried to squeeze his revolutionary musical imagination into the traditional mold of French grand opera. The result is an opera that sounds both familiar (in its surface duplication of the most common grand opera formulas) and musically innovative (in the sense of capturing Virgil's drama in music of inspired originality). As mentioned earlier, it's subject presented a problem because mythology and ancient history had long before faded from the operatic

---

6. Cairns, 1975, 468.

stage as new, more middle-class (i.e., less well-read) audiences came to replace the more aristocratic audiences of the previous century. Thus, the majestic grandeur of the depiction of the siege of Troy in acts 1 and 2 failed to make the kind of impression Berlioz had hoped for. As the curtain goes up on act 1, the Greeks have just abandoned their ten-year siege of the city and have left behind a strange, gigantic wooden horse. With the Greeks' disappearance, a crowd of Trojans swarms out of the city to celebrate their apparent victory. This scene is set as a standard opening chorus. Although such opening choruses are absolutely traditional, Berlioz's music is unique. He placed demands on his chorus members that went far beyond anything they would have encountered at the Opéra. Here, he wrote a five-part chorus in full contrapuntal style, with each voice often singing a line that was different and independent from its neighbors. Further compounding the difficulty of this counterpoint is the tempo at which it must be sung: the dotted quarter = MM138 (i.e., more than two beats per second). At that speed a series of eighth notes with separate syllables on each note becomes a tongue twisting challenge of immense proportions. Also unique was Berlioz's entrusting to winds and brass, rather than the usual strings, much of the orchestral accompaniment for this opening scene.

Following this opening chorus, Cassandra enters to sing her first aria. Here we have one of Berlioz's most drastic alterations of his literary source. Virgil's *Aeneid* hardly mentions Cassandra; her name appears only three times in a total of over one thousand lines of poetry. In the *Aeneid*, the role of the prophet-of-doom falls instead to the Trojan priest Laocoön, who warns his people of the lurking danger in the Greek horse, and even hurls his javelin at the wooden sculpture in an attempt to rouse his people to action against it. But because no French grand opera of that time existed without a dramatic heroine (a prima donna), Berlioz needed to manufacture an important role for one of the women in the story, and Cassandra probably fit that role better than any of her companions. This attachment to Cassandra was surely also motivated by his own life-long idolization of such visions of noble, self-sacrificing feminine perfection. Both Cassandra and Dido (the heroine of acts 3--5) are women of the kind that Berlioz longed to meet in real life but never did. Furthermore, Cassandra may also have assumed the allegorical role of the misunderstood visionary—a role with which Berlioz would have personally identified in an autobiographical way. But while Cassandra may appear to be a traditional heroine, the style of her music is far from traditional—at least far from the more decorative style of many of the works of Meyerbeer. Berlioz poured out Cassandra's forebodings in an aria, "Malheureux roi," built out of irregular phrase lengths, and lacking the usual melodic gracefulness of other French grand operas. Especially evident in this aria is Berlioz's deliberate recall of the old-fashioned melodic style of his childhood idol Gluck, long since forgotten and disparaged by Parisian audiences of the 1850s and '60s. Cassandra's opening phrase (Ex. 16-1) consists of a pickup and one full measure, followed by a pick-up leading to two measures, all totaling an unusual five-measure phrase.

Example 16-1. Cassandra, "Malheureux roi."

Having made up the role of Cassandra, Berlioz then had to create a love interest for her. So again he picked on only a couple of lines in Virgil that mention Corebus as Cassandra's betrothed. Suddenly out of nothing, this completely minor character now has a major love duet with Cassandra. The music of this duet is simply spectacular in its ability to delineate character: Cassandra in her distraught hysterical mood, and Corebus in the classic male role of reassuring counselor. But it is quite clear that this duet (and even the entire role of Corebus) really exists simply to allow Berlioz to expand upon the depiction of his heroine and to give her more to do in the opera. The rest of the first act is all firmly rooted in traditional French grand opera, with scenes and dialogue invented by Berlioz from little more than the faintest hints in Virgil to fulfill the needs of the genre. First comes the procession of the Trojan King and his court: a five-minute parade accompanied by some glorious choral music. Then we have a short ballet depicting the public games and entertainments in celebration of the Trojan victory. This is an example of what is usually referred to in French opera as the *divertissement* (diversion), literally an entertainment for the characters in the opera (but also, of course, for the audience in the theater). The drama continues with another element drawn from traditional grand opera: the pantomime. Here, the widow and son of the slain Trojan hero Hector come forward to receive the blessing of the King. Neither of them sings, but their actions are accompanied by the chorus and a solo clarinet that plays some of the most plangent and sorrowful music Berlioz ever wrote.

In making his adaptation of Virgil, Berlioz clearly invented scenes such as this one, not found in his literary source, just to make his opera conform to tradition. But most of the opera, including some of its most effective scenes, was adapted directly from Virgil's poetry. Such is the case with the story of the death of Laocoön who, upon throwing his spear at the Greek horse, was suddenly attacked and eaten alive by two giant sea monsters. Berlioz places the story of his death in the mouth of Aeneas, who dashes in breathless to announce it, in a most extraordinary aria, to the assembled crowd. Berlioz unfolds the story (which he calls a "narration"[7]), in a single sweeping melodic line that rises higher and higher in the tenor range as it moves to an almost painful climax, and is supported by an orchestral accompaniment that pulses with an extremely rapid, rhythmically animated accompaniment, like an excited heartbeat.

Example 16-2. Aeneas's "narration."

The effect of this narration on the assembled crowd is one of stunned mumbling. The choral number in which the crowd responds marks an extreme contrast with Aeneas's narration. In a slow tempo, Berlioz weaves a complex contrapuntal web of diverse thoughts as the Trojan people try

---

7. Berlioz is here drawing on a tradition of French baroque opera wherein action offstage is often reported or narrated onstage by a single character.

to comprehend the mystery. But this chorus is symptomatic of his peculiar approach to writing opera, and is worth exploring just a little further. A single, seemingly unimportant line in Virgil ("a strange terror takes its way through every heart") catches the composer's attention, and he decides that this is a moment in the drama that demands musical elaboration. This, of course, is what music does best: it gives expression to intangible emotions that are associated with tangible objects or events. So Berlioz feels the terror of the crowd that is suggested in Virgil's poetry, and elaborates it into a six-minute piece in which the Trojan people try to comprehend the death of Laocoön. The question is: how can Berlioz justify making so much out of so little? For him, this terror was clearly meaningful, but is this really an important event in the unfolding of the epic drama? And if not, why did he choose to spend so much time on such a seemingly ancillary event? The music itself is highly dramatic, as anyone can hear, even if the moment it represents may not be. This suggests that Berlioz's aesthetic of opera went beyond the usual setting to music of the major "events" of the drama, to include the setting of seemingly inconsequential lines that the composer found pregnant with musical potential, and therefore important for the overall dramatic effectiveness of the opera.

The final scene of the act brings us back to more traditional French grand opera techniques. Here, the frightened Trojan people rush off to get the horse and drag it into the city, while Cassandra, alone onstage, raves ineffectively about the danger that lies ahead. The offstage chorus produces the effect of distant music heard against Cassandra's onstage music, thus creating the spatial relationships that were so important in French grand opera. Gradually the procession dragging the horse comes closer, and the music gets louder as the spatial relationship changes. The scene ends with the chorus pulling the horse away toward the city—growing softer as they do—while Cassandra is left onstage railing at what she knows to be certain disaster awaiting her unsuspecting countrymen.

Example 16-3. Finale of act 1.

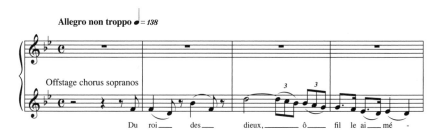

Example 16-3 *(continued)*

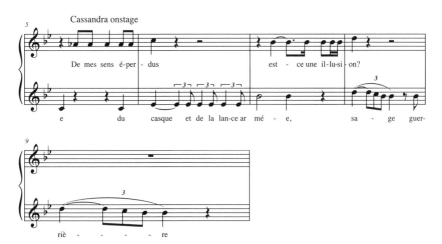

Having created the character of Cassandra out of the merest hint in Virgil, Berlioz was then faced with the dilemma of how to dispose of her in the second act. Virgil was of little help here, since he never actually explains what becomes of any of the Trojan women other than Hector's widow, who is taken prisoner. This ambiguity left Berlioz more or less on his own to find an appropriately operatic end to Cassandra. Perhaps he took his cue from a short passage in book 3 of the *Aeneid*, where Cassandra is referred to with the lines:

> O happy past all others, virgin daughter / of Priam, made to die beside our foeman's / tomb, underneath the towering walls of Troy; / O you, for whom no lots were cast, who never / as captive touched the couch of a conquering master! (417–21)

Although this explains what happened to Cassandra (she dies), it doesn't explain exactly how it happened. For the solution to how she was going to die, Berlioz turned to an earlier model of French grand opera: Rossini's *Le siège de Corinthe*, produced in Paris in 1826. There, Berlioz found a scene that suited his purposes exactly. In this opera, an army of Turks lay siege to the Greek city of Corinth. The leader of the Turks, Maometto, loves the Greek princess Pamira, who has rejected his offer of marriage and peace between their respective countries. Angered by this, Maometto vows to take her and the city by force. In the final scene, the Greek defenders have been defeated, and as the Turks are heard victorious in the background, Pamira decides to kill herself and exhorts her companions to do the same. When

Maometto enters, he is greeted by Pamira and the other Greek women, daggers in hand, stealing the final victory for themselves. This, to be sure, is exactly how act 2 of *Les Troyens* ends. If one were simply to substitute Cassandra for Pamira, Rossini's finale would become the glorious group suicide that closes Berlioz's act 2.

During the intermission following act 2, Berlioz skips over all the rest of the story of the fall of Troy—how Aeneas and his men escaped the Greek massacre and set sail for Italy, where they are destined to build a new empire. As act 3 opens, we find Aeneas blown off course and shipwrecked on the northern coast of Africa in the city of Carthage, which is ruled by the beautiful widowed queen, Dido. The opening scene depicts the spectacle of her empire through the use of a large chorus of Carthaginian people, the procession of Dido's court, and the procession of builders, farmworkers, and sailors—all of which are fully expected elements of any French grand opera. Dido's entry march (Ex. 16-4) is especially regal with its steadily marching bass line under simple blocked harmonies in the chorus, all reminiscent of marches in some much better-known grand operas such as Verdi's *Aida*.

Example 16-4. Dido's procession.

After a duet between Dido and her sister Anna, in which Dido reminds us of her vow never to marry again, the stage is set for the arrival of Aeneas and his men. This brings with it more processions, as the shipwrecked Trojans march in seeking refuge and bearing gifts for the queen. But Aeneas is not at their head. He is instead disguised as one of the regular Trojan warriors. Berlioz then invents a surprise attack on Carthage by the Numidian chieftain Iarbas. This conveniently allows Aeneas to drop his disguise and step forward in full armor to offer Dido help in defeating the invaders. But because this scene is nowhere to be found in the *Aeneid*, Berlioz may again have looked elsewhere for help with creating this finale. There is an almost identical scene in an earlier French opera by Grétry, *La caravane du Caire* (1783), in which Egyptian soldiers announce an attack by invading Arabs. The hero of that opera, who is at that point a captive slave, wins his freedom by stepping forward and offering to fight beside his Egyptian captor to successfully repel the attack. Did Berlioz know this earlier opera by Grétry? Evidence suggests he did. The work was in production at the Paris Opéra through the late 1820s, and Berlioz mentions it in chapter 15 of his *Memoirs* in connection with his student years at the Conservatoire.

Perhaps the most fascinating aspect of the history of the first production of *Les Troyens* is the story behind the huge pantomime that opens act 4. This scene, called the "Royal Hunt and Storm," is Berlioz's musical-dramatic equivalent of lines in Virgil that describe a hunting party interrupted by a storm that forces Dido and Aeneas to take refuge in a cave. There, while they wait for the weather to clear, they physically consummate their growing love for each other. Although the technique of pantomime was common in French opera, nothing of this magnitude had ever been seen before in the theater. The detailed scenario as conceived by Berlioz appears as follows.

An African forest at morning. At the back, a high rock; below, the opening to a cave. A small stream flows along the rock until it disappears into a natural basin bordered with rushes and reeds. Two naiads appear for an instant and vanish; a moment later they can be seen bathing in the pool. Royal hunt. Hunting calls are heard far off in the depths of the forest. The frightened naiads hide in the reeds. Tyrian huntsmen pass leading dogs on leashes. Young Ascanius [Aeneas's son] gallops across the stage on horseback. The sky darkens; it begins to rain. The storm grows. It becomes a tempest, with sheets of rain, hail, lightning, and thunder. Repeated hunting calls are heard amid the tumult of the elements. The huntsmen scatter in different directions. Finally Dido and Aeneas appear . . . Both are on foot. They enter the cave. Immediately the nymphs of the forest appear, with disheveled hair, on top of the rock, and run back and forth, crying out and making extravagant gestures. In the midst of their cries, one word can from time to time be heard: "Italy." The stream swells and becomes a foaming torrent. Several other waterfalls form at different points on the rock and mingle their noise with the roar of the storm. Satyrs and sylvans, with fauns, perform grotesque dances in the darkness. A tree is struck by lightning, shatters and catches fire. The wreckage of the tree falls on the stage. The satyrs, fauns, and sylvans pick up the flaming branches and dance with them in their hands, then disappear with the nymphs into the depths of the forest. The storm passes. The clouds lift.

Notice, in this pantomime, all the elaborate and very specific scenic instructions that would have made for a spectacular effect had they been carried out as the composer wanted. But alas they were not.[8] As he wrote in his *Memoirs*,

> Instead of several real waterfalls, I was given a painted representation of a stream. The leaping satyrs were represented by a troupe of twelve-year-old girls, who brandished no flaming branches in their hands because the fire marshal forbade them for fear of a conflagration. There were no nymphs flying disheveled through the forest with cries of Italy. Even the stage thunder could scarcely be heard. And when this miserable travesty came to an end, the scene-shifter always needed at least forty minutes to change his scenery. So I myself asked for the interlude to be removed.[9]

Just as well perhaps, because audiences and critics alike failed to appreciate the symbolic significance of this monumental scene. Berlioz, of course, blamed this failure on the poor staging, but it may have been partly the composer's fault as well, since nothing in the pantomime actually explains what Dido and Aeneas are doing in the cave during the storm. Therefore, the dramatic point of the scene is easily lost on an audience like Berlioz's that would probably not have been familiar with the *Aeneid*, and as a result, would have had no point of reference for understanding what was happening onstage.

The importance of this scene is that it demonstrates Berlioz's

---

8. Nor are they carried out in some modern productions. The most recent staging at the New York Metropolitan Opera reduced all of these meaningful scenic details to a minimalist representation of the royal hunt, in which Dido and Aeneas were seen swinging on ropes high above the stage.

9. Cairns, 1975, 490–91.

prowess as an instrumental dramatist. The interlude is, in fact, a miniature symphonic tone poem for orchestra, not unlike his *Symphonie fantastique* or other programmatic orchestral works, in which the drama lies wholly in the instrumental parts, without the aid of voices and texts. This kind of instrumental drama gives us a clue to the significance of Berlioz as a composer of opera, which is that he envisioned opera not as a sung play, but as a discontinuous mixture (a mélange) of vocal *and* instrumental numbers based on selected dramatic moments in an original poetic or literary source that he found "musicable." By "musicable," I mean capable of being translated into the language of music. Did Berlioz care if these moments failed to unfold a perfectly continuous narrative? No. Like Shakespeare's historical plays (after which he claimed *Les Troyens* was modeled), this opera skips over large distances of time and place to capture the essential framework of the drama in a series of autonomous musical vignettes (or as the French would say, *tableaux*). The drama of *Les Troyens* is in many ways similar to the drama in his *La damnation de Faust* (see chapter 9), where the essential action lies in the music itself rather than in the action onstage. In this regard, Berlioz's opera is unusual to say the least. It looks both forward and backward from its place in the middle of the nineteenth century. Deeply indebted to the tradition of French grand opera of the first half of the century, *Les Troyens* is also steeped in the more rarefied air of an avant-garde musical style and a unique vision of what opera is. While the external trappings of *Les Troyens* seem to suggest the continuation of a firmly established tradition, the actual musical expression of that tradition thoroughly confused audiences of Berlioz's day. Like most avant-garde composers, Berlioz adopted a style that pushed the envelope of both performance technique and audience comprehension. In the area of rhythmic invention, his music was extremely difficult, animated, and unpredictable. His melodies were equally strange, modeled as they were on the old-fashioned style of Gluck, in which tunefulness was not a high priority. His orchestration was also remarkably inventive, relying on the use of strange new instruments (such as saxhorns) and unorthodox wind and brass sounds. And his complex choral writing was far in advance of anything heard in Paris at that time. So although Berlioz may have been writing what he thought was a French grand opera, he may actually have been fulfilling his early prediction to play the part of an "Attila come to ravage the musical world." His was a musical style that virtually laid waste to a tired old tradition with the sharply honed sword of a revolutionary new musician. Out of the devastation that was left behind arose *Les Troyens*, perhaps the greatest French grand opera of the nineteenth century.

PART IX
VERISMO OPERA

CHAPTER 17

BIZET'S CARMEN: A SOCIOLOGICAL INTERPRETATION

Georges Bizet, the composer of *Carmen*, would probably have reacted with shock and disbelief had he lived long enough to hear the recording of his famous "Habanera" made in 1997 by the Broadway musical theater soprano Rebecca Luker. Her rendition, from an album entitled simply *Aria*, stripped Bizet's original of its orchestral accompaniment and substituted an electronically synthesized background that gave the work an entirely new, somewhat eerie, and decidedly modernistic sound. This reinterpretation of what had become over the years a classic of the operatic repertoire catapulted the "Habanera" from the opera house directly into the world of pop music, and served as both a reminder and demonstration of the tremendous breadth of audience appeal that *Carmen* has sustained over the 135 years since it was composed.

But this immense popularity accrued only gradually, and mostly outside of France. At home in 1875, Parisian music critics greeted the opera with outright derision, declaring its premiere a fiasco. The reason for this failure, which seems so illogical from a modern point of view, had to do with the reaction of a specific audience, at a particular time, and in a particular theater. Building on this hypothesis, I intend to explore here the context in which *Carmen* first appeared, to arrive at a new understanding of the opera based upon its true social-political meaning.

For audiences today, this opera, Bizet's most popular, is usually thought of as an early example of *verismo*: the first, in fact, of this new style of "realism" that was to become so popular in literature, painting, and music of the late nineteenth century. The principal ingredients of verismo opera are low class characters involved in everyday events that lead to passionate, often violent action and tragic endings. On this count, *Carmen* seems to have it all: the heroine and all her cohorts are certainly members of the lower class, and her demise at the hands of her jealous lover is nothing if not violent.

Equally important for the popularity of this opera today is its Spanish setting, which brings to the music the element of exoticism, or "local color" as it is also known. Exoticism played an important part in the development of nineteenth-century musical styles, as composers began increasingly to incorporate materials borrowed from different ethnic and folk traditions into the mainstream of Western European fine art music. Germans wrote gypsy music (Brahms), Frenchmen wrote Spanish music (Debussy), and Russians wrote Italian and Arabian music (Tchaikovsky and Rimsky-Korsakov, respectively). In the world of opera, exoticism manifested itself in the appearance of librettos featuring the simple peasant people of little-known places such as Poland, Scotland, Turkey, China, or (as with *Carmen*) Spain.

Although today such examples of exoticism may seem somewhat quaint and innocent, for nineteenth-century Parisians they carried a much more potent message, one ripe with overtones of social criticism that served two quite opposite and seemingly contradictory purposes: either to condemn or to glorify the bourgeoisie. As a condemnation, exoticism represented an antidote for repressive Catholic, bourgeois European cultural mores. In this light, foreign folk cultures that were the subject of most musical exoticism were understood to be freer from the sexual and moral constraints that fettered Western European social behavior. On the other hand, as a glorification of the bourgeoisie, exoticism often served to demonstrate the cultural superiority of the middle class by depicting all native people as intellectually inferior, superstitious, uncivilized, and culturally ignorant. In *Carmen*, for instance, the gypsy girls smoke cigarettes, fight like wild animals, and spend their time telling fortunes, all of which might be interpreted as signs of their social inferiority.

Having lost sight of these nineteenth-century meanings of cultural exoticism, audiences today tend to see *Carmen* mostly as a harmless piece of verismo melodrama infused with some colorful folk-flavored Spanish music. But a look at Prosper Merimée's short story on which Bizet's libretto is based can help clarify its author's true intent and lead to new ways of understanding this opera. Merimée's original story, first published in the *Revue des deux mondes* in 1846, explores the theme of social and ethnic conflict, with the ultimate goal of demonstrating the cultural superiority of France. Merimée tells the story of Carmen through the eyes of an amateur French archaeologist, a man of learning and cultural sophistication who is traveling through Spain, where he first encounters a bandit named José. The intellectually superior Frenchman befriends his lawless acquaintance and helps him avoid arrest by the authorities. The archaeologist then travels to Cordoba, where he meets another exotic figure, the gypsy Carmen. She, even more than José, is a socially inferior, lawless, exotic, almost uncivilized native whose lifestyle, behavior, and speech stand in sharp contrast with that of the culturally superior, well-educated Frenchman. As the story unfolds, the reader discovers that Carmen and José were once lovers as well as partners in crime. In the process of telling this story, Merimée reveals more of José's background: his aristocratic origins, his enlistment in the army, his murder of two men, his seduction by Carmen, and her repeated infidelities. It becomes clear that Merimée's primary intention is to contrast both of these unsavory characters with his very proper French archaeologist, and thereby to stereotype his Spanish subjects as culturally inferior people.

In his novella, Merimée also sets up another conflict of a racial nature. Carmen is not just a member of the laboring class, the disenfranchised poor, she is a gypsy, a racially inferior breed of human not much different, in terms of nineteenth-century prejudices, from the equally reviled Jews. Although for readers today, the appearance of gypsies in art and literature inevitably calls up images of a fun-loving, superstitious, nomadic people, in nineteenth-century France there was nothing harmless or quaint about such people. Merimée's portrayal of Carmen was meant to be unsavory in every possible way, in so far as she, and all her gypsy friends, are depicted not only as nomadic thieves and swindlers, but also as witches who practice the black art of sorcery, thus lending them an air of the pagan and ungodly.

Lastly, Merimée's *Carmen* is also a story of gender conflict. Curiously though, this conflict plays out in a reversal of the usual gender roles—Carmen, herself, is remarkably unfeminine and José is equally unmasculine. Carmen smokes cigarettes, and is a thief, a smuggler, and a whore. Her job in the factory where she works is loaded with Freudian sexual imagery: she cuts off the tips of the cigars that she manufactures, which symbolically places her in the role of one who emasculates men. And if José is the hero of the story, he certainly commands little respect. In the 1840s, when Merimée wrote his novella, the traditional image of the hero in literature was firmly based on the model presented in the works of Lord Byron: that of a dashing, commanding, charismatic, slightly inscrutable loner. From this point of view, Merimée's hero is actually an antihero. José's murder of Carmen must be understood not as the result of a fatal flaw in the character of a great hero (which is how it is sometimes described), but rather, as the last desperate act of an impotent man who has been emasculated by a stronger woman.

Bizet and his librettists took Merimée's story and made several radical changes that altered both its dramatic effect and symbolic meaning by diluting much of the ethnic, social, and sexual pungency of the original. In Bizet's opera, the French narrator is eliminated and José becomes a much more sympathetic character, first seen not as a murdering bandit on the run from the authorities, but as a middle-class army corporal. Bizet's José then is not an aristocrat gone bad, but a simple member of the European bourgeoisie building a career in the military. The fact that the archaeologist is cut from the story and that José is not introduced at the outset as a dangerous outlaw effectively soften the dramatic intention of Merimée's original story. No longer does the story depend upon the contrast set up between the culturally superior Frenchman and his socially inferior Spanish acquaintances. Instead, in its operatic transformation, the story now turns only on the contrast built between Carmen and José. In a sense, Bizet has made José play the role of the superior Frenchman by emphasizing his middle-class respectability in distinction to Carmen's bohemian wildness. But as a replacement for the sophisticated archaeologist, José is only partly effective. No matter how cleaned up and gentrified he becomes in Bizet's hands, he is still too much of a cultural simpleton to replace the effete Frenchman of the original story. Thus, Bizet's elimination of the French narrator, along with his recasting of José, blunts the point of using exoticism as a cultural slur aimed at the Spanish and the gypsies. Instead, the meaning of the exoticism shifts to a celebration of unfettered social freedom, in which bandits and gypsies represent unspoiled native spirits who can entice and ensnare weaker middle-class dupes like José. Here, then, is one possible reaction that Bizet's audience might have had to the opera—to understand it as a critique of French bourgeois values through the glorification of socially disreputable characters such as Carmen. Because Bizet's opera places José in the metaphoric role of the bourgeoisie in general, his complete collapse under the spell of Carmen could only have been seen as a total rebuff of those middle-class values by which audiences at the Opéra-Comique lived. Under these circumstances, such an opera was sure to insult the very audience for which it was intended, and in the process, to create a scandal that was destined to overturn the whole world of French opera at that time.

To understand why the theater management, and Bizet himself, would have taken such a chance, it becomes necessary to digress slightly into the nature and variety of French opera in the years between 1850 and 1875—the period that produced most of the operas with which Bizet's audience would have been familiar. During that time, the two principal Parisian opera houses produced entirely different repertoires. The Opéra put on serious French grand operas by such composers as Meyerbeer and Halévy. These were operas conceived on a gigantic scale, almost always in five long acts, usually based on subjects drawn from modern history, and featuring the extensive use of large choruses and spectacular scenic effects. The Opéra-Comique, on the other hand, put on simple comic works by popular composers such as Boieldieu, Auber, and their less famous compatriots. In contrast, these operas were often based on contemporary sentimental romantic stories, and were musically less sophisticated and otherwise smaller in every way than their serious counterparts. These different repertoires were further distinguished by the manner in which composers treated the sections of their librettos that contained dialogue. Such sections are extremely important to any opera, because dialogue allows the dramatic action to move forward through the sharing of information between characters or with the audience. For these important moments of the drama, opéra comique relied exclusively on the use of spoken dialogue, whereas grand opera always employed sung recitative.

By the third quarter of the nineteenth century, this strict bifurcation of the operatic repertoire had begun to stifle composers who had new ideas, resulting in the desire to create new forms of musical-dramatic entertainment that would offer some much needed variety. One of these was the wildly popular satirical operettas of Offenbach, which deliberately poked fun at the serious operas so reverently canonized by Parisian high society. The other, even more important, alternative genre was the opéra lyrique, a kind of romantic tragedy constructed on a scale somewhat smaller than that seen in grand opera, and concentrating more on the personal interaction of its principal characters rather than on the broad relationships of large groups of people caught up in historical-political conflicts. This new kind of "lyric" opera is best represented by the works of Gounod, in particular his *Faust* and *Roméo et Juliette.*

In 1870 the management of the Opéra-Comique, facing competition for audiences from the several new alternative musical theaters, and realizing that their theater had become calcified as what might be called a "family theater," finally decided that they needed to make some changes if they were to survive. They invited Bizet to initiate that change, and suggested several subjects, none of which he really liked. His counterproposal to the management was for the setting of Merimée's *Carmen,* an idea that perhaps struck everyone concerned as making more of a change than was necessary, and one that they accepted only with great reluctance. Because this new work was to be produced at the Opéra-Comique, Bizet adopted the traditional form of French comic opera in which spoken dialogue alternates with musical numbers. But the subject matter of Merimée's novella so departed from the usual comic fare produced at that theater that one could rightly say that this opera single-handedly destroyed (or at the very least, remade) the whole tradition of comic opera in France.

Furthermore, Bizet's insistence on setting Merimée's *Carmen* to music created a major dilemma for the management of the theater, because of the disreputable nature of the story and its characters. To make this seedy tale even remotely acceptable for a family theater, the directors insisted that Bizet make some alterations to soften the effect of the original. He agreed to these:

- Besides softening Carmen's character to make her less of an outlaw, Bizet invented the character of Micaëla, a typical female ingenue drawn from the world of traditional nineteenth-century French opéra comique. Micaëla serves the dual purpose of giving the audience something familiar to hold on to and of functioning as a contrast to the wicked heroine.
- In addition to changing the focus of José from bandit to military man, Bizet further softened him by portraying him as a bit of a mama's boy as well. Throughout the opera, the image of his mother always pulls him away from the dangerous lure of Carmen and a life of degradation.
- The death/murder scene at the end was played down by placing it against, and counterbalancing it with, the festive background of a bullfight.

These changes were insufficient, however, to calm the fears of the management. They begged Bizet to eliminate the murder altogether, but both he and the singers refused. Eventually one of the codirectors actually resigned partly in protest over the opera's frightening vulgarity. It went on nonetheless, and received the kind of reaction the directors had feared. Everything that today looks so innocent to audiences caused a furor in 1875 among the very bourgeois audience and critics whose values it so blatantly ridiculed. The conclusion is clear: that while the Opéra-Comique did manage to extricate itself from the routine of triviality into which it had fallen over the years, it also never anticipated the magnitude of the change this opera wrought on comic opera in France.

Turning now to other issues that bear upon the sociological meaning of *Carmen*, one of the most relevant facts to be borne in mind is that it exists in two different versions: the original for the Opéra-Comique with spoken dialogue, and the revised version for international consumption in which sung recitative replaces the spoken dialogue of the first version. Which version an opera company chooses to produce will determine what kind of operatic experience its audience is going to have, and, to some extent, how much of Merimée's original meaning will filter through to that audience. While arguments can be made to support either version, listeners must understand that Bizet's original, with spoken dialogue, has several distinct and undeniable advantages over the revised version with recitatives. First, the spoken dialogue allows for much more detail about the background of the characters to be communicated to the audience than does the drastically shortened text of the sung recitatives. The use of spoken dialogue, for instance, allows José to give his superior officer a fairly detailed description of Carmen and the trouble she caused in the tobacco factory, including the report that "with the knife with which she cuts cigar ends, the young lady [Carmen] drew a St. Andrew's cross on the other's face." This kind of specificity is lost in the version of the opera with sung recitatives, because much less text can be dispatched when it has to be sung as opposed to when it is spoken.

The second advantage of the original version is that in an opera where speaking and singing are kept separate, the move from speech to lyrical expression in the form of song carries a special significance. These lyrical moments are the emotionally charged high points of the drama. In this regard, special note must be taken of the fact that in Bizet's original version, José makes his first entrance onstage in a spoken dialogue with corporal Moralès, talking about a young woman (Micaëla) who was asking about him only a few minutes earlier. Then Lieutenant Zuniga questions José about the tobacco factory and the young women who work there. Finally Micaëla enters and tells José she has been sent by his mother. Only at this point, with the line, "Tell me about my mother," does José break from speech into song, because the subject of his mother is one that, for him, is loaded with intense emotion. Had he been singing all along, this sudden change would have carried no special significance. But here the change underlines the importance of this dramatic moment for José.

The difference between speaking and singing is also important at other points in the drama. When Lieutenant Zuniga questions Carmen, which is done in dialogue, her response is not to talk but to sing, as a kind of diversionary tactic:

ZUNIGA [*spoken*]:
Well then? What have you to say? Speak up, I'm waiting.

CARMEN [*sung*]:
Tra la la la la
Cut me up, burn me. I'll tell you nothing!
Tra la la la la
I defy everything.

In this situation, Carmen is deliberately not cooperating with Zuniga's investigation; that is, she isn't "talking" to him. To place emphasis on this diversionary technique, Bizet has her sing instead. But the meaning of her singing here is lost in the version of the opera in which she sings all the time. Likewise, when José commands Carmen (in spoken dialogue) not to talk to him when she is in his custody after being arrested, she again sings instead. She is thus able to obey his command not to speak while also ignoring his directive for her not to communicate with him. But in the revised version, in which everyone sings all the time, this slip into song becomes meaningless.

No examination of Bizet's *Carmen* would be complete without an analysis of the impact of Carmen herself on the social-political meaning of the opera. Bizet's genius with regard to the effective depiction and deployment of Carmen throughout the drama can be seen in the way he sets up her introduction. The opera starts with a chorus of soldiers singing in a style that would have been thoroughly familiar to audiences of the Opéra-Comique—simple, regular, almost innocent, and delivered *leggieramente* (lightly). Next, Bizet introduces Micaëla, who has come in search of José. Dramatically speaking, she functions as the standard ingenue of opéra comique, a character of sweetness and innocence, who serves, in this particular case, as a contrast and foil to the wicked heroine. Musically speaking, Micaëla's portrayal is equally as simple and innocent as that of the opening chorus. In fact, part of her response to one of the army guards who invites her into the guardhouse where she can wait for José to come on duty, is to mimic the cute little tune (Ex. 17-1) that the soldiers used to assure her that José would be arriving soon.

Example 17-1. Micaëla's response to the chorus of soldiers.

To this point in the opera, Bizet's music has held the audience firmly in the familiar world of traditional opéra comique, where simple, regular, attractive music was the norm. Only after establishing this familiar musical ground does Bizet bring Carmen onstage. Here for the first time the music turns to the minor mode and looses its sense of clear tonality as the composer introduces the first sample of his musical exoticism—a version of Carmen's "fate" motif (Ex. 2).

Example 17-2. "Fate" motif.

A rhythmic variation of this theme appears in the orchestra as a chorus of soldiers notices and comments on Carmen's arrival. Here for the first time, Bizet's music sounds different, alerting his audience to the fact that Carmen is not from the same world as Micaëla and José, and suggesting, as well (through the use of the interval of the augmented second from B to A-flat in the minor mode), a potential danger in this new, obviously alien character.

Carmen's arrival leads directly to one of the most famous numbers in the opera, the "Habanera" (Ex. 17-3), the music of which was borrowed and adapted by Bizet from a popular Afro-Cuban cabaret tune of the time by Sebastián Iradier. Small chance that Bizet's audience would have recognized this particular tune, since respectable middle-class Parisians were not regular patrons of the cabaret theaters. But they must surely have recognized the general style of the music and its suggestion of licentiousness. Such distinctions between cabaret music and the usual style of the Opéra-Comique, although meaningful in 1875, are all but lost on modern audiences, for whom there is nothing at all naughty about this tune. Even the melodic chromaticism that so colors Bizet's melody with slinky sexuality will likely remind today's audiences more of *Tristan und Isolde* than of nineteenth-century cabaret music. We have, in effect, lost touch with the sociological meaning that this cabaret-style aria had for listener's in a Parisian family theater in 1875, because our own ears have been spoiled by a familiarity with the chromaticism of later nineteenth-century music, especially that of Wagner, for whom such chromaticism had the altogether different implication of romantic longing.

Example 17-3. "Habanera."

Example 17-3 *(continued)*

bien en vain qu'on l'ap - pel-le, s'il lui con - vient____ de__ re - fu - ser!

The fact that Carmen's song is a cabaret tune also suggests that she is "performing" for the crowd. In fact, the real Carmen is hard to find behind all the performing she does throughout this opera. Usually in opera, singing is understood to replace real-world speech. That is, all verbal communication is accomplished through the medium of song. But there are times in opera when singing is meant to represent just that—a song. It must therefore say something about Carmen that Bizet has her so often "singing" in this latter sense. Even the title of this opening number is ripe with significance: the habanera is a kind of Cuban song and dance. Carmen is therefore giving the world a "song and dance," both in the literal sense of a performance, and in the figurative sense of foisting something phony on an unexpecting world.

At the point when Carmen makes her next entrance, she has been arrested by Zuniga and placed in the custody of José who, as mentioned above, commands her not to speak. To communicate with him without disobeying his order, she decides to sing instead. Here, too, Carmen operates in a performance mode, adopting another Spanish song and dance form, the "Seguidilla."

Example 17-4. Carmen's "Seguidilla."

Près des rem-parts de Sé - vil - - - le, chez___ mon a - mi___ Lil-las Pas-tia,

Continuing into act 2, this "song and dance" routine takes on even greater importance as Carmen and her gypsy friends sing and dance for the patrons of Lillas Pastia's tavern. By now the audience has begun to suspect that the real Carmen is hidden behind the facade of a performer, and that Bizet must be deliberately portraying this woman as someone who cannot be trusted, or, at the very least, has something to hide. The first time we see Carmen in a role other than that of a performer is when she tells her friends that she cannot accompany them on a smuggling mission because she is in love once again. Is this meant to suggest that she is genuinely in love with

José because she is finally not putting on a show—a first brief glimpse of the real person behind the performer? Or is the real Carmen the mysterious one who, when José finally appears at the tavern, entertains him with yet another song and dance?

Besides impressing the audience with Carmen's role as a performer (and her concomitant insincerity), these numerous instances of singing and dancing are also clearly meant to suggest that performers are people who are in control of an audience. Carmen's continual "performing" throughout the opera thus closely corresponds to the theme of domination that was so central to Merimée's original story. Carmen controls and dominates José (and others) through her performances in much the way that Merimée's archaeologist dominates the lower class characters of the original story. This is especially true in the tavern scene of act 2, where her seductive song and dance puts José into an irresolvable dilemma (should he go AWOL and follow Carmen, or return to the barracks like a good boy?) that finds expression in the almost pitiful pleading of his famous "Flower Song" (Ex. 17-5):

Act 2, tavern scene.

JOSÉ:	JOSÉ:
La fleur que tu m'avais jetée	The flower that you threw at me
Dans ma prison m'était restée	I kept in my prison cell
Flétrie et sèche, cette fleur	Withered and dried, that flower
Gardait toujours sa douce odeur;	Kept its sweet smell;

....

Car tu n'avais eu qu'à paraître,	For you only had to appear,
Qu'à jeter un regard sur moi,	To throw a glance my way,
Pour t'emparer de tout mon être.	To ensnare my whole being.
O ma Carmen!	O my Carmen!
Et j'étais une chose à toi!	And I was completely yours!
Carmen, je t'aime!	Carmen, I love you!

| CARMEN: | CARMEN: |
| Non! Tu ne m'aimes pas! | No! You don't love me! |

| JOSÉ: | JOSÉ: |
| Que dis-tu? | What are you saying? |

CARMEN:	CARMEN:
Car si tu m'aimais,	Because if you loved me,
Là-bas tu me suivrais!	You would follow me!

....

JOSÉ:
Quitter mon drapeau ... déserter ...
C'est la honte ... c'est infamie!
Je n'en veux pas!

CARMEN:
Eh bien! Pars!

JOSÉ:
Carmen, je t'en prie!

JOSÉ:
Quit my flag ... desert ...
It's shameful ... infamous!
I want none of it!

CARMEN:
Very well then! Leave!

JOSÉ:
Carmen, I beg you!

Example 17-5. José's "Flower Song."

This is surely José's lowest point in terms of strength of character and self-respect. His music boldly proclaims the impotence he suffers in the presence of Carmen. Especially important in this regard is the climactic high note near the end of his flower song. Bizet marks it *pianissimo* in the score, but all too often tenors sing it full voice, in typical heroic style. But José is no hero, and a loud high note is just what Bizet didn't want here.

So if the domination of foreign nationals was a subject that the French bourgeoisie found attractive (as found in Merimée's original story), then this opera would have shocked its audience on a most fundamental level. It is the bourgeois José, not Carmen, who is dominated and reduced to groveling, not only in his "Flower Song" but also in the final duet:

JOSÉ:
Je ne menace pas! J'implore ... je supplie!
Notre passé, Carmen, je l'oublie!
Oui, nous allons tous deux

JOSÉ:
I do not threaten; I implore, I beg!
I'll forget our past, Carmen.
Yes, we'll both

Commencer une autre vie,	Begin another life
Loin d'ici, sous d'autres cieux!	Far from here, under other skies!

The only other character of importance in this opera is, of course, Escamillo, the bullfighter, who is actually brought to life in the opera after only getting a third-person mention in Merimée's story (i.e., in the novella, he never actually appears as a character with lines to say). Most likely the reason Bizet increased the prominence of his role in the opera was to create a male foil for José, similar to the female foil that he created for Carmen with the invention of Micaëla. And, of course, the toreador provides Bizet with an excuse to inject more local color into his music. We first meet this character in act 2 at Lillas Pastia's tavern. As he arrives in town, via a parade of admirers, he is invited to join the merrymaking in the tavern. There he meets and falls in love with Carmen, and sings his famous "Toreador Song." The real value of Escamillo, however, becomes most apparent at the end of the opera, in the scene in which José murders Carmen. This violent act takes place outside the arena where Escamillo is performing. Bizet thus brings into direct opposition the poignant difference of musical styles associated with Escamillo and the bullfight on the one hand, and José's murder of Carmen on the other. This kind of musical superimposition of opposites was a common French operatic technique, used to create dramatic tension through the juxtaposition of violently contrasted and conflicting musical materials. Bizet's music cleverly suggests that Escamillo lies at the root of José's murder of Carmen. But on a deeper level, this conflation of musical opposites may have been designed to invite audiences to draw a parallel between the confrontation of a matador and his bull and the confrontation of José and Carmen. In both of these face-offs, a man tries to assert his dominance over a powerful animal by stabbing it (or her) to death.

More than 125 years after the premiere of *Carmen*, commentators continue to insist that this is an opera about love and jealousy. But viewed this way *Carmen* is messy and inconsistent. How, for instance, is José to be understood? Is he a tragic hero in the mold of Verdi's Otello: a great man plagued by insecurities who falls victim to jealousy? Not in the least. Verdi worked hard to establish Otello's heroism before exposing us to his horrible demise. Bizet, on the other hand, did no such thing for José, who is never presented as a strong character with a tragic flaw, but rather as nothing more than a spineless simpleton.

And what about Carmen? Is she just a domineering, femme fatale who falls victim to a fate beyond her control? In part, yes. Is she, like Verdi's Lady Macbeth, a character whose drive to dominate eventually extracts its own tragic subconscious self-punishment? Not at all. Unlike Verdi, Bizet offers up a heroine who dies without reason, more in a willful act of suicide than in submission to fate. Carmen is warned to avoid the lurking José in the last scene of the opera (the bullfight), but she deliberately engages him and almost dares him to kill her. Objectively speaking, there would seem to be better ways to be free of José, if that was what she really wanted.

In general, then, this opera works best if understood on the level of a social/political allegory, but probably not the one Merimée intended. José's character makes sense only if seen as a metaphor for the weak, hypocritical value system of the French bourgeoisie, the very audience whom this opera was intended to shock. In the end, José becomes the victim of his own weakness and his uncertain devotion to a corrupt and indefensible moral code. Carmen's death, in turn, also only makes sense on a metaphoric level. As a symbol for the oppressed, socially disenfranchised minorities of the world, Carmen must sing, "Let me be free, or kill me." In this way she carries a potent political message about the power of self-sacrifice to defeat injustice.

While this view of *Carmen* studiously avoids the usual interpretation of the work as a piece of popular verismo exoticism, it also attempts to offer an alternative understanding of the opera as a social-political allegory designed to shock audiences at the Opéra-Comique out of their bourgeois complacency in 1875. This alternative view is offered here as a potential means to get beyond the superficial attractiveness of Bizet's music and to examine what this opera's shocking verismo style might have meant to its composer, to nineteenth-century Parisians, and, just as important, to audiences today.

CHAPTER 18

The opposite ends of the nineteenth century differ remarkably in their philosophical outlook, and as a result, in their music style. The early years of the century were marked by a buoyant optimism among creative artists—an optimism rooted in the discovery of the self, the projection of personal emotions in art, and a belief that art might somehow transform society. Manifestos in support of a new art appeared in the form of printed declarations such as the preface to Victor Hugo's *Cromwell*, calling for the overthrow of the formal rigidity of the past, and in purely musical forms such as Berlioz's *Symphonie fantastique*, which single-handedly revolutionized the genre of the symphony as it had been known up to that time. This revolution had held out a new hope for what art might become in the new era of the common man. But this flame of optimism was eventually extinguished at the other end of the century by a feeling of pessimism that overtook the world upon the realization that life was not going to change so easily. Perhaps the philosophy of Arthur Schopenhauer as expounded in his treatise *Die Welt als Will und Darstellung (The World as Will and Idea*, 1819), had already planted the seeds of discontent and pessimism with talk of the eternal pain of the world caused by a relentless life force motivated by inextinguishable desire. By the last decades of the nineteenth century, artists of all kinds began to come to grips with the myth of a world made perfect through art, and in place of this utopian fantasy, had embraced a gloomier, doubt-riddled view of life. It is the desire to show the world for what it really is that produced the entirely new movement of "realism" in literature, art, and music after 1850.

Realism, also known as *naturalism*, and in Italy as *verismo*, began as a literary movement in France in the mid-nineteenth century. Responding to the darker side of the growing industrial revolution and related ills in society, French authors began to abandon the highly romanticized historical dramas popular earlier in the century, and to take up subjects drawn from less idealized accounts of everyday life with an almost brutally realistic depiction of the ugly and sordid aspects of existence. Alexandre Dumas fils

---

1. Joseph Kerman's term in *Opera as Drama*.

touched on these issues of societal decay when he wrote the play *La dame aux camélias*, which in 1853 was turned into the opera *La traviata* by Verdi. Part of the failure Verdi suffered with the premiere of this opera had to do with its contemporary setting and the subject matter of prostitution (which audiences seemed to think Verdi was condoning). Issues of sex, violence, and prostitution, which had become matters of everyday Parisian life during the Second Empire (ca. 1850–70), became the excuse for other French writers to explore less attractive, less romanticized depictions of contemporary life. These writers included Honoré de Balzac, Émile Zola, and especially Gustave Flaubert, whose *Madame Bovary* was published in 1856.

The realism movement spread to the visual arts after 1850, as painters such as Gustave Courbet in his *A Burial at Omans* (1850) and Vincent Van Gogh in *The Potato Eaters* (1885) began depicting seemingly unpainterly subjects drawn from the most ordinary and sometimes poverty-stricken parts of contemporary society.

Eventually realism moved into the world of opera as well. Although Verdi's *La traviata* is rarely thought of as a verismo opera because of its depiction of life at the highest echelons of Parisian society, the opera, like Dumas's play on which it is based, does expose a sordid, unhealthy side of that society that qualifies it at least as a first step in the direction of verismo. Perhaps the first truly verismo opera was Bizet's *Carmen*, written in 1875. (See chapter 17.) It dealt with the lowest classes of society (smugglers, gypsies who work in a cigar factory, and low-ranking military men who go AWOL) and their amoral and illegal activities, including robbery and murder. The violent end of this opera, in which José stabs Carmen to death, is typical of the characteristics of late-nineteenth-century verismo opera: low-class characters involved in passionate and usually violent action.

From France, verismo spread south to Italy, where several important composers became caught up in this new style of opera. One of the first was Pietro Mascagni, whose *Cavalleria rusticana* of 1890 is usually mentioned as an important example of this style. Among these Italian composers of verismo opera, Giacomo Puccini is perhaps the best known today. With a total of only twelve operas written over a career that spanned approximately forty years, Puccini can hardly be said to have been prolific. But few composers had so many long-running successes on opera stages around the world. There may be only about four of Puccini's operas that are not regularly performed these days—a remarkable measure of his popularity. Puccini is generally thought of as an exponent of the verismo style; however, one would actually be hard pressed to find many of his works that qualify as part of this particular operatic subgenre. An opera such as *La bohème*, for instance deals with the lower classes of society and with the struggles of everyday life, but is missing the violent action that we usually expect in a verismo opera. Likewise, *Turandot* is a fine example of an opera full of violence, but its characters are drawn from the land of fairytale make-believe.

For this reason the best example of a verismo opera among Puccini's oeuvre is surely *Tosca* (1900). This opera has everything that a fan of verismo could ever ask for: two suicides, an attempted rape, a torture scene, a murder, and an execution. The libretto, written by the team of Luigi Illica and Giuseppe Giacosa, is, not surprisingly, based on a French play by Victorien Sardou titled *La Tosca* (1887). With this play, and Puccini's opera based upon it, one might say that verismo not only reached its zenith, but perhaps even overstepped its boundaries. Here, the realistic treatment of everyday life that is so essential a characteristic of this genre borders on the melodramatic. Sardou prided himself on being a disciple of the "well-made plays" of Eugène Scribe (Meyerbeer's librettist), but the frequently heard complaint that this play is a little too well made is not unfounded. Realism implies believability, and much of what happens in *Tosca* stretches our credibility: the ferocity of Tosca's jealousy, the villainy of Scarpia, and Cavaradossi's ill-advised vocal support for Napoleon in the presence of a royalist police chief, are all just a bit too exaggerated as dramatic gestures to strike audiences as truly realistic—at least not realistic in the same manner as something like *La bohème*. This may have been what the musicologist Joseph Kerman meant when he referred to this opera as a "shabby little shocker." Of course, the fact that this drama succeeds as an opera is largely to be credited to the power of Puccini's music. So despite the fact that *Tosca* may well be the ultimate verismo drama, which in itself produces a certain element of theatrical sensationalism that audiences find irresistible, the more important question to be dealt with in an analysis of this opera is that of how the music facilitates or contributes to the creation of its dramatic effectiveness; that is, how this opera "works."

This brings us to the question of what kind of an opera Puccini wanted to write. Perched as he was on the cusp of musical modernity, and aware of the many musical traditions that surrounded him in 1900, he was faced with a choice: to what extent was his new work going to adopt the traditional Italian understanding of opera as a dramatic dialogue interspersed with moments of lyrical introspection, and to what extent was it going to adopt the more modern (i.e., Wagnerian) approach to opera as a continuous vocal narrative in arioso supported by a symphonic development of leitmotifs; that is, a sung play? This dilemma is mirrored in the correspondence between one of the librettists, Giacosa (himself a well respected dramatist), and the composer. In true modern fashion, Giacosa expressed his desire to make Sardou's drama into a libretto that plumbed the psychological depths of its characters, whereas Puccini, for his part, was more concerned about making sure the libretto contained a sufficient number of emotional moments in which the tenor or soprano could deliver stunningly beautiful melodies of the kind he was so good at writing. The battle lines were thus drawn, but what was the outcome? How modern was *Tosca* going to be?

Before determining which aesthetic of opera drove Puccini's creativity in this new work, and how he resolved the differences between what he and his librettists wanted, it might be helpful to briefly review the basic differences between the two principal competing styles and techniques of opera at the end of the nineteenth century: those of Wagner and late Verdi, both of which bore directly upon the choices that Puccini had to make in writing *Tosca*. Given the fact that the basic goal of all opera composers at that time was to bring to the genre the more realistic unfolding of dramatic action that characterized a spoken stage play, the compositional techniques of Verdi and Wagner resemble each other more than most of us might imagine. For Verdi, of course, the idea of great singing propelled him toward a conception of opera as a musical drama in which particularly meaningful moments—those most intensely emotional in nature—were treated in an expansive lyricism. But toward the end of his career, these became the exceptional moments in a texture that otherwise took the form of a flexible arioso of asymmetrical, unpatterned phrases that more closely approximate the rhythm of speech. In this regard, Verdi tends (here and there) to sound much like Wagner. But unlike Wagner, Verdi mixed into this general arioso style some larger ensemble numbers (trios, quartets, choruses) that promote the older Italian understanding that an opera should logically contain group displays of emotion, in which the drama comes to a full stop as singers express those emotions in an ensemble set piece. At the root of this combination of arioso and set pieces in Verdi's last masterpieces, lies the ghost of the old Italian number opera, with vestiges of individual musical numbers (set pieces) operating on an almost subliminal level, their lines of demarcation ironed out and smoothed over with orchestral bridgework.

Meanwhile, Verdi's use of the orchestra to accompany the singers again relies heavily on the Italian tradition of asking nothing more from the orchestra than quiet, unobtrusive accompaniment of the solo voices on stage. Of course, Verdi moved far beyond this principle in his journey from *Oberto* to *Falstaff*, and by the end of his career, he came to realize that the orchestra could be employed as a powerful tool in the establishment of dramatic moods in opera. Nevertheless, most of Verdi's orchestral writing remains accompanimental in nature. While no longer unobtrusive, at the end of his career it still functioned mostly in the role of commentator on the drama that unfolded in the vocal parts above it.

Wagner approached the writing of opera with a somewhat different set of aesthetic principles. He did not believe in expansive vocal lyricism, because for him, music drama was not the product of a collection of "songs." Nor, for the same reason, did he make room for large ensembles in his operas. As a result, Wagner's vocal writing is almost exclusively limited to solo arioso. In place of the once glorious voice, he elevated the importance of the orchestra in his operas, giving it the role of chief bearer of the main melodic material of the drama. This new concept of the dominance of the orchestra led to the coining of the term *symphonic opera* as a way of describing the new balance of power in Wagner's music dramas. But while it is true that long stretches of music are controlled by a continuous orchestral texture of developing leitmotifs that suggests the compositional process of a symphonic development section à la Beethoven, it is equally true that there are in Wagner's works long stretches of uninteresting, purely accompanimental orchestral music that no one would ever tolerate in a real symphony. So Wagner's operas, like Verdi's, hint at a division that distinguishes between musical styles that approximate (without ever actually duplicating) the old speechlike recitative on the one hand, and the more lyrical set piece on the other.

Given the operatic precedents Puccini faced, the argument about the inclusion of lyrical moments in the libretto would suggest that he leaned in the direction of the Italian approach as he began writing his new opera. Indeed one can see the librettists acceding to the desires of the composer as they adapted Sardou's drama to give Puccini what he wanted. A typical example appears near the beginning of act 1 in the duet between Cavaradossi and Tosca that takes place when she visits him in the church where he has been working on a religious painting. This confrontation contains exactly the kind of texts that Puccini wanted in order to allow his singers extended sections of lyricism, and it is telling to see how these lyrical moments in the libretto compare to the original scene between these two characters in the play. In both the play and the opera Tosca comes on stage suspicious about why the door to the church is locked. She thinks she heard Cavaradossi talking with someone, and believes it to be another woman. Tosca thus enters in an agitated state of mind, but Puccini's music gives the impression, as Cavaradossi insists, that everything is perfectly fine. Thus the duet begins with the lyrical orchestral melody seen in Ex.18-1.

Example 18-1. Orchestra melody in Tosca-Cavaradossi duet, act 1.

This melody continues through the point where Tosca, now reassured, places some flowers at the foot of a statue of the Madonna in a short pantomime. From here, the play and the opera diverge significantly, and the reason they do can be traced to the librettists' need to create those moments of lyricism Puccini wanted. At this point in the play, Tosca tells Cavaradossi that they can't meet that evening because the concert she has been ordered to perform will be long and is to be followed by a ball that she must attend. In the opera, on the other hand, she says just the opposite, telling Cavaradossi that the concert will be short and that they can meet afterward and escape for a romantic rendezvous at his country villa. This then leads to Tosca's elaborate description of the beauties of the country house, with text that was added to Sardou's conversation just to allow Tosca to have her lyrical moment. And here, Puccini takes advantage of the opportunity handed to him, allowing the vocal part itself to become amply lyrical, as seen in Ex. 18-2.

Example 18-2. First lyrical section in act 1 duet.

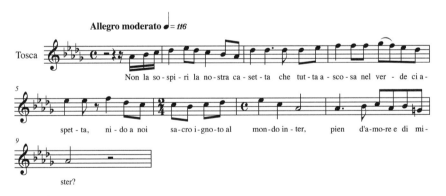

Both the play and the opera then proceed to the part of the encounter between these characters when Tosca notices the painting of Mary Magdalene on which Cavaradossi is working. She recognizes in this painting the face of its model, the Marchesa Attavanti, and flies into another jealous rage. But the librettists added here a few lines for Cavaradossi to soothe Tosca's ruffled feathers by praising her dark eyes. These new lines, not found in the play, are the only other section of this duet to receive an extended lyrical vocal setting, as seen in Ex. 18-3.

Example 18-3. Second lyrical section in act 1 duet.

The comparison of the play with the libretto thus reveals that Giacosa and Illica adapted Sardou's play fairly loosely, manipulating the original to shorten the drama and reduce some of its complexities, but also to supply Puccini with reflective moments that could be treated lyrically. Besides this duet in act 1, the librettists also added the lines in act 2 that became Tosca's famous aria, "Vissi d'arte," and the entire opening of act 3, including the song of the offstage shepherd boy and Cavaradossi's equally famous aria "E lucevan le stelle"—all major moments of lyricism in the completed opera.

The interjection of new material of a more reflective nature into the original dialogue of Sardou's play produced a libretto that obviously played into Puccini's strength as a composer of melodies of searing intensity and beauty. This fact has always obscured the real nature of his compositional technique, however. To any attentive listener, *Tosca* sounds similar enough to many of the masterpieces of Verdi to lend it an aura of comfortable familiarity. Over the years, Puccini has thus been understood by most opera lovers to be a disciple of Verdi and an upholder of the basic Italian values of vocal supremacy in opera. While I would not challenge the basic validity of this view, I will suggest that this easy association with the Italian school of opera has tended to obscure the subtleties of Puccini's style and has misled our understanding of his compositional technique. Behind all those gorgeous melodies lurks far more of the influence of Wagner than

most opera audiences are aware. Puccini's receptivity to elements of the
Germanic style surely reflects the growing sense among all turn-of-the-
century composers that the opera of the future would continue to rely
on the resources of a large, colorful orchestra as the source of powerful
musical-dramatic effects. In the particular case of *Tosca*, the elevation of the
orchestra to a position of central importance is accomplished through the
adoption of several of the techniques of Wagner's music dramas, first and
foremost of which is the use of specific themes and motifs to tag the various
characters and events in the drama. Although Puccini's motifs often take
form as far more expansive melodies than Wagner's leitmotifs, their use
does produce an opera in which large sections of music find the principal
melodic material located in the orchestra. This, in turn, creates the overall
effect of an opera that mimics a symphony.

The first few scenes of act 1 of *Tosca* can be used to illustrate this
symphonic approach in greater detail. The opera opens with a powerful brass
motif that later becomes associated with the villain, Scarpia (Ex. 18-4).

Example 18-4. Scarpia's motif.

As the curtain rises, Angelotti enters the church anxiously looking
for something. His initial entrance is accompanied by the rhythmically
unsettled, frantic music seen in Ex.18-5.

Example 18-5. Angelotti's motif.

As he continues his search, his actions are accompanied by a more
subdued motif in the orchestra that suggests a release of tension (Ex. 18-6).

Example 18-6. Angelotti's "search" motif.

The last four measures of this melody are developed in the orchestra as the search continues. This developmental technique is the essence of any truly symphonic style in opera. Exs. 18-5 and 18-6 are then repeated as Angelotti finally finds the key, left for him by his sister, to a chapel where he can hide.

Next the sacristan enters doing his chores. Like Angelotti, most of the sacristan's activities onstage are pantomimed to the accompaniment of new melodic material in the orchestra. The beginning, middle, and end of the music that accompanies the sacristan's activity can be seen in Ex.18-7.

Example 18-7. Sacristan's motif.

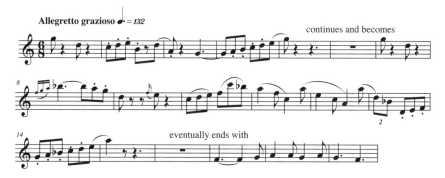

The orchestra then moves into a bell-like passage that imitates the ringing of the angelus bell, as the sacristan falls to his knees to pray. He finishes and Cavaradossi enters, goes up to the painting of Mary Magdalene that he has been working on, and pulls off the cover to the accompaniment of another attractive tune in the orchestra (Ex. 18-8).

Example 18-8. "Painting" motif

In true symphonic fashion, however, this new theme is derived by Puccini from the opening of the sacristan's theme (Ex. 18-7) by starting on the second beat of the first measure of that theme (d^2) and taking the first note of each beat thereafter (c^1, b^1, a^1, g^1) and then proceeding to the rising scale that follows. This kind of thematic derivation demonstrates an interest on Puccini's part in the modern symphonic techniques of thematic transformation found in the German (Wagnerian) school of opera writing.

The unveiling of the painting leads to a discussion between the sacristan and Cavaradossi about the unknown woman who served as a model for this portrait. The motif in the orchestra that supports this conversation (Ex. 18-9) is again derived from (or at least distantly related to) the last few measures of Ex. 18-7 (the sacristan's theme), by virtue of the fact that both involve a stepwise arrangement of the melodic interval of the major third (f^1 to a^1 in ex. 7 and f-sharp^1 to a-sharp^1 in Ex. 18-9).

Example 18-9. Conversation about painting.

Up to this point in act 1 the orchestra has had total possession of all the principal melodic material, while the voices have had only short arioso-like phrases to sing, occasionally doubling the orchestral melody underneath. What follows, however, again represents one of those situations in which the librettists added lines to the play to satisfy Puccini's need for reflective emotional moments that would allow him to write more symmetrical and tuneful melodies, imitating the sound of an old-fashioned set piece. As Cavaradossi paints, he muses on the difference between the beauty of the mysterious woman he used as a model for his Mary Magdalene painting and that of his girlfriend, Tosca. This extended solo section ("Recondita armonia") is the first place in the opera where the solo voice has the principal melodic material, and for this reason it stands out from everything around it like an independent musical unit that might be called an aria. But in typical Puccini fashion, this vocal melody is sung in unison with the orchestra, thus making it unclear who actually owns the tune, the singer onstage or the instruments in the pit. The "aria" begins with an orchestral introduction based on the melody in Ex. 18-10.

Example 18-10. Orchestral introduction to Cavaradossi's "Recondita armonia."

Two more tunes make up the vocal part of this little "aria": Exs. 18-11 and 18-12.

Example 18-11. First vocal theme of Cavaradossi's "Recondita armonia."

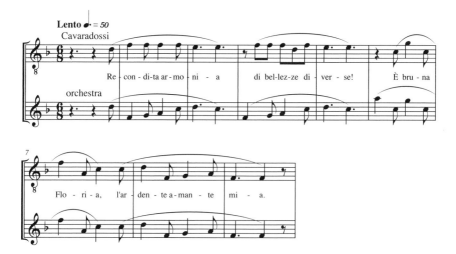

Example 18-12. Second vocal theme of Cavaradossi's "Recondita armonia."

Of these, the more important is the second, which has a second phrase (mm. 6–9) that is clearly derived from mm. 11–14 of the sacristan's music as seen in Ex. 18-7. (The notes f^2-c^2 and e^2-c^2-a^1 are a common element in each theme.) This kind of motivic derivation in which one theme metamorphoses into another again testifies to Puccini's adoption of a symphonic technique in *Tosca* that is reminiscent of the basic manipulation of leitmotifs found in Wagner's operas.

Tosca exemplifies the manner in which Puccini is often said to have been a composer who borrowed freely from styles and techniques he found around him, but it also demonstrates the manner in which he created a style uniquely his own. Large sections of the opera are carried in a vocal arioso not unlike that found in either the works of Verdi or Wagner, but the orchestral support under this arioso is usually far more tuneful than what one hears in either of those earlier composers. At the same time, the peak moments of emotional intensity are given over to vocal melody of an extreme lyricism—the kind of melodies that etch themselves in the collective memory of opera audiences, generation after generation. It is these melodies that place Puccini's operas in a category all their own. Even Verdi had given up writing such tunes in his last operas, and Wagner so distrusted pure melody that none of his mature works contains anything nearly as songful. While the illusion of a continuous opera resulting from set pieces blended together declaims Puccini's Italian roots, and the continuous importance of the orchestra as the primary purveyor of melodic material recalls the style of Wagner, the final result in *Tosca* is an opera that differs from both of these models and marks Puccini as an important innovator in the history of early twentieth-century opera.

PART X
FAIRY-TALE OPERA

CHAPTER 19

PUCCINI'S *TURANDOT*: THE (UN)SOLVED RIDDLE

Puccini's *Turandot* is such a well-known and beloved opera, writing about it in any new and meaningful way poses a major challenge. My goal in this chapter, then, is to organize the approach to this subject around the question (rarely addressed by other writers) of the opera's strengths and weaknesses as a piece of music drama in relation to the late-nineteenth-century musical milieu out of which it grows. As explained in the chapter on *Tosca*, Puccini was a composer usually thought to have carried forward the principles of Italian opera as seen in the late works of Verdi. To be sure, Verdi and Puccini bare a chronological relationship that produces an unbroken line of opera in the closing years of the nineteenth century. Verdi's last masterpiece, *Falstaff*, was premiered in 1893, the very same year that Puccini produced his first great opera *Manon Lescaut*. Despite the overlapping of their compositional careers, Verdi and Puccini do not sound the same (something that even the most careless listener cannot help noticing); and this difference can be traced in part to the younger composer's adoption of some of the principles of symphonic opera (as outlined in the chapter on *Tosca*). Whereas Wagner's revolutionary theories about opera had a profound effect on composers throughout Europe and beyond in the last half of the nineteenth century, their impact on Puccini was moderated somewhat by the fact that he, like most Italians, loved singing, pure and simple. With the exception of a few hard-core Wagner disciples, most Italian composers reacted to the German master as did Verdi, who upon being labeled a copier of Wagner late in his career, angrily retorted that opera and symphony are two distinctly different genres, and that it was a mistake to mix the two. Although Verdi decried the growing trend toward writing symphonic opera, it was nevertheless patently clear to anyone with ears that after 1850 even he was beginning to use the orchestra in a new way that lifted it out of its old role of simple vocal accompaniment and made it into an active participant in the musical drama onstage. In this regard, Puccini simply picked up the hint of Wagner in the last works of Verdi and carried the symphonic torch forward into the new century. But in accepting the idea of an increased role for the orchestra in opera, Italian composers (Puccini included) never fully accepted that part of the Wagner aesthetic that ceded the prominence of the voice to the orchestra. They remained, for the most part, secure in their conviction that opera was a collection of emotional highpoints set to tuneful musical moments strung together on a thread of recitative or arioso. This basic principle continued to define Italian opera, including many of the late works of Verdi, throughout most of the nineteenth century.

Despite their adherence to this ageing formula, such composers as Verdi and Puccini were very much aware of the dramatic weaknesses of their native operatic style. As a result, they began to question such fundamental Italian characteristics as the constant interruption of both music and drama by applause, and the lack of any large-scale musical form. Verdi was one of the first to overcome these inherent deficiencies in Italian opera by finding ways of maintaining musical continuity through the greater use of arioso and the blending of one set piece into the next via short orchestral bridges that created at least the illusion of musical continuity. In his hands, the new Italian model became that of a continuous arioso, out of which there arose here and there short moments of lyricism—not really arias per se, but fleeting melodic high points. Act 2 of *Otello* contains a typical example in the duet in which Iago attempts to arouse Otello's suspicion about Desdemona. Coming out of the bridge that connects the preceding quartet to this duet, the vocal writing is all in an arioso style, but by m. 12 where the tempo slows, the music lapses into a more regular phrase structure and a slightly more tuneful melody, making this section stand out as a lyrical moment amidst the general arioso style of most of the rest of the duet. In this limited regard, Wagner and Verdi worked along similar lines, toward similar musical-dramatic goals.

Example 19-1. Otello's solo in act 2 duet with Iago: arioso moving to full melody.

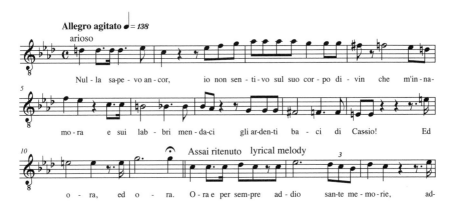

Example 19-1 *(continued)*

dio____ su - bli-mi in - can - ti del pen - sier! Ad - dio schie - re ful -

gen - ti ad-dio vit - to - rie, dar-di vo-lan - ti___ e vo-lan-ti cor-sier!

Concerning the subject of long-range musical form, Verdi also experimented with the use of returning melodic motifs—not the leitmotifs of Wagner, but his own system of thematic recall. In *La traviata*, for example, he introduced an important melodic idea in the little love duet between Alfredo and Violetta during the opening party scene in act 1. Later in this act that same theme returns in the middle of Violetta's aria "Ah fors'è lui," right after she sings the cabaletta in which she rededicates her life to pure pleasure and rejects the idea of a true love. The effect of the appearance of the theme from the love duet here in the aria is to force Violetta aggressively to reject Alfredo's avowal of love by repeating her cabaletta devoted to pleasure. In this way, Verdi created a logical dramatic motivation for the old-fashioned practice of repeating cabalettas. Motivic coherence of this type is termed *thematic recall*, and is designed literally to recall an earlier, related moment in the drama that has some bearing on the later dramatic situation in which the theme is brought back. Puccini therefore had access to both Verdi's technique of thematic recall and to Wagner's system of symphonically developed leitmotifs as he began work on *Turandot*, which was to be his last opera.

In the final analysis, we might best think of Puccini as a composer in whose operas the various priorities of Italian or German opera are brought into alignment and synthesized into a new style. In *Turandot*, we find Verdi's older Italian style modernized through the adoption of some new techniques rooted in the work of Wagner. This eclectic opera, left unfinished at its composer's death in 1924, draws not only upon the techniques of Verdi and Wagner, but also on innovations found in the works of other major composers of the early twentieth century, including Stravinsky, Berg, Debussy, and Schoenberg. Despite these broad contemporary influences, *Turandot* remains very much an opera cast in the spirit of the nineteenth century. We will return to the subject of Puccini's musical style after first taking a look at the libretto for this opera.

The subject of *Turandot* is unlike that of any other Puccini opera. It is not a verismo plot with characters drawn from everyday life (like *La bohème*), or of characters caught up in violent action of some kind (as in *Tosca*). Nor is it a tragedy of two lovers parted by death (again as in *La bohème*). After some tragic events, this opera ultimately concludes happily. Yet despite this happy ending and the incorporation of some stock comic characters in the form of the three ministers Ping, Pang, and Pong, it is clearly not a comedy. So what is this story? Very simply, a fairy tale, one that first appeared in Italy as a play that its author Carlo Gozzi described as a dramatic fable. Gozzi had borrowed this subject from one of the tales in *1001 Arabian Nights*, which accounts for the exoticism and Asian setting of the subject. In reality, fairy tales often make difficult subjects for operatic adaptation. They frequently deal with unpleasant subjects, such as child abuse or child abandonment, and equally unsavory characters such as wicked stepmothers or wolves that devour both pigs and people. The repertoire of fairy tales is full of such examples of horror and unpleasantness; and the story of Turandot is no exception.

At this point it might be useful to review the plot of the libretto with an eye to identifying the potential problems that such a story might present a composer wishing to make an opera out of it. Central to the story is the beautiful Chinese princess, Turandot, who offers herself in marriage to any man who can answer three riddles. But the price of failure is the forfeiture of his head. In this gruesome fashion, the princess satisfies her legendary hatred of men. So right away Turandot would appear to be the villainess of the story. The opera opens in the midst of an execution scene, as the princess's last suitor is about to be beheaded. Amid the crowd assembled to witness the execution, we meet the opera's hero, Prince Calaf, who stumbles upon his long-lost blind father, Timur, and his servant girl, Liù. We learn that Liù has long devoted herself to Timur because years earlier Prince Calaf smiled at her, and she has been in love with him ever since. But instead of being touched by this devotion and grateful for Liù's attention to his father, Calaf is distracted by the arrival of the beautiful but cruel princess Turandot. He decides then and there that he loves Turandot and wants to try to win her hand by answering the riddles. This, by measure of even the most modest dramatic standards, is the first of several problems that this libretto created for its composer. Admittedly, in opera, handsome young men often fall in love with physical beauty as though it was the only measure of attractiveness in a woman. But this is an especially egregious case of crass physicality. Liù, who has earned Calaf's love by devotedly caring for his blind father all these years, is callously overlooked in favor of a mean, misanthropic ice queen. What hope is there that Puccini, or any composer, could, through his music, make us like such an insensitive brute as this?

As the plot unfolds in act 2 Turandot presents Calaf with her three riddles, and, to her amazement and horror, he gets them all right. But not wanting to force Turandot into an unwanted marriage, he offers to sacrifice his own life if she can discover his name before the next daybreak. So Calaf's callous insensitivity toward Liù is balanced by this completely illogical altruism designed to spare a misanthropic sadist the embarrassment of having to marry a strange man.

In act 3 Calaf discovers that Turandot has threatened mass murders of her own people unless someone can learn the name of the mysterious prince. Here, the nature of fairy tales creates more problems for the opera composer. One might hope that the threat of mass executions would cause Calaf to abandon his pursuit of Turandot. But no, determined to possess her, he forges ahead with his challenge despite the pleas of the ministers and the populace. How can Puccini possibly make a sympathetic hero out of a character who is so self-serving? Calaf falls so far short of the classic definition of a hero, that only a major musical miracle (on the part of Puccini) could rescue him from total audience alienation.

Next, guards drag in Timur and Liù, suspecting (correctly) that they know the prince's name. Liù protects the old man by announcing that only she knows Calaf's name, but that she will not reveal it. Soldiers then begin to torture her to extract the information everyone wants, but she resists, telling Turandot that it is her love for Calaf that gives her strength. Here, of course, Liù becomes, inadvertently, the heroine of the opera. Her self-sacrificial goodness steals both the show and all our sympathy. Meanwhile, Calaf again misses his chance to act heroically. As Liù is tortured, he makes only a half-hearted objection. Finally she ends her own suffering by stealing a knife from one of the soldiers and stabbing herself. Now that the only sympathetic character in the opera is dead, the story might just as well end. (And this, in fact, is exactly where Puccini stopped composing, or more accurately, got stuck.) But no, the fairy tale is not over quite yet. The bloodless Turandot and the insensitive Calaf are left onstage alone. He grabs her and kisses her, and like magic, she melts into an adoring girl, suddenly soft and pliant. Because this is a fairy tale, we are expected to accept this magic at face value. Fairy tales are, after all, full of such moments of transformation. But from a purely dramatic point of view, Turandot's sudden change of character strains our willingness to take this story seriously on any level—even a metaphoric one. We are left with only a couple of not very plausible interpretations of the situation: either Turandot loved Calaf all along—which is completely out of character for her—or Calaf's kiss possesses magical powers somewhat on the order of the love potion in Wagner's *Tristan und Isolde*. (This latter hypothesis may not be as farfetched as it first sounds, because Puccini himself entered a cryptic marginal note in his sketches for this part of the opera saying "Then Tristan.") Turandot, having melted in Calaf's arms, now begs him to leave and demand no more of her. Again the prince surprises us by offering up his name so that Turandot may be the final victor in this senseless battle of the sexes. But of course, she is now a changed woman, no longer capable of hating men and demanding executions. So she announces that his name is Love, and they live happily ever after.

The point of retelling this whole story is simply to show how deep a dramatic hole Puccini had to dig himself out of even before he began writing a note of music. If the goal of opera is to use music to draw us into the characters, so that we sympathize with their weaknesses, cringe at their horrible choices of action, and finally cry at the resulting tragedy, then it might seem as though nothing would rescue this plot from its banal triviality or the story's characters from their hollow insensitivity. But, in fact, Puccini's music does just that. So let's take a look at what his musical magic consists of.

In comparing his style to that of Verdi, we can hear, right from the start of the opera, some of the internationalization and modernization of Italian opera that took place around the turn of the century. Puccini begins with a short but forceful four-note melodic gesture in the orchestra. This motif, like the one that opens *Tosca*, is associated in typical Wagnerian fashion with a person or idea in the drama—in this case Turandot. It reappears at points in the first act where her cruelty and obsessive hatred of men are the subjects. Its presentation in the orchestra also recalls Wagner in its use of powerful brass instruments and tremendous volume.

Example 19-2. Motif for Turandot's cruelty.

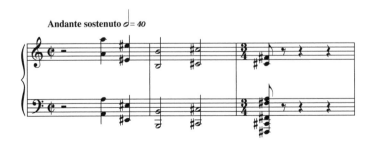

Despite the use of loud brass instruments at the beginning and in many other places throughout the opera, Puccini did not blindly adopted

Wagner's penchant for placing the center of interest in the orchestra, at the expense of beautiful singing. Instead, we might say he cleverly adapted Wagner's orchestral technique to his own Italian purposes by being careful not to require his singers to sing over top of this mountain of sound. In good Italian fashion, he pulls back the volume of the orchestra when the vocalists begin to sing. In this regard, Puccini's use of the orchestra stands on a middle ground somewhere between that of Verdi and Wagner. Like a true Italian, he continued to see opera as a vocal genre, never allowing the orchestra to overwhelm the singers as it so often seems to do in Wagner's works. Yet at the same time, there *was*, as mentioned earlier, something attractive about the largeness of sound in a Wagner opera to which nearly all late-nineteenth-century composers were drawn. As a result, *Turandot* is an opera that requires rather larger voices and greater volume than do most of the operas of Verdi.

The modernization of Italian opera can also be seen in Puccini's harmonic vocabulary. The music that follows the opening orchestral leitmotif, and establishes the mood of horror associated with the ritual of the three riddles, is clearly bitonal in nature. This means that the chords imply two simultaneous and different tonal centers or keys: in this case D minor in the lower parts (bass clef), and C-sharp major in the upper parts (treble clef).

Example 19-3. Bitonal harmony.

This bitonal sound itself becomes a unifying theme in the opera, reappearing whenever the subject of the horror of the riddles is being discussed. In act 2, when Calaf asks to be given a chance to answer Turandot's riddles, the mandarin reads him the "rules" of the game, sung to the same bitonal accompaniment. Then Puccini opens the last act by repeating this bitonal material. At that point in the drama Turandot has just declared that there will be mass murders of the populace unless someone can discover the name of the mysterious prince. So this bitonal harmony has a very specific and consistent dramatic meaning throughout the opera, as do the leitmotifs of Wagner. The difference is that Puccini's repetition of this motif does not involve the process of thematic transformation that underlies the symphonic technique of Wagner.

Another aspect of the opening motif worth mentioning is its relationship to the compositional techniques of another modern composer, Claude Debussy. Here the connection involves Puccini's adoption of non-Western scales, one of which is the unusual six-note scale made up of nothing but whole steps.

Example 19-4. Whole-tone scale.

Debussy employs this scale frequently in his music because of its exotic, non-Western sound; and Puccini was surely doing the same. Because this opera takes place in China, many of the melodic motifs are based either on this whole tone scale or on the Asian pentatonic scale. The resulting non-Western sound is especially predominant in much of the choral writing and in Liù's first big solo, in which she tries to dissuade Calaf from challenging Turandot.

Example 19-5. Liù's aria "Signore ascolta."

As explained earlier, most composers of opera were searching for ways of creating greater musical continuity in their work. Puccini was no exception. The fact that a performance of *Turandot* presents relatively few pauses in its musical flow that would allow an audience to jump in to applaud their favorite singers, demonstrates how Wagner did not have a monopoly on this particular operatic concern, as so many opera aficionados seem to think. In fact, Puccini's method of creating continuity is similar to that of both Verdi and Wagner in its dependence upon arioso as the principal vocal technique, wherein large sections of music are based on a repeating melody in the orchestra while the voices engage in fairly uninteresting arioso. And as in Verdi (but not Wagner), these sections eventually lead, without a break, to real moments of lyricism that are sometimes full-blown arias, but are just as often only brief lyrical peaks in the musical texture where Puccini uses one of his spectacularly memorable tunes to bring the scene to a musical-dramatic climax. A prime example is Turandot's famous act 2 "aria" "In questa reggia," in which she tells the sad story of Princess Lou-Ling, who many years before was conquered, mistreated, and dragged off by foreign warriors. Ever since Turandot has been seeking revenge on all men. This particular vocal piece is not truly an aria. It begins and continues for a long time with fairly uninteresting vocal arioso used for the narration of Lou-Ling's story.

Example 19-6a. Arioso portion of "In questa reggia."

Only at the end of the text that Puccini was setting did he allow himself to well up into truly magnificent tunefulness as the voice and orchestra come together to make a melodic climax of immense power. "In questa reggia" is thus a prime example of how a glorious melody can arise seamlessly from a surrounding arioso texture in a way that doesn't break the flow of the music.

Example 19-6b. "In questa reggia," main melody.

Example 19-6b *(continued)*

This technique of rising out of arioso momentarily into a true melody is something like the style of Verdi and Wagner, except that the melody, when it arrives, is always far more lyrical in Puccini's operas (as a comparison of Exs. 19-1 and 19-6b will demonstrate). In fact, most of Puccini's success as an opera composer is due in no small part to his gift for writing melodies like that of "In questa reggia"—melodies that etch themselves indelibly in our musical memories. One might say that Puccini's entire compositional technique is melody based. Ironically perhaps, these melodies are often not found in the vocal parts, but are placed in the orchestra while the voices are given over to a fairly uninteresting arioso style. But at moments of special textual significance, Puccini usually allowed the voice to double the orchestral melody to heighten the music's expressivity, as in "In questa reggia." The same technique can be heard at the very opening of the opera, in the scene where we first meet Timur, Liù, and Calaf (Ex. 19-7). It is based on the following orchestral melody:

Example 19-7. Orchestra tune underlying opening scene of act 1.

Example 19-7 *(continued)*

Much of the vocal music superimposed over this tune is in an arioso style. But at especially important moments in the unfolding of the drama, we can hear the voices pick up a part of the orchestral tune, as when Calaf sings, "Oh father, yes, I've found you." This style of continuous orchestral melody only occasionally doubled by the voices is a technique that Puccini made into his own stylistic signature. Most opera lovers find this style of repeating orchestral tunes extremely attractive, especially when the melodies are as gorgeous and memorable as his. But some have criticized Puccini's operatic technique, calling it a style based on "indiscriminate lyricism."[1] The claimed danger here is that the continual use of great tunes repeated over and over (whether in the voices or in the orchestra) eventually produces a dulling effect on the audience's sensibilities. This, in a nutshell, is the basis of the continual academic attack on Puccini that one occasionally hears or reads about.

Italian opera just wouldn't be Italian opera without the inclusion of independent set pieces such as arias and duets. Although Wagner eliminated all such pieces in his sweeping attempt to reform opera into something more realistic (at least in terms of how it unfolds onstage), Italian composers like Verdi and Puccini were faced with a dilemma brought about by their conflicting needs for greater musical flow and continuity on the one hand, and their love, on the other hand, of these concertlike musical numbers in which the action stops and the singer elaborates in song on the depth of his or her feelings at that moment. As a result, the continuous flow of a Puccini opera is, like Verdi's, somewhat illusory. Hidden behind the seamless orchestral music are many old-fashioned arias and duets of the kind Italian audiences always loved, some more obvious than others. Calaf's famous "Nessun dorma," sung at the beginning of act 3 in anticipation of his triumph over Turandot, is perhaps the best example in this opera of a real Italian aria, although even this "aria" is blended at both ends into its surrounding musical context (à la Verdi), so as to make it less obvious and to keep the dramatic momentum from being interrupted by the traditional full stop at the end. The aria is introduced by an orchestral bridge (of the kind we saw in Verdi's *Otello*), which is itself

---

1. See the several sections on Puccini in Joseph Kerman's *Opera as Drama.*

preceded by an offstage chorus singing the words *nessun dorma* (no one sleeps). This bridge then flows seamlessly into Calaf's repetition of those words at the beginning of his aria.

Example 19-8. Bridge to "Nessun dorma."

Similarly, the aria's end is blurred by the use of one of Puccini's greatest musical inventions: the orchestral postlude. The aria comes to a clear climax with a closing cadence, at which point one would expect the whole thing to be over, and for there to be a chance to vigorously applaud the tenor. But Puccini keeps the music going after this final cadence with what is usually referred to as an orchestral peroration: a climatic repetition of the main tune of the aria in the orchestra alone, playing at full volume. This is an extremely effective way to extend the climax of the aria and build an instrumental bridge to the next musical number.

Example 19-9. End of "Nessun dorma."

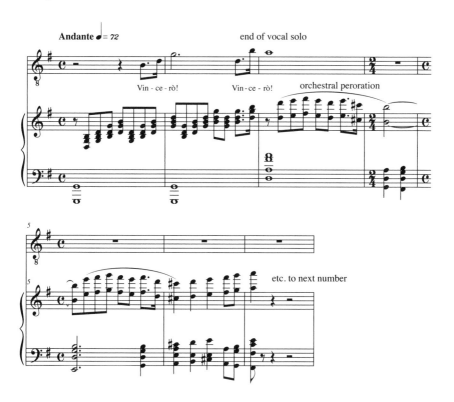

To finish this discussion of *Turandot* we can return to the question, thus far avoided, of how Puccini's attractive music redeems the flagrant insensitivity of the hero to the suffering of those around him. How does this music lead us into a sympathetic relationship with Calaf? Can we understand, through the music, why he behaves the way he does? Indeed we can. There is in Puccini's music a searing emotional intensity, which indicates that Calaf is a man caught in the throes of an uncontrollable passion. He is effectively blinded by this passion to the needs of everyone around him. His totally irrational, overardent need to possess Turandot, to hope that she is something other than what she portrays herself to be, is all part of a fantasy that constitutes Calaf's tragic flaw. Out of the actions that stem from this character flaw come the usual bad things that happen in a tragedy—in this case, Liù's death. The difference between a true tragedy and a fairy tale, of course, is that fairy tales have happy endings. Indeed, Calaf's irrational passion, captured so perfectly in his music, turns Turandot into a loving person, and leads the plot to a happy ending. It is Puccini's music that makes Calaf's obsession with Turandot believable. With melodies that touch our heart and excite our passions, Puccini allows his audience to experience those emotions that the printed word alone can never capture. Through the power of music, disbelief evaporates.

The climax of this opera lies near its end, in the final duet in which Turandot's resistance melts away under the extreme ardor of our hero. For the opera to succeed, Puccini's music must now make Turandot's transformation convincing. Unfortunately, this is the part of the opera that Puccini didn't write. He died before being able to complete more than a few sketches for the final duet. What we hear today at the end of the opera is music written by Franco Alfano, a colleague of Puccini. Unfortunately, Alfano was not a composer of Puccini's caliber, and what the opera needs to make the fairy tale succeed, is just what we are missing here. Puccini broke off his work with the death of Liù. This death scene contains much of the kind of music that makes a dramatic situation memorable, as the following example of the music that accompanies Liù's final farewell to life and love easily demonstrates.

Example 19-10. Liù's farewell.

But the opera does not end with the death of Liù. The composer must get us through the final passionate scene in which Calaf rips off Turandot's veil and dares to take her in his arms and kiss her. Her violent opposition and struggle are then instantly transformed, as if by magic, into tender acquiescence. But for this melodramatic end of the story, Puccini left little other than a note to himself that he must find yet another transcendent melody for this important duet. At the time of his death, Puccini hadn't found that melody, nor was Alfano able to do so (despite a very valiant attempt). This final duet is thus dressed up with some music that was borrowed from earlier scenes in the opera (especially "In questa reggia") and some other music that simply seems to flail about in the manner of something passionate, but without the climactic effectiveness that a truly great, show-stopping tune would have produced in this most important moment of the drama. The other problem with Alfano's musical realization of this scene is that the transformation of Turandot occurs almost in an instant, as if something magical had happened when Calaf kissed her. One might rationalize this instant transformation by claiming that such magic befits a fairy tale, but this stepping out of reality again removes the opera from the world of the believable. Individual listeners will disagree, of course, about the dramatic effectiveness (or lack thereof) of this part of the opera, as well as with my suggestion that the speed of Turandot's transformation is in itself a problem. So in keeping with the spirit of controversy surrounding the end of this opera, I will offer yet another provocative hypothesis. The prevalent fantasy about this opera is that Puccini was working feverishly toward its completion when death suddenly cut short his final inspiration. But it is more likely that Puccini failed to finish the opera not because death stole him away at the moment of epiphany, but rather because he himself was unable to find the right music to make the libretto convincing. Puccini reached the point where Liù stabs herself (the point where he stopped composing) several years before his death. He then spent his remaining years searching (unsuccessfully) for the music that he needed to make the end an effective theatrical experience. So the frequent lamentations over the fact that Alfano's ending is not as effective as the rest of the opera is really a case of misplaced frustration in view of the fact that Puccini himself was unable to solve the problem of how to bring the opera to a memorable close. Recognizing the problem here, the Italian composer Luciano Berio tried in 2001 to improve what Alfano left us by rewriting the final scene of the opera. Berio's avowed goal was not to replace what Alfano had done, but to modify it enough to improve its theatrical effectiveness. His solution to the transformation of Turandot was to make her change of character take place over a much longer span of time, and to write enough music to allow us to feel the meltdown in her heart and to experience the mix of emotions that would probably accompany such a critical dramatic moment in an opera. While this idea seems well motivated, the creation of so much new music to augment what Alfano had written, considerably lengthens the moment of the fateful kiss of transformation, leaving the theater's staging director with the major problem of finding something for the singers to do onstage during this lengthy orchestral interlude. And while Berio's revision might represent a slight improvement on Alfano's final duet, it still fails to solve the problem of how to create the great tune that Puccini was looking for— the one that would galvanize the entire final scene. At least Alfano had the common sense to borrow a theme from Calaf's "Nessun dorma" aria for the opera's closing chorus. These final choral lines are a paean to love, and for the last words, "Gloria a te," Alfano borrowed the part of Puccini's melody that had originally been set to the word *vincerò*, as if to suggest, perhaps, that love itself is the final victor.

PART XI

THE INFLUENCE OF WAGNER

CHAPTER 20

Reflect for a moment upon this operatic axiom: that Wagner and Debussy are as different as any two composers who lived in the same century could possibly be. Yet the fact remains that in the world of opera, the French masterpiece, *Pelléas et Mélisande* (completed 1902), seems, even upon a cursory look, to be built upon a foundation of essentially Wagnerian principles. If one were asked to name an opera that has no arias, duets, choruses, or other ensemble numbers, one that uses an elaborate system of leitmotifs, one that is characterized by a recitative-like semideclamatory melodic vocal style, and whose plot is meant to reflect universal truths and communicate a philosophical message through allegorical metaphors, the most logical response would be to name one of Wagner's *Ring* cycle operas, or perhaps his *Tristan und Isolde*. But in actuality Claude Debussy's *Pelléas et Mélisande* is equally as good a response to the question of which opera best fits this list of stylistic characteristics.

Herein lies one of the most fascinating of all operatic paradoxes: that Debussy, who lamented the influence of Wagner on all late nineteenth-century French music, should have, in his only completed opera, come so close to duplicating the very style he so desperately worked to avoid. The truth of the matter is that this great opera is far more like the works of Wagner than Debussy would ever have admitted, and that try as he might, Debussy, the great French impressionist, was ultimately unable to completely exorcise the ghost of Wagner from his own work.

To make sense out of this paradox and to understand Debussy's connection to Wagner, it may be helpful to sort through some biographical facts. As a gifted young pianist, Debussy entered the Paris Conservatoire in 1872 at the age of ten. Despite early signs of promise for a career as a concert pianist, he was unable to win any of the Conservatoire's big piano prizes, and was thus forced to redirect his musical studies to the area of composition. In this new arena he was far more successful, winning the coveted Prix de Rome in 1884. After fulfilling the terms of his "prize" (a requisite stay of two years at the French Academy in Rome), he returned to Paris via Bayreuth. Like most of his compatriots, he had fallen under the spell of Wagner's music, and a pilgrimage to the Festspielhaus (Wagner's theater built especially for productions of the *Ring* cycle) was absolutely de rigueur for anyone who wanted to be counted as a disciple of the German master. But even in the midst of these years of German idolatry, Debussy seemed to realize that Wagner's influence on French music carried some inherent dangers. While Wagner was to be admired, he was, perhaps, not to be copied, or as Debussy himself so aptly put it: "I began to have doubts about the Wagnerian formula, or, rather, it seemed to me that it was of use only in the particular case of Wagner's own genius."[1] In Debussy's view, if French composers were going to retain a national individuality, they were going to have to find their own solutions to the questions of form and style in music. In effect, Debussy was struggling with the need to define himself as a French composer in the face of what was perhaps the most overwhelming musical influence of the nineteenth century. Although the composer Eric Satie claimed to have first put Debussy on the trail of a unique French style, and even to have suggested the methods of impressionist painters such as Monet and Renoir as a model,[2] it is more likely that Debussy was already on the way to disentangling his music from that of Wagner even while he was still an ardent admirer of the German master.

Before exploring how he might have done this, a short digression into the world of impressionist painting and its possible relationship to music is in order. First of all, it must be remembered that Debussy himself hated the association that was always drawn between his music and the painting of Monet, Manet, and others. Perhaps he was responding to the fact that the term Impressionist originally carried a pejorative connotation as it was first applied to a new and misunderstood school of French painters in the 1880s. More likely, though, he simply did not want to be seen as an imitator of anything or anybody. Nonetheless there are some useful parallels between impressionist art and the music of Debussy—most particularly, the reliance on vibrant color to replace traditional techniques of formal construction. The paintings of Monet and his colleagues are works in which straight lines are noticeably absent, resulting in the depiction of objects without traditional linear boundaries of demarcation. Instead, as anyone who has ever seen one of these paintings up close knows, small daubs of vibrant color are arranged in a way that suggests the forms of objects in the real world. Much as impressionist painters abandoned formal depiction that relied on straight lines, Debussy abandoned musical form that had traditionally grown out

---

1. From a program note written by Debussy for the premiere of *Pelléas* in 1902 and reprinted in François Lesure, 1977, 74.

2. Wilkins, 1980, 110; also reprinted in Orledge, 1990, 47.

of a patterned (i.e., predictable) repetition of melodic motifs that created a recognizable thematic design. In its place, he substituted the musical equivalent of Monet's color: unusual timbres and harmonic constructions that rejected past syntactical meanings in favor of new colorful juxtapositions. Without a pattern of returning themes, Debussy's music can at first sound formless, at least from the traditional Germanic point of view in which musical structure is thought to grow out of the repetition and development of melodies and a traditional arrangement of functional harmonies. To a large extent, Debussy upset and then reordered the traditional German musical hierarchy that valued theme, development, and tonality over the "less important" musical elements of rhythm, meter, and color. Like the impressionist painters, he rejected earlier methods of creating form and relied on color and supple, unpredictable rhythms to build his new French music. But while many of the characteristics of Debussy's mature style seem closely related to the techniques of impressionist painters, we must not lose sight of the fact that in creating this uniquely French music, he was also drawing on sources he found outside of France, in Russian and Javanese music that came to his attention early in his career. In 1880, while still a student at the Paris Conservatoire, Debussy had toured Russia as a member of a piano trio. It was there that he came into contact with the music of some of the composers of the so-called Mighty Five, the Russian nationalists who were themselves struggling to break free of foreign influences on their music. Within this group, Nikolai Rimsky-Korsakov and Modest Mussorgsky were perhaps the most interesting—at least for Debussy. It was in their music that the young Frenchman discovered the unusually colorful sound of the octatonic scale. Unlike the seven-note scale that had served as the foundation of Western European music for three hundred years, the octatonic scale, as its name suggests, contains eight notes in an octave, outlining a pattern of alternating whole and half steps. Although the music that Rimsky-Korsakov and Mussorgsky constructed using this scale grabbed Debussy's attention and sparked his interest in the early 1880s, its influence on the development of his own compositional style seems to have lain dormant for several years, until it was awakened in 1889 by another chance encounter with an exotic music of a different type.

That was the year in which Debussy first heard the gamelan music of Java, brought to Paris via the Universal Exhibition, a giant festival of art and culture from around the world. The gamelan is a large ensemble consisting primarily of various kinds of metallic pitched percussion instruments, such as gongs, bells, and xylophones that were native to Southeast Asia, especially Java and Bali. The sound of these "orchestras" differed from that of

Western ensembles in nearly every possible way. And the style of the music itself seems, to Western ears, totally foreign: having no melody (at least none that anyone can sing), no perceptible meter (i.e., no arrangement of alternating strong and weak beats), and a rhythm that is fluid, unpatterned, and seemingly improvisational. If one were to ask what it is about gamelan music that sounds so unlike the music of Wagner, the answer would be "just about everything," but especially the rhythm, the lack of melody, and the strange instrumental colors. These are exactly the musical elements with which Debussy was eventually able to contradict the influence of Wagner in his own mature music. Despite the rather exotic influences of Javanese music and all the possible connections with impressionist painting, however, the example of Wagner proved alarmingly resilient in Debussy's work, especially when it came time for him to write an opera. This move into the world of dramatic music came about through his reading in 1892 of Maurice Maeterlinck's play, *Pelléas et Mélisande*, to which Debussy was attracted by its symbolist style, a mode of literary expression in which the deeper meaning of a drama is never made overtly manifest, but is only suggested through the use of recurrent motifs or symbols.

To understand these symbols and their impact on Debussy's setting of the play to music, a short review of the plot of the opera will be useful. The action—what little there is of it—takes place in an unspecified place called Allemonde (literally, "all the world") in an unspecified time long ago. As the story opens, Prince Golaud, a middle-aged man, is lost in a forest where he is hunting. He stumbles upon a young woman named Mélisande, who is also lost. After questioning her unsuccessfully about who she is and why she is sitting alone in the middle of the forest, Golaud convinces her to come away with him. In scene 2, which takes place some time later, Golaud brings Mélisande home as his wife. At their castle, which is situated deep in a dark forest, she meets Golaud's grandfather (who is blind), his mother, and his younger half brother, Pelléas. Partly because Mélisande and Pelléas are close in age, they begin to spend time together, gradually becoming deeply attached to each other, although this latter fact is never acknowledged or even recognized by either of them. A love between them develops over the course of the opera, as does Golaud's suspicion and jealousy. One event in particular sets in motion the tragic culmination of the action: Mélisande's symbolic loss of her wedding ring, which she carelessly drops in a deep well in the castle. This turning point in the dramatic action further fuels Golaud's jealousy, which comes to a climax in act 4, scene 4, when the enraged husband surprises the young lovers during a clandestine midnight rendezvous in the forest outside the castle. He jumps out of the bushes where he was hiding, murders Pelléas and wounds his wife, who is pregnant with his child and dies shortly after giving birth.

The dramatic events as outlined here involve several important recurring motifs or symbols. For example, nearly everyone in the opera is either lost, blind, or in the dark (both literally and figuratively). No one seems to understand what is happening to them, or why. They are all passive victims of an inexorable fate that directs their lives. Darkness and obscurity, therefore, become important symbols of this lack of awareness in the unfolding drama. Maeterlinck's use of these symbols in conjunction with the three principal characters in the drama must have suggested to Debussy the use of equivalent musical motifs, which again brought the composer face to face with the specter of Wagner, whose whole technique was founded upon an elaborate system of such manipulated themes (leitmotifs).

Clearly the composition of this opera pushed Debussy into a creative crisis from which he could escape only by articulating in concrete terms his relationship to the style and technique of Wagner. This he did in the early 1890s by setting down his objections to what he called the "Wagnerian formula." His reservations concerned four specific musical areas, and amounted to what might be called Debussy's operatic "credo":

- **Rhythm:** "Music has a rhythm whose secret force shapes the development. The rhythm of the soul, however, is quite different—more instinctive, more general, and controlled by many events. From the incompatibility of these two kinds of rhythm, a perpetual conflict arises, for the two do not move at the same speed. Either the music stifles itself by chasing after a character, or the character has to sit still on a note to allow the music to catch up with him."[3]
- **Melody:** "A character cannot always express himself melodically: *dramatic* melody has to be quite different from what is generally called melody. . . . Melody is anti-lyrical. It cannot express the varying states of the soul, and of life. Essentially it is suited only to the song that expresses a simple feeling. It must be understood that melody, or song, is one thing, and that lyrical expression is another. It is illogical to think that one can make a fixed melodic line hold the innumerable nuances through which a character passes. I want the vocal

---

3. From a review of Alfred Bruneau's opera *L'Ouragan* in *La revue blanche*, 1901; Francois Lesure, 1977, 36.

expression to remain lyrical without being absorbed by the orchestra."[4]

- **Symphonic development:** "Music in opera is far too predominant. A prolonged symphonic development will always be at odds with the fluidity of the dramatic action. I have endeavored to render the successive impulses and moods of the characters as they are produced, without making laborious efforts to follow a symphonic development which by its very nature will sacrifice emotional development to an arbitrary musical design."[5]

- **Leitmotifs:** "In Wagner's works each character has, one might say, his own "calling card,"—his leitmotif—which must always precede him. I must confess that I find this procedure somewhat gross and obvious. A character should not be a slave to his leitmotif like a blind man is a slave to his dog."[6]

These became the principles upon which the musical setting of Maeterlinck's play began in 1893. By the time the opera was finished and ready for production in 1902, Debussy felt obliged proudly to announce to the Parisian press that his compositional method owed nothing to Wagner. Of course, had this really been true, and had he not been personally tormented with the influence of Wagner in his own work, it is not likely that he would have felt the need to deny the connection with such vociferous passion.

An investigation of *Pélleas et Mélisande* might well begin, then, with a look at how Debussy put into effect (or didn't, as the case may be) these basic operatic principles. The first two—rhythm and melody—represent areas in which his music most violently contradicted that of Wagner and the whole German tradition. (Again, the influence of the Javanese gamelan should be kept in mind.) In creating a new world of rhythm and melody for opera, Debussy began by making one pivotal decision regarding his libretto: the daring choice to use Maeterlinck's play directly as his sung text, and not, as was usually the case, to have a poetic adaptation drafted by a librettist. This decision to use a prose, rather than a poetic, text was motivated largely by the composer's desire to avoid the sing-song rhythms of poetry in favor

---

4. From program notes for the premiere and from an interview with Robert Le Flers on *Pelléas* from *Le Figaro*, May 16, 1902. Reprinted in Lesure, 1977, 75, 79.

5. From a conversation between Debussy and his teacher, Ernest Guiraud, as quoted in Orledge, 1982, 49.

6. Lesure, 1977, 80–81, and Evans Jr., 1909, 361.

of the more realistic rhythms of the spoken language. In the process, he was able to avoid what he called "the predominance of music in opera," to which he so strongly objected. One of the most important operatic innovations in *Pelléas et Mélisande* is, then, this prose libretto. It results in a new kind of music drama, which the eminent musicologist Joseph Kerman once referred to as "sung play."[7] The difference between a sung play and a traditional opera can be heard in Debussy's music as soon as the curtain goes up on act 1. The interaction between Golaud and Mélisande at the beginning of the opera is carried out in a vocal rhythm that is determined by the rhythm of the French language, not by the rhythm of song. That is to say, there are no repeating rhythmic patterns of the kind that one usually finds in song. Instead there is an infinitely variable and unpredictable rhythm that tries to imitate the natural flow of the French language; and this speech rhythm is supple in a way that musical rhythm rarely is.

But Debussy's notation of these speech rhythms can be deceptive and misleading for the unwary singer. If performed in accordance with the traditional rules of strong and weak beats implied by the musical meters that Debussy notated in his score, the effect will turn out totally wrong. The following musical examples demonstrate the problem:

Example 20-1.

U - ne   pe - ti - te   fil - le   qui pleure au bord de l'eau

Example 20-2.

El - le   ne   m'en - tend   pas

These examples are drawn from the opening scene of act 1, where Golaud questions Mélisande about her identity. The music here is in the very common meter of 4/4. Traditionally in this meter, the first and third beats are stressed more heavily than the second and fourth beats. But a performance of Ex. 20-1 based upon this traditional placement of stress would result in an accent falling on the first syllable of the word *petite*, which of course makes no sense at all in French. Similarly, the phrase in

---

7. The chapter on Debussy in Kerman, 1952, is titled "Opera as Sung Play.

Ex. 20-2 places the musical accent on the second syllable of *elle* because the beginning of any beat in a single measure (in this case the fourth beat) is always the strongest part of a fractional subdivision of that beat. But this normal placement of the accent produces the sound "el-LE" (capital letters indicate the stress), which makes no sense. In spoken French, the final *le* of *elle* is actually silent, and in sung French it is always vocalized very weakly. The first person to draw attention to this conflict between musical and textual accents in Debussy's opera was the composer Richard Strauss, who in the early years of the twentieth century set out to write his opera *Salome* in French, the language in which Oscar Wilde had written the play on which that libretto was based. Since Strauss knew little about how to set French to music, he wrote to his friend, the French novelist Romain Rolland, seeking advice. Their exchange of letters on the subject of the musical quality of the French language is comical, irritating, and enlightening all at the same time.

> STRAUSS: When singing in French, must mute syllables at the end of words be stressed?
>
> ROLLAND: The mute *e* is one of the great difficulties of the French language. One must really be careful not to eliminate it: it is one of the principal charms of our poetry; but it is very rare for a foreigner to have a real feeling for it. It's not so much a sound as a resonance, an echo of the preceding syllable, which vibrates, hovers, and gently dies away in the air. If you have not already got the score, I urge you most strongly to get hold of *Pelléas et Mélisande* by Claude Debussy, the music of which follows Maeterlinck's text very closely . . .
>
> STRAUSS: Well, I have had the Debussy score sent to me, but here too I find the same unconcern about declamation that has always so much surprised me in all French music. Why do the French sing differently from the way they speak? When speaking, does one say: PEtite or peTIte? [Strauss inserts Ex. 1 into his letter.] Debussy also writes elLE ne m'entend pas. This can't possibly be right. [Strauss inserts Ex. 2 at this point.] Here in Germany, Wagner has revived a feeling for the sense of language. France seems to me to be still bogged down in the artificiality of eighteenth-century tragedy.
>
> ROLLAND: I hardly know how to reply to you. I would have too much to say, and I would be afraid of being rather harsh. May I say it in a friendly way? You Germans really are astonishing; you don't understand anything about our poetry, not a thing; and yet you pass judgment on it with imperturbable complacency. . . . I can see that you have no feeling for our literary French language at all. You imagine that it's like yours.

> Our language has no connection with yours. You have very marked
> stresses, very strong and continual contrasts between the accent and
> unaccent, between the strong and the weak syllable. . . . And it's precisely
> in the interval that separates the strong from the weak that our poetry
> lies. It has an infinite number of shades in the half-tone—accents much
> less stressed than yours are, but much more varied, more supple, more
> flexible. In the example, "Elle ne m'entend pas," there is no stress on the
> word "elle." The barline does not mean anything.[8]

From this testy exchange of letters, one can deduce that the answer
to the question of how to place the musical accents in Debussy's vocal
melodies is to disregard the traditional rules of musical meters. A singer
must be trained to ignore measure lines and other traditional signs of strong
musical accents, and to allow textual accents to determine the placement of
these stresses.

So in terms of rhythm and melody (items 1 and 2 of the "credo"), Debussy
was able to create a style that owed little if anything to Wagner. But the
third and fourth points of the credo—the symphonic development and the
use of leitmotifs—are another story altogether. Here, Debussy's attempt to
exorcise the ghost of Wagner from his music was less successful. In avowing
that *Pelléas et Mélisande* owed little to the style and technique of Wagner,
Debussy managed to fool the vast majority of reviewers at the opera's premiere
into taking him at his word. But today there is little chance that anyone with
a score in hand will not notice that there are, in fact, leitmotifs attached
to every major character in the opera. It is this appearance in Debussy's
music of one of Wagner's most characteristic compositional techniques that
demands a closer examination, as the application of leitmotifs in *Pelléas et
Mélisande* would seem to contradict everything that Debussy was trying to
accomplish in building a new French style of opera.

The invention of the leitmotif is often laid at the feet of the great
French composer Hector Berlioz, whose famous *Symphonie fantastique* of
1830 contained a single theme that represented his unrequited love interest,
the actress Harriet Smithson. This theme, called an *idée fixe* (fixed idea) by
Berlioz, reappears throughout the five movements of his symphony in ever
changing guises, but always with reference to the same woman. Here then is
the beginning of the Wagnerian system of "leading motifs": short melodic
ideas that are associated with particular people or things throughout an
opera, and which reappear in transformation with new but associated

---

8. Myers, 1968, 32--38.

meanings. A few of the most important leitmotifs in *Pelléas et Mélisande* include the following:

Example 20-3a. Forest (fate) motif.

Example 20-3b. Golaud motif.

Example 20-3c. Pelléas motif.

Example 20-3d. Mélisande motif.

Looking at these motifs, one understands why so many of the French music critics at the premiere in 1902 failed to recognize their existence in this opera. Unlike Wagner's leitmotifs, whose strong rhythmic patterns and memorable melodic shapes all but hit the listener in the face, Debussy's have so little character that they mostly escape recognition altogether. *Pelléas et Mélisande* is an opera in which the leitmotifs might be said to be transparent, in the sense that one hears right through them as though they had no impact on our perception of the work as a whole. It is this transparency that belies the fact that this opera is actually full of leitmotifs. The implicit irony here is that in adopting a compositional technique from the very person he was attempting to reject, Debussy aimed to create an entirely different musical effect.

The success of this new "effect," however, hinged upon the question of how Debussy's leitmotifs were going to be employed. If the music were to sound different from Wagner's, then the leitmotifs would have to be used differently. What purpose, then, would they serve? For Wagner, leitmotifs were the melodic source material for a symphonic development of themes that were continually repeated, and transformed into new, but related, themes. The musical texture of a Wagner opera thus imitated the unfolding of the development section in a symphonic sonata form. That is to say, Wagner operas work like gigantic symphonic tone poems, or like the development section of a Beethoven symphony. For Debussy, the use of leitmotifs brought him face to face with the issues of motivic development and the relationship of these motifs to the overall form of the opera. As seen in his credo, one of Debussy's primary objections to Wagner's style was that, in his opinion, a protracted symphonic development of musical themes ran counter to the need of the drama to be able to capture the instantaneous and quixotic changes of mood through which characters move. If the musical logic of such a symphonic development was not up to the task of following the nuances of emotional change, then Wagner's use of leitmotifs was somehow misguided.

Debussy's struggle with this question of how to avoid the Wagnerian implication of leitmotifs manifested itself in the early sketches he made for *Pelléas et Mélisande*. These first drafts, which date from 1893, show him planning large sections of the orchestral accompaniment around the repetition and development of melodic motifs: a technique that clearly recalled the style of Wagner. Debussy apparently recognized the trap into which he had inadvertently fallen, stopped himself, and threw out the entire first draft of act 4, scene 4 (the famous love duet with which he had begun work on the opera) for this very reason.[9] In fact, the general trajectory of Debussy's compositional process with this opera was to delete long passages of a developmental nature and replace them with insertions of additional leitmotifs, thereby keeping the music free to change emotional direction at any moment. Despite Debussy's attempt to avoid the Wagnerian formula of building an opera on the use of symphonic techniques, and his fairly indignant criticism of Wagner's "obvious" use of motifs to accompany the entrance of characters, Debussy's own opera, in its finished form, actually does much the same thing. This inescapable reliance on the techniques of German opera, can be seen in act 1, scene 1, where Debussy begins by setting out three important motifs: the "forest," "Golaud," and "Mélisande." The last of these (Mélisande) is expanded and developed as in Ex.20-4.

Example 20-4. Mélisande's motif developed.

9. In a letter to the composer Ernest Chausson, Debussy wrote, "And worst of all the ghost of old Klingsor, alias R. Wagner, kept appearing in the corner of a bar, so I've torn the whole thing up. I've started again and am trying to find a recipe for producing more characteristic phrases." Lesure and Nichols, 1987, 54.

A comparison of this excerpt with the motif as it appeared in its original form (Ex. 20-3d), will reveal that in this repetition of the theme Debussy has taken the melodic skip of the third (from C-sharp to E in the original) and expanded it into a descending series of such skips. As scene 1 unfolds, this technique of expanding a melodic interval continues. At the point where Golaud questions Mélisande about whether someone has mistreated her, the orchestra plays the melody illustrated in the first line of Ex. 20-5, and then further develops that melody as in line 2:

Example 20-5. Further development of Mélisande's motif.

All of this clearly shows the composer consciously manipulating a melodic motif through expansion and development of the basic idea of the falling, oscillating third. Despite Debussy's claims to the contrary, this compositional technique clearly recalls Wagner's symphonic process, and shows how potent the influence of the German master was on the composition of *Pelléas et Mélisande*, even as Debussy worked tirelessly to minimize this influence. In sifting through all the evidence, the conclusion becomes obvious: that although Debussy may have worked diligently to exorcize the spirit Wagner from his new opera, to avoid a compositional process that would produce a musical form with a life of its own, and whose unfolding was determined by a purely musical rather than a purely dramatic logic, he was only partly successful in doing so, and the goal of creating a new kind of dramatic music, about which he had spoken so often and so clearly, continued to elude him in these middle years of his career.

No discussion of the debt that Debussy owed to Wagner in the writing of *Pelléas et Mélisande* can pretend to be complete without some notice of the purely orchestral interludes that fill the space between the scenes of each act. While much of Debussy's semirecitative-like vocal writing seems to float on a sea of rather formless orchestral accompaniment (which, as the composer suggested, is musically directionless in a way that allows it to respond to the evanescent changes of mood and spirit through which his characters continually move), the opera nonetheless also contains these curious instrumental interludes that constitute the one major exception to

Debussy's antisymphonic aesthetic. Here, when no characters appear on stage and the curtain is down, Debussy allows himself to explore the purely musical potential of his various leitmotifs in an orchestral texture that again reminds us of Wagner and the many beautiful symphonic interludes in his *Ring* cycle operas. The very first interlude in *Pelléas et Mélisande* gives ample evidence of this symphonic process in operation. It begins with a restatement of Golaud's motif and then moves into an accompanimental figure of triplet eighth notes based on the interval of the second that characterizes that motif.

Example 20-6. Interlude accompaniment derived from Golaud's motif.

Superimposed over this accompaniment are statements of the forest motif, which are extended and developed.

Example 20-7. Forest motif developed.

Shortly thereafter, Debussy repeats and develops Mélisande's motif as well.

Example 20-8. Mélisande's motif developed.

The interlude ends with a final statement and development of Golaud's motif, as seen in Ex. 20-9. The entire interlude thus has a motivic continuity that is not nearly as apparent in the rest of the opera.

Example 20-9. Golaud's motif developed.

Despite all this talk of Wagnerisms in *Pelléas*, only a fool would claim that Debussy sounds like Wagner. For one thing, the reappearance of the important leitmotifs in *Pelléas et Mélisande* is always disguised by alterations that affect their rhythm, harmony, or orchestration. Perhaps this is why early reviewers never picked up on their appearance in this opera. Debussy was a master at reclothing his thematic material in ways that completely changed their identity. One of his favorite techniques in this regard was to repeat a leitmotif note for note, but to harmonize it not just with new chords but with a totally different harmonic vocabulary. In this way, a theme that had appeared originally in octatonic dress might return wearing a whole-tone harmonic disguise. The harmonies derived from these different scales (octatonic vs. whole-tone) are often so radically different that the melody they accompany becomes unrecognizable. Ex. 20-10 illustrates just one such reclothing of the leitmotif for Golaud.

Example 20-10a. Golaud motif—harmonization based on octatonic scale on A.

Example 20-10b. Golaud motif—harmonization based on whole-tone scale on B.

Equally foreign to the spirit of German music is Debussy's overall sense of restraint and understatement. Despite all its Wagnerian techniques, *Pelléas et Mélisande* is French by virtue of this restraint. A wonderful demonstration can be found in the famous fourth scene of act 4. This is the scene in which Pelléas meets Mélisande late at night in the park outside the palace. It is during this meeting that they finally state openly their love for each other. The scene is therefore equivalent to a traditional operatic love duet, which if we were thinking of Wagner, might be something like the scene at the end of act 1 of *Die Walküre* where Siegmund and Sieglinde finally recognize that they love each other. In general, operatic duets in which the hero and heroine (usually a tenor and a soprano) declare their mutual love have always been characterized by lots of loud, passionate, lyrical singing, accompanied by an equally frenzied orchestra. It seems as though composers could not set the words "I love you" to music without having recourse to the sound of surging strings, panting brass, and weeping woodwinds all going full tilt behind singers caught in the throws of vein-popping vocal ecstasy. From this point of view, then, Debussy's love duet in act 4 is a declaration of war against traditional opera. Instead of music, music, and more music, Debussy gives us speech, climaxing ever so briefly in song, punctuated by silence. This, in fact, is the only opera I know in which the hero and heroine arrive at the climax of the duet—their declaration of mutual love—almost whispering in the total absence of an orchestral accompaniment. To the extent that silence is the opposite of music, this duet confirms Debussy's belief that "music in opera is far too predominant." Here, emotional understatement replaces emotional excess, and silence replaces song to underline a dramatically critical moment. Only a composer desperately in search of an antidote to Wagner could ever have imagined such a love duet.

From this examination of Debussy's struggles with the ghost of Wagner (who died, incidentally, exactly a decade before Debussy began work on *Pelléas et Mélisande*), there emerges a picture of a composer's unique path to the resuscitation of a French operatic style that had been lost in the last quarter of the nineteenth century. Yes, Debussy did borrow certain operatic techniques from Wagner: the idea of a continuous musical structure not divided into set pieces (arias, duets, etc.), the use of leitmotifs, a less tuneful melodic style, and an allegorical subject. But the genius of Debussy was that he was able to use so many of these seemingly German techniques to create a uniquely French operatic style. As any good cook will tell you, it's not the ingredients in great food that matter as much as it is the chef who knows how to assemble them in a unique fashion. Musically speaking, there is no better French chef than Debussy, and no better French cuisine than *Pelléas et Mélisande*.

PART XII

APPROACHES TO TWENTIETH-CENTURY OPERA

CHAPTER 21

LOOKING AHEAD WHILE LOOKING BACK:
BARTÓK, BERG, AND BRITTEN

INTRODUCTION: THE PROBLEM

If one were asked to make a list of the most significant composers in the early twentieth century—those who revolutionized music through innovative contributions that put music on a new path after 1900—that list might contain names such as Schoenberg, Stravinsky, Debussy, Bartók, Ives, Berg, and Webern. Now, if asked to make a similar list of prominent composers of opera in the same period—those whose involvement with the genre seemed to constitute a significant portion of their compositional activity—that list would be quite different, because not one of the composers on the first list would have qualified for inclusion in the second list as well. This simply suggests that the most revolutionary composers of the new century showed relatively little interest in opera as a genre that could accommodate their new music (whatever that was). The question, of course, is why? And of what significance is this observation to our understanding of twentieth-century opera?

There may be several reasons why avant-garde composers in the early years of the twentieth century avoided the genre of opera in their attempt to invent a new musical language. First, opera is one of the most expensive genres to put into live performance, and the financial risks associated with the production of a new opera in an unfamiliar "modern" style are enormous. Second, the amount of time (and hence also money) needed for both singers and instrumentalists to learn a difficult new score could also have discouraged the production of operas involving musical complexities of pitch and rhythm with which most performers were not comfortable. Lastly, some composers who were exploring new more dissonant styles early in the twentieth century may have felt that the human voice was not the performance medium best suited to negotiating the dissonance and atonality of their new music. Unlike instruments such as the piano, violin, or flute, the human voice cannot reproduce a notated pitch simply by putting a finger down in the proper position on a keyboard or fingerboard. Singers cannot sing without first hearing the pitches they want to reproduce in their heads. Dissonant, atonal music makes this extremely difficult, and as a result operas written in a "modern" style can be nearly impossible to perform accurately. For all these reasons and more, those composers who chose to write opera in the twentieth century tended for the most part to adopt a more conservative and traditional approach to the genre. Composers such as Puccini, Poulenc, and Britten, to name just three, found that opera suited their less revolutionary styles. These were composers whose music seemed to imply that the human voice was ill-suited to the angularity and dissonance of atonal music, especially in a large-scale genre such as opera.

Much of the early twentieth-century operatic repertoire still heard today in theaters around the world tends to be drawn from works that have their roots in stylistic developments of the late nineteenth century. One of those developments included the goal, shared by composers of different nationalities, to make opera more realistic in its moment-to-moment unfolding and to make it flow with the same continuity one finds in a spoken drama. To this end, set pieces were eliminated or minimized, arioso replaced song in solo vocal lines, and orchestral accompaniments played an increasingly important role in underlining the drama. Despite this unanimity regarding musical-dramatic theory, the process through which this new aesthetic was carried out in the real world differed from one country to another. At the end of the nineteenth century, three important variations on this dramatic theme arose and remained somewhat distinct: the French (represented by Debussy), the German (represented by late Wagner and Strauss), and the Italian (represented by late Verdi). Of these various approaches to opera, that of Debussy came closest to capturing the effect of a sung play, in which the libretto was written in prose, there are no set pieces of any kind, and the vocal parts are comprised almost entirely of semimelodic arioso. Debussy's music attempts to capture the rhythm of the French language, and his orchestra captures the rapid changes of mood through which characters move without superimposing any kind of large-scale musical form on the opera as a whole. By contrast, the Wagnerian approach to writing music drama places far greater significance on the orchestra, which presents most of the important melodic material of the opera in a web of symphonically developed leitmotifs. It is this issue of a symphonic continuity dominating large portions of an opera that separates Wagner's aesthetic from Debussy's (see chapter 20 for more details). In Italy, Verdi also relied on arioso to create continuity in his late works, but also blended traditional set pieces into this arioso structure in a way the masked their beginnings and endings and created the illusion of continuously unfolding music and drama. Each of these national styles found proponents among twentieth-century composers struggling to find a secure footing for the development of new operatic styles in the future. What follows here is a look at three masterpieces of twentieth-century opera, each based to some extent on one or another of these earlier models.

THE DEBUSSY MODEL: BARTÓK'S
DUKE BLUEBEARD'S CASTLE

The model of "opera as sung play," most effectively espoused by Debussy, was first explored in the new century by the Hungarian composer Béla Bartók, whose one and only opera, *Duke Bluebeard's Castle* (1911) duplicates many of the essential ingredients of Debussy's unusual operatic formula. The story of Duke Bluebeard and his last wife, Judith, is not based on modern history or contemporary literature. Nor is it drawn from an episode in the everyday life of the common folk. Instead, the libretto for this opera, like that for *Pelléas et Mélisande*, is a contemporary allegory based on symbolic, legendary characters set in no particular place at no particular time (except for the implication of something far away and long ago). Debussy's characters symbolize blind unawareness, whereas Bartók's represent male guardedness in the face of female inquisitiveness, or more simply, the opposition of closed and open aspects of human nature. When Judith asks for one after another of the keys to the locked doors in the castle, what she finds behind each is a part of Bluebeard's life that he prefers to keep hidden. Judith's insatiable desire to know everything about her new husband, of course, ends in disaster, from which we must draw our own conclusions. In only one act, Bartók takes the two characters of his opera on an emotional journey that unfolds exclusively in conversation between them, as Judith pries deeper and deeper into the life Bluebeard so desperately wants to hide from her. The librettos for both *Pélleas* and *Bluebeard* read like plays in which the drama unfolds in conversations between characters, with no concession made to the old-fashioned need in opera to allow for moments of reflection (arias) or moments of group emotional expression (ensembles). In Bartók's one-act opera, both music and text unfold in a through-composed fashion that avoids thematic repetition and standard musical forms of any kind. In this regard, *Bluebeard* reminds us of that part of Debussy's operatic aesthetic that decried obvious musical forms as incapable of capturing the continuously changing "rhythm of life."

Both Debussy and Bartók were composers for whom musical rhythm grew innately out of the rhythm of the language in which they worked. In Debussy's case, his French text was drawn directly from a prose play by Maeterlinck. The libretto therefore has none of the metric accentuation associated with poetry, and Debussy's setting of this text carefully duplicates the rhythm of the spoken language in all its suppleness and irregularity. Bartók's libretto (by Béla Belázs) is similarly irregular in its metric organization, duplicating the effect of prose. And the rhythm of the Hungarian language, which is characterized by many words having a strong accent on a short first syllable (like the English word *never*), is consistently mirrored in Bartók's musical rhythms.

Lastly, musical form and vocal style were compositional parameters that both of these composers worked to revitalize. Debussy once referred to his music as having a form that grew out of a "rhythm of colors and time," without ever really clarifying exactly what he meant by that. But the result is an opera that seems to progress by stream of consciousness through the continual presentation and restatement of motifs that never develop or progress toward a musical climax or point of arrival. Working in conjunction with this kaleidoscope of orchestral themes is Debussy's vocal style based on his theory that melody was not synonymous with lyricism. Rarely does Debussy's style of melody blossom into full song, aiming instead for the sound and effect of musically heightened speech similar to the vocal recitatives of the very earliest operas of Monteverdi. Bartók's style seems to reflect the same lack of concern with large-scale form and traditional vocal melody we see in Debussy. In fact, Bartók's score seems, on first hearing, even less organized in its musical structure than does Debussy's. Not only does it avoid independent musical units that might be understood as set pieces, but its large-scale musical structure cannot, like Debussy's, be hung on a repetitive arrangement of leitmotifs. The music has, as a result, more the effect of a film score, unfolding moment by moment as dictated by the necessities of the drama. In this regard, Bartók's music comes even closer perhaps than does Debussy's to the ideal of opera as sung play. Similarly, Bartók's vocal style copies that of Debussy in its avoidance of long lyrical lines, in favor of short melodic phrases that encompass a limited range of pitches in a free and supple rhythm reminiscent of the speech rhythms of *Pelléas et Mélisande*.

Given this close relationship to Debussy's aesthetic of opera, one might ask how Bartók was able to modernize the genre (i.e., to bring it into the twentieth century) while remaining true to his model and to the lyrical potential of the human voice. The answer lies in the relationship of his compositional technique to his work as an ethnomusicologist. Early in his career, Bartók devoted himself to discovering and bringing to light the folk music of his native country. He spent several years traversing the backwoods of Hungary with a crude recording device in an attempt to document the true nature of this unknown musical tradition. Bartók then used what he learned about the folk music of his country to inform his work as a contemporary composer, becoming in the process, what might be called the father of twentieth-century musical nationalism.

To understand how Bartók's work with folk music affected his general compositional style, we need to examine some aspects of *Duke Bluebeard's Castle* in greater detail. Harmony, for example, was a musical parameter in which musical modernism had made significant innovations. The chromatic harmony of Wagner in the late nineteenth century had been expanded by his German disciple Arnold Schoenberg, who eventually created an "atonal" harmonic vocabulary in which the distinction between consonance and dissonance was formally abandoned, and in which any combination of pitches was "allowable" in music without regard to traditional concepts of harmonic tension and resolution. Bartók must have understood that one could not write new music governed by old rules of harmony, but he was not ready to abandon tonality altogether, at least not in an opera. His solution to the question of how to move ahead with a modernized harmonic style was to create a sound world based not exclusively on traditional uses of major, minor, or chromatic scales, but one that combined these old scale forms with the unique folk scales he discovered in his work with Hungarian peasants. These new scales (known as *modes*) were then often combined in a manner that brings two different tonalities together (bitonality), producing a confluence of similar and dissimilar pitches that has a "spicy" yet still familiar tonal sound. The very beginning of the opera presents a fine example of this technique. The first sixteen measures of the score consist of an orchestral bass part that outlines an F-sharp natural minor scale (commonly found in folk music) as seen in Ex. 21-1.

Example 21-1a. F-sharp natural minor scale (aeolian mode).

Example 21-1b. Orchestral opening of opera.

In m. 16, the higher orchestral instruments enter playing a series of parallel thirds drawn from an entirely different scale often associated with folk music—something that sounds like an A natural minor scale altered with raised fourth and sixth degrees:

Example 21-2a. Folk scale.

Example 21-2b. First bitonal entrance of orchestra.

The parallel thirds in the upper parts, along with all the notes that are common to the two scales, create a mostly consonant and quasi-tonal sound to the music, while the few notes that clash between the two scales (the C-natural vs. C-sharp) add a twentieth-century pungency that modernizes the sound of the opera without threatening to derail its overall tonal feeling. In other spots, Bartók's music relies on just one folk scale at a time, such as the F-sharp harmonic minor scale that appears at rehearsal 11 in the score. But here the harmony also takes on a dissonant sound caused by the inclusion of a harmonic leitmotif (the half-step dyad G-sharp and A) that represents "blood" throughout the opera.

Example 21-3. Dissonant motif added to an F-sharp harmonic minor scale.

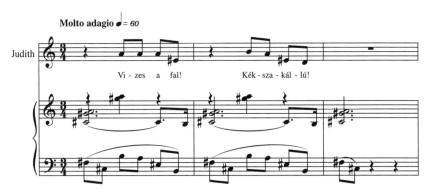

Finally, much of the music in *Bluebeard's Castle* is based on the traditional chromatic scale, so common in nearly all late-nineteenth-century music. But Bartók's selection of pitches from this twelve-note chromatic scale allows him to create a modal sound that is fully in keeping with the overall folk-like vocabulary of the opera. Example 4 illustrates the eighth and ninth measures after rehearsal 22 in the score, where every note of the chromatic scale, except an A-sharp, is employed, but in a manner that produces a modal sound centered around the tonic of G-sharp.

Example 21-4. Modal harmony derived from chromatic scale.

In much the same manner that Bartók was able to modernize his harmonic language without having to resort to the fully dissonant style of some of his early twentieth-century colleagues such as Schoenberg, he was also able to manufacture an equally modern vocal style without embracing the aesthetic of angularity and atonality characteristic of much of the avant-garde music of his generation. Here, too, Bartók relied on his familiarity with Hungarian folk music, using this untapped resource to design melodies that are imminently singable because of their connection to an oral folk tradition. If one were to listen objectively to the vocal parts in *Bluebeard's Castle*, the general impression regarding Bartók's melodies would probably be that he, like Debussy, cared little about tunes that one could hum at the end of an evening's performance. Some of the most salient characteristics of this untuneful vocal writing are its many repeated notes, its limited vocal range, and the frequent use of short phrases of only two or three measures each. Furthermore, none of these short phrases ever seems to repeat or coalesce into larger units of melodic organization. In this sense, Bartók's melodic writing seems again to duplicate that of Debussy, and to be designed in a more or less through-composed style. Yet at the same time, one senses some kind of unity at work behind this melodic style; that is, the material of the vocal parts seems somehow to be organically unified on a subliminal level that prevents both the perception of melodic regularity and, at the same time, protects against the total disintegration of the vocal lines into a state of melodic entropy. Closer analysis of Bartók's style reveals the presence of a simple melodic formula in this opera that the composer subjects to infinite variations, thus creating a web of relationships between the various melodic materials without actually building what might be termed a family of leitmotifs. This basic formula consists of an arrangement of repeated notes, stepwise motion, and small skips. A common iteration of this formula begins with a few repeated notes followed by some stepwise motion and a downward skip at the end (Ex. 21-5).

Example 21-5. Iterations of the basic melodic formula.

Other variations of this prototype include those melodies that leave out one of the three parts: either the repeated notes, the stepwise motion, or the skip.

Example 21-6a. Formula variations: without repeated notes.

Example 21-6b. Formula variation: without stepwise motion.

Example 21-6c. Other formula variations.

These variations do not constitute thematic development in the manner of Wagner, because they are not dependent on specific intervallic relationships. Instead, such "variations" are created through the manipulation of three specific types of melodic motion, all of which are further connected by a kind of rhythmic uniformity caused by the use of only a few different repeating values: mostly eighths and quarters. Thematic relationships such as these give the opera a musical unity that is less obvious than that created by the repetition and development of leitmotifs, and allow this unity to develop almost unnoticed over vast lengths of musical time. Because it works on such a subliminal level, this kind of musical cohesion, which creates an overarching similarity of melodic style throughout the opera, does not interfere with the composer's attempt to project, on a conscious level, the sense of an uninterrupted flow of ideas that mimics the dramatic structure of a spoken play. *Duke Bluebeard's Castle* stands out, then, as a successful modernization of the operatic model first established by Debussy. Accordingly, it might best by described as the Hungarian *Pelléas*, and like its French predecessor, a true masterpiece of drama in music.

II. THE WAGNER MODEL: ALBAN BERG'S WOZZECK

By the end of the nineteenth century, the Wagnerian model of symphonic opera had spread throughout Europe. This kind of opera rejected the old role of the orchestra as an accompaniment to the vocal soloists onstage—a relationship between instruments and voices that had dominated opera since its inception in the seventeenth century—and replaced it with a new aesthetic that relegated the vocal parts to the position of just another line in the overall musical texture that was now dominated by the orchestra. Of course, the idea of an orchestra carrying the principal motivic material of an opera in a freely developing symphonic texture usually worked better in theory than in practice; and, as pointed out elsewhere in this book, rarely produced an orchestral texture that one could truly claim equaled the independent continuity of a real symphony. Nevertheless, the dream of controlling the overall form of an opera with a large-scale symphonic structure was one that appealed to many composers of the early twentieth century, because it seemed to offer an efficient method for achieving the operatic ideal of an uninterrupted musical continuity for which most composers were striving. Foremost among these advocates of symphonic opera in the twentieth century was Alban Berg, whose *Wozzeck* (1921) is a prime example of the technique of Wagner and Strauss carried to a new level of complexity and sophistication.

Wozzeck, the first of Berg's two operas (the other being *Lulu*, left unfinished at his death in 1935), combines two different operatic themes that were popular at the turn of the twentieth century: expressionism and realism (verismo). Its libretto was drawn by Berg himself from a play by Georg Büchner, a pre-Marxist writer and political activist who lived a tragically short life from 1813 to 1837, when he died of typhus. His play, titled *Woyzeck*, dealt with the life of a regimental soldier whose mistress, with whom he has had a child, is cheating on him, and whose life in the army is marked by exploitation at the hands of both his captain, for whom he functions as a personal servant, and the regimental doctor, who uses him as the subject of unusual dietary experiments. Berg selected fifteen of the twenty-five scenes in the play to set directly to music, creating a libretto, like that for Strauss's *Salome* and Debussy's *Pelléas*, written in prose. To the extent that Wozzeck himself is a somewhat dim-witted man whose actions are more instinctual than rational, the opera treats the typical expressionist themes of the unexplored subconscious motivations of human behavior. Like Salome, Wozzeck is a character propelled to gruesome acts of violence by a psyche of which he is completely unaware. The libretto also deals, allegorically, with the subject of the exploitation of the masses at the hands of a selfish, manipulating upper class. As such, the story of Wozzeck is one dealing with the lowest stratum of society caught in poverty and driven to acts of passion and violence—exactly the kind of subject on which the verismo movement was based. For any composer wanting to present both the expressionist and realistic elements of a drama, the problem would have been one of finding the appropriate musical style to depict the mental obsessions, the tortured psyche, and the violence inherent in this type of subject matter. But for Berg, the question of finding an appropriate musical style proved not to be an issue, since his teacher, Schoenberg, had already established a style for this kind of subject in his expressionist monodrama, *Erwartung* (for soprano and orchestra, 1909). That was the so-called free atonal style, which Berg then adopted for his new opera.

When Schoenberg abandoned tonality in a series of revolutionary works written in 1908, and replaced it with what is usually known as *free atonality*, he inadvertently brought to the process of composition an unforeseen problem: that of how to create long-range form in a new atonal musical world. Tonality served many functions in music, foremost among which was the creation of a sense of direction, a moving away, through modulation, from a point of departure, toward a new point of arrival, and finally back again to the point of origin. This tonal motion caused music to function in a teleological fashion and to take on a shape that stretched across the full duration of the work. In earlier opera, of course, this sense of tonal motion away from and back to a central point of repose was never especially important, because each individual piece had its own key, and the organization of those keys had more to do with practicalities of singers and singing than with matters of long-range tonal design stretching over three acts. But as opera became more symphonic in the late nineteenth century, composers (especially Wagner) became concerned with the tonal structure of their works as part of an attempt to organize the newly important instrumental component of opera into satisfying shapes.

Because Berg borrowed his teacher's free atonal style for the writing of *Wozzeck*, he borrowed along with it the same problem of how to create form in music without a tonal center. His solution in this opera, as is generally well known, was to adopt an elaborate structure of different instrumental forms that could be used to underpin the unfolding drama in the vocal parts. Berg himself explained exactly what these forms were in each act of his opera. Act 1 (the dramatic exposition) consists of five scenes that introduce the various characters. Each of these scenes is accompanied by a different form: a dance suite, a rhapsody, a military march and lullaby, a passacaglia, and a rondo. The second act (the dramatic development), also contains five scenes and is organized like a five-movement symphony, with a sonata, a fantasia and fugue, a largo, a scherzo, and a rondo. And the five scenes of the last act are all organized as inventions: on a theme, a note, a rhythm, a chord, and a perpetual rhythm. Then to weld together all the scenes in each act, Berg decided to write instrumental interludes, like those in Debussy's *Pelléas et Mélisande*, to keep the music going while the curtain is down between scenes. The superimposition of abstract instrumental forms on a continuously unfolding drama might at first seem to suggest that Berg was making the same compositional mistake that Debussy found in the operas of Wagner: the use of fixed musical forms to capture the moment-to-moment vacillation of human moods that the text of an opera will inevitably expose. Or, to put it another way, the Wagnerian development of musical ideas will have a logic (i.e., form) of its own that will nearly always conflict with the musical depiction of life in real time. In defense of Berg, however, it has been observed (most cogently by Douglas Jarman in his Cambridge Opera Handbook on *Wozzeck*) that the instrumental forms selected by Berg often present musical material "that is of a kind that is traditionally associated with the kind of activity depicted on stage."[1] Examples include the "military march and lullaby" in the third scene of act 1 where Marie watches the passing of a military parade that includes the drum major in whom she is interested and then proceeds to her singing a lullaby to the child she has had with Wozzeck. Similarly, the use of a *Ländler* (a folk waltz) for the

---

1. Jarman, 1989, 43.

scherzo movement of act 2, scene 4 suits the fact that the action takes place in a tavern where dancing is expected. Yet at the same time, Berg did use abstract instrumental forms that occasionally seem to bear little relation to the underlying dramatic action of a particular scene. The baroque dance suite that accompanies act 1, scene 1 would seem to present such a case. This act serves as an introduction to each of the characters in Wozzeck's life, none of whom has anything to do with dancing. Nevertheless, there are at least two good explanations for why he was able to employ these various abstract musical forms throughout his opera. The first is that in many cases the instrumental form he chose for each scene mimics the sequence of events as they unfold in the drama onstage. A fine example is scene 1 in act 2, in which Berg employs a sonata form to depict Wozzeck's growing suspicion of Marie, aroused when he finds her wearing some new earrings that she claims to have found, but which were actually given her by the drum major who seduced her at the end of act 1. A classical sonata form of the kind one could find in the instrumental works of a composer such as Mozart might at first seem ill-suited to the needs of a developing stage action because a sonata has a particular, fixed formal design. Throughout the history of classical and romantic music that form consisted of three large sections: the exposition, development, and recapitulation. The exposition begins with a primary theme, then makes a transition to a secondary theme in a new key, and sometimes closes with a final thematic idea. The development section then takes the themes of the exposition and reworks them through sequences, contrapuntal combinations, and truncation, all while constantly modulating through different keys. The musical instability of the development section then leads to the recapitulation, in which all the material of the exposition is repeated, but now without leaving the home (tonic) key. Although this fairly predictable structure may seem too rigid to accommodate the needs of a continuously developing drama, sonata form had for years (at least since the days of Mozart) been recognized as a dramatic form in and of itself. The exposition introduces the listener to the principal melodic idea, but then juxtaposes that with a contrasting melodic idea in a new key. Dramatically speaking this presents the listener with two different (often competing) characters. In the classical period, the exposition of a sonata was always repeated before moving on to the development section, which functions as the part of the form in which the themes (or characters) of the exposition interact and literally confront one another. The tension of this confrontation leads eventually to a resolution in the recapitulation, where all parties involved (i.e., all the themes) converge on a unified tonality, thus bringing the dramatic journey to a satisfying conclusion. Berg must have recognized that the dramatic action of act 2, scene 1 suited this particular formal design perfectly. The scene opens with Marie admiring her new earrings in a mirror, while also trying to put her son to sleep. The opening theme of the sonata form (Ex. 21-7) is that which accompanies her satisfaction with the earrings.

Example 21-7. Sonata form first theme.

A short transition occurs at the point where the little boy becomes restless, and Marie tells him to close his eyes. She then sings him a lullaby, which becomes the new contrasting second theme of the sonata form (Ex. 21-8).

Example 21-8. Lullaby as sonata, second theme.

In the style of all symphonic opera, this lullaby proves to be a transformation of the lullaby sung by Marie to her child in act 1. This original appearance of the lullaby can be seen in Ex. 21-9.

Example 21-9. Original lullaby in act 1, sc. 3.

The fact that one lullaby is a variation on the other demonstrates that in addition to the numerous instrumental forms Berg chose to underpin the fifteen scenes of his opera, he also created a series of leitmotifs in the manner of Wagner and Strauss, which reappear from one scene to another effectively pulling what might otherwise have been a series of discrete abstract forms into a symphonically unified whole. As Marie's child closes his eyes, she returns to admiring herself in the mirror. This return to the original action with which the scene began brings us to the traditional repeat of the exposition. Fortunately, the entire sequence of events that took place during the initial statement of the exposition is now repeated. The child stirs off his mother's lap (transition theme) causing her to sing him the lullaby again (repeating the second theme). The development section of the sonata form marks a major new division of the musical structure that corresponds to the arrival of Wozzeck, who has come to give Marie some money. The musical confrontation, instability, and unpredictability of a traditional development section is all mirrored in the confusion that now occurs onstage, as Wozzeck points to the earrings and suspiciously questions Marie about where she got them. The resolution of the tension in this part of the scene is not achieved until Wozzeck leaves. Here, Berg brings back the opening theme to begin the recapitulation that accompanies Marie's musings on her own infidelity, and the remainder of the recapitulation is given over to the instrumental interlude that leads to the next scene, thereby allowing the audience to contemplate the meaning of what just happened onstage. The dramatic action of the scene—exposition of contrasting situations, dramatic development, and denouement—thus aptly mirrors the dialectic structure (thesis, antithesis, synthesis) of the instrumental sonata form that Berg used to carry the action.

The second reason that Berg was able to employ these various instrumental forms as an organizational tool in his opera was that many of the forms he chose have a fairly loose and unprescribed formal design. Act 1, scene 2 is a rhapsody, a form which, as the name suggests, implies something rhapsodic or loosely organized. The passacaglia that accompanies scene 4 also carries no specific musical form beyond the fact that a single theme is presented and then continuously varied without the need to follow any prescribed pattern of tempo or style. In act 2, the fantasia, the largo, and the scherzo are also all instrumental forms with which no specific formal design is usually associated, thus leaving Berg free to organize his orchestral material to suit the nature of the action onstage. Here, the third scene, the largo, makes a fine example. The term *largo* is frequently seen as a label on slow movements of classical and romantic symphonies; but it designates only a slow tempo, without implying anything about the actual formal design of the movement. In this scene, Wozzeck accuses Marie of cheating on him without actually naming the drum major as her partner in sin. Accordingly, Berg took the opportunity to create an instrumental form for this slow movement that was partly based on themes borrowed from the scenes in act 1 that included the drum major (scene 3 where Marie first expresses an interest in him, and scene 5 in which he seduces her). Some of the important melodic shapes and rhythms from those two scenes are transformed to become part of the orchestral texture of this slow movement in act 2. Here we have another manifestation of an overarching symphonic technique at work in this opera. The mere suggestion of the drum major in this argument between Wozzeck and Marie in scene 3 inevitably calls up melodic material associated with his appearance in earlier scenes, and the musical form of the largo is sufficiently supple and variable so that bits of his thematic material can easily be dropped into this new movement.

By far the instrumental forms that are most free are the inventions of act 3. The term *invention* suggests a contrapuntal study (such as Bach's Two-Part Inventions) in which a theme is worked out in a logical design of some kind. Therefore, an invention will treat a single thematic idea in a freely developmental fashion. Act 3 of *Wozzeck* is a collection of five inventions (one for each scene), all based on different kinds of musical material: a theme, a single note (B), a rhythm, a six-note chord, and a perpetual rhythm. In each of these scenes, the basic kernel of an idea is continuously present, unifying the musical development. In scene 2, Wozzeck and Marie are walking by a pond when a rising red moon puts the thought of blood into Wozzeck's unstable mind. Suddenly he pulls out a knife and slits Marie's throat. Musically, this scene, an "invention on a note," is organized around the growing prominence of the note B, which comes to represent the idea of murder. The note appears discretely at first, becoming louder and more insistent as the moment of the murder approaches, finally climaxing in a continual, pounding repetition in the timpani as Wozzeck commits the murder and Marie drops lifeless to the ground. As he leans over her dead body, he utters one last word, Tot (dead), ironically sung on the note C. In the tonal music of earlier centuries a B leading to, and resolving on, a C would suggest a traditional V-I cadence in the key of C major. And the little musical joke here is that the continual repetition of the note B in this scene takes on the meaning of murder, which leads to the note C as the manifestation of its completion, much as the note B in tonal music functions as a "leading tone" resolving to and completing itself in the tonic note C. One might want to observe, of course, that this allusion to tonal procedures of the past suggests that buried under the veneer of dissonant harmonic modernity in this opera is a conscious glance back to the late-romantic era in which Berg had his roots. Certainly, Berg's harmonic vocabulary leans far more heavily on tonal procedures of the past than did that of his teacher, Schoenberg, as the large orchestral interlude between the last two scenes of this act amply demonstrates. Berg undoubtedly chose to make this interlude—an invention on the key of D minor—the most tonal section of the opera because it represents the climax of the whole drama. At this point in the opera, Marie has been murdered and Wozzeck has drowned in an attempt to cover up the evidence of his guilt. Now, with both of the opera's protagonists dead, the audience sits through what is by far the longest interlude (in which most of the major leitmotifs return in one final mélange), during which they are expected to contemplate the meaning of the tragic conclusion to the drama. As if to underline the significance of this instrumental interlude, Berg highlighted it by placing it in a clearly perceptible tonal center. At the conclusion of this tonal interlude, all that remains is the final scene, in which Wozzeck's little boy is seen playing with some friends, when one of them enters and announces the discovery of Marie's body. Not quite understanding, the child remains behind as his friends run off to see what all the excitement is about. The perpetual rhythm on which this last invention is based causes the top notes of the final chord of the opera to oscillate between two sets of pitches in a fashion that suggests not an ending through a final cadence, but rather, a nonending in a chord that could continue oscillating forever. Dramatically this equivocal end to the opera might be Berg's way of hinting that the tragedy of the poor and disenfranchised, about whom Büchner wrote, is one that has no end. Now that the parents are dead, the child's destiny will simply be to duplicate their tragedy in a new generation, and on into the foreseeable future.

In writing *Wozzeck*, Berg leapt bravely into the world of atonal music as a way to define the opera of the new century. The problem with this style of opera is that the human voice does not produce pitches the way a piano or a clarinet does. As explained earlier, a singer cannot simply place his or her fingers in the proper position and get the desired note. With the human voice, if a singer can't hear the note in his or her head before singing it, there is no way of finding that specific pitch. Because Berg's style is so dissonant and so full of difficult leaps, the task of finding the right notes becomes daunting. The vocal parts need to be learned from rote and repeated over and over again to get the right pitches in the ear.

One could understand the development of this especially difficult vocal style as the culmination of the general trajectory of German symphonic opera from the beginning of the nineteenth century into the first decades of the twentieth. To be sure, *Wozzeck* is not a beautiful opera, nor is it easy to sing. But it is an intensely moving, and in some ways disturbing work, which depends for its success, as does all symphonic opera, on the central role of the orchestra in creating the drama in the music. In the absence of a traditional tonal harmonic vocabulary, and in the absence of any kind of vocal lyricism, we cannot be surprised that Berg should have chosen to organized his opera with the superimposition of abstract instrumental forms and related symphonic techniques. These techniques represent yet another solution to the problem of how to write opera in the modern era.

III. THE VERDI MODEL: BENJAMIN BRITTEN'S *PETER GRIMES*

If anyone were going to carry the torch of Italian opera into the twentieth century, chances are it would be an Englishman like Benjamin Britten. Of the three operatic models inherited from the late nineteenth century, Verdi's was perhaps the most traditional, especially in terms of its inclusion of set pieces that allowed for old-fashioned lyrical singing in the form of arias and ensemble numbers. The fact that this more traditional operatic aesthetic would have appealed to English composers will come as no surprise to anyone who knows the generally conservative streak that runs through the history of English music. In fact, attitudes toward music in England from the end of the Renaissance (ca. 1600) to the dawn of the twentieth century seem to have been marked by an overall conservatism that resulted in English composers simply following trends established elsewhere in Europe, without ever really developing a unique style of their own.

Benjamin Britten could easily have become a product of this English conservatism, were it not for the fact that at age eleven he came to the attention of Frank Bridge, who took him on as a student. Bridge was at the time breaking away from the academic conservatism of nineteenth-century English music in an attempt to expose himself to the more modern techniques of composers such as Bartók, Stravinsky, and Schoenberg. It was through Bridge's influence that Britten came to know the works of these composers, particularly Berg's *Wozzeck*, a performance of which in 1934 caused the young composer to make a trip to Vienna in hopes of studying with its composer. Britten was eventually to develop a compositional style that modernized the sound of English music while also remaining faithful to some of its traditional roots. Over the course of his career he composed thirteen operas, and made a worldwide reputation for himself as the most significant English composer of opera since Purcell nearly two hundred years earlier.

It was on a trip through the United States between 1939 and 1942 that Britten read an article by E. M. Forster about the British poet George Crabbe, and became fascinated with his poem "The Borough." A portion of the poem was devoted to a depiction of the fisherman Peter Grimes, a brutal, antisocial misfit who mistreated three different orphan boys who served consecutive terms as his apprentice. In Crabbe's poem, Grimes is a man of no redeeming social value, a complete outcast from village life in the small coastal town where he lived. Montague Slater turned Crabbe's poem into a libretto that painted a slightly different image of this central character—one that was more sympathetic and less obviously sociopathic. This new vision of the hero suited Britten, who himself was something of an outcast (as a pacifist, a conscientious objector, and a homosexual), and who regularly treated in his music the theme of the sacrifice of innocence at the hands of a misunderstanding society. Slater's libretto for this opera differed significantly from those for *Pelléas*, *Bluebeard's Castle*, and *Wozzeck*, despite the fact that Grimes was very much a Wozzeck-like character in his alienation from society, and very much like Pelléas in his inability to understand or control his own destiny. Unlike these other operas, *Peter Grimes* includes a large role for the chorus (the villagers) who are almost always set in opposition to Peter: the group against the individual. With the chorus at the center of the opera, ensemble singing was naturally going to be a featured part of the musical fabric of the opera, therefore giving the work a more old-fashioned sound than those operas that unfold mostly in dialogue between individual characters in the manner of Wagner or Debussy.

The opera begins with a prologue that takes place in a courtroom where a judge is hearing evidence in an inquisition surrounding the death of Peter Grimes's young apprentice. Along with Peter and the judge, local townspeople fill the courtroom, mostly out of curiosity. Although the verdict of the judge is that the boy died in "accidental circumstances," Peter is upset about the gossiping that is sure to pursue him even after the court has exonerated him. Once the courtroom is cleared, Ellen Orford, the local schoolmistress and Peter's only friend in town, remains behind to comfort and reassure him. The musical disposition of this entire opening scene depends mostly upon an arioso style of vocal writing similar to that found in Italian opera of the nineteenth century. The orchestral accompaniment introduces an important motif at the beginning and repeats this idea periodically throughout the prologue (see Ex. 21-10).

Example 21-10. Orchestral motif.

Out of the general arioso that is sung over this orchestral part, there arises in spots something more melodic—not quite an aria per se, but certainly a few lines of music that have a more tuneful melodic profile. Such is the case with the lines sung by the judge:

Peter Grimes, I here advise you—do not get another boy apprentice.
Get a fisherman to help you—big enough to stand up for himself.

This melodic section, illustrated in Ex. 21-11, is clearly based on the introductory motif with which the prologue began:

Example 21-11. Prologue.

The end of the trial scene becomes something of a miniature ensemble in which Peter's impassioned response to the judge is intermingled with comments from the chorus as everyone present sings together. Then once the courtroom is cleared, Ellen and Peter sing their duet. Here, Britten steps further into the world of modernism by writing a bitonal piece that has no orchestral accompaniment. Each singer is assigned a distinct key—Peter in F minor, Ellen in E major—which they must hold in perfect intonation against those notes in the other key that conflict with their own. Ex. 21-12 reproduces an excerpt in which the bitonal technique can clearly be seen.

Example 21-12. Bitonal duet.

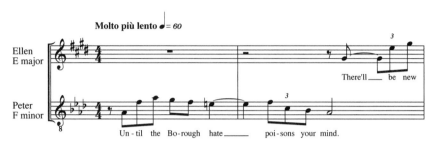

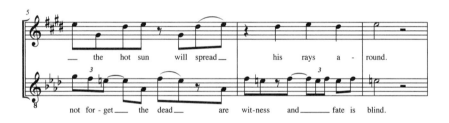

Without the support of the orchestra to help each singer stay on pitch and hold the key, a performance of this duet becomes a true challenge. The technique is not being used here just to demonstrate how modern a composer Britten was. The bitonality of the duet has a dramatic relevance, metaphorically expressing the fact that Peter and Ellen are of two different minds on the subject of his reputation: his more pessimistic, hers more optimistic. Significantly, at the end of the duet the two keys merge into one, as the E major of Ellen's part takes over Peter's F minor (end of Ex. 21-12), in a symbolic representation of his grudging acceptance of her offer of help. As the duet finishes on the unified tonic of E, the orchestra finally enters on the same pitch to begin the first interlude that connects the prologue to the first scene of act 1. If the singers have gone even slightly off key during their a cappella duet, the entrance of the orchestra on the pitch E will embarrass them when the last note they sing does not match the note on which the orchestra enters. Few listeners appreciate either the difficulty of this part of the prologue or the vocal skill required to capture the musical metaphor Britten constructed here.

Standing back to look at the whole of the prologue, we can see that its first half consists of a section of music that mixes soloists and the chorus singing in a variety of styles from arioso, to lyrical melody and full ensemble, all accompanied by orchestral motifs that support, but do not eclipse, the vocal parts. This is then followed by a second part comprised of a traditional-looking duet in which both singers join together in a true ensemble. Taken together, both parts of the prologue constitute what in nineteenth-century Italian opera would have been termed a *gran scena e duetto*. The Italian word *scena* means "scene," and was used by composers to describe a part of the drama that contained several solo characters along with the chorus involved mostly in conversation that moves the plot forward (therefore with narrative, not reflective, text). Such sections were primarily organized around a combination of vocal arioso supported by interesting accompanimental motifs in the orchestra and sections of choral singing combined with the soloists. The *gran scena* became one of several methods that composers used to create musical continuity by blending together different kinds of singing in one uninterrupted unit of dramatic narrative. Usually a *gran scena* led to a standard musical number of some kind, often an aria or duet, just as it does here in *Peter Grimes*. In relation to the model of Italian opera then, the Britten's prologue is a modernized copy of a standard nineteenth-century form.

Following the prologue comes the first orchestral interlude: a depiction of the sea at dawn. The basic motif of this instrumental section (Ex. 21-13) continues into the next scene as the curtain rises on the depiction of bustling activity at daybreak in the fishing village.

Example 21-13. Interlude 1.

Dramatically, this scene serves to introduce the audience to the main characters in the opera: Bob Boles (a Methodist fisherman), Auntie (who runs the local tavern), her "nieces" (who seem to be prostitutes who work out of the tavern), Balstrode (a retired sea captain), Ned Keene (the apothecary), Mrs. Sedley (the town busybody), and Horace Adams (the village rector). Little snippets of conversation among all these characters move the drama forward in a very mundane prose style. Musically, however, these conversations take place as simple arioso that is interwoven into the fundamental choral substance of the scene. The text for the chorus differs from that for the individual characters in two important ways: it is poetry instead of prose, and it functions in a more abstract, allegorical, and therefore less realistic manner. The opening choral lines are as follows:

> Oh hang at open doors the net, the cork,
> While squalid sea dames at their mending work.
> Welcome the hour when fishing through the tide
> The weary husband throws his freight aside.

The orchestral accompaniment for this chorus consists of a continuation of the melodic material of the first interlude. Again thinking in terms associated with earlier nineteenth-century number opera, the opening of this scene would simply have been labeled a "chorus." The inclusion of the solo characters as interjections laid over (or between) the basic choral parts causes the musical technique here to remind one more of French grand opera (where soloists and chorus were regularly mixed together like this) than it does of Italian opera. But regardless of its national identity, this opening scene of act 1 is clearly an elaborated choral set piece.

As the chorus finishes, Grimes enters asking for help hauling his boat on shore. At first there is little response, as the crowd shuns him. Finally Captain Balstrode and Ned Keene lend a hand. As they turn the capstan to haul in Grimes's boat, everyone has something to say about the situation, which takes musical shape as a small ensemble. This, in turn, is followed by what looks in Italian operatic terms like a *scena ed aria*, which is to say another section of dialogue between some of the characters leading to an aria, here for Ellen Orford. As before, the dialogue moves the drama forward, now in a conversation that reveals that Ned Keene has made arrangements for Grimes to get another boy from the local orphanage to serve as his new apprentice. The problem, however, is that the local errand man, Hobson, refuses to pick the boy up at the workhouse and bring him back to Grimes, until Ellen steps forward and volunteers (much to the dismay of the crowd) to help with the task. All of this dramatic action unfolds in the scena, carried out in the usual arioso style, leading to a moment of reflection in which Ellen justifies her actions in an aria (Ex. 21-14).

Example 21-14. Ellen's aria.

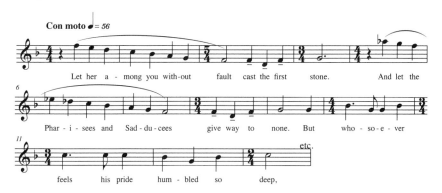

The *scena ed aria* pattern not only reminds us of the Italian operas of Donizetti and Verdi, but the specific manner in which Britten handles the end of the aria recalls the compositional technique of Puccini, who frequently built instrumental bridges linking the ends of arias to the musical numbers that followed. Such bridges usually consisted of an orchestrated repetition of the main melody of the aria with some kind of vocal arioso superimposed over it. In the case of Ellen's aria, Britten does more or less the same, using a repetition of the orchestral accompaniment from the aria to support a short conversation between Ned Keene and Mrs. Sedley about some medicine of hers that is out of stock in his shop and must be fetched by Mr. Hobson from another nearby town. With this little dialogue that uses the music of the preceding aria, the composer disguises the end of the aria, and forces the music to move forward without interruption.

The first scene of act 1 then closes with two more easily recognizable set pieces: a large choral-solo ensemble and a duet. The ensemble begins as Captain Balstrode observes that a storm is approaching, and everyone has a reaction to this news. Again Slater's libretto distinguishes these large choral sections from the dialogue of the soloists by making the group texts more abstract and poetic:

Now the flood tide
And the sea-horses
Will gallop over
The eroded coast
Flooding, flooding
Our seasonal fears.

As the crowd disperses, taking refuge from the approaching storm, only Grimes and Balstrode remain behind. Balstrode's suggestion that Peter should leave town and take some other kind of seafaring job leads to an argument between them that rises in pitch as the storm itself gathers intensity. This duet is laid out in a mostly conversational style based on the same use of arioso that Verdi had perfected in his late operas. In keeping with that technique, Britten often rises out of arioso into moments of true lyricism, especially for those texts in which Peter tries to explain and justify himself. His reliving of the death of his apprentice is an effective example in which the following lines are set to music of heightened lyricism as seen in Ex. 21-15.

> Picture what that day was like,
> That evil day!
> We strained into the wind,
> Heavily ladened.
> We plunged into the wave's
> Shuddering challenge.

Example 21-15. Peter's solo in duet.

The duet closes with a truly allegorical gesture of isolation, as the exasperated Balstrode walks off into the pub, leaving Peter to finish the duet alone, musing on the possibility of a better life with Ellen.

Taking a broader view of the opening of the opera up to this point (the end of scene 1), we can see the obvious connection between Britten's compositional technique and the operas of nineteenth-century Italian composers such as Verdi. Like those earlier works, *Peter Grimes* is, underneath its surface continuity, a number opera in disguise, not all that different from Verdi's *Otello* or Puccini's *Tosca*. Britten cleverly used the orchestral interludes to help create the illusion of a continuously unfolding music by associating the themes of the interludes with the accompaniments of the vocal parts in the surrounding scenes. Thus, the first interlude (between the prologue and act 1) contributes its motivic figures to the accompaniment of the choral scene that follows, and the music of the "storm" ensemble and final duet of act 1, scene 1, becomes the material on which the second interlude is built. Britten's solution to the problem of how to write a twentieth-century opera (at least here at the beginning of his career) was clearly to rely on the tradition of vocal lyricism that had been so important for Italian opera of the past. That meant opera as a drama communicated through a string of lyrical moments, connected by less melodically interesting dialogue that took the form of arioso. The overall structure of the opera up to the end of scene 1 could be diagrammed (in nineteenth-century Italian terms) as follows:

> *Scena e duetto*—the prologue in court
> Chorus—introduction of villagers
> Choral/solo ensemble—entrance of Grimes and reaction to his need for help
> *Scena ed aria*—plan to get Grimes a new apprentice with Ellen's help
> Choral/solo ensemble—storm approaches, group reaction
> *Duetto*—Balstrode and Grimes argue about what Grimes should do next

Final justification for this view of *Peter Grimes* as an offshoot of the Verdian tradition comes from Britten himself, who published a short introduction to his opera at the time of its first performance in 1945, in which he discussed the matter of his compositional technique in this work:

> I am especially interested in the general architectural and formal problems of opera, and decided to reject the Wagnerian theory of "permanent melody" for the classical practice of separate numbers that crystallize and hold the emotion of a dramatic situation at chosen moments.[2]

As in the works of the Italian masters who established this operatic ideal, true recitative makes only rare appearances, because its lack of melodic interest hampered composers' ability to avoid breaking the opera into small independent bits of lyrical music. Like the other two operas under consideration here (*Wozzeck* and *Duke Bluebeard's Castle*), *Peter Grimes* is a

---

2. Brett, 1983, 149

work that meets the minimal standards of modern opera to imitate the style of a spoken stage play; but unlike those earlier operas, both of which took a more radical approach to the rapprochement with literary drama, *Peter Grimes* stands alone in its prominent use of the chorus and its insistence on the continuing viability of discrete units of vocal lyricism, whether as "arias," or as smaller sections within duets and ensembles. In the final analysis, one might find something comforting in this attachment to such a familiar and attractive tradition. Like Bartók, Berg, and Britten, composers who wanted to write opera in the twentieth century had to come to grips with the same basic questions: (1) Is it important for opera to be, at least in part, lyrical and tuneful; (2) what should be the role of the orchestra; (3) does opera need to have a long-range musical form; (4) can or should opera work like a spoken play? Answers to these questions first emerged at the end of the nineteenth century, and formed the point of departure from which many composers of twentieth-century opera worked. Vestiges of the past inhabit and inform the creative minds of all modern composers of opera, even to this day. The challenge for modern audiences is to try to identify the source of any specific contemporary operatic style in the hope of better understanding how its composer has balanced the various competing issues through which the genre of music drama defines itself. As always, attentive, informed listening pays large dividends in terms of greater appreciation of opera, the most extravagant of musical art forms.

GLOSSARY

arioso

A vocal style that lies somewhere between the speechlike quality of recitative and the full lyricism of an aria. Arioso usually contains asymmetrical phrases, very little text repetition, and an orchestral accompaniment built on the repetition of a single melodic motif.

bel canto

A style of singing practiced by the great castrati of the eighteenth century and passed on to singers of both genders in the following century. Its characteristics include the production of beautiful tone quality, long legato phrases, technical virtuosity, and the ability to add improvised ornamentation to the written melody.

cadence

The end of a musical phrase at which point the music pauses briefly.

cavatina

In Italian opera, the opening slow section of a large aria. In French opera and Italian opera buffa, an aria of small proportions.

commedia dell'arte

An improvised, slapstick form of masked theatrical entertainment popular from the sixteenth to the eighteenth century. It included several stock character types such as an old doctor, a pair of young lovers, a servant girl, and a captain.

chromaticism

Music that employs notes drawn from all twelve notes that can be found within an octave.

chords

The result of stacking several notes (usually three or four) on top of one another.

consonance

A pleasant sounding combination of notes.

counterpoint

The combination of two or melodies sounding together.

dissonance

A harsh sounding combination of notes. In the eighteenth and nineteenth centuries, dissonance added harmonic "spice" to music, but always "resolved" to consonances. In the twentieth century, dissonance was used without the softening of consonant resolution.

divertissement

Scenes of decorative entertainment within a French grand opera.

dyad

A two-note chord.

fioriture

Literally "flowers." Decorative ornaments in a melodic line, including turns, trills, mordents, and short melismas. These could be written by the composer or added by singers as improvisations.

free atonality

The use of any combination of notes drawn from the chromatic scale to form harmonies in which traditional dissonances no longer need to be "resolved" (i.e., move directly to consonances).

grand opera

A style of French serious opera in

the nineteenth century. It featured historical plots, large choruses, elaborate scenic effects, and ballet.

homophonic

A musical texture in which one melody is accompanied by harmony made up of chords.

invention

In the eighteenth century, a free polyphonic composition based on imitative counterpoint. More generally, any musical form based on a single theme treated freely.

key

A sense of musical gravitation around a central note produced by a standard pattern of whole and half steps that make up all major and minor scales. These patterns can be built on any of the twelve possible notes in an octave, thereby producing twelve different gravitational centers (tonal centers). Each center is known as a key.

melisma

Setting one syllable of text to many notes.

meter

The sequence of alternating strong and weak pulses that underlies all Western music.

modality

An arrangement of the notes of a scale to form a pattern of whole and half steps that differs from the usual arrangement found in major or minor scales. Modal scales are common in several types of European folk music.

modulation

A change of key.

octave

An interval between two notes that represents a 2:1 ratio in the frequency of the pitches. These pitches sound like the same note in different registers of the voice. Usually octaves are divided into scales of seven or twelve notes.

"park and bark"

A singers' term for those moments when the action in a libretto comes to a pause to allow the singer to stand in front of the audience ("park") and simply sing his or her heart out ("bark").

patter aria

An aria in which the text is set to a series of mostly repeated notes in a very fast tempo, giving the effect of a tongue-twisting exercise. These arias were mostly written for low male voices, and were common in comic opera.

perfect pitch

The ability to identify the exact pitch of any note simply by hearing it played or sung.

polyphonic

A musical texture in which two or more melodies sound together.

primo tempo

The opening slow section of music (after the introductory recitative) in a duet. It consists usually of a solo for each character followed by a joint duet.

Prix de Rome

An arts competition run by the French government in painting, sculpture and music. In music the competition required the composition of a dramatic cantata with orchestra. The winner was sent to Rome to study for two years and was awarded a five-year stipend to support his or her career.

recitative, secco

The most speechlike vocal music, used in opera for the delivery of dialogue. It consists of many repeated notes with little melodic shape, accompanied only by a harpsichord. This style of recitative was found mostly in the eighteenth century.

recitative, accompanied

A slightly more tuneful style of recitative, accompanied by the full orchestra.

rhythm

Any series of note durations (i.e., whole notes, half notes, quarter notes, etc.). Sometimes these durations form repeating patterns (as in much dance music, for instance), while at other times the durations may seem random and unpatterned.

scena

In Italian opera seria, a scene in which multiple characters interact, usually in a combination of arioso, chorus, and lyrical singing. The scena often leads to a set piece such as an aria or duet.

sequence

The immediate repetition of a melodic motive at a higher or lower pitch level.

set piece

An independent musical number of a lyrical nature, such as an aria, duet, or ensemble. These numbers always have a clear beginning and end that create pauses in the flow of the drama.

sonata form

A standard form of instrumental music in the eighteenth and nineteenth centuries, consisting of an exposition of two or three themes stated in different keys, a development of those themes, and a recapitulation in which the themes are restated in the home (tonic) key of the piece.

Sprechgesang

A German term used to describe a semimelodic style of vocal writing similar to Italian arioso. The term usually describes the style of melody found in the operas of Wagner.

Sprechstimme

Literally "spoken voice." A technique employed in the twentieth century and invented by Arnold Schoenberg. The singer must hit the note indicated in the music and then let the voice fall away to a speaking intonation.

stretta

The fast, energetic closing section of an Italian ensemble number.

tonality

The establishment of a particular key. (See "key.")

trouser role

The part of a teenage boy played by a female, usually a mezzo-soprano. The tradition was common in Italian opera buffa, but also appears in such operas as Gounod's *Faust* and Strauss's *Der Rosenkavalier.*

BIBLIOGRAPHY

ANDERSON, EMILY, tr. and ed. *The Letters of Beethoven.* 3 vols. London: Macmillan, 1961.

_____, tr. and ed. *The Letters of Mozart and His Family.* 3rd ed. London: Macmillan, 1985.

BERLIOZ, HECTOR. Preface to *Roméo et Juliette.* 1839.

_____. (Abbreviated CG) *Correspondance générale,* vol. 1. Ed. Pierre Citron. Paris: Flammarion, 1972.

BRETT, PHILIP. *Benjamin Britten: Peter Grimes.* Cambridge Opera Handbooks. New York, Cambridge University Press, 1983.

BUDDEN, JULIAN. *The Operas of Verdi,* vol. 2. New York: Oxford University Press, 1978.

_____. *The Operas of Verdi,* vol. 3. New York: Oxford University Press, 1981.

CAIRNS, DAVID, ed. and tr. *The Memoirs of Hector Berlioz.* New York: W. W. Norton, 1975.

EVANS, EDWIN, JR. "Debussy's *Pelléas et Mélisande,*" *Musical Standard* 31 (June 5, 1909).

GIROUD, VINCENT. *French Opera: A Short History.* New Haven, CT: Yale University Press, 2010.

GOETHE, WOLFGANG VON. *Faust,* Part I. Rev. ed. Trans. Peter Salm. New York: Bantam Books, 1985.

JARMAN, DOUGLAS. *Alban Berg: Wozzeck.* Cambridge Opera Handbooks. New York: Cambridge University Press, 1989.

KERMAN, JOSEPH. *Opera as Drama.* New York: A. Knopf, 1952.

KIMBELL, DAVID. *Verdi in the Age of Italian Romanticism.* New York: Cambridge University Press, 1981.

LAWTON, DAVID. "On the *Bacio* Theme in *Otello,*" *19th Century Music* 1, no. 3 (March, 1978): 211–20.

LESURE, FRANÇOIS. *Debussy on Music.* New York: A. Knopf, 1977.

LESURE, FRANCOIS, AND ROGER NICHOLS, eds. *Debussy Letters.* Cambridge, MA: Harvard University Press, 1987.

MYERS, ROLLO, ed. *Richard Strauss & Romain Rolland Correspondence.* Berkeley, CA: University of California Press, 1968.

ORLEDGE, ROBERT. *Debussy and the Theater.* New York: Cambridge University Press.

_____. "Satie and Debussy." In *Satie the Composer.* New York: Cambridge University Press, 1990.

OSBORNE, CHARLES. *Letters of Giuseppe Verdi.* New York: Holt, Rinehart, and Winston, 1971.

_____. *The Complete Operas of Verdi.* New York: A. Knopf, 1979.

SHAKESPEARE, WILLIAM. *Othello.* New York: Methuen Press, 1958.

_____. *Romeo and Juliet.* New York: Methuen Press, 1980.

SOLOMON, MAYNARD. *Beethoven*. 2nd ed. New York: Schirmer Trade Books, 2001.

SPAETHLING, ROBERT. *Mozart's Letters, Mozart's Life*. New York: W. W. Norton, 2000.

WILKINS, NIGEL. *The Writings of Erik Satie*. London: Eulenburg, 1980.

INDEX